Lecture Notes in Computer Science 15186

Founding Editors

Gerhard Goos
Juris Hartmanis

Editorial Board Members

Elisa Bertino, *Purdue University, West Lafayette, IN, USA*
Wen Gao, *Peking University, Beijing, China*
Bernhard Steffen ⓘ, *TU Dortmund University, Dortmund, Germany*
Moti Yung ⓘ, *Columbia University, New York, NY, USA*

The series Lecture Notes in Computer Science (LNCS), including its subseries Lecture Notes in Artificial Intelligence (LNAI) and Lecture Notes in Bioinformatics (LNBI), has established itself as a medium for the publication of new developments in computer science and information technology research, teaching, and education.

LNCS enjoys close cooperation with the computer science R & D community, the series counts many renowned academics among its volume editors and paper authors, and collaborates with prestigious societies. Its mission is to serve this international community by providing an invaluable service, mainly focused on the publication of conference and workshop proceedings and postproceedings. LNCS commenced publication in 1973.

Alberto Gomez · Bishesh Khanal · Andrew King ·
Ana Namburete
Editors

Simplifying Medical Ultrasound

5th International Workshop, ASMUS 2024
Held in Conjunction with MICCAI 2024
Marrakesh, Morocco, October 6, 2024
Proceedings

Editors
Alberto Gomez ⓘ
Ultromics Ltd.
Oxford, UK

Andrew King ⓘ
King's College London
London, UK

Bishesh Khanal ⓘ
Nepal Applied Mathematics and Informatics
Institute for Research
Lalitpur, Nepal

Ana Namburete ⓘ
University of Oxford
Oxford, UK

ISSN 0302-9743 ISSN 1611-3349 (electronic)
Lecture Notes in Computer Science
ISBN 978-3-031-73646-9 ISBN 978-3-031-73647-6 (eBook)
https://doi.org/10.1007/978-3-031-73647-6

© The Editor(s) (if applicable) and The Author(s), under exclusive license
to Springer Nature Switzerland AG 2025, corrected publication 2025

This work is subject to copyright. All rights are solely and exclusively licensed by the Publisher, whether the whole or part of the material is concerned, specifically the rights of translation, reprinting, reuse of illustrations, recitation, broadcasting, reproduction on microfilms or in any other physical way, and transmission or information storage and retrieval, electronic adaptation, computer software, or by similar or dissimilar methodology now known or hereafter developed.
The use of general descriptive names, registered names, trademarks, service marks, etc. in this publication does not imply, even in the absence of a specific statement, that such names are exempt from the relevant protective laws and regulations and therefore free for general use.
The publisher, the authors and the editors are safe to assume that the advice and information in this book are believed to be true and accurate at the date of publication. Neither the publisher nor the authors or the editors give a warranty, expressed or implied, with respect to the material contained herein or for any errors or omissions that may have been made. The publisher remains neutral with regard to jurisdictional claims in published maps and institutional affiliations.

This Springer imprint is published by the registered company Springer Nature Switzerland AG
The registered company address is: Gewerbestrasse 11, 6330 Cham, Switzerland

If disposing of this product, please recycle the paper.

Preface

Ultrasound is one of the most accessible imaging modalities in the world. Even in low- and middle-income countries (LMICs) with limited resources for their healthcare sectors there are many clinics and healthcare centres which have ultrasound scanners. Ultrasound machines are low-cost compared to many other imaging modalities and with the increasing availability of mobile ultrasound probes the reach of ultrasound imaging is increasing. However, ultrasound is also one of the most challenging imaging modalities to use, with significant skill and experience required to obtain good quality images and interpret them. This raises a need for techniques to facilitate simplification of the ultrasound imaging process, so that the clinical benefits of ultrasound are accessible, affordable, reliable and widespread throughout the world. The Fifth International Workshop on Advances in Simplifying Medical Ultrasound (ASMUS 2024) aimed to address this need. ASMUS was held in conjunction with the Medical Image Computing and Computer- Assisted Intervention (MICCAI) conference in Marrakesh, Morocco, and acted as the endorsed workshop of the MICCAI Special Interest Group on Medical Ultrasound. Each year, ASMUS acts as a forum to bring together multiple stakeholders from academia, industry and healthcare institutions to report and discuss the latest advances in the simplification of ultrasound imaging. The audience regularly features senior figures with unparalleled experience and insight into the field as well as early career researchers who bring a fresh perspective on the challenges faced. The work presented covers the full spectrum of ultrasound imaging, from acquisition and reconstruction through to analysis and interpretation. A wide range of healthcare applications are considered, including cardiac imaging, placenta assessment, fetal screening, prostate imaging and image-guided interventions. The workshop is a vibrant forum featuring high-quality oral and poster presentations, active and open discussions and live demonstrations of the latest technology. This year ASMUS received a record-breaking 34 submissions which underwent peer-review. Each submission was double-blind reviewed by a minimum of two (and an average of 3.5) reviewers from the program committee, supplemented as needed by additional reviews from the program chairs. The chairs chose the final papers to be accepted based on these reviews, considering the scientific soundness, novelty and clinical relevance. Of the 34 submissions, 22 were accepted for presentation at the workshop and 21 of these are included in this proceedings volume. This year MICCAI and ASMUS were held for the first time on the African continent. For researchers working in ultrasound in particular, this represented an excellent opportunity to engage with stakeholders in parts of the world that stand to benefit most from the simplification of ultrasound imaging. ASMUS seized this opportunity and the program this year had a particular focus on LMIC-related challenges. Our keynote speaker was Youssef Bouyakhf, the CEO of DeepEcho, who was born and raised in Morocco and now works to improve ultrasound-based fetal diagnosis using AI. The workshop also featured a vibrant panel discussion on the use of ultrasound in LMICs, which we hope will inspire researchers to engage with the particular problems and challenges faced in Africa and LMICs in other parts of the world. We would like to take this opportunity to express our gratitude to the ASMUS program committee for their commitment, hard work and expertise, which were crucial in ensuring the high quality of the papers presented. We are also grateful to our organising committee and advisory boards for their invaluable advice and support throughout the process of organising the workshop. Finally, we owe a huge debt of gratitude to our delivery team for being so efficient and helpful in taking care of the many practical and time-consuming aspects of workshop organisation.

September 2024

Alberto Gomez
Bishesh Khanal
Andrew King
Ana Namburete

Organization

Program Committee Chairs

Gomez, Alberto	Ultromics, UK
Khanal, Bishesh	NAAMII, Nepal
King, Andrew	King's College London, UK
Namburete, Ana	University of Oxford, UK

Organizing Committee

Abolmaesumi, Purang	University of British Columbia, Canada
Aylward, Stephen	Kitware, USA
Boctor, Emad	Johns Hopkins University, USA
Hu, Yipeng	University College London, UK
Kainz, Bernhard	FAU Erlangen-Nürnberg, Germany, and Imperial College London, UK
Meng, Qingjie	University of Birmingham, UK
Mousavi, Parvin	Queen's University, Canada
Ni, Dong	Shenzhen University, China
Noble, Alison	University of Oxford, UK
Wein, Wolfgang	Imfusion, Germany
Zimmer, Veronika A.	Technical University of Munich, Germany
van den Heuvel, Thomas	Radboud University, Netherlands

Delivery Team

Adhikari, Rabin	NAAMII, Nepal
Bransby, Kit	Queen Mary University, UK, and Ultromics, UK
Yuan, Zhen	King's College London, UK

Advisory Board

Diao, Babacar	Cheikh Anta Diop University of Dakar, Senegal
Fichtinger, Gabor	Queen's University, Canada
Hajnal, Joseph	King's College London, UK

Navab, Nassir	Technical University of Munich, Germany
Razavi, Reza	King's College London, UK
Rhode, Kawal	King's College London, UK
Taylor, Russ	Johns Hopkins University, USA
de Korte, Chris	Radboud University Nijmegen, Netherlands

Program Committee

Adhikari, Rabin	NAAMII, Nepal
Alsharid, Mohammad	Khalifa University of Science and Technology, UAE
Bonmati, Ester	University of Westminster, UK
Bransby, Kit	Queen Mary University of London, UK, and Ultromics, UK
Chintada, Bhaskara Rao	Harvard Medical School, USA
Ellethy, Hanem	University of Queensland, Australia
Fenster, Aaron	Robarts Research Institute, Canada
Gleed, Alexander	Weill Cornell Medicine, USA
Gomez, Alberto	Ultromics, UK
Gu, Ang Nan	University of British Columbia, Canada
Hu, Yipeng	University College London, UK
Irshad, Samra	Kyung Hee University, South Korea
Kainz, Bernhard	FAU Erlangen-Nürnberg, Germany, and Imperial College London, UK
Karunanayake, Nalan	Memorial Sloan Kettering Cancer Center, USA
Khanal, Bishesh	NAAMII, Nepal
King, Andrew	King's College London, UK
Lee, Brian	Philips Research, USA
Li, Qi	University College London, UK
Min, Zhe	Shandong University, China, and University College London, UK
Noble, Alison	University of Oxford, UK
Oliveira, Jorge	Ultromics, UK
Parra Raad, Jaime	King's College London, UK
Shakya, Mahesh	NAAMI, Nepal
Stojanovski, David	King's College London, UK
Thapaliya, Safal	NAAMII, Nepal
Thorley, Alex	University of Birmingham, UK, and Ultromics, UK
Ungi, Tamas	Queen's University, Canada
Vasconcelos, Francisco	University College London, UK

Venturini, Lorenzo	King's College London, UK, and Fraiya, UK
Wang, Shuangyi	Chinese Academy of Sciences, China
Wein, Wolfgang	Imfusion, Germany
Yuan, Zhen	King's College London, UK

Sponsors

Fraiya Ltd.	https://fraiya.com/
Imfusion GmbH	https://www.imfusion.com/
Ultromics, Ltd.	https://www.ultromics.com/
ThinkSono, Ltd.	https://thinksono.com/

Contents

Image Acquisition, Synthesis and Enhancement

Unsupervised Physics-Inspired Shear Wave Speed Estimation in Ultrasound Elastography 3
   Ali Kafaei Zad Tehrani, E. G. Sunethra Dayavansha, Yuyang Gu, Ion Candel, Michael Wang, Rimon Tadross, Yiming Xiao, Hassan Rivaz, Kai Thomenius, and Anthony Samir

Simplifying Prostate Elastography Using Micro-ultrasound and Transfer Function Imaging 14
   Reid Vassallo, Tajwar Abrar Aleef, Vedanth Desaigoudar, Qi Zeng, David Black, Brian Wodlinger, Miles Mannas, Peter C. Black, and Septimiu E. Salcudean

Do High-Performance Image-to-Image Translation Networks Enable the Discovery of Radiomic Features? Application to MRI Synthesis from Ultrasound in Prostate Cancer 24
   Mohammad R. Salmanpour, Amin Mousavi, Yixi Xu, William B. Weeks, and Ilker Hacihaliloglu

PHOCUS: Physics-Based Deconvolution for Ultrasound Resolution Enhancement 35
   Felix Duelmer, Walter Simson, Mohammad Farid Azampour, Magdalena Wysocki, Angelos Karlas, and Nassir Navab

Tracking, Registration and Image-guided Interventions

PIPsUS: Self-supervised Point Tracking in Ultrasound 47
   Wanwen Chen, Adam Schmidt, Eitan Prisman, and Septimiu E. Salcudean

Structure-aware World Model for Probe Guidance via Large-scale Self-supervised Pre-train 58
   Haojun Jiang, Meng Li, Zhenguo Sun, Ning Jia, Yu Sun, Shaqi Luo, Shiji Song, and Gao Huang

An Evaluation of Low-Cost Hardware on 3D Ultrasound Reconstruction Accuracy 68
   Étienne Léger, Niki Najafi, Houssem-Eddine Gueziri, D. Louis Collins, and Marta Kersten-Oertel

Learning to Match 2D Keypoints Across Preoperative MR
and Intraoperative Ultrasound 78
  Hassan Rasheed, Reuben Dorent, Maximilian Fehrentz,
  Tina Kapur, William M. Wells III, Alexandra Golby, Sarah Frisken,
  Julia A. Schnabel, and Nazim Haouchine

Automatic Facial Axes Standardization of 3D Fetal Ultrasound Images 88
  Antonia Alomar, Ricardo Rubio, Laura Salort, Gerard Albaiges,
  Antoni Payà, Gemma Piella, and Federico Sukno

Segmentation

C-TRUS: A Novel Dataset and Initial Benchmark for Colon Wall
Segmentation in Transabdominal Ultrasound 101
  Ramona Leenings, Maximilian Konowski, Nils R. Winter, Jan Ernsting,
  Lukas Fisch, Carlotta Barkhau, Udo Dannlowski, Andreas Lügering,
  Xiaoyi Jiang, and Tim Hahn

Label Dropout: Improved Deep Learning Echocardiography Segmentation
Using Multiple Datasets with Domain Shift and Partial Labelling 112
  Iman Islam, Esther Puyol-Antón, Bram Ruijsink, Andrew J. Reader,
  and Andrew P. King

Introducing Anatomical Constraints in Mitral Annulus Segmentation
in Transesophageal Echocardiography 122
  Børge Solli Andreassen, Sarina Thomas, Anne H. Schistad Solberg,
  Eigil Samset, and David Völgyes

Interactive Segmentation Model for Placenta Segmentation from 3D
Ultrasound Images 132
  Hao Li, Baris Oguz, Gabriel Arenas, Xing Yao, Jiacheng Wang,
  Alison Pouch, Brett Byram, Nadav Schwartz, and Ipek Oguz

Enhanced Uncertainty Estimation in Ultrasound Image Segmentation
with MSU-Net 143
  Rohini Banerjee, Cecilia G. Morales, and Artur Dubrawski

Classification and Detection

Multi-site Class-Incremental Learning with Weighted Experts
in Echocardiography 157
  Kit M. Bransby, Woo-Jin Cho Kim, Jorge Oliveira, Alex Thorley,
  Arian Beqiri, Alberto Gomez, and Agisilaos Chartsias

Masked Autoencoders for Medical Ultrasound Videos Using ROI-Aware
Masking 167
   Ádám Szijártó, Bálint Magyar, Thomas Á. Szeier, Máté Tolvaj,
   Alexandra Fábián, Bálint K. Lakatos, Zsuzsanna Ladányi,
   Zsolt Bagyura, Béla Merkely, Attila Kovács, and Márton Tokodi

Uncertainty-Based Multi-modal Learning for Myocardial Infarction
Diagnosis Using Echocardiography and Electrocardiograms 177
   Yingyu Yang, Marie Rocher, Pamela Moceri, and Maxime Sermesant

Fetal Ultrasound Video Representation Learning Using Contrastive
Rubik's Cube Recovery 187
   Kangning Zhang, Jianbo Jiao, and J. Alison Noble

LoRIS - Weakly-Supervised Anomaly Detection for Ultrasound Images 198
   Marco Colussi, Dragan Ahmetovic, Gabriele Civitarese,
   Claudio Bettini, Aiman Solyman, Roberta Gualtierotti, Flora Peyvandi,
   and Sergio Mascetti

Unsupervised Detection of Fetal Brain Anomalies Using Denoising
Diffusion Models 209
   Markus Ditlev Sjøgren Olsen, Jakob Ambsdorf, Manxi Lin,
   Caroline Taksøe-Vester, Morten Bo Søndergaard Svendsen,
   Anders Nymark Christensen, Mads Nielsen,
   Martin Grønnebæk Tolsgaard, Aasa Feragen, and Paraskevas Pegios

Diffusion Models for Unsupervised Anomaly Detection in Fetal Brain
Ultrasound 220
   Hanna Mykula, Lisa Gasser, Silvia Lobmaier, Julia A. Schnabel,
   Veronika Zimmer, and Cosmin I. Bercea

Correction to: Unsupervised Physics-Inspired Shear Wave Speed
Estimation in Ultrasound Elastography C1
   Ali Kafaei Zad Tehrani, E. G. Sunethra Dayavansha, Yuyang Gu,
   Ion Candel, Michael Wang, Rimon Tadross, Yiming Xiao, Hassan Rivaz,
   Kai Thomenius, and Anthony Samir

Author Index 231

Image Acquisition, Synthesis and Enhancement

Unsupervised Physics-Inspired Shear Wave Speed Estimation in Ultrasound Elastography

Ali Kafaei Zad Tehrani[1(✉)], E. G. Sunethra Dayavansha[2], Yuyang Gu[2], Ion Candel[2], Michael Wang[3], Rimon Tadross[3], Yiming Xiao[4], Hassan Rivaz[1], Kai Thomenius[2], and Anthony Samir[2]

[1] Department of Electrical and Computer Engineering, Concordia University, Montreal, Canada
ali.kafaeizadtehrani@mail.concordia.ca, hrivaz@ece.concordia.ca
[2] Massachusetts General Hospital, Harvard Medical School, Boston, USA
asamir@mgh.harvard.edu
[3] General Electric Healthcare, Chicago, USA
[4] Department of Computer Science and Software Engineering, Concordia University, Montreal, Canada

Abstract. Shear wave elastography (SWE) is a promising tool to quantify tissue stiffness variations with increasing applications in tissue characterization. In SWE, the tissue is excited by an acoustic radiation force pulse sequence induced by an ultrasound probe. The generated shear waves propagate laterally away from the push location. The shear wave speed (SWS) can be measured to estimate elasticity, which is a physical property that can be used to characterize the tissue. SWS estimation requires two steps: speckle tracking from radiofrequency (RF)/IQ data to obtain particle displacement or velocity, and SWS estimation from the estimated velocity, which aims to find the speed of wave propagating in the lateral direction. The SWS can be calculated by comparing the velocity-time profiles at two locations separated by a few millimeters. In the supervised deep learning methods of SWS estimation, simulation data generated by finite element analysis is employed to train the network. However, the computational cost and complexity of modeling the wave propagation contribute to the limited practicality of supervised methods. In this paper, we present an unsupervised physics-inspired learning method for SWS estimation using equations governing the wave propagation in a viscoelastic medium. The proposed method does not require any finite element simulated data, and training data is synthetically generated using forward modeling of the wave propagation equation. Furthermore, unlabeled experimental data is utilized to

---

The original version of the chapter has been revised. Reference missing and now has been corrected. A correction to this chapter can be found at https://doi.org/10.1007/978-3-031-73647-6_22

Supplementary Information The online version contains supplementary material available at https://doi.org/10.1007/978-3-031-73647-6_1.

train/fine-tune the network. We validated the proposed method using experimental data imaged by different machines and data created by placing pork fat on top of a phantom. The findings validate that the suggested approach can demonstrate comparable (or superior) performance compared to the traditional cross-correlation method.

Keywords: Shear wave elastography · unsupervised physics-inspired learning · viscoelastic medium

1 Introduction

Shear wave elastography (SWE) is a promising and quantitative technique for tissue characterization that can be applied to determine the severity of disease and treatment monitoring [14]. In SWE, an acoustic radiation force pulse sequence is utilized to generate laterally propagating shear waves with transient displacements. These displacements are tracked to measure the shear wave speed (SWS) and converted to shear modulus to display an elastogram [3,16].

Deep learning techniques have been widely employed in quasi-static ultrasound elastography [20,22] and both main steps of SWE: tracking velocity from RF/IQ data [6,8,21] and estimating SWS from velocity data [1,9,13]. Supervised techniques were mainly used for the SWS estimation. Simulation data generated from finite element analysis software was utilized to train a network in a supervised fashion [1]. However, unsupervised learning is favored due to the high cost of generating simulation data, and the availability of ample experimental data for network training. In this paper, Synthetic data generation, which does not require finite element analysis, is introduced, enabling the creation of diverse datasets within a short timeframe. An unsupervised training method is also proposed enabling learning from available unlabeled experimental data.

2 Datasets and Metrics

2.1 Devices and Phantoms

The GE Logiq E10 (General Electric Healthcare, USA) ultrasound system and a Verasonics Vantage 256 system (Verasonics Inc., USA) were used in these experiments. The system parameters are tabulated in the Supplementary Materials.

The I/Q data for shear wave propagation was obtained from the CIRS elasticity QA phantoms of model 049 and 049A (CIRS Inc., Norfolk, VA). A soft inclusion (Type I) and a hard inclusion (Type IV) in 049A phantom with respective ground truth SWS values of $1.6\,\text{m/s}$ and $4.9\,\text{m/s}$ were used in the experiments when using the GE LE10 system. Here, the ground truth SWS of the background was $2.5\,\text{m/s}$. Additionally, the 049 phantom with respective ground truth SWS values of $2.8\,\text{m/s}$ and $5.2\,\text{m/s}$ in the background and the hard inclusion were used when using the Verasonics system. Inspired by [18,19], we created another dataset by placing a pork fat layer with a thickness of around 10 mm on top of the 049 phantom to mimic obese patients. Adding the pork fat introduces aberration artifacts and decreases the signal-to-noise ratio (SNR). Any data from this phantom was not included in the unsupervised training dataset. The photo of this experiment is provided in the Supplementary Materials.

2.2 Pre-processing

The speckle tracking methods are widely used for motion estimation [2], and in this study, a 1-D Kasai technique [10,15] was utilized. The acquired I/Q data was used to estimate the velocity by measuring the relative phase shift to obtain the particle velocity-time profiles at each location in the imaged region. To minimize the effect of unwanted motion, a high-pass motion filter with a cut-off frequency of 150 Hz was used. The filtered particle velocity data is then normalized to be zero mean with a standard deviation of 1.

3 Materials and Methods

3.1 Conventional Method for SWS Estimation

The cross-correlation methods provide an effective method for estimating time delay between different locations. Here, a 1-D cross-correlation method was used [23]. The generated displacement-time profiles with a spatial tracking location offset of 2.8 mm were subsequently processed to compute the time delays at each spatial location.

3.2 Modeling the Shear Wave Propagation

The relationship between the velocity waveforms of two points v_1 and v_2 that are $2\Delta_x$ laterally apart can be described as [7,17]:

$$v_2(t) = v_1(t) * w(\Delta x, t) \tag{1}$$

where $v_1(t)$ is the velocity waveform at the lateral point $x - \Delta x$, and $v_2(t)$ is the velocity waveform at the lateral point $x + \Delta x$. The interaction between the two velocity waves is modeled by a transfer function (w). Assuming that there is no geometric spreading and the material is elastic, w can be simply described as $\delta(t - 2\Delta x/C_s)$ with SWS denoted as C_s, which means that $v_2(t) = v_1(t - 2*\Delta x/C_s)$. However, this model is too simplistic, and a more generalized model is to assume the medium is viscoelastic (following the Kelvin-Voight model), w becomes frequency dependent and can be obtained in the frequency domain by [7,17]:

$$W(\Delta x, \mu, f) = exp\left\{\frac{-j4\pi f|\Delta x|}{\sqrt{(\mu/\rho)}}\right\} \tag{2}$$

where ρ is the density of the material (we assume $\rho = 1000$ for soft tissue), and μ is the elasticity which has real and imaginary parts. The real part depends on SWS (C_s), and the imaginary part is proportional to the viscosity (η_s):

$$\mu(f) = \rho C_s^2 + j2\pi f \eta_s \tag{3}$$

Assuming $\eta_s = 0$, the material becomes elastic. The imaginary part linearly depends on frequency (f) and viscosity (η_s) which has been found useful in

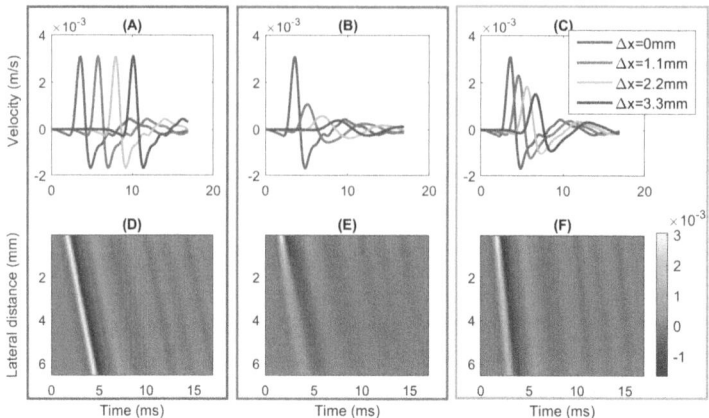

Fig. 1. 1D representation of propagation of velocity profiles using Eq. 1 and 2 with SWS of 2.0 m/s and viscosity of 0 Pa.Sec (A), SWS of 2 m/s and viscosity of 2 Pa.Sec (B), and SWS of 4 m/s and viscosity of 2 Pa.Sec (C). (D–F) are the 2D representation of the lateral position versus time of (A)–(C). The slope of the line corresponds to the SWS, and the attenuation depends on SWS and viscosity.

tissue characterization [4,5]. Examples of wave propagation using Eqs. 1 and 2 are depicted in Fig. 1 (A, B, and C). Finally, $v_2(t)$ can be obtained by:

$$v_2(t) = fft^{-1}\left\{fft(v_1(t)) \times W(\Delta x, \mu(C_s, \eta_s))\right\} \quad (4)$$

The equation can be compared with the warping operation (moving a feature map or an image by a known displacement field), which has been widely employed in unsupervised optical flow training [12]. The difference is the presence of viscosity, which introduces attenuation and phase changes. We called this operation viscoelastic warping to emphasize their similarities.

Simulation Data Generation Using the Viscoelastic Model: The equations modeling the shear wave propagation can be used to generate simulation data with known SWS and viscosity. It should be noted that the viscoelastic equations (Eqs. 1 and 2) only model how the wave deforms when it propagates through the medium. Therefore, we need to get the first velocity ($v_1(t)$) from experimental phantom velocity data and transform it by the known SWS and viscosity using the viscoelastic equations. We obtained the first velocity from the Verasonics machine imaging a uniform phantom and found it more similar to the initial velocity of other scanners than the synthetically generated initial velocity using finite element analysis. We generated several lateral points with fixed spacing of d_x to simulate uniform phantoms having fixed SWS and viscosity parameters. Algorithm 1 illustrates the procedure to generate simulation data using this technique. SWS and viscosity are sampled uniformly from 0.5–7 m/s and 0–4 Pa.Sec to mimic soft tissues. Six thousand samples were generated for training the network. Figure 1 (D, E, and F) shows a few examples of the generated data (time versus lateral distance) using Algorithm 1. The simulation

Algorithm 1. Generation of simulation data for training

input: SWS (C_s), Visc (η_s), Maximum distance X_m, lateral resolution (d_x), and v_1
output: $patch \in R^{W \times T}$

$c \leftarrow 0$
for $\Delta x = d_x/2$ to $X_m/2$ step d_x **do**:
  $W \leftarrow exp\left\{\frac{-j4\pi f|\Delta x|}{\sqrt{(\mu/\rho)}}\right\}$
  $v_2(\Delta x, t) \leftarrow fft^{-1}(W \times fft(v_1))$
  $patch(c, t) \leftarrow v_2(\Delta x, t)$
  $c \leftarrow c + 1$
end for

---

took 2.7 sec on average for each sample on an i7 CPU using the viscoelastic equation. While, it takes 1440 sec using Comsol finite element software.

3.3 Proposed Method

Having the velocity data $v \in R^{D \times W \times T}$, where D, W, and T represent axial, lateral, and time dimensions, respectively. The goal is to obtain SWS ($C_s \in R^{D \times W}$) and viscosity maps ($\eta_s \in R^{D \times W}$). Instead of comparing two velocity profiles, we followed a patch-based approach similar to [9,13]. The advantage is that more observations are provided to the networks compared to having two velocities. A patch around the sample of interest with the size $0.9mm \times 2.8mm \times 16msec$ is selected. Since data has three dimensions, 3D Convolutional Neural Networks (CNN) can be employed. However, to reduce the computational costs and benefit from pre-trained available 2D networks, we converted the data to 2D by considering axial points as different channels (we considered only 3 adjacent axial samples to have three channels). The patch is also upsampled in the lateral direction (from 14 points corresponding to 2.8 mm to 96), which gives the size of $3 \times 96 \times 256$. In order to obtain SWS and viscosity maps, the network is utilized for each sample of interest separately and the estimated values are combined.

An essential aspect to consider is the number of lateral and axial samples in each patch. We utilized 14 samples laterally and 3 samples axially, equivalent to 2.8 mm and 0.9 mm, respectively. We explored the possibility of increasing axial samples to 7 while decreasing lateral samples to 7, but no improvements were observed in doing so.

Supervised Training: Given that the SWS and viscosity of the synthetically generated dataset are known, The network can learn in a supervised fashion. The following loss function is used for supervised training.

$$loss = L_1(\widehat{Cs}, Cs_{GT}) + \lambda \times L_1(\widehat{\eta s}, \eta s_{GT}) \quad (5)$$

where L_1 denotes smooth L_1 loss, $\hat{x}$ denote the estimated parameters, and λ is the weight for viscosity and it was set empirically to 0.2.

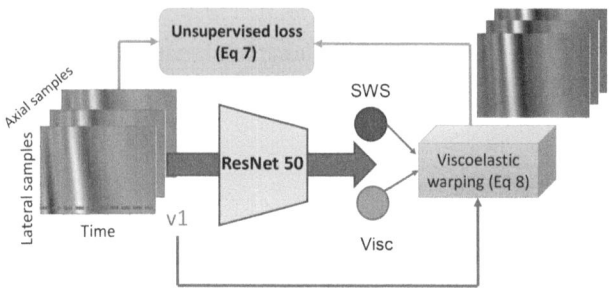

Fig. 2. The graphical representation of the training procedure. The velocity corresponding to the first lateral sample (v_1) is transformed using viscoelastic warping (Eq 8).

Unsupervised Training: The explained viscoelastic warping can be employed as the loss function, which can be written for two distinct velocity profiles (v_1 and v_2) as:

$$loss = L_1(v_2(t), \widehat{v_2(t)}), \tag{6}$$
$$\widehat{v_2(t)} = fft^{-1}\{fft(v_1(t)) \times W(\Delta x, \mu(C_s, \eta_s))\},$$

where μ is the complex elasticity (Eq. 3), and viscoelastic warping is employed to obtain $\widehat{v_2(t)}$. This loss function (Eq. 6) should be extended for the patch in which several velocity profiles belonging to different lateral distances (Δx) exist. The equation can be extended by:

$$loss = \frac{1}{N}\sum_{i=1}^{N} L_1(v_2(t)^i, \widehat{v_2(t)^i}), \tag{7}$$

where N is the number of lateral samples, and $\widehat{v_2}^i$ is obtained by:

$$\widehat{v_2}^i(t) = fft^{-1}\{fft(v1) \times W(\Delta x^i, \mu(C_s, \eta_s))\}, \tag{8}$$
$$\Delta x = \frac{1}{2}[d_x, 2d_x, 3d_x, ..., X_m],$$

where X_m is the maximum lateral distance. The simple explanation of the loss function is that the viscoelastic warping is employed to move $v_1(t)$ for all lateral distances (the superscript i) using the estimated SWS and viscosity, and the average L_1 loss comparing the $v_2(t)^i$ and $\widehat{v_2(t)^i}$ is employed as the final loss value.

Training and Network Architecture: We utilized ResNet50 and changed the last layer to have two outputs (SWS and viscosity). The first layer is also altered by replacing the strides of 2 with 1 to avoid loss of information. The graphical representation of the network and the training procedure is provided

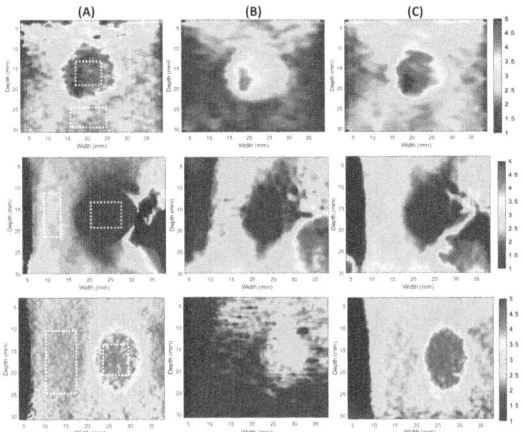

Fig. 3. Experimental phantom SWS maps estimated by cross-correlation (A), supervised training (B), and unsupervised training (C) for a phantom having an inclusion with SWS of 4.9 m/s imaged by GE E10 machine (top), type 1 inclusion with SWS of 1.6 m/s imaged by Verasonics machine (middle), and type 4 inclusion with SWS of 5.2 m/s imaged by Verasonics machine (bottom).

in Fig. 2. The network architecture employed in [9,13] can also be employed instead of the utilized ResNet50.

For supervised training, we employed 6000 samples generated by Algorithm 1. The network was trained for 100 epochs with AdamW [11] as the optimizer and learning rate of 1e-4 which reduced by half every 20 epochs. For unsupervised training, 2000 patches were used, and we made sure that different parts of the phantom in training and testing were employed to avoid data leakage. The network was fine-tuned for 20 epochs with a learning rate of 1e−5, which halved every 5 epochs.

4 Results

Contrast to Noise Ratio (CNR), and Bias error are employed as quantitative metrics, and they are defined as:

$$CNR = \sqrt{\frac{2(E(\widehat{Cs_b}) - E(\widehat{Cs_t}))^2}{\sigma_b^2 + \sigma_t^2}}, \qquad Bias = E(\widehat{Cs} - Cs_{gt}), \qquad (9)$$

where $\widehat{Cs_b}$, $\widehat{Cs_t}$ denote the estimated SWS of the target and background windows, respectively. The $E(.)$, and σ^2 denote the average and variance. CNR is computed for small overlapping patches inside the selected windows, and the mean and standard deviation are reported.

The supervised method performed well on simulation test data (mean absolute error of SWS and viscosity are 0.080 m/s and 0.085 Pa.Sec, respectively).

Table 1. The evaluated methods' CNR values (highest in bold).

	GE E10 Type 4	Verasonics Type 1	Verasonics Type 4	Verasonics with Pork fat layer
cross-correlation	10.76±2.55	**21.82±4.10**	11.77±2.97	**4.04±0.73**
Supervised method	6.78±3.42	6.13±2.46	4.93±1.36	1.24±1.015
Unsupervised method	**13.31±3.06**	11.87±1.46	**12.92±3.64**	1.84±1.01

Table 2. Bias errors (lowest absolute value is in bold) of the evaluated methods, and the percentage with respect to the true value.

	GE E10 Type 4		Verasonics Type 1		Verasonics Type 4		Verasonics with Pork fat layer	
Method	Background	Target	Background	Target	Background	Target	Background	Target
cross-correlation	**-0.09 (-4%)**	**-0.39 (-8%)**	-0.33 (-12%)	-0.28 (-18%)	-0.51 (-18%)	-1.18 (-23%)	**-0.19 (-18%)**	**-1.63 (-30%)**
Supervised method	-0.50 (-20%)	-1.42 (-29%)	-0.22 (-8%)	**0.09 (6%)**	-0.97 (-35%)	-2.6 (-50%)	-0.73 (-26%)	-3.3 (-0.63%)
Unsupervised method	-0.17 (-7%)	-0.41 (-8%)	**-0.08 (-3%)**	0.19 (12%)	**-0.38 (-14%)**	**-0.82 (-16%)**	-0.26 (-9%)	-2.20 (-42%)

The SWS maps of experimental phantom test data of the compared methods are illustrated in Fig. 3. The unsupervised method (C) provides a better delineation than the supervised one (B). Furthermore, the supervised method failed to provide an acceptable SWS map for type IV inclusion imaged by Verasonics (third row), and had a high bias for type IV inclusion imaged by GE E10 (first row).

Comparing cross-correlation and the unsupervised method, cross-correlation has a better delineation in Type I inclusion (middle row). However, there is an underestimation bias for Type IV inclusion imaged by Verasonics, whereas the unsupervised method obtains SWS values closer to the true SWS (5.2 m/s for the inclusion in the bottom row). The quantitative results are given in Tables 1 and 2. The target and background windows to calculate the quantitative results are

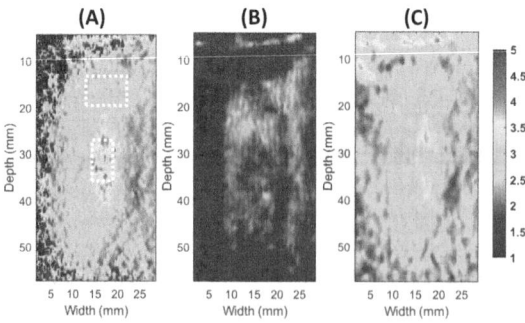

Fig. 4. SWS maps of the phantom with pork fat layer on top, estimated by cross-correlation (A), supervised training (B), and unsupervised training (C).

highlighted in Fig. 3. Unsupervised training has shown to be advantageous; it has substantially higher CNR and lower Bias error than supervised training in most cases. In GE E10 Type 4 and Verasonics Type 4, the unsupervised method has a higher CNR than cross-correlation method. Although cross-correlation has a higher CNR in Verasonics Type 1 (Table 1), the unsupervised method has lower bias error values in the background (-0.08 vs -0.33) and target (0.19 vs -0.28) compared to cross-correlation. The viscosity was not the main aim of this paper, we provided the estimated viscosity maps in the Supplementary Materials.

The estimated SWS maps of the phantom with pork fat on top are depicted in Fig. 4. The supervised method failed in this challenging case. The cross-correlation method managed to detect the inclusion but has noisy and unreliable values on the left side. The unsupervised method managed to detect the SWS values of the left side, but the inclusion is not as visible as the one in cross-correlation.

5 Conclusion

In this paper, we present an unsupervised physics-inspired learning method for SWS estimation using equations governing the wave propagation in a viscoelastic medium. The training data is synthetically generated using forward modeling of the wave propagation equation without requiring finite element analysis. Furthermore, unlabeled experimental data was utilized to fine-tune the network. The proposed method was validated using experimental data imaged by different machines and low SNR, aberrated phantom data. The findings validated that the suggested approach was superior to the supervised training, and enabling utilization of real data for training. This work demonstrates the potential of deep neural networks in SWS estimation. Incorporating more diverse training data and using a more complex wave propagation model can further improve the estimation of the network.

Acknowledgments. We acknowledge the support by GE Healthcare, Government of Canada's New Frontiers in Research Fund (NFRF), [NFRFE-2022-00295] and Natural Sciences and Engineering Research Council of Canada (NSERC).

References

1. Ahmed, S., Kamal, U., Hasan, M.K.: Dswe-net: A deep learning approach for shear wave elastography and lesion segmentation using single push acoustic radiation force. Ultrasonics **110**, 106283 (2021)
2. Ashikuzzaman, M., Héroux, A., Tang, A., Cloutier, G., Rivaz, H.: Displacement tracking techniques in ultrasound elastography: From cross-correlation to deep learning. IEEE Transactions on Ultrasonics, Ferroelectrics, and Frequency Control (2024)
3. Bamber, J., Cosgrove, D., Dietrich, C.F., Fromageau, J., Bojunga, J., Calliada, F., Cantisani, V., Correas, J.M., D'Onofrio, M., Drakonaki, E., et al.: Efsumb guidelines and recommendations on the clinical use of ultrasound elastography. part

1: Basic principles and technology. Ultraschall in der Medizin-European Journal of Ultrasound **34**(02), 169–184 (2013)
4. Bhatt, M., Moussu, M.A., Chayer, B., Destrempes, F., Gesnik, M., Allard, L., Tang, A., Cloutier, G.: Reconstruction of viscosity maps in ultrasound shear wave elastography. IEEE transactions on ultrasonics, ferroelectrics, and frequency control **66**(6), 1065–1078 (2019)
5. Bhatt, M., Yazdani, L., Destrempes, F., Allard, L., Nguyen, B.N., Tang, A., Cloutier, G.: Multiparametric in vivo ultrasound shear wave viscoelastography on farm-raised fatty duck livers: human radiology imaging applied to food sciences. Poultry science **100**(4), 100968 (2021)
6. Chan, D.Y., Morris, D.C., Polascik, T.J., Palmeri, M.L., Nightingale, K.R.: Deep convolutional neural networks for displacement estimation in arfi imaging. IEEE transactions on ultrasonics, ferroelectrics, and frequency control **68**(7), 2472–2481 (2021)
7. Chen, X.: Enhancing ultrasound shear-wave viscoelastography by advanced signal processing and deep learning. Ph.D. dissertation, Eindhoven University of Technology (2024)
8. Delaunay, R., Hu, Y., Vercauteren, T.: An unsupervised learning-based shear wave tracking method for ultrasound elastography. In: Medical Imaging 2022: Ultrasonic Imaging and Tomography. vol. 12038, pp. 149–155. SPIE (2022)
9. Jin, F.Q., Carlson, L.C., Feltovich, H., Hall, T.J., Palmeri, M.L.: Sweinet: Deep learning based uncertainty quantification for ultrasound shear wave elasticity imaging. arXiv preprint arXiv:2203.10678 (2022)
10. Kasai, C., Namekawa, K., Koyano, A., Omoto, R.: Real-time two-dimensional blood flow imaging using an autocorrelation technique. IEEE Transactions on sonics and ultrasonics **32**(3), 458–464 (1985)
11. Loshchilov, I., Hutter, F.: Decoupled weight decay regularization. arXiv preprint arXiv:1711.05101 (2017)
12. Meister, S., Hur, J., Roth, S.: Unflow: Unsupervised learning of optical flow with a bidirectional census loss. In: Proceedings of the AAAI conference on artificial intelligence. vol. 32 (2018)
13. Neidhardt, M., Bengs, M., Latus, S., Gerlach, S., Cyron, C.J., Sprenger, J., Schlaefer, A.: Ultrasound shear wave elasticity imaging with spatio-temporal deep learning. IEEE Transactions on Biomedical Engineering **69**(11), 3356–3364 (2022)
14. Nightingale, K.R., Palmeri, M.L., Nightingale, R.W., Trahey, G.E.: On the feasibility of remote palpation using acoustic radiation force. The Journal of the Acoustical Society of America **110**(1), 625–634 (2001)
15. Pinton, G.F., Dahl, J.J., Trahey, G.E.: Rapid tracking of small displacements with ultrasound. IEEE transactions on ultrasonics, ferroelectrics, and frequency control **53**(6), 1103–1117 (2006)
16. Shiina, T., Nightingale, K.R., Palmeri, M.L., Hall, T.J., Bamber, J.C., Barr, R.G., Castera, L., Choi, B.I., Chou, Y.H., Cosgrove, D., et al.: Wfumb guidelines and recommendations for clinical use of ultrasound elastography: Part 1: basic principles and terminology. Ultrasound in medicine & biology **41**(5), 1126–1147 (2015)
17. van Sloun, R.J., Wildeboer, R.R., Wijkstra, H., Mischi, M.: Viscoelasticity mapping by identification of local shear wave dynamics. IEEE transactions on ultrasonics, ferroelectrics, and frequency control **64**(11), 1666–1673 (2017)
18. Song, P., Urban, M.W., Manduca, A., Greenleaf, J.F., Chen, S.: Coded excitation plane wave imaging for shear wave motion detection. IEEE transactions on ultrasonics, ferroelectrics, and frequency control **62**(7), 1356–1372 (2015)

19. Song, P., Zhao, H., Urban, M.W., Manduca, A., Pislaru, S.V., Kinnick, R.R., Pislaru, C., Greenleaf, J.F., Chen, S.: Improved shear wave motion detection using pulse-inversion harmonic imaging with a phased array transducer. IEEE transactions on medical imaging **32**(12), 2299–2310 (2013)
20. Tehrani, A.K., Ashikuzzaman, M., Rivaz, H.: Lateral strain imaging using self-supervised and physically inspired constraints in unsupervised regularized elastography. IEEE Transactions on Medical Imaging **42**(5), 1462–1471 (2022)
21. Tehrani, A.K., Dayavansha, E.S., Gu, Y., Jakovljevic, M., Wang, M., Tadross, R., Rivaz, H., Thomenius, K., Samir, A.E.: Advancements in shear wave elastography with neural networks and multi-resolution approaches. In: 2023 IEEE International Ultrasonics Symposium (IUS). pp. 1–4. IEEE (2023)
22. Tehrani, A.K., Rivaz, H.: Displacement estimation in ultrasound elastography using pyramidal convolutional neural network. IEEE transactions on ultrasonics, ferroelectrics, and frequency control **67**(12), 2629–2639 (2020)
23. Wiseman, L.M., Urban, M.W., McGough, R.J.: A parametric evaluation of shear wave speeds estimated with time-of-flight calculations in viscoelastic media. The Journal of the Acoustical Society of America **148**(3), 1349–1371 (2020)

Simplifying Prostate Elastography Using Micro-ultrasound and Transfer Function Imaging

Reid Vassallo[1](✉), Tajwar Abrar Aleef[1,2], Vedanth Desaigoudar[1], Qi Zeng[3,4], David Black[3], Brian Wodlinger[5], Miles Mannas[6], Peter C. Black[6], and Septimiu E. Salcudean[1,3,6]

[1] School of Biomedical Engineering, University of British Columbia, Vancouver, BC, Canada
rvassallo@prostatecentre.com
[2] Synthesis Health, Maple Ridge, BC, Canada
[3] Department of Electrical and Computer Engineering, University of British Columbia, Vancouver, BC, Canada
[4] Boston Children's Hospital, Harvard Medical School, Cambridge, MA, USA
[5] Exact Imaging, Markham, ON, Canada
[6] Department of Urologic Sciences, University of British Columbia, Vancouver, BC, Canada

Abstract. Prostate cancer is one of the most commonly diagnosed cancers worldwide, yet working towards more accurate and cost-effective detection strategies for this disease remains an active area of research. This includes introducing a new method called micro-ultrasound (microUS), which has equal performance to the gold standard multiparametric magnetic resonance imaging for prostate biopsy guidance. Cancerous lesions are often stiffer than their healthy surroundings, and this tissue stiffness can be imaged using elastography. Clinical strain elastography generally uses manual compression of the tissue via the probe face; however, this method is highly user-dependent and can result in unreliable images due to the complexity and steep learning curve to apply ideal compression. Here, we implement and validate a relative elastography method called transfer function (TF) imaging, which uses automatic tissue compression from a voice coil motor attached to the microUS probe for excitation, and calculates the tissue's relative stiffness from its frequency response to this excitation. We demonstrate our method's improved repeatability compared to manual strain elastography using quantitative and qualitative evaluations performed using a commercial quality assurance elasticity phantom. Overall, this method makes elastography much simpler for clinicians, further enabling its use in guiding prostate biopsy procedures.

Keywords: Micro-ultrasound · Elastography · Prostate cancer

1 Introduction

Prostate cancer (PCa) is the fourth most commonly diagnosed cancer worldwide [5], with rates expected to rise until 2040 due in part to an aging population and rising life expectancy worldwide [10]. However, despite its relatively high prevalence, limitations persist in the detection and diagnosis of this disease. Many of these limitations can be traced back to the inability of conventional ultrasound (US) to accurately and reliably identify PCa tumours, as only approximately 50% of PCa lesions are detectable by US [17]. This results in a series of biopsy samples being taken from predefined locations in the prostate to search for the disease, rather than targeting specific suspicious areas [15]. In turn, this systematic sampling technique leads to some cases of clinically significant PCa going undetected, as well as clinically insignificant PCa being overdiagnosed [9]. Together, this results in a relatively poor sensitivity of 48% [1]. Addressing this shortcoming has been an active area of research, and has led to multiparametric magnetic resonance imaging (mpMRI) becoming the gold standard for PCa imaging. However, mpMRI remains an expensive and relatively inaccessible method for disease detection. Another effort to improve this has been the development of the ExactVu™ micro-ultrasound (microUS) system (Exact Imaging, Markham, ON, Canada), which uses a higher transmit frequency of up to 29 MHz (compared to typical 9–12 MHz [11]), allowing it to have an improved spatial resolution of up to 70 μm [6]. Meta-analyses have shown that B-mode microUS alone can guide targeted prostate biopsies as well as mpMRI [24], although a randomized controlled trial is underway to confirm these findings (NCT05220501) [12]. There has recently been additional work to further improve the utility of microUS, including deep learning-based image analysis [20], quantitative US [18], volumetric imaging [23], and elastography [3].

Since tumours are often stiffer than their surrounding healthy tissue [22], elastography using conventional US has been an active area of development for PCa imaging [2,4]. US-based elastography has been a component of previous multiparametric US systems, and contributed to these systems being able to detect PCa better than B-mode alone [13].

A popular method of US-based elastography is shear wave elastography, which provides quantitative estimates of tissue stiffness [2,4]. However, these estimates are only valid if a volumetric image is obtained due to the unknown shear wave direction in the tissue [26]. This makes it difficult to obtain these images in real-time to guide prostate biopsy procedures, as the geometric constraints of a transrectal US (TRUS) probe mean that a matrix array to obtain real-time three dimensional (3D) images are not yet available, and working around this requires additional complexity. However, when trying to pinpoint suspicious areas for PCa in a patient, it is sufficient to be able to identify areas which are relatively stiffer than their surrounding tissue rather than requiring specific quantitative values of absolute stiffness. This relative stiffness information can be provided by strain elastography, which is a technically simpler method.

Current implementations of strain elastography using microUS have relied on manual tissue compression using the probe face, but this is known to have higher inter-observer variability than automated methods [16] due to its complexity and steep learning curve. In an effort to overcome this known limitation of strain elastography, it has previously been demonstrated that relative tissue stiffness can be elucidated from the transfer function (TF) of the tissue's response to an automatically generated vibration [8], even being implemented in real-time [19]. This simplification of the method can allow for much less user-dependent stiffness imaging, which could make it much easier to be clinically adopted.

In this work, the TF elastography method is implemented for the first time using the ExactVu™ microUS system, using a probe-mounted voice coil motor for tissue excitation. The repeatability of this method (as a measure of simplicity for the user) is compared against manual strain elastography using the ExactVu™ using a commercial quality assurance phantom. In summary, the main contributions of this work are: the first implementation of TF-based elastography using microUS and the first integration of probe-mounted voice coil-drive multi-frequency excitation for strain imaging using microUS.

2 Methods

2.1 System Overview

Hardware Setup. To acquire freehand elastography images, some additional hardware is required with the ExactVu™ microUS system. The tissue is excited with a linear voice coil motor which is rigidly affixed to the TRUS probe such that the direction of motion is approximately perpendicular to the imaging array. The excitation frequencies and their relative phases are controlled by a function generator (33220A, Agilent Technologies, USA), and amplified by a previously described custom control box, [4], which uses a Lepy LP-2020A signal amplifier (Lepai, Shenzhen, China). The overall intensity of the signal, and thus the tissue excitation, can be changed by using either a physical knob on the control box or within the custom software controlling the function generator. This setup can be seen in Fig. 1.

Imaging and Excitation Parameters. The voice coil is driven using a sum of sinusoids from 1–10 Hz, with phase offsets chosen to produce a waveform without major constructive interference between the frequencies such that the local maxima are relatively uniform in amplitude. To do so, the phase offsets were sampled randomly from a uniform distribution between 0 and 2π until the above condition was met. These same phase offsets were then used for every imaging session. This excitation can be described as:

$$\sum_{n=1}^{10} sin(2\pi nt + \theta_n) \quad (1)$$

where t represents time (in seconds) and θ_n represents the phase offset for each frequency.

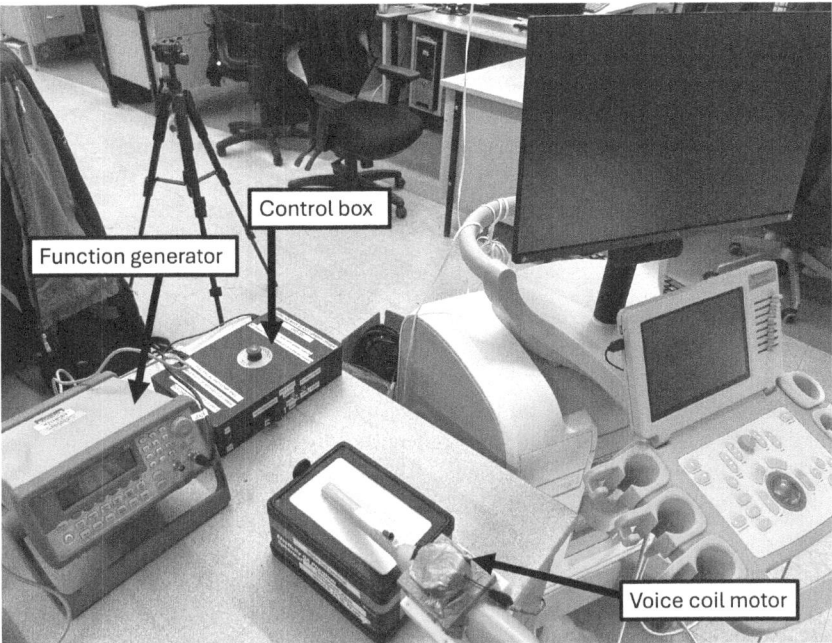

Fig. 1. Our imaging setup including the ExactVu™ microUS device, imaging phantom, and mechanical excitation hardware.

The majority of PCa tumours occur in the peripheral zone [14], which should be sufficiently covered by the imaging depth of 30 mm chosen for this work. A single focal zone was used, set at approximately 25 mm. Our choice of settings resulted in a frame rate of 25 Hz, ensuring that even our maximum excitation frequency (10 Hz) fell below the Nyquist frequency for this frame rate (12.5 Hz). The cine capture feature of the ExactVu™ system was used, and the radiofrequency (RF) data was saved and transmitted automatically over the network to another computer for immediate processing and display.

Image Processing. Tissue displacement is tracked in the RF images using a speckle tracking algorithm [25], and this was then used to calculate the frequency response of the tissue to estimate relative elasticity values, as described below.

The mechanical properties of tissue can be modelled by a one-dimensional model of springs, dampers, and masses which are assembled as Voigt elements, as previously explored in [7]. If this linear network is excited by a waveform consisting of a single frequency, we expect the displacements and local strains will maintain the same frequency, but have different amplitudes and phase lags. This will hold true if the excitation consists of multiple frequencies, as in our case, and the spectra of displacements and strains will cover the same range of frequencies as the input.

The TF between the applied force and displacements has been previously studied [21], including the case where the applied force cannot be accurately measured. In this case, the displacements are taken relative to a common reference location in the image. When this common reference location, arbitrarily chosen as the center of the image in our case, is defined as element j, and the ith element is the block of pixels currently under investigation, the TF of this system is defined as:

$$H_i^j(\omega) = \frac{P_{x_i x_j}(\omega)}{P_{x_i x_i}(\omega)} \tag{2}$$

where $P_{x_i x_i}(\omega)$ is the power spectral density of element $x_i(t)$, and $P_{x_i x_j}(\omega)$ is the cross-spectral density between elements i and j.

Tissue stiffness can be estimated by averaging the magnitude of this TF over a range of low frequencies where it is approximately constant. Here, we calculated the TF, $H_i^j(\omega)$, using 20 image frames. Each patch used for analysis was 28 RF samples in the axial direction, with 50% overlap.

Manual Strain Imaging. To validate TF imaging using microUS, we compared it to manual strain imaging, which has been previously implemented on the ExactVu™ system [3]. To briefly recap this previous implementation, compression was manually applied using the probe face at a frequency of approximately 1 Hz, and tissue displacement (δ) was tracked using the same speckle tracking algorithm as our TF method [25]. The strain (ϵ) was then calculated by finding the spatial derivative of $|\delta|$ along the axial direction of each RF line, described by

$$\epsilon = \frac{d|\delta|}{dx} \tag{3}$$

A Gaussian smoothing filter with an anisotropic kernel (with sigma values of 5 along the x axis and 3 along the y axis) was applied to ϵ in an effort to reduce noise in the resulting image.

2.2 Phantom Validation

Validation of this method was performed using a commercial quality assurance elasticity phantom, namely the CIRS 049 (Computerized Imaging Reference Systems, Norfolk, VA, USA). Imaging was performed on its four small (10 mm diameter) spherical inclusions. The stiffness of each inclusion increases from Type 1 to Type 4, with Type 4 being the stiffest. Imaging was performed freehand in order to best mimic the expected future clinical environment.

Results are based on 10 acquisitions using the TF method and 3 acquisitions (each consisting of 59 frames) using manual compression for each inclusion.

Quantitative Evaluation. We compared our TF method to manual strain imaging using strain ratio (SR) and contrast to noise ratio (CNR), as defined in [3], in order to obtain a pseudo-quantitative assessment of the resulting images.

The interquartile range (IQR), which is the difference between the 75th and 25th percentile values, of these two metrics (SR and CNR) were calculated and are presented in Table 1.

The inclusion and background were manually segmented in MATLAB (The Mathworks, Natick, MA, USA), where the inclusion was a circular region of interest (ROI) drawn to include the spherical inclusion's imaged cross section, and the background ROI was a rectangle in a representative section of the image to one side of the inclusion. These were drawn for each TF image output, but because of the high variability in manual strain images, as seen in Fig. 3, the segmentation was done on the best frame of the series and then mapped to the remaining 58 strain elastography frames.

Qualitative Evaluation. Qualitative evaluation between manual strain and TF imaging was performed by comparing the best and worst images from each method, to get a sense of the variability in the images. The determination of the best and worst frames was done subjectively by considering how visible the inclusions were in each frame.

3 Results

3.1 Quantitative Evaluation

The results of our quantitative evaluation are shown graphically in Fig. 2, and IQR values are shown in Table 1. In almost all cases the inter-image variability, as determined by the IQR for SR and CNR measurements, is demonstrably better for our TF method.

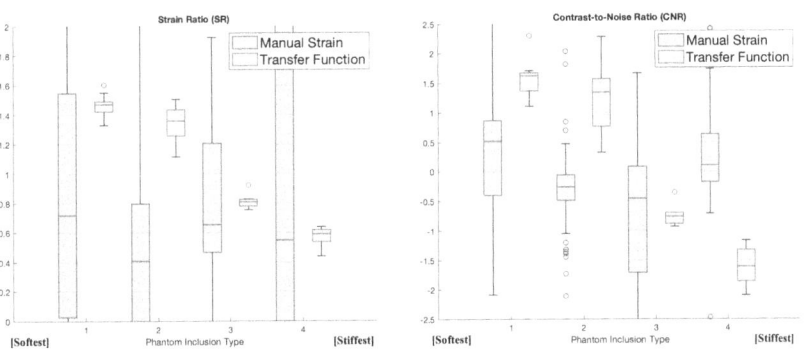

Fig. 2. Boxplots comparing the SR and CNR values of the same phantom inclusions imaged using our proposed TF based method and previously published manual strain elastography using ExactVu™ microUS. IQR values of these boxplots are shown in Table 1

Table 1. Interquartile range (IQR) values for four inclusions, imaged with both elastography methods. The lower IQR for each inclusion is bolded.

	Strain Ratio IQR		Contrast to Noise Ratio IQR	
	Transfer Function	Manual	Transfer Function	Manual
Inclusion 1	**0.07**	1.52	**0.30**	1.27
Inclusion 2	**0.18**	1.69	0.80	**0.43**
Inclusion 3	**0.05**	0.74	**0.19**	1.79
Inclusion 4	**0.08**	2.87	**0.54**	0.82

3.2 Qualitative Evaluation

A qualitative comparison of the best and worst frames for TF and manual strain imaging can be seen in Fig. 3. To further highlight the improved repeatability of our TF method, the display parameters were kept constant between all four displayed TF images, but were adjusted for the manual strain images individually to match the contrast of the TF images for display purposes.

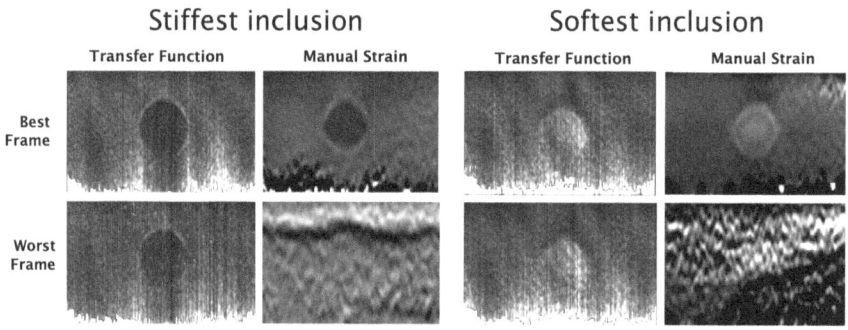

Fig. 3. A qualitative comparison of the best and worst frames acquired using the TF and manual strain methods for the softest and stiffest inclusions. This demonstrates the improved repeatability of the TF method, as compared to manual strain elastography.

4 Discussion

In this work we describe and validate the first known implementation of TF-based elastography using the ExactVu™ microUS system in order to simplify the acquisition of elastography images for PCa detection. We demonstrate its ability to accurately identify inclusions which have different mechanical properties than their surroundings, and particularly that it can do this with less variability between images than manual strain elastography, and should require less user training. As can be seen in Fig. 3, this system is more effective at identifying inclusions which are stiffer than their surroundings, rather than lesions which are softer. This has relevance to our proposed clinical application of PCa detection, as cancers tend to be stiffer than their surroundings, rather than softer [22]. Although a major component of the novelty of this work is the implementation of TF imaging using state-of-the-art microUS, this method can be implemented on any system which can provide access to RF image data.

4.1 Limitations

There are some limitations to this study, which are necessitated by the differences between TF-based and manual strain elastography. The TF method uses a series of 20 frames to calculate the frequency response of the tissue. However, manual strain just uses the displacement measured between two adjacent frames in the time series. Having more frames included in each TF image may inherently improve its reliability as a form of averaging, but we were unable to control for this effectively since it is part of the proposed benefit of this method.

4.2 Future Work

Future work will include optimization of this method to allow for real-time implementation, such that it can be used to guide prostate biopsy procedures. We also plan to integrate the voice coil motor into a system similar to the one proposed in [4] for clinical imaging. It has also been shown that the phase of the TF can be used to determine the viscosity of the tissue under investigation [7], which can provide an additional parameter to identify areas suspicious for harbouring PCa.

5 Conclusion

We demonstrate the first implementation of TF-based strain imaging using microUS. We compared this to previously-published manual strain elastography using the same microUS system using both quantitative and qualitative methods, demonstrating our method's improved repeatability, which we expect will allow for better eventual clinical adoption.

Acknowledgments. This work was funded by the Canadian Institutes of Health Research (CIHR) and the Natural Sciences and Engineering Research Council (NSERC) through a CHRP grant. We also acknowledge the support from the Charles A. Lazlo Chair in Biomedical Engineering held by Professor Salcudean.

Disclosure of Interests. Brian Wodlinger is employed by Exact Imaging, creators of the ExactVu™ system. All other authors have no competing interests to declare.

References

1. Ahmed, H.U., Bosaily, A.E.S., Brown, L.C., Gabe, R., Kaplan, R., Parmar, M.K., Collaco-Moraes, Y., Ward, K., Hindley, R.G., Freeman, A., et al.: Diagnostic accuracy of multi-parametric mri and trus biopsy in prostate cancer (promis): a paired validating confirmatory study. The Lancet **389**(10071), 815–822 (2017)
2. Aleef, T.A., Lobo, J., Baghani, A., Mohammed, S., Eskandari, H., Moradi, H., Rohling, R., Goldenberg, S.L., Morris, W.J., Mahdavi, S.S., et al.: Multi-frequency 3d shear wave absolute vibro-elastography (s-wave) system for the prostate. IEEE Transactions on Medical Imaging (2023)
3. Aleef, T.A., Vassallo, R., Zeng, Q., Mahdavi, S.S., Wodlinger, B., Mannas, M., Black, P.C., Salcudean, S.E.: Implementation of shear wave and strain elastography with micro-ultrasound. In: 2023 IEEE International Ultrasonics Symposium (IUS). pp. 1–6. IEEE (2023)
4. Aleef, T.A., Zeng, Q., Moradi, H., Mohammed, S., Curran, T., Honarvar, M., Rohling, R., Mahdavi, S.S., Salcudean, S.E.: 3d transducer mounted shear wave absolute vibro-elastography: Proof of concept. IEEE Transactions on Ultrasonics, Ferroelectrics, and Frequency Control (2023)
5. Bray, F., Laversanne, M., Sung, H., Ferlay, J., Siegel, R.L., Soerjomataram, I., Jemal, A.: Global cancer statistics 2022: Globocan estimates of incidence and mortality worldwide for 36 cancers in 185 countries. CA: a cancer journal for clinicians **74**(3), 229–263 (2024)
6. Dias, A.B., O'Brien, C., Correas, J.M., Ghai, S.: Multiparametric ultrasound and micro-ultrasound in prostate cancer: a comprehensive review. The British Journal of Radiology **95**(1131), 20210633 (2022)
7. Eskandari, H., Salcudean, S.E., Rohling, R.: Viscoelastic parameter estimation based on spectral analysis. IEEE transactions on ultrasonics, ferroelectrics, and frequency control **55**(7), 1611–1625 (2008)
8. Eskandari, H., Salcudean, S.E., Rohling, R., Baghani, A., Frew, S., Gordon, P.B., Warren, L.: Identifying malignant and benign breast lesions using vibroelastography. In: 2013 IEEE International Ultrasonics Symposium (IUS). pp. 25–28. IEEE (2013)
9. Grossman, D.C., Curry, S.J., Owens, D.K., Bibbins-Domingo, K., Caughey, A.B., Davidson, K.W., Doubeni, C.A., Ebell, M., Epling, J.W., Kemper, A.R., et al.: Screening for prostate cancer: Us preventive services task force recommendation statement. Jama **319**(18), 1901–1913 (2018)
10. James, N.D., Tannock, I., N'Dow, J., Feng, F., Gillessen, S., Ali, S.A., Trujillo, B., Al-Lazikani, B., Attard, G., Bray, F., et al.: The lancet commission on prostate cancer: planning for the surge in cases. The Lancet **403**(10437), 1683–1722 (2024)
11. Klotz, C.L.: Can high resolution micro-ultrasound replace mri in the diagnosis of prostate cancer? European urology focus **6**(2), 419–423 (2020)
12. Klotz, L., Andriole, G., Cash, H., Cooperberg, M., Crawford, E.D., Emberton, M., Gomez-Sancha, F., Klein, E., Lughezzani, G., Marks, L., et al.: Optimization of prostate biopsy-micro-ultrasound versus mri (optimum): A 3-arm randomized controlled trial evaluating the role of 29 mhz micro-ultrasound in guiding prostate biopsy in men with clinical suspicion of prostate cancer. Contemporary Clinical Trials **112**, 106618 (2022)
13. Mannaerts, C.K., Wildeboer, R.R., Remmers, S., van Kollenburg, R.A., Kajtazovic, A., Hagemann, J., Postema, A.W., van Sloun, R.J., J. Roobol, M., Tilki, D., et al.: Multiparametric ultrasound for prostate cancer detection and localization:

correlation of b-mode, shear wave elastography and contrast enhanced ultrasound with radical prostatectomy specimens. The Journal of urology **202**(6), 1166–1173 (2019)
14. McNeal, J.E., Redwine, E.A., Freiha, F.S., Stamey, T.A.: Zonal distribution of prostatic adenocarcinoma: correlation with histologic pattern and direction of spread. The American journal of surgical pathology **12**(12), 897–906 (1988)
15. Mottet, N., Bellmunt, J., Bolla, M., Briers, E., Cumberbatch, M.G., De Santis, M., Fossati, N., Gross, T., Henry, A.M., Joniau, S., et al.: Eau-estro-siog guidelines on prostate cancer. part 1: screening, diagnosis, and local treatment with curative intent. European urology **71**(4), 618–629 (2017)
16. Mulabecirovic, A., Vesterhus, M., Gilja, O.H., Havre, R.F.: In vitro comparison of five different elastography systems for clinical applications, using strain and shear wave technology. Ultrasound in medicine & biology **42**(11), 2572–2588 (2016)
17. Ohori, M., Kattan, M.W., Utsunomiya, T., Suyama, K., Scardino, P.T., Wheeler, T.M.: Do impalpable stage t1c prostate cancers visible on ultrasound differ from those not visible? The Journal of urology **169**(3), 964–968 (2003)
18. Rohrbach, D., Wodlinger, B., Wen, J., Mamou, J., Feleppa, E.: High-frequency quantitative ultrasound for imaging prostate cancer using a novel micro-ultrasound scanner. Ultrasound in medicine & biology **44**(7), 1341–1354 (2018)
19. Salcudean, S.E., French, D., Bachmann, S., Zahiri-Azar, R., Wen, X., Morris, W.J.: Viscoelasticity modeling of the prostate region using vibro-elastography. In: Medical Image Computing and Computer-Assisted Intervention–MICCAI 2006: 9th International Conference, Copenhagen, Denmark, October 1-6, 2006. Proceedings, Part I 9. pp. 389–396. Springer (2006)
20. Shao, Y., Wang, J., Wodlinger, B., Salcudean, S.E.: Improving prostate cancer (pca) classification performance by using three-player minimax game to reduce data source heterogeneity. IEEE Transactions on Medical Imaging **39**(10), 3148–3158 (2020)
21. Turgay, E., Salcudean, S., Rohling, R.: Identifying the mechanical properties of tissue by ultrasound strain imaging. Ultrasound in medicine & biology **32**(2), 221–235 (2006)
22. Tuxhorn, J.A., Ayala, G.E., Smith, M.J., Smith, V.C., Dang, T.D., Rowley, D.R.: Reactive stroma in human prostate cancer: induction of myofibroblast phenotype and extracellular matrix remodeling. Clinical Cancer Research **8**(9), 2912–2923 (2002)
23. Vassallo, R., Aleef, T.A., Zeng, Q., Wodlinger, B., Black, P.C., Salcudean, S.E.: Robotically controlled three-dimensional micro-ultrasound for prostate biopsy guidance. International Journal of Computer Assisted Radiology and Surgery **18**(6), 1093–1099 (2023)
24. You, C., Li, X., Du, Y., Peng, L., Wang, H., Zhang, X., Wang, A.: The microultrasound-guided prostate biopsy in detection of prostate cancer: A systematic review and meta-analysis. Journal of Endourology **36**(3), 394–402 (2022)
25. Zahiri-Azar, R., Salcudean, S.E.: Motion estimation in ultrasound images using time domain cross correlation with prior estimates. IEEE Transactions on Biomedical Engineering **53**(10), 1990–2000 (2006)
26. Zeng, Q., Mohammed, S., Aleef, T.A., Pang, E.H., Hu, C., Jago, J., Rohling, R., Salcudean, S.E.: Multifrequency liver shear wave absolute vibro-elastography with an xmatrix array-2d vs. 3d comparison study. In: 2022 IEEE International Ultrasonics Symposium (IUS). pp. 1–4. IEEE (2022)

Do High-Performance Image-to-Image Translation Networks Enable the Discovery of Radiomic Features? Application to MRI Synthesis from Ultrasound in Prostate Cancer

Mohammad R. Salmanpour[1](✉), Amin Mousavi[2], Yixi Xu[3], William B. Weeks[3], and Ilker Hacihaliloglu[1,4]

[1] Department of Radiology, University of British Columbia, Vancouver, BC, Canada
m.salmanpour@ubc.ca
[2] Department of Computer, Islamic Azad University, Abhar BranchAbhar, Iran
[3] AI for Good Research Lab, Microsoft Corporation, Redmond, WA, USA
[4] Department of Medicine, University of British Columbia, Vancouver, BC, Canada

Abstract. This study investigates the foundational characteristics of image-to-image translation networks, specifically examining their suitability and transferability within the context of routine clinical environments, despite achieving high levels of performance, as indicated by a Structural Similarity Index (SSIM) exceeding 85%. The evaluation study was conducted using data from 794 patients diagnosed with Prostate cancer (PCa). To synthesize MRI from Ultrasound (US) images, we employed five widely recognized image-to-image translation networks in medical imaging: 2D-Pix2Pix, 2D-CycleGAN, 3D-CycleGAN, 3D-UNET, and 3D-AutoEncoder. For quantitative assessment, we report four prevalent evaluation metrics: Mean Absolute Error (MAE), Mean Square Error (MSE), Structural Similarity Index (SSIM), and Peak Signal to Noise Ratio (PSNR). Moreover, a complementary analysis employing Radiomic features (RF) via Spearman correlation coefficient was conducted to investigate, for the first time, whether networks achieving high performance (SSIM > 85%) could identify low-level RFs. The RF analysis showed 75 features out of 186 RFs were discovered via just 2D-Pix2Pix algorithm while half of RFs were lost in the translation process. Finally, a detailed qualitative assessment by five medical doctors indicated a lack of low-level feature discovery in image-to-image translation tasks. This study indicates current image-to-image translation networks, even with a high performance (SSIM > 0.85), don't guarantee the discovery of low-level information which is essential for the integration of synthesized MRI data into regular clinical practice.

Keywords: Ultrasound-to-MRI Translation · Radiomic Feature Analysis · Prostate Cancer

1 Introduction

Ultrasound (US) imaging offers real-time, cost-effective, and bedside diagnostic capabilities. Recent advancements in transducer technology have propelled the adoption of point-of-care ultrasound (POCUS), extending its utility across various clinical domains and beyond hospital settings, particularly in resource-constrained environments [1]. However, persisting challenges including low signal-to-noise ratio (SNR) and the prevalence of imaging artifacts continue to hinder the optimal utilization of both traditional cart-based and POCUS imaging systems [1]. Recently, image-to-image translation methods have been investigated to overcome these problems.

In [2], authors proposed synthesizing pseudo-CT images from US scans.[3] investigated pseudo-anatomical display images generated from ultrasound data. [4] explored a generative attention network for synthesizing X-ray spine images from US scans. Additionally, [1] introduced a self-supervised method for synthesizing MRI fetal brain images from US scans. Quantitative analysis of the synthesized images encompassed the evaluation of key metrics, including MAE, MSE, SSIM, and PSNR [5]. Since these metrics are not always sufficient to capture the complexity of the data and the underlying biological processes [6–9], certain studies have examined the enhancements achieved in downstream tasks, such as image classification or segmentation [10, 11].

Radiomic features (RF), encompassing spatial distribution, shape, intensity, and texture of radiological structures within the translated images, could offer complementary insights to these metrics. Such analysis could ensure that critical diagnostic information such as changes and characteristics in tissues is not lost in the translation process [12]. However, to date, no study has explored the significance of RF analysis in the context of image synthesis.

Therefore, this study aims to compare RFs extracted from the original high-resolution data with those from translated US images (synthesized MRI images), examining the visual similarity of images at detailed information (low feature) levels. Furthermore, this effort represents one of the initial studies into this area, particularly concerning US data. Specifically, we focus our attention on Prostate cancer (PCa), the second most common cancer in men and the fifth leading cause of cancer-related deaths [13]. We make the following contributions: 1) We investigate the synthesis of MRI-like images from US data, utilizing five widely employed deep learning (DL) methods for medical image synthesis: 2D-CycleGAN, 2D-Pix2pix, 3D-CycleGAN, 3D-AutoEncoder, and 3D-UNET [14]. Notably, this marks the first attempt to synthesize prostate MRI images from US data, with a specific focus on the detection of malignant lesions in PCa. 2) We extend the conventional quantitative analysis by investigating the capability of high-performing networks, achieving SSIM scores exceeding 85%, in identifying low-level RFs. This novel exploration sheds light on the intricate relationship between image quality metrics and the extraction of clinically relevant features, providing valuable insights for future research in medical image analysis. 3) We contribute to the qualitative evaluation domain by engaging five experienced medical professionals in assessing the synthesized MRI images. Their qualitative insights provide a nuanced understanding of the clinical utility and perceptual fidelity of the synthesized images, offering valuable feedback for refining and validating the proposed synthesis methodologies.

2 Material and Methods

Patient Data and Preprocessing Steps. We employed 794 patients with PCa who had US, T2-weighted MRI, and masks delineated on both images from The Cancer Imaging Archive (dataset name: Prostate-MRI-US-Biopsy) [15]. US scans were performed with Hitachi Hi-Vision 5500 7.5 MHz or the Noblus C41V 2–10 MHz end-fire probe while MR imaging was performed on a 3 T Trio, Verio or Skyra scanner (Siemens, Erlangen, Germany). All US and MRI images were already registered by our clinical collaborators, cropped to $128 \times 128 \times 64$ cubic millimeters from the prostate gland center, normalized using the min-max function, and then utilized in training.

DL-Based Image Translation. Five image-to-image translation algorithms were investigated to synthesize MRI from US images: 2D-CycleGAN, 2D-Pix2Pix, 3D-CycleGAN, 3D-AutoEncoder, and 3D-UNET [14]. The dataset with 794 patients was split into 3 sections including 75% for training, 10% for training validation, and 15% for external testing. The performance of the networks is assessed through 4 evaluation metrics: MAE, MSE, SSIM, and PSNR. We performed 3-fold cross-validation and reported average in all the experiments. Network parameters are listed in the supplemental file. Individual 2D slices from the 3D volumetric data were used as input for the 2D models. The 3D volume was then reconstructed by integrating these 2D slices. Thus, the assessment of all images generated by both 2D, and 3D networks was based on 3D volumetric data.

RF Analysis. Radiomics feature generator within ViSERA (*visera.ca*), extensively standardized in reference to the Image Biomarker Standardization Initiative [16] was utilized to extract a total of 186 standardized RFs, including 2 local intensity (LI), 18 intensity-based statistics (IS), 23 intensity histogram (IH), 7 Intensity-Volume Histogram (IVH), and 136 texture features containing gray level co-occurrence matrix (GLCM; 50 features), gray level run-length matrix (GLRLM; 32 features), gray level size zones (GLSZM; 16 features), gray level distance zone matrix (GLDZM; 16 features), neighborhood gray-tone difference matrix (NGTDM, 5 features), and neighboring gray level dependence matrix (NGLDM; 17 features). RF analysis was conducted using the Spearman correlation function and paired t-test. This analysis encompassed 186 RFs extracted from the segmented prostate gland of both the original and synthetic MRI images. Moreover, we did not utilize any morphological features in this study due to the utilization of identical masks for extracting such characteristics from various images, encompassing original and synthetic MRIs.

Qualitative Analysis. In the qualitative validation process, we initially present 15 synthetic MRI images randomly selected from the external testing dataset to five medical doctors with over five years of experience (row 2 in Table 1). Their task is to differentiate between original and synthetic prostate MRI images (row 3 in Table 1). Following this, we provide the medical doctors with specified original and synthetic MRI images and pose eight additional questions to them, prompting them to visually compare and evaluate the synthetic MRI images in relation to the original MRI and US images (rows 4–11 in Table 1). To ensure the reliability and validity of our qualitative analysis questions, we designed them and had them reviewed by an independent professional. The evaluating doctors were blinded to the imaging source (original vs. synthesized MRI) during their assessments. Additionally, we performed an average Inter-Item Correlation statistical test to validate the survey's internal consistency, reliability, and validity.

3 Results and Discussions

DL-Based Image Translation Quantitative Assessment. As shown in Fig. 1 (i), 2D-Pix2Pix network significantly outperformed the other four networks, with an average MAE of 0.026 ± 0.007, MSE of $\sim 0.001 \pm 0.001$, SSIM of 0.855 ± 0.032, and PSNR of 28.831 ± 2.067 (P-values < 0.01, paired t-test, compared to the performance provided from other networks). 2D-CycleGAN had an average MAE of 0.141 ± 0.037, MSE of 0.040 ± 0.018, SSIM of 0.372 ± 0.129, and PSNR of 14.538 ± 2.200, while 3D-CycleGAN had an average MAE of 0.192 ± 0.018, MSE of 0.062 ± 0.011, SSIM of 0.301 ± 0.034, and PSNR of 12.124 ± 0.726. In addition, 3D-UNET and 3D-AutoEncoder provided average MAEs of 0.119 ± 0.021 and 0.102 ± 0.022; MSEs of 0.025 ± 0.009 and 0.019 ± 0.008; SSIMs of 0.466 ± 0.059 and 0.553 ± 0.068; and PSNRs of 16.259 ± 1.578 and 17.499 ± 1.761, respectively. Figure 1 (ii) displays images generated by 2D-Pix2Pix networks for four test patients, highlighting qualitative results with high SSIM values and demonstrating the closeness between the original and synthesized MRI images.

RF Analysis. Koo and Li [17] provided a guideline that categorizes correlation coefficients as follows: i) below 0.50 is poor, ii) 0.50–0.75 is moderate, iii) 0.75- 0.90 is good, and iv) above 0.90 is excellent. Therefore, this research employed a threshold of 0.50 to distinguish between groups. Therefore, in our RF analysis, as shown in Fig. 2., feature similarity amounts enabled us to divide RFs into 3 sub-sections, i) Group 1: the low-level RFs were successfully discovered by synthetic MRI images generated through majority of algorithms, ii) Group 2: the low-level RFs were successfully discovered from synthetic MRI images generated by 2D-Pix2Pix algorithm only, and iii) Group 3: the low-level RFs extracted from synthetic MRI images were not successfully discovered, even with high performance algorithm 2D-Pix2Pix.

As shown in Fig. 2. (i), most algorithms, even with low performance (SSIM < 0.6), enable the generation of synthetic MRI images, leading to the discovery of 18 RFs including 1 IS, 2 NGLDM, 4 GLRLM, 2 GLSZM, 6 GLDZM, and 3 NGTDM features. As depicted in Fig. 2. (ii), the analysis revealed that 75 RFs extracted from synthetic MRI images produced by 2D-Pix2Pix network (demonstrating high performance with SSIM > 0.85) exhibited a proportional relationship between the quantitative performance of network and the discovery of low-level features. Thus, Group 2 includes 75 RFs with correlation > 0.5 including 5 IS, 17 IH, 2 IVH, 26 GLCM, 6 NGLDM, 12 GLRLM, 3 GLSZM, 3 GLDZM, and 1 NGTDM. Moreover, Group 3 demonstrated that none of the algorithms, including the one with high performance, facilitated the discovery of 93 low-level features, including 2 LI, 12 IS, 6 IH, 5 IVH, 24 GLCM, 9 NGLDM, 16 GLRLM, 11 GLSZM, 7 GLDZM, 1 NGTDM features (see Fig. 2. (iii)).

i) Distribution of four evaluation metrics

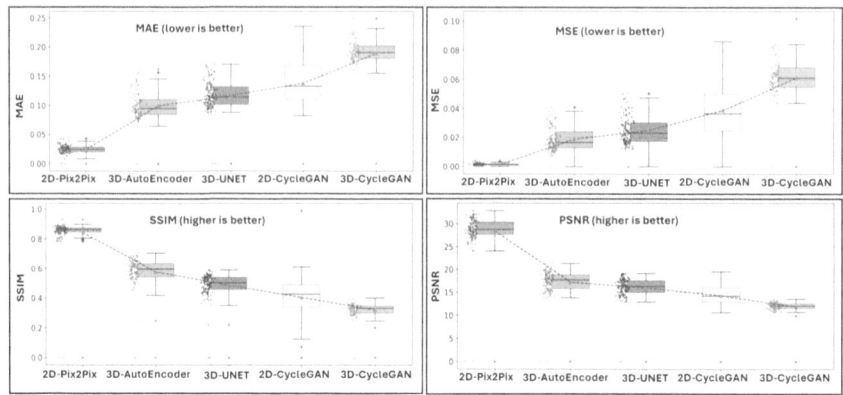

ii) Four examples

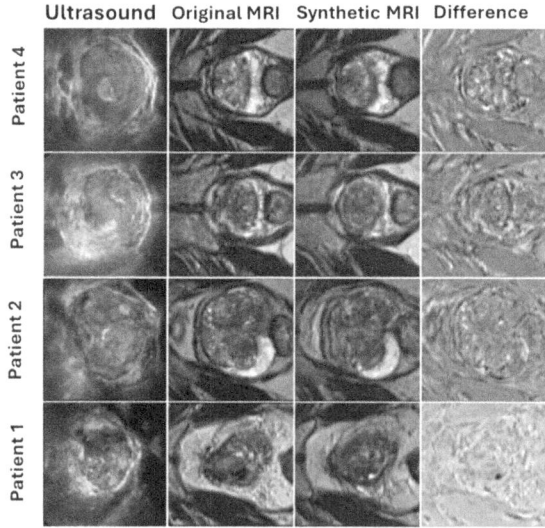

Fig. 1. (i) A distribution of four quantitative evaluation metrics: MAE, MSE, SSIM, and PSNR for 2D-Pix2Pix, 2D-CycleGAN, 3D-CycleGAN, 3D-AutoEncoder, and 3D-UNET in synthesizing MRI images from US images, (ii) four examples of synthetic MRI images provided by 2D-Pix2Pix. Rows show Ultrasound, Original MRI, Synthetic MRI, difference between original and synthetic MRI images. Columns show different patients. All synthetic images had SSIMs > 0.85. **High resolution of this figure is provided in "Code and Data Availability" section.**

Qualitative Analysis. The qualitative evaluation of synthetic MRI images, guided by feedback from experienced medical practitioners, was centered on assessing the fidelity of anatomical delineation and tissue contrast compared to original MRI counterparts. Five doctors assessed the perceptual clarity of anatomical structures, precision of boundary delineation, and the presence of any discernible artifacts, crucial factors underpinning

Application to MRI Synthesis from Ultrasound in Prostate Cancer

Fig. 2. Different Radiomic feature (RF) groups provided by RF Analysis. i) Group 1 showed 18 low-level RFs successfully discovered by synthetic MRI images generated through majority of algorithms, ii) Group 2 showed 75 low-level RFs were successfully discovered from synthetic MRI images generated by 2D-Pix2Pix, and iii) Group 3 showed synthetic MRI images generated by the current generative networks couldn't discovered 93 low-level RFs. **High resolution of this figure is provided in "Code and Data Availability" section.**

the integration of synthetic MRI into clinical practice. Doctors' evaluations were highly consistent, with an average Inter-Item Correlation Coefficient of 0.99, affirming the survey's reliability. As mentioned previously, each doctor possessed extensive expertise exceeding five years in the interpretation of diverse medical imaging modalities including MRI and US (Table 1, row 2). All five experts could discriminate synthetic MRI from original MRI (row 3). Despite average SSIM > 0.85, all doctors believed that the quality of synthetic MRI images (in terms of detailed information) was not comparable with the original ones (row 4).

Furthermore, practitioners remarked upon the salient presence of artifacts within synthetic MRI images, serving as a distinguishing hallmark vis-à-vis their authentic counterparts (row 5). All experts believed that diagnosis using the synthetic MRI (even with SSIM > 0.85) is difficult, compared to original MRI images (row 6). Although all doctors believed that synthetic MRI images added no value compared to the original MRI (row 7), some experts expressed that synthetic MRI images added value to the diagnosis process compared to US images (row 8) in terms of anatomical structure. Nonetheless, the majority consensus underscored the perceptible discrepancies in resolution and contrast levels between synthetic and original MRI images (row 9). Collectively, practitioners underscored the lack of detailed anatomical information, particularly pertaining to low-level features, within synthetic MRI images - a pivotal focus of this inquiry. Thereby, they were convinced that there are potential clinical benefits of using synthetic MRI images and strongly support the integration of synthetic MRI technology into regular clinical practice if the synthetic MRI images include detailed information (rows 10 and 11). One notable benefit is that synthetic MRIs can improve diagnosis in emergency situations where access to MRI scans is limited.

Discussions. We have shown that RF analysis is vital to address the limitations of standard metrics such as MAE, MSE, SSIM, and PSNR in image-to-image translation tasks. RFs extend beyond above metrics, offering a more comprehensive analysis that identifies important characteristics such as shape, intensity, texture, and patterns that are used for diagnostics. These features are pivotal for unraveling the underlying biological and pathological information, providing a richer understanding of the intricacies within the synthesized medical images [12]. Our analysis investigates that translated images retain clinically relevant information, bridging the gap between statistical accuracy and clinical utility, which is often overlooked by conventional evaluation metrics. We believe that this deeper level of analysis is essential in a clinical context, as it can reveal subtle changes and characteristics in tissues that might be crucial for accurate diagnosis, disease monitoring, and treatment planning [12]. By integrating RFs, we ensure that the image translation networks are not only statistically accurate but also effective and meaningful in real-world medical applications, enhancing the reliability and utility of these technologies in healthcare settings [18].

RF analysis in this study indicated that RFs can be divided into three sections in US to MRI translation, including i) a set of low-level features (RFs) that can be discovered by the majority of networks, even with low-performance algorithms, ii) a set of low-level features that can be discovered by high-performances networks only, and iii) a set of low-level features currently undetectable by any existing networks (high or low performance networks). RF analysis, beyond conventional metrics quantifying overall

Table 1. Qualitative analysis of synthetic MRI by 5 medical doctors (D).

Questions (Q), Scoring system: 0 = zero, 1 = low, 2 = intermediate, 3 = high, 4 = very high	D 1	D 2	D 3	D 4	D 5
Q1: What is your medical specialty and how many years of experience do you have in interpreting MRI and ultrasound images? (years)	> 5	> 6	> 5	> 5	> 5
Q2: How many doctors could discriminate the synthetic MRI from the original MRI properly? (15 external testing images existed)	15	15	15	15	15
Q3: After specifying synthetic and original MRI for you, how would you rate the overall quality of synthetic MRI images compared to original MRI?	1	2	1	1	1
Q4: Are there any noticeable artifacts or inaccuracies in the synthetic MRI images?	4	2	4	4	3
Q5: How confident are you in making a diagnosis based on synthetic MRI images versus original MRI?	1	1	1	1	1
Q6: Do synthetic MRI images offer any additional diagnostic information compared to the original MRI images? How much?	0	0	0	0	0
Q7: Do synthetic MRI images offer any additional diagnostic information compared to the original Ultrasound images? How much?	2	2	3	2	3
Q8: How do you assess the resolution and contrast of the synthetic MRI images, compared to original MRI images?	1	2	1	2	2
Q9: In your opinion, how much are the potential clinical benefits of using synthetic MRI images?	4	3	3	4	3
Q10: Would you support the integration of synthetic MRI technology into regular clinical practice? How much?	4	4	4	4	4

error and similarity, obviously shows that current translation networks, even 2D-Pix2Pix with SSIM > 85% are not able to discover half of RFs (93 out of 186 RFs in Group 3). Group 1 showed that 18 RFs out of 186 features can be discovered by the majority of algorithms, even with low-performance algorithms while Group 2 indicated that just 75 RFs can be roughly restored by high-performance translation networks (2D-Pix2Pix).

Thus, the identification of RFs is contingent upon the efficacy of algorithms such as MAE, MSE, SSIM, and PSNR. Notably, algorithms demonstrating superior performance, exemplified by 2D-Pix2Pix, facilitate the synthesis of MRI images, thereby enabling the discernment of certain low-level RFs. Despite the marked significant enhancement observed in the similarity index of RFs derived from synthetic MRI images generated by 2D-Pix2Pix in comparison to other image-to-image algorithms across various groups (P-Value < 0.05, paired t-test), there persists a pressing imperative to refine image-to-image translation networks to optimize the performance of low-level features.

Qualitative analysis indicated that differences in quality, existing artifacts, resolution, and contrast between synthetic and original MRI images enabled all doctors to successfully discriminate between the synthetic and original MRI images. Furthermore, all doctors expressed that diagnosis using the synthetic MRI (even with SSIM > 0.85), compared to original MRI images, is difficult and the synthetic MRI images didn't cover all low-level features which are essential for successful diagnosis. Thus, it can be concluded that translation networks with high performances didn't guarantee appropriate discovery of low-level features. However, some doctors expressed that the synthetic MRI images added value to the diagnosis process beside US images. They believed that enhancing the detailed information in synthetic MRI images is necessary for integrating synthetic MRI technology into regular clinical practice. This is especially important in low-resource settings where access to traditional MRI is challenging, as pursued in this study.

Our RF analysis indicated that 74% of IH features belonged to Group 2, which highly depends on network performance. These features offer a comprehensive quantitative analysis of tumor traits in medical images, improving cancer diagnosis and assessment. By quantifying pixel intensities, they reveal details about tumor heterogeneity, the microenvironment, and responses to treatment, indicating cellular complexities. Statistics like Mean, Variance, Skewness, and Kurtosis analyze the distribution's tendency and shape, while Median, Mode, and Percentiles examine the data's central aspects and variability. Additionally, metrics such as Entropy, Uniformity, and Gradient evaluate image texture and edges, crucial for assessing tissue characteristics and aiding diagnosis.

GLCM features, complementing visual assessment, are a statistical method to analyze image texture. In this study, 53% of GLCM features belonged to Group 2 while the remaining 47% of features went to Group 3, indicating disabilities of the current networks to discover these kinds of features. These features quantify the co-occurrence of gray levels at specific offsets, providing information about homogeneity, contrast, and other textural properties of images. Radiologists use GLCM features to differentiate between healthy and abnormal tissues, aiding in disease detection and prognosis.

Most NGTDM features fell into Group 1, showing a general consistency with network performance. These features examine the local differences in gray-tone intensities in medical images, offering crucial texture information that improves the accuracy of visual assessments. This assists in differentiating between malignant and benign lesions, thereby enhancing diagnostic decisions. All features of LI and most features of IS fall under Group 3. These characteristics help measure minor changes in the intensity of individual pixels in tumor areas, enhancing visual evaluations. Furthermore, IVH features, indicating the relationship between a gray level area and the fraction of the volume of the histogram, offer a comprehensive perspective on the distribution of intensity, assisting medical professionals in grasping the diversity within tumors. Further, the majority of GLRLM, GLSZM, NGLDM, and GLDZM belonged to Group 3. These features provide insights into tumor heterogeneity, spatial patterns, and microstructure, guiding clinical decisions and patient management.

A recent study [19] has developed a novel technique for enhancing MRI-to-CT image conversion, utilizing a loss function derived from GLCM to reproduce texture features more accurately in generated CT images. This method surpasses traditional pixel-based approaches by focusing on improving texture quality, potentially offering significant benefits to medical image synthesis and its clinical applications. Considering that RFs derived from multiple imaging techniques provide extra information for various purposes, the selection of the most pertinent features for inclusion in the loss function grows more complicated and will be left for a future study. Additionally, we plan to extend our research to larger datasets and other medical imaging datasets. We also aim to explore newer architectures, such as diffusion models, to broaden the applicability of our findings in future studies.

4 Conclusions

In summary, this study, employing RF and qualitative analysis conducted by five experienced physicians, determined that synthetic MRI images produced by existing image-to-image translation algorithms, despite achieving a high SSIM performance > 0.85, fail to facilitate the detection of crucial low-level features essential for accurate diagnosis and decision-making processes. Consequently, there is a pressing need for further refinement of image-to-image translation networks to enhance the performance of low-level features. Future work will involve exploring diffusion model-based analysis and developing loss functions that integrate radiomic features (RF) into their design, aiming to enhance the rate of feature discovery.

Acknowledgments. This work was supported by the Mitacs Accelerate program (AWD-024298-IT33280), the NSERC Discovery Grant (RGPIN-2023–03575), The Canadian Foundation for Innovation (CFI)- John R. Evans Leaders Fund (JELF) program grant number 42816, and Microsoft's AI for Good Lab.

Disclosure of Interests. The authors have no competing interests to declare that are relevant to the content of this article.

Code and Data Availability. All relevant information: RF names, codes, high resolution figures and tables are available on: https://github.com/MohammadRSalmanpour/MRI-to-US-Translation_MICCAI/.

References

1. J. Jiao, A. Namburete and et al, "Self-supervised ultrasound to MRI fetal brain image synthesis," IEEE Transactions on Medical Imaging, vol. 39, no. 12, pp. 4413-24, 2020.
2. H. Sun, Z. Lu and et al, "Research on obtaining pseudo CT images based on stacked generative adversarial network," Quant Imaging Med Surg, vol. 11, no. 5, p. 1983–2000, 2021.
3. L. Barkat, M. Freiman and H. Azhari, "Image Translation of Breast Ultrasound to Pseudo Anatomical Display by CycleGAN," Bioengineering, vol. 10, no. 3, p. 388, 2023.
4. W. Jiang, C. Yu and et al, "Ultrasound to X-ray synthesis generative attentional network (UXGAN) for adolescent idiopathic scoliosis," Ultrasonics, vol. 126, p. 106819, 2022.
5. 6. U. Sara, M. Akter and et al, "Image Quality Assessment through FSIM, SSIM, MSE and PSNR—A Comparative Study," Journal of Computer and Communications, vol. 7, no. 3, pp. 8-18, 2019.

6. 7. L. Zhang, L. Zhang and et al, "FSIM: A Feature Similarity Index for Image Quality Assessment," IEEE Transactions on Image Processing, vol. 20, no. 8, pp. 2378-2386, 2011.
7. 8. A. Liu, W. Lin and M. Narwaria, "Image quality assessment based on gradient similarity," IEEE Transactions on Image Processing, vol. 21, no. 4, p. 1500–1512, 2012.
8. 9. X. Zhang, X. Feng and et al, "Edge strength similarity for image quality assessment," IEEE Signal Processing Letters, vol. 20, no. 4, p. 319–322, 2013.
9. 10. L. Zhang, Y. Shen and H. Li, "A visual saliency-induced index for perceptual image quality assessment," IEEE Transactions on Image Processing, vol. 23, no. 10, p. 4270–4281, 2014.
10. 11. A. Alotaibi, "Deep Generative Adversarial Networks for Image-to-Image Translation: A Review," Symmetry, vol. 12, no. 10, p. 1705, 2020.
11. 12. Y. Pang, J. Lin and et al, "Image-to-Image Translation: Methods and Applications," IEEE Transactions on Multimedia, vol. 24, pp. 3859-3881, 2022.
12. 13. S. Rizzo, F. Botta and et al, "Radiomics: the facts and the challenges of image analysis," European Radiology Experimental, vol. 2, no. 1, pp. 1-8, 2018.
13. 14. H. Sung, J. Ferlay and et al, "Global cancer statistics 2020: GLOBOCAN estimates of incidence and mortality worldwide for 36 cancers in 185 countries," CA Cancer J Clin, Vols. 209-249, p. 71, 2021.
14. 15. V. de Souza, B. Marques and et al, "A review on generative adversarial networks for image generation," Computers & Graphics, vol. 114, pp. 13-25, 2023.
15. Natarajan, S., et al.: Prostate MRI and ultrasound with pathology and coordinates of tracked biopsy (Prostate-MRI-US-Biopsy) (version 2). Cancer Imaging Arch. **10** (2020)
16. Zwanenburg, A., et al.: The image biomarker standardization initiative: Standardized quantitative radiomics for high-throughput image-based phenotyping. Radiology **295**(2), 328–338 (2020)
17. 18. T. Koo and M. Li, "A Guideline of Selecting and Reporting Intraclass Correlation Coefficients for Reliability Research," J Chiropr Med, vol. 15, no. 2, p. 155–163, 2016.
18. 19. Y. Qin, L. Zhu and et al, "Review of radiomics-and dosiomics-based predicting models for rectal cancer," Frontiers in Oncology, vol. 12, p. 913683, 2022.
19. Yuan, S., et al.: A novel loss function to reproduce texture features for deep learning-based MRI-to-CT synthesis. Med Phys 1–12 (2023)

PHOCUS: Physics-Based Deconvolution for Ultrasound Resolution Enhancement

Felix Duelmer[1,2,3,4](✉), Walter Simson[5], Mohammad Farid Azampour[1,2], Magdalena Wysocki[1,2,6], Angelos Karlas[7,8], and Nassir Navab[1,2]

[1] Chair for Computer-Aided Medical Procedures and Augmented Reality, School of Computation, Information and Technology, Technical University of Munich, Munich, Germany
[2] Munich Center for Machine Learning (MCML), Munich, Germany
[3] Institute of Biological and Medical Imaging, Helmholtz Zentrum Munich, Neuherberg, Germany
[4] Chair of Biological Imaging, School of Medicine, Technical University of Munich, Munich, Germany
felix.duelmer@tum.de
[5] Department of Radiology, School of Medicine, Stanford University, Stanford, USA
[6] LUMA Vision GmbH, Munich, Germany
[7] Department for Vascular and Endovascular Surgery, Rechts der Isar University Hospital, Technical University of Munich, Munich, Germany
[8] German Centre for Cardiovascular Research, Munich, Germany

Abstract. Ultrasound is widely used in medical diagnostics allowing for accessible and powerful imaging but suffers from resolution limitations due to diffraction and the finite aperture of the imaging system, which restricts diagnostic use. The impulse function of an ultrasound imaging system is called the point spread function (PSF), which is convolved with the spatial distribution of reflectors in the image formation process. Recovering high-resolution reflector distributions by removing image distortions induced by the convolution process improves image clarity and detail. Conventionally, deconvolution techniques attempt to rectify the imaging system's dependent PSF, working directly on the radio-frequency (RF) data. However, RF data is often not readily accessible. Therefore, we introduce a physics-based deconvolution process using a modeled PSF, working directly on the more commonly available B-mode images. By leveraging Implicit Neural Representations (INRs), we learn a continuous mapping from spatial locations to their respective echogenicity values, effectively compensating for the discretized image space. Our contribution consists of a novel methodology for retrieving a continuous echogenicity map directly from a B-mode image through a differentiable physics-based rendering pipeline for ultrasound resolution enhancement. We qualitatively and quantitatively evaluate our approach on synthetic data, demonstrating improvements over traditional methods in metrics such as PSNR and SSIM. Furthermore, we show qualitative enhancements on an ultrasound phantom and an in-vivo acquisition of a carotid artery.

Keywords: Ultrasound Image Formation · Ultrasound Deconvolution · Point-spread-function · Implicit Neural Representation in Ultrasound

1 Introduction

Medical ultrasound (US) imaging examines biological tissue using acoustic sound waves to create images based on the received echoes. The relatively low frequency and limited aperture size compared to other imaging modalities like CT and MRI reduce the diffraction-limited resolution of ultrasound imaging. This limitation affects the diagnostic efficacy of ultrasound imaging, making it challenging to identify small tumors or subtle tissue abnormalities accurately.

Deconvolution models describe techniques to improve image resolution in ultrasound imaging, by modeling the point-spread-function (PSF) of the imaging system and convolving the image with its inverse [6]. Deconvolution has been proven useful in various medical tasks such as tissue characterization [1], prostate cancer detection [9], and microbubble localization [3]. The basis of this approach is a model of the imaging formation process as a spatially invariant convolution of the PSF with the echogenicity map, which represents the tissue reflectivity function (TRF). The PSF of an imaging system encapsulates all parameters of the imaging system, such as transducer geometry and frequency response. By modeling the inverse process of this idealized imaging system via deconvolution, the underlying TRF can be recovered. In theory, deconvolution eliminates an acquisition-specific influence on the final B-mode image and addresses the resolution challenges associated with a limited bandwidth of the transducer.

In general, deconvolution can be divided into blind (unknown PSF) [4] and non-blind (known PSF) approaches [2]. Even though knowing the PSF reduces the solution space, deconvolution is an ill-posed problem where multiple possible solutions exist for one target. One approach to this problem is to formulate the deconvolution as a Maximum A Posteriori (MAP) estimation, as proposed in [1]. It provides a structured approach but limits the solution to the given priors and can be noise-sensitive. Newer methods employ neural networks to execute the deconvolution process [7], demonstrating the potential to recover high-quality images from sparse signals. Recently, implicit neural representations (INR) have gained attention as a continuous and adaptable mapping function between spatial coordinates and a sensor space [16]. At the core, the weights of an MLP are optimized to minimize the difference between regressed and target sensor data. INRs have been successfully applied in the medical domain for sparse-view CT reconstruction [14,18] or for novel view synthesis in ultrasound imaging using a physics-based rendering [15].

Inspired by the recent work, we propose to leverage INRs to learn the continuous underlying echogenicity map from a B-mode image in order to enhance resolution. Our approach utilizes a deconvolutional method, based on a modeled PSF, and integrates a fully differentiable rendering pipeline. This allows us to estimate the echogenicity map by comparing predicted and acquired B-mode images. We evaluate the effectiveness of our framework using synthetic, in-vitro, and in-vivo US data. Our contributions are as follows:

1. a novel methodology to retrieve the continuous echogenicity map of soft tissue anatomy by learning its implicit neural representation
2. a physics-informed, differentiable rendering pipeline that models the ultrasound formation process

2 Methods

2.1 Image Formation Process

Following [5,12,17], we model the pulse-echo time series data as a linear system that can be estimated as:

$$y(z,t) = h(z,t) * \gamma(z) + n(t), \tag{1}$$

where y is the beamformed radio frequency (RF) data per channel based on time t and distance z from the transducer to the interrogated point. h represents the PSF, γ denotes the underlying echogenicity map, n is positive zero-mean Gaussian noise, and $*$ signifies a convolution. To remove the dependency on time t, we assume a constant speed of sound of $v_{SoS} = 1.54$ mm/μs and can, therefore, write everything in spatial coordinates, given a known signal frequency f_s. This simplifies the equation to:

$$y(z \mid f_s, v_{SoS}) = h(z) * \gamma(z) + n(z) \tag{2}$$

To acquire a realistic PSF, we follow [13] in their representation of the imaging system as a convolution of the transmit and receive aperture functions multiplied with the axial pulse in k_s-space. We present the PSF function in the spatial domain as the outer product $\otimes$ of the axial h_{ax} and lateral h_{lat} pressure distribution:

$$h(x', z') = h_{lat}(x') \otimes h_{ax}(z') \tag{3}$$

Due to aperture growth and synthetic aperture focusing of modern US machines, we assume an isotropic PSF function in the image, thereby removing the dependence on z in Eq. 2. We furthermore introduce independent axial and lateral spatial variables x' and z'. The lateral pressure distribution at the focal distance r of a beam can be estimated by the convolution of the Fourier transform of the receive and transmit aperture functions [13]. Assuming a uniform apodization function, we model the aperture functions as:

$$A_T(t, f_s, D) = A_R(t, f_s, D) = t \cdot f_x \cdot rect(1/D) \tag{4}$$

where A_T and A_R refer to the aperture function of the transmit and the receive signal, respectively, and lateral aperture extent D. The evaluation of the lateral signal at an arbitrary focal point $f_x(x) = x/(\lambda z)$ can be written as:

$$h_{lat}(x' \mid \lambda, D, r) = \mathcal{F}(A_T) * \mathcal{F}(A_R) = D^2 \text{sinc}^2\left(\frac{Dx'}{r\lambda}\right) \tag{5}$$

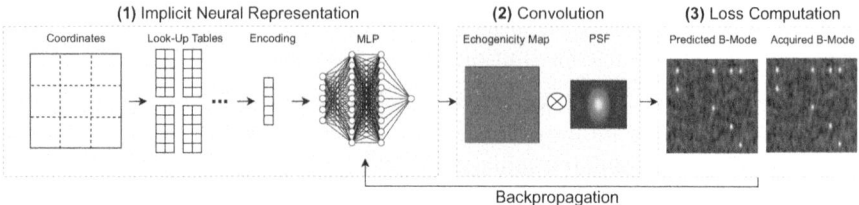

Fig. 1. General outline of the proposed framework:**(1)** encoding of the input location based on a multi-resolution look-up table, which forms the input to the MLP (inspired by [11]). The neural network predicts the echogenicity map. **(2)** convolution of the echogenicity map γ with the PSF h. **(3)** computation of the loss and backpropagation to update the MLP.

where λ is the wavelength and $\mathcal{F}$ represents the Fourier transform. To have a non-negative PSF and remove envelope detection in our pipeline, we model the axial signal as a Gaussian following [2]:

$$h_{ax}(z' \mid \sigma_z) = exp(-\frac{z'^2}{2 * \sigma_z^2}) \qquad (6)$$

with σ_z corresponding to a scaling factor based on the number of cycles for the axial pulse. Due to the simplification and assumptions, we limit the environment to comply with the first-order Born approximation theorem, similar to [4,10,12,13]. This implies that an echo of a target only affects the target and does not influence any other backscattering signal [5].

2.2 Proposed Framework

Our framework consists of three components for approximating the continuous echogenicity map of the tissue, as described in Fig. 1. First, an INR that predicts a scalar echogenicity value s for a given spatial location $x \in \mathbf{R}^2$. Second, a differentiable rendering pipeline convolving a PSF with the predicted echogenicity map. Third, the backpropagation of the computed loss function for updating the parameters in the INR.

In the first step, the input space is divided into multiple grids of L different resolution levels, where the vertex indices are used to perform a hash-based table lookup. In this table, an F-dimensional trainable feature vector is stored. The feature tables have a fixed size of T entries. A bilinear interpolation weighs the inputs based on the respective location in the grid. Finally, the concatenation of the different resolution levels forms the input $\theta \in \mathbf{R}^{LF}$ to the MLP. Based on this encoding, the MLP predicts the echogenicity value s. Performing the convolution of the echogenicity map with the PSF, we get the envelope data e.

$$e(x, z) = h(x', z') * s(x, z) \qquad (7)$$

Mimicking the image formation process of B-mode images, we perform log compression on the envelope data to get the B-mode image in decibels. To constrain the INR, we include three different loss functions that can be separated into regularizing the output and regularizing the echogenicity map.

$$\mathcal{L} = \lambda \text{SSIM}(I', I) + (1-\lambda) \sum_{i \in I} (I'(i) - I(i))^2 + \epsilon TV(S) \qquad (8)$$

Similar to [15], we employ SSIM and L2 loss as a similarity measurement between the predicted Image I' and its acquired counterpart I. Additionally, we use a total variation loss for regularizing the predicted echogenicity map S. This has been shown to be useful in the regularization of deconvolutional algorithms [2] and enhanced results for us as well. We empirically determined that the best results were acquired by setting $\lambda = 0.5$ and $\epsilon = 1e-4$.

2.3 Richardson-Lucy Algorithm

As a comparison, we use the Richardson-Lucy algorithm [8], which has been shown to be efficient for ultrasound deconvolution [2]. The Richardson-Lucy algorithm is an iterative algorithm that refines image f with each step n by applying:

$$f_{n+1} = \left(\frac{d}{h * f_n} * \bar{h}\right) \cdot f_n \qquad (9)$$

where d represents the target image. h and $\bar{h}$ denote the PSF and the complex conjugate of the PSF, respectively.

2.4 Data

In Silico Data: To compare our method with the baseline, we use the general-purpose ultrasound phantom from CIRS (model 054GS). For synthetic and real data evaluation, we reconstructed the structure of the CIRS phantom based on available measurements[1] and estimated unknown parameters to visually match the outline of the acquired b-mode of the phantom.

Axial and Lateral Resolution Targets: We use the close proximity targets on the CIRS phantom to evaluate the axial and lateral resolution capability of our approach. In total, 12 nylon wires are spread out at a depth of 3 cm. The wires have a diameter of 80 microns, and the closest wires are 0.25 mm apart from each other.

Cylindrical Inclusions: The grayscale targets, located at a depth similar to that of the resolution targets, consist of six cylindrical inclusions aligned side by side, each measuring 8 mm in diameter. We visualize three central cylinders with a contrast of (+6, +3, -3) in decibels in comparison to the background.

---

[1] https://www.cirsinc.com/wp-content/uploads/2020/12/054GS-UG-062119.pdf.

Synthetic Image Formation Process: In order to create the echogenicity map, we take the structures and the mean intensities based on the decibels defined above and then apply Rayleigh distribution-based variations to the different labels. The scale parameter σ is calculated based on the relation between the mean μ of the distribution $f(x \mid \sigma)$ and the scale given by $\mu(f(x \mid \sigma)) = \sigma\sqrt{\frac{\pi}{2}}$.

$$f(x \mid \sigma) = \frac{x}{\sigma^2} e^{-x^2/(2\sigma^2)}, \quad x \geq 0, \tag{10}$$

After the convolution of the generated echogenicity map with a PSF, we perform log compression on the data to get the synthetic B-mode image. For the synthetic imaging, we create a PSF based on a central frequency of 10 MHz, an f-number of 2 (ratio of the focal distance to the diameter of the aperture), and an axial pulse length based on 5 cycles.

In-Vitro and In-Vivo: Data were acquired using a Siemens Juniper Acuson ultrasound system with a 12L3 linear probe. Images were retrieved from the ultrasound machine using a frame grabber. To eliminate distortions, the phantom was submerged in a water bath, and all post-processing features like tissue harmonic imaging were disabled to produce unprocessed B-mode images. For the in-vivo study, a B-mode image of a healthy volunteer's carotid artery was obtained under an approved institutional review protocol.

3 Experiments and Results

3.1 Implementation Details

The MLP and the learnable feature tables were written in Pytorch. We achieved the best ratio of performance and accuracy when setting the number of the learnable parameter table size to 2^{22} using only a single-dimensional feature per entry and 15 resolution levels. Using the learnable tables, the MLP can be rather small, so we set it to 2 layers with 64 neurons as proposed by [11]. Similarly, for optimization, we used Adam as an optimizer with a learning rate of 0.01. Due to the possibility that the pixel resolution may not be sufficiently high, we incorporated oversampling of the spatial grid to meet the Nyquist criteria. To improve continuity, we implemented random sampling between grid points. Convergence was usually reached after 5000 iterations. All the training was done on a single workstation with an NVIDIA RTX 4070 Ti. The code for this work can be found on GitHub[2].

3.2 Synthetic Dataset

In Fig. 2, we compare the ground truth echogenicity map and the predicted ones from the Richardson-Lucy algorithm and our proposed methodology. Both

---
[2] https://github.com/Felixduelmer/phocus.

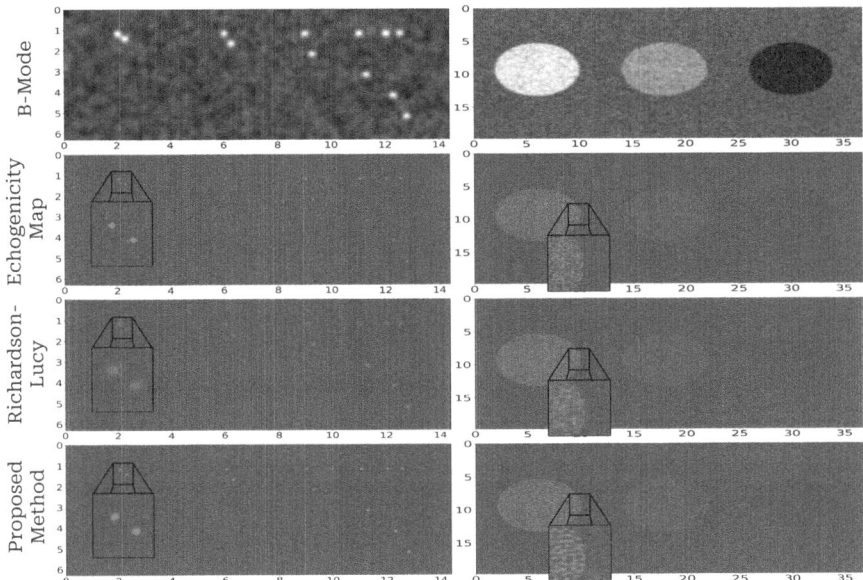

Fig. 2. The left column represents the axial and lateral resolution targets, and the right column displays the cylindrical inclusions.

methods operate on the same PSF. As the Richardson-Lucy algorithm predicts the echogenicity map directly in log-compressed space, we perform log compression on our prediction and on the ground truth map. Figure 2 highlights, within the enlarged red bounding boxes, that the proposed method generates high-resolution images. Unlike the Richardson-Lucy algorithm, our approach delivers sharper edges and achieves clearer target separation. Accordingly, we observe better values for Peak Signal-to-Noise Ratio (PSNR) and Structural Similarity Index (SSIM), when comparing the ground truth maps with the predicted echogenicity map (see Table 1).

Table 1. Quantitative evaluation of the deconvolution algorithms

	Cylindrical Inclusions		Wire Targets	
	PSNR	SSIM	PSNR	SSIM
Richardson-Lucy	16.89	0.21	17.35	0.06
Proposed Method	**17.85**	**0.29**	**17.85**	**0.07**

3.3 Wire Target In-Vitro

Following the synthetic results we evaluate the feasibility of our approach on real B-mode data. In order to obtain the PSF, we performed a grid search by varying the f-number from 1.0 to 4.0 in steps of 0.5 and the number of cycles for

Fig. 3. Predicted echogenicity map (center) of the B-mode image (left). The right side shows the result of the minimum enclosing circles' algorithm on the filtered and clustered image.

the transmit pulse from 1 to 5 and selected the best results. As can be seen in Fig. 3, the targets are notably smaller and are clearly separable. For quantitative evaluation, we perform an intensity thresholding at 20%, filter for noise, and then perform a clustering. Consequently, we calculate the cluster centers and the respective radius for each cluster. Following this process, we end up with 10 of the 12 expected targets, a mean radius of 0.053 mm, and a standard deviation of 0.01 mm which is close to the expected 0.04 mm value.

3.4 Carotid Data In-Vivo

Lastly, we demonstrate our approach on the carotid of a volunteer. As can be seen in Fig. 4, we can reconstruct the B-mode image with the predicted echogenicity map. Additionally, the intima layer in the carotid is more clearly visible on the echogenicity map. Evaluating the predicted map, we reconstruct the B-mode image with a baseband and harmonic frequency to display the generalization ability of our proposed method. In this way, we show a tighter speckle and sharper resolution.

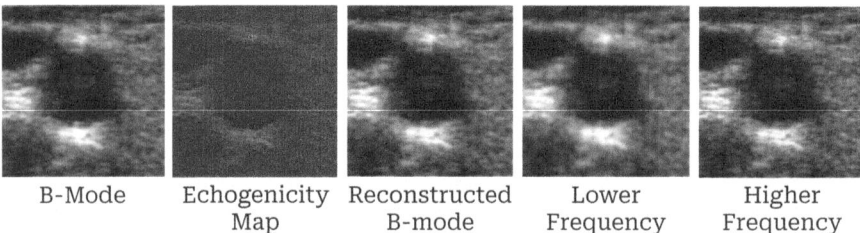

B-Mode Echogenicity Map Reconstructed B-mode Lower Frequency Higher Frequency

Fig. 4. In-Vivo carotid data: the acquired B-mode image with 8 MHz central frequency, the predicted echogenicity map, and the reconstructed B-Mode image at the same frequency, at 6 MHz, and at 10 MHz

4 Discussion and Conclusion

We present a framework for enhancing ultrasound imaging resolution, focusing on the integration of physical sound propagation principles with advanced computational techniques on commonly available B-mode images. Unlike conventional approaches that work on RF data, our work introduces a methodology for retrieving the echogenicity map directly from the B-mode image.

However, our approach faces challenges inherent to the ill-posed nature of the problem, such as image alterations from post-processing parameters introduced by the ultrasound machine (e.g., log-compression factor). Additionally, determining the correct PSF through grid search is computationally expensive. A learnable PSF could, therefore, simplify the application of our approach in the future.

In conclusion, this work introduces a novel methodology to retrieve the continuous echogenicity map by learning its implicit neural representation based on a differentiable rendering pipeline that models the ultrasound formation process. The presented approach enhances the quality of ultrasound imaging and can open the door for future improvements in medical diagnostics.

References

1. Alessandrini, M., Maggio, S., Porée, J., De Marchi, L., Speciale, N., Franceschini, E., Bernard, O., Basset, O.: A restoration framework for ultrasonic tissue characterization. IEEE transactions on ultrasonics, ferroelectrics, and frequency control **58**(11), 2344–2360 (2011)
2. Dalitz, C., Pohle-Frohlich, R., Michalk, T.: Point spread functions and deconvolution of ultrasonic images. IEEE transactions on ultrasonics, ferroelectrics, and frequency control **62**(3), 531–544 (2015)
3. Foroozan, F., O'Reilly, M.A., Hynynen, K.: Microbubble localization for three-dimensional superresolution ultrasound imaging using curve fitting and deconvolution methods. IEEE Transactions on Biomedical Engineering **65**(12), 2692–2703 (2018)
4. Goudarzi, S., Basarab, A., Rivaz, H.: A unifying approach to inverse problems of ultrasound beamforming and deconvolution. IEEE Transactions on Computational Imaging **9**, 197–209 (2023)
5. Jensen, J.A.: A model for the propagation and scattering of ultrasound in tissue. The Journal of the Acoustical Society of America **89**(1), 182–190 (1991)
6. Jensen, J.A.: Deconvolution of ultrasound images. Ultrasonic imaging **14**(1), 1–15 (1992)
7. Khan, S., Huh, J., Ye, J.C.: Unsupervised deconvolution neural network for high quality ultrasound imaging. In: 2020 IEEE International Ultrasonics Symposium (IUS). pp. 1–4. IEEE (2020)
8. Lucy, L.B.: An iterative technique for the rectification of observed distributions. Astronomical Journal, Vol. 79, p. 745 (1974) **79**, 745 (1974)
9. Maggio, S., Palladini, A., De Marchi, L., Alessandrini, M., Speciale, N., Masetti, G.: Predictive deconvolution and hybrid feature selection for computer-aided detection of prostate cancer. IEEE transactions on medical imaging **29**(2), 455–464 (2009)

10. Michailovich, O., Tannenbaum, A.: Blind deconvolution of medical ultrasound images: A parametric inverse filtering approach. IEEE Transactions on Image Processing **16**(12), 3005–3019 (2007)
11. Müller, T., Evans, A., Schied, C., Keller, A.: Instant neural graphics primitives with a multiresolution hash encoding. ACM transactions on graphics (TOG) **41**(4), 1–15 (2022)
12. Ng, J., Prager, R., Kingsbury, N., Treece, G., Gee, A.: Modeling ultrasound imaging as a linear, shift-variant system. ieee transactions on ultrasonics, ferroelectrics, and frequency control **53**(3), 549–563 (2006)
13. Walker, W.F., Trahey, G.E.: The application of k-space in pulse echo ultrasound. IEEE transactions on ultrasonics, ferroelectrics, and frequency control **45**(3), 541–558 (1998)
14. Wang, H., Zhou, M., Wei, D., Li, Y., Zheng, Y.: Mepnet: a model-driven equivariant proximal network for joint sparse-view reconstruction and metal artifact reduction in ct images. In: International Conference on Medical Image Computing and Computer-Assisted Intervention. pp. 109–120. Springer (2023)
15. Wysocki, M., Azampour, M.F., Eilers, C., Busam, B., Salehi, M., Navab, N.: Ultranerf: neural radiance fields for ultrasound imaging. In: Medical Imaging with Deep Learning. pp. 382–401. PMLR (2024)
16. Xie, Y., Takikawa, T., Saito, S., Litany, O., Yan, S., Khan, N., Tombari, F., Tompkin, J., Sitzmann, V., Sridhar, S.: Neural fields in visual computing and beyond. In: Computer Graphics Forum. vol. 41, pp. 641–676. Wiley Online Library (2022)
17. Zemp, R.J., Abbey, C.K., Insana, M.F.: Linear system models for ultrasonic imaging: Application to signal statistics. IEEE transactions on ultrasonics, ferroelectrics, and frequency control **50**(6), 642–654 (2003)
18. Zha, R., Zhang, Y., Li, H.: Naf: Neural attenuation fields for sparse-view cbct reconstruction. In: International Conference on Medical Image Computing and Computer-Assisted Intervention. pp. 442–452. Springer (2022)

Tracking, Registration
and Image-guided Interventions

PIPsUS: Self-supervised Point Tracking in Ultrasound

Wanwen Chen[1(✉)], Adam Schmidt[2], Eitan Prisman[3], and Septimiu E. Salcudean[1,4]

[1] Department of Electrical and Computer Engineering, The University of British Columbia, Vancouver, BC, Canada
{wanwenc,tims}@ece.ubc.ca
[2] Intuitive Surgical Inc., Sunnyvale, CA, USA
[3] Division of Otolaryngology, Department of Surgery, The University of British Columbia, Vancouver, BC, Canada
[4] School of Biomedical Engineering, The University of British Columbia, Vancouver, BC, Canada

Abstract. Finding point-level correspondences is a fundamental problem in ultrasound (US), enabling US landmark tracking for intraoperative image guidance and motion estimation. Most US tracking methods are based on optical flow or feature matching, initially designed for RGB images. Therefore domain shift can impact their performance. Ground-truth correspondences could supervise training, but these are expensive to acquire. To solve these problems, we propose a self-supervised point-tracking model called PIPsUS. Our model can track an arbitrary number of points at pixel-level in one forward pass and exploits temporal information by considering multiple, instead of just consecutive, frames. We developed a new self-supervised training strategy that utilizes a long-term point-tracking model trained for RGB images as a teacher to guide the model to learn realistic motions and use data augmentation to enforce tracking from US appearance. We evaluate our method on neck and oral US and echocardiography, showing higher point tracking accuracy when compared with fast normalized cross-correlation and tuned optical flow. Codes are available at https://github.com/aliciachenw/PIPsUS.

Keywords: Point tracking · Ultrasound · Self-supervised learning · Landmark tracking

1 Introduction

Intraoperative ultrasound (US) in head and neck surgery is an emerging tool that helps surgeons localize tumors and important anatomy such as arteries. Keypoint

---

Supported by NSERC Discovery Grant and Charles Laszlo Chair in Biomedical Engineering held by Dr. Salcudean, VCHRI Innovation and Translational Research Awards, and the University of British Columbia Department of Surgery Seed Grant held by Dr. Prisman. This work was completed when Dr. Schmidt was at the University of British Columbia.

tracking can assist surgeons in finding and keeping tissue of interest in the US plane and estimating relative transducer motion [25]. Moreover, finding point-level correspondences in US can benefit many clinical applications, such as large strain estimation and image registration, where deformation can be modeled by the motion of control points. Sparse feature matching and optical flow are two different methods of finding point correspondences. The former requires designing feature descriptors and is usually limited to keypoints that are detected by a detector, while the latter estimates dense pixel-level motion for consecutive frames instead of long-term motion. Recent work in particle video [8,26] predicts the motion of densely-sampled points based on feature correlation and pixel motion, exploits both sparse feature matching and optical flow and achieves high accuracy in long-term pixel tracking.

Though point tracking has been studied in RGB images, its implementation in US is difficult. Most models for RGB images are trained on labeled datasets [6] or simulated images [26]. However, it is difficult to simulate 2D US videos because of the complexity of the physical interaction between sound waves and tissue. Labeling corresponding points is time-consuming and expensive, and requires training labelers to understand the particulars of US such as artifacts.

Targeting the problems above, we enable point tracking in US utilizing a particle video representation with a self-supervised training strategy. Our novelty includes: (1) A new particle video model for online tracking of any number of points at the same time in US image sequences; (2) A new self-supervised teacher-student learning strategy: a teacher model that can view entire clips is used to train our model to estimate frame-by-frame motion.

2 Related Work

Feature and Template-based Matching in US: Feature matching has been used to track landmarks in US. Early methods used detectors and descriptors for RGB images such as FAST [24] and SIFT [14]. However, these methods do not consider the special texture of US. Some methods use handcrafted features for US [2,4] but do not achieve real-time performance. Recent success of deep learning-based keypoint matching in RGB images raises interest in their applications to US, such as in Zhao *et al.* [25] and Shen *et al.* [19]. However, labels or external sensors are required for their supervised training.

Self-supervised or unsupervised learning has been investigated to reduce the effort of labeling. In [23], an autoencoder is trained to reconstruct patches and the latent space vector for each patch is used as feature for tracking. Learning from data augmentation [13,22] and contrastive learning with teacher-student learning [12] have also been employed. However, these methods have been tested on a limited number of landmarks (usually on the CLUST dataset which has 1–5 annotated landmarks for each sequence [5]). Compared with these methods, our model can track an arbitrary number of points in one forward pass.

Optical Flow: Optical flow estimates dense pixel-level motion and is similar to our work, but it is not widely applied in US. Classical optical flow methods

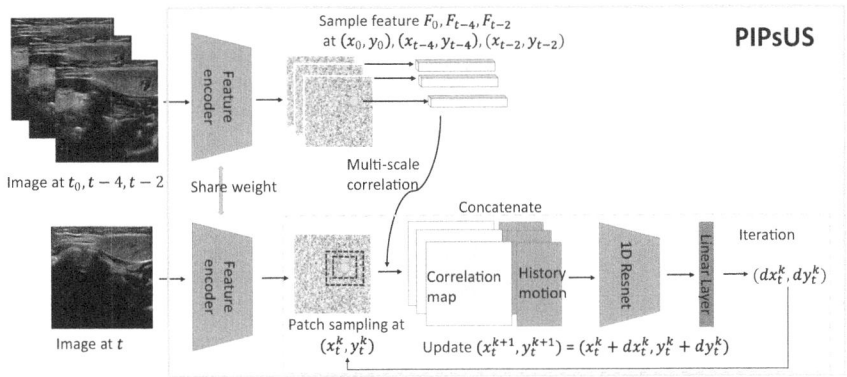

Fig. 1. PIPsUS architecture: PIPsUS enables streaming evaluation of point motion, estimating point motion at time t using motion and image feature history. The model encodes history and current images and samples the features of the tracked points on history feature maps. The correlation maps of the history feature and current feature maps are concatenated with the history motion. A 1D-Resnet encodes the information and a linear layer iteratively predicts the tracking update.

such as Lukas-Kanade [15], optimization-based flow [18], or in combination with block-matching [3] have been used for US, and deep learning optical flow such as LiteFlowNet [1], FlowNet [7] and PDD-Net [16] have also been investigated. However, these models only consider consecutive frames, making them more sensitive to drift and presenting artifacts in long-term tracking. Unlike optical flow, our method uses features and motion history to improve tracking performance.

Track-any-point in RGB: Our work is inspired by tracking-any-point (TAP), estimating pixel correspondences in videos. TAP models such as PIPs [8], TAP-Net [6], and PIPs++ [26] are usually trained with real labels or simulated scenes. Wang et al. [21] proposed a new TAP model that is supervised by optical flow. However, most established TAP models infer whole sequences, limiting the usability in intra-operative US tracking. We developed an online point-tracking model and a new learning strategy to train the model without manual labels.

3 Methods

PIPsUS Model. We propose a model named Persistent Independent Particles in US (PIPsUS) to track points in US, as shown in Fig. 1. PIPsUS is inspired by PIPs++ [26], an improved model of Persistent Independent Particles (PIPs) [8], where pixel motions are modeled as moving particles in videos. However, PIPs++ inspects the entire video to predict point trajectories, so it can not predict in a streaming manner, and the computation and memory cost increase regarding the length of the videos. The main advantage of our model PIPsUS is that it estimates motion in a streaming manner to keep computation and memory costs constant, allowing it to run intra-operatively with fewer memory resources. It first has a feature encoder that encodes the US images into feature maps. We use the same ResNet-based encoder as PIPs++ to reuse the pre-trained weights to accelerate convergence. Features of the tracked points are sampled at prior frames by $F_i = bilinear sampling(I_i, \mathbf{p}_i = (x_i, y_i))$, where $i \in \{0, t-4, t-2\}$. Sampling from multiple frames allows the model to learn the original and current appearance of tracked points. The encoder also encodes the image I_t to generate a dense feature map. The new point location $\mathbf{p}_t = (x_t, y_t)$ is estimated using an iterative method that showed great success in RAFT [20] and PIPs++. We assume zero-motion to start, so the initial location $\mathbf{p}_t^0 = (x_t^0, y_t^0)$ is $\mathbf{p}_{t-1}$. For each iteration k, we sample an $R \times R$ patch in the current frames's feature map at $\mathbf{p}_t^k$ as $P^0, P^1, ..., P^L$, where L is the number of resolution layers. Feature F_i is correlated with these patches and the resulting correlation maps at each resolution are concatenated and reshaped into n $L \times R^2$ vectors, where n is the number of points. Since the point motion should be consistent, we concatenate the most recent motion flow $\mathbf{p}_t^k - \mathbf{p}_{t-1}, \mathbf{p}_t^k - \mathbf{p}_{t-2}, \mathbf{p}_t^k - \mathbf{p}_{t-3}$ and use a sinusoidal position embedding [8] to generate motion vectors to enable the model viewing recent motion. A 1D-Resnet then encodes the concatenated motion and correlation vectors, and a linear layer is used to predict the update $\Delta \mathbf{p}_t^k$. We update $\mathbf{p}_t^{k+1} = \mathbf{p}_t^k + \Delta \mathbf{p}_t^k$ for the next iteration. To start the inference when there is no enough previous frame, we pad the video with I_0 and $\mathbf{p}_0$ since our model needs image and location history.

Self-supervised Teacher-Student Training: To train the model without manual labels, we use two different pseudo-ground truth labels:

(1) PIPs++ teacher labels: We use point trajectories predicted by PIPs++ as labels to guide PIPsUS to predict the point motions. We use a weighted Huber loss because it is more robust against outliers than L1 loss, preventing the model from overfitting possible wrong predictions in PIPs++:

$$L_t = \mu_t \sum_{k=0}^{K} w_k HuberLoss(\mathbf{p}_t^{gt}, \mathbf{p}_t^k) \quad (1)$$

w_k is an increased weight with update iteration $w_k = \gamma_{Iter}^{K-k-1}$ to encourage the model to learns the update function. The weight $\mu_t = \gamma_{Time}^{T-t-1}$ increases with time to encourage the model to reduce drifting. We set $\gamma_{Iter} = 0.8$ and $\gamma_{Time} = 0.95$.

(2) Simulation labels: We randomly transform ultrasound images with translation, intensity modulation, and noise addition to generate US videos with known motions. The loss is similar to Eq. 1 but with $\gamma_{Time} = 1$, and we choose L1 loss since the motion under our transformations is known.

We use simulation to warm up the model, then train the model with PIPs++ labels plus 50% of the simulated labels and validate on PIPs++ labels. We implement a zero-flow regularization with zero-motion videos to regularize model

Table 1. Number of collected videos and generated sequences in OUS dataset.

		Videos	Frames	# generated sequences	# keypoints per sequence
Pips++	Train	174	65 ± 42	452	18.75 ± 14.33
	Valid	57	112 ± 70	278	14.50 ± 11.20
	Test	45	116 ± 82	225	8.88 ± 8.19
Sim	Train	212	41	199	20.53 ± 13.78
	Test	59	41	49	13.00 ± 9.57

Table 2. Number of videos and generated sequences used in EchoNet dataset.

		Videos	Frames	# generated sequences	# keypoints per sequence
Pips++	Train	200	173 ± 46	1620	69.88 ± 19.97
	Valid	50	168 ± 38	392	68.65 ± 17.58
	Test	50	175 ± 47	410	75.87 ± 21.33
Sim	Train	200	41	200	75.36 ± 20.41
	Test	50	41	50	81.72 ± 24.36

prediction. The input motion history has a 70% chance of being the accurate flow with added Gaussian noise and 30% to be the model's previous prediction. As a proof-of-concept experiment, the keypoints are detected by SIFT, with the contrast threshold as 0.08 and the edge threshold as 4. However, our model is not limited to SIFT in training and inference.

4 Experiments

Data: (1) Neck and oral US (OUS): This is a private dataset containing 2D US sequences collected from 19 patients who underwent transoral robotic surgery, from January 2022 to October 2023 at the Vancouver General Hospital (Vancouver, BC, Canada). This study received ethics approval from the UBC Clinical Research Ethics Board (H19-04025). A BK3500 and a 14L3 linear 2D transducer (BK Medical, Burlington, MA) were used in the operation room for US imaging and a Polaris Spectra (Northern Digital, ON, Canada) was used to track the US transducer. PLUS [10] was used to record the US videos. The image depth is 4 cm at 9 MHz, with a frame rate of 5.76 ± 0.89 fps. For each patient, the US scan included the neck, oropharynx, and the base of tongue (BOT) on the cancerous side, before and after the tongue retraction. Data from 12 patients are used for training, 4 patients for validation, and 3 patients for testing. We did not include the BOT scan for PIPs++ ground truth, since it mainly contains out-of-plane motions along the neck, but we kept the BOT images in the simulated sequences. For the PIPs++ labels, we split the recorded sequences into 20 frame-long sequences. For the simulated labels, we used the first frame in the videos to generate 41 frame-long sequences. Images were resized to 256 × 256. The final amount of data is summarized in Table 1.

(2) EchoNet [17]: EchoNet is a public dataset containing 2D videos of US cardio motion, shared under the Stanford University Dataset Research Use Agreement. We randomly select 200 videos for training, 50 videos for validation, and 50 videos for testing. Images were resized to 256 × 256. We use the same method in OUS to generate US sequences and the dataset statistics is shown in Table 2.

Training Details: The models were trained on an NVIDIA Tesla V100 and implemented in python 3.8, PyTorch-2.1.0, and CUDA-11.8. The weight of the encoder was initialized with the public weight of PIPs++. AdamW optimizer was used with a learning rate of 5e-4 for warmup, and 1e-4 for self-supervised teacher-student tuning. We warmed up the model with 10 epochs and then the model was trained with our self-supervised learning method for 50 epochs. The models with the lowest loss on the validation set were selected. The image batch size was 1 because the number of keypoints per batch varies.

Table 3. Quantitative evaluation on OUS. The L2 error is in pixels. ** The average time for PIPs++ to run inference on each sequence (20 frames) is 0.08 s.

Method	Simulation		Real Data		
	L2	NCC	L2	NCC	FPS
Fast NCC	6.65 ± 6.25	0.83 ± 0.19	22.84 ± 27.91	0.82 ± 0.19	145.2
RAFT	21.49 ± 21.20	0.80 ± 0.21	14.65 ± 14.57	0.80 ± 0.21	60.2
PIPs++	**0.94 ± 0.72**	**0.95 ± 0.10**	N/A	N/A	N/A**
PIPsUScorr	1.28 ± 1.19	0.94 ± 0.12	12.10 ± 16.95	**0.84 ± 0.19**	43.3
PIPsUS	1.10 ± 0.88	**0.95 ± 0.11**	**9.04 ± 11.79**	**0.84 ± 0.19**	34.6

Table 4. Quantitative evaluation on EchoNet. The L2 error is in pixels. ** The average time for PIPs++ to run inference on each sequence (20 frames) is 0.13 s.

Method	Simulation		Real Data		
	L2	NCC	L2	NCC	FPS
Fast NCC	6.40 ± 6.60	0.83 ± 0.22	5.05 ± 10.56	0.93 ± 0.13	19.3
RAFT	12.27 ± 11.25	0.80 ± 0.24	4.32 ± 3.60	0.86 ± 0.20	70.0
PIPs++	**0.90 ± 0.75**	**0.96 ± 0.11**	N/A	N/A	N/A**
PIPsUScorr	1.26 ± 1.21	0.95 ± 0.12	**2.27 ± 2.62**	**0.94 ± 0.11**	39.0
PIPsUS	1.07 ± 1.04	0.95 ± 0.11	2.40 ± 3.15	**0.94 ± 0.11**	15.4

5 Results

We compare our models with fast normalized cross-correlation (NCC) template matching [11], fine-tuned RAFT [20], PIPs++, and conduct an ablation study. PIPsUS has correlation maps and motion history in the input, while PIPsUScorr only sees the correlation. RAFT was fine-tuned with US using mean square loss between target images and optical flow-wrapped source images for 5 epochs. We choose RAFT because it outperforms LiteFlowNet and FlowNet [20], and PDD-Net [16] is originally designed for 3D registration. We evaluated the performance on simulated US sequences with smooth random affine motions and intensity changes and real US sequences. Due to the lack of ground truth labels on real US, we compare with teacher model PIPs++ pseudo ground truth, similar to [9]. The quantitative evaluation includes L2 error and image-patch NCC, as shown in Table 3 for OUS and Table 4 for EchoNet. The L2 error evaluates the absolute tracking accuracy, while the NCC quantifies the keypoint patch similarity.

In the simulation, PIPs++ has the highest accuracy and patch similarity, but PIPsUS is comparable to PIPs++ both on the OUS and EchoNet. PIPsUS and PIPsUScorr all demonstrate a large improvement in accuracy and similarity compared with fast-NCC and RAFT. However, PIPs++ needs to infer the whole video sequences, while PIPsUS can infer the point location in a frame-by-frame manner, making PIPsUS preferable in online applications such as intra-operative landmark tracking. In the real US, PIPsUS achieves the highest accuracy on OUS. PIPsUScorr performs the best on EchoNet, but PIPsUS is comparable. Again, PIPsUS and PIPsUScorr achieve higher accuracy and patch similarity in both datasets compared with Fast-NCC and RAFT. All methods perform better on EchoNet than OUS, and we expect this is because echocardiography contains smaller in-plane motions from standard views while freehand OUS contains larger motions and points can be out-of-plane. Thus, tracking points in EchoNet is easier. Figure 2 shows the trend of L2 error; fast NCC and RAFT are both sensitive to drift. PIPs-like models view the features at different times, so their performance degrades slowly. The results show the advantages of investigat-

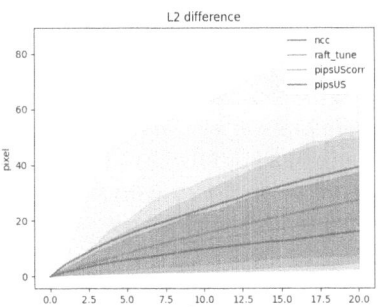 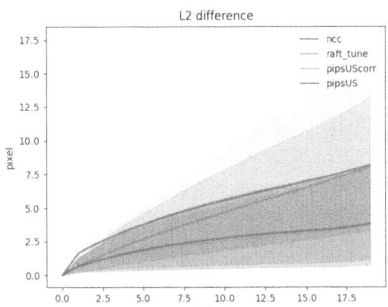

Fig. 2. L2 in different frames on real US sequence. Left: on OUS, right: on EchoNet. The line is average L2 and the shadow is 10 and 90 percentile.

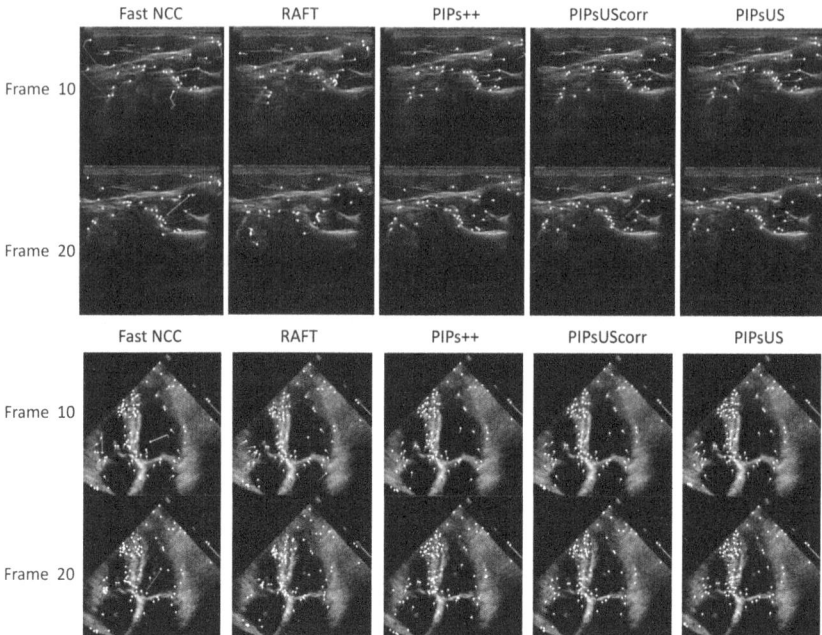

Fig. 3. Examples of tracked point trajectories in different frames on OUS (top 2 rows) and EchoNet (bottom 2 rows). The point is the current predicted keypoint locations and the colored line is the trajectory history. On OUS, in Frame 20 of PIPsUScorr and NCC, a point is correlated to a faraway location. By using point motion history, PIPsUS avoids this.

ing multiple frames instead of just consecutive frames. The comparison between PIPsUS and PIPsUScorr shows that the motion history can improve motion estimation in OUS but not in EchoNet. We hypothesize that motion history can help generate a reasonable prediction when points have larger motion and are temporally out-of-plane, so its advantage is not shown in echocardiography where features remain in-plane. This is also shown in Fig. 3 which displays images of the tracked points and trajectories in OUS and EchoNet. More visualization is provided in the supplemental materials. We also evaluate the survival rate, which is the percentage of points that have an L2 error smaller than 50, as defined in [26]. In real EchoNet, the survival rate of the points at the end of sequences is 97.27% for fast NCC, and 100.00% for other methods. For OUS, the survival rate is 67.95% for fast NCC, 88.89% for RAFT, 90.27% for PIPsUScorr and 95.19% for PIPsUS, showing that PIPsUS is better at keeping track of points in OUS, which has more complicated motions.

Limitations and Future Work: Though we show improved tracking, disappearing and reoccurring detection is required for longer-term landmark tracking, which will be the next step in our investigation. We did not investigate other data augmentation methods, and US physics-based augmentation might improve the model's robustness against deformation, shadows, and artifacts. Our model relies on feature correlation and temporal information without the awareness of point saliency. Integrating segmentation maps might allow the model to focus on tracking anatomically salient landmarks. Also, SIFT may not detect all anatomically meaningful keypoints, and we expect that new detectors can be designed to find more suitable keypoints for tracking. These limitations have not been addressed in previous US point tracking either.

6 Conclusions

We propose a new model utilizing particle video to track an arbitrary number of points utilizing dense feature maps and particles' previous motion with constant memory cost, and can track points in an on-line manner. We develop a self-supervised teacher-student training strategy to train our model to learn without manual labeling. Our model achieves higher accuracy compared with fast NCC and fine-tuned RAFT, and it is more robust to temporal drift.

References

1. Al-Battal, A.F., Lerman, I.R., Nguyen, T.Q.: Object detection and tracking in ultrasound scans using an optical flow and semantic segmentation framework based on convolutional neural networks. In: ICASSP 2022-2022 IEEE International Conference on Acoustics, Speech and Signal Processing (ICASSP). pp. 1096–1100. IEEE (2022)
2. Alkhatib, M., Hafiane, A., Tahri, O., Vieyres, P., Delbos, A.: Adaptive median binary patterns for fully automatic nerves tracking in ultrasound images. Computer methods and programs in biomedicine **160**, 129–140 (2018)
3. Chuang, B.I., Hsu, J.H., Kuo, L.C., Jou, I.M., Su, F.C., Sun, Y.N.: Tendon-motion tracking in an ultrasound image sequence using optical-flow-based block matching. Biomedical engineering online **16**, 1–19 (2017)
4. Dall'Alba, D., Fiorini, P.: Bipco: ultrasound feature points based on phase congruency detector and binary pattern descriptor. International journal of computer assisted radiology and surgery **10**, 843–854 (2015)
5. De Luca, V., Banerjee, J., Hallack, A., Kondo, S., Makhinya, M., Nouri, D., Royer, L., Cifor, A., Dardenne, G., Goksel, O., et al.: Evaluation of 2d and 3d ultrasound tracking algorithms and impact on ultrasound-guided liver radiotherapy margins. Medical physics **45**(11), 4986–5003 (2018)
6. Doersch, C., Gupta, A., Markeeva, L., Recasens, A., Smaira, L., Aytar, Y., Carreira, J., Zisserman, A., Yang, Y.: Tap-vid: A benchmark for tracking any point in a video. Advances in Neural Information Processing Systems **35**, 13610–13626 (2022)
7. Evain, E., Faraz, K., Grenier, T., Garcia, D., De Craene, M., Bernard, O.: A pilot study on convolutional neural networks for motion estimation from ultrasound images. IEEE transactions on ultrasonics, ferroelectrics, and frequency control **67**(12), 2565–2573 (2020)
8. Harley, A.W., Fang, Z., Fragkiadaki, K.: Particle video revisited: Tracking through occlusions using point trajectories. In: European Conference on Computer Vision. pp. 59–75. Springer (2022)

9. Ihler, S., Kuhnke, F., Laves, M.H., Ortmaier, T.: Self-supervised domain adaptation for patient-specific, real-time tissue tracking. In: Medical Image Computing and Computer Assisted Intervention–MICCAI 2020: 23rd International Conference, Lima, Peru, October 4–8, 2020, Proceedings, Part III 23. pp. 54–64. Springer (2020)
10. Lasso, A., Heffter, T., Rankin, A., Pinter, C., Ungi, T., Fichtinger, G.: PLUS: Open-source toolkit for ultrasound-guided intervention systems. IEEE Transactions on Biomedical Engineering **61**, 2527–2537 (2014)
11. Lewis, J.: Fast normalized cross-correlation. Industrial Light & Magic **10**, 7 (2001)
12. Liang, H., Ning, G., Zhang, X., Liao, H.: Semi-supervised anatomy tracking with contrastive representation learning in ultrasound sequences. In: 2023 IEEE 20th International Symposium on Biomedical Imaging (ISBI). pp. 1–5. IEEE (2023)
13. Liu, F., Liu, D., Tian, J., Xie, X., Yang, X., Wang, K.: Cascaded one-shot deformable convolutional neural networks: Developing a deep learning model for respiratory motion estimation in ultrasound sequences. Medical image analysis **65**, 101793 (2020)
14. Machado, I., Toews, M., Luo, J., Unadkat, P., Essayed, W., George, E., Teodoro, P., Carvalho, H., Martins, J., Golland, P., et al.: Non-rigid registration of 3d ultrasound for neurosurgery using automatic feature detection and matching. International journal of computer assisted radiology and surgery **13**, 1525–1538 (2018)
15. Makhinya, M., Goksel, O.: Motion tracking in 2d ultrasound using vessel models and robust optic-flow. Proceedings of MICCAI CLUST **20**, 20–27 (2015)
16. Nicke, T., Graf, L., Lauri, M., Mischkewitz, S., Frintrop, S., Heinrich, M.P.: Real-time optical flow estimation on vein and artery ultrasound sequences based on knowledge-distillation. In: International Workshop on Biomedical Image Registration. pp. 134–143. Springer (2022)
17. Ouyang, D., He, B., Ghorbani, A., Lungren, M.P., Ashley, E.A., Liang, D.H., Zou, J.Y.: Echonet-dynamic: a large new cardiac motion video data resource for medical machine learning. In: NeurIPS ML4H Workshop: Vancouver, BC, Canada (2019)
18. Ouzir, N., Basarab, A., Lairez, O., Tourneret, J.Y.: Robust optical flow estimation in cardiac ultrasound images using a sparse representation. IEEE transactions on medical imaging **38**(3), 741–752 (2018)
19. Shen, C., He, J., Huang, Y., Wu, J.: Discriminative correlation filter network for robust landmark tracking in ultrasound guided intervention. In: Medical Image Computing and Computer Assisted Intervention–MICCAI 2019: 22nd International Conference, Shenzhen, China, October 13–17, 2019, Proceedings, Part V 22. pp. 646–654. Springer (2019)
20. Teed, Z., Deng, J.: Raft: Recurrent all-pairs field transforms for optical flow. In: Computer Vision–ECCV 2020: 16th European Conference, Glasgow, UK, August 23–28, 2020, Proceedings, Part II 16. pp. 402–419. Springer (2020)
21. Wang, Q., Chang, Y.Y., Cai, R., Li, Z., Hariharan, B., Holynski, A., Snavely, N.: Tracking everything everywhere all at once. arXiv preprint arXiv:2306.05422 (2023)
22. Wang, Y., Fu, T., Wang, Y., Xiao, D., Lin, Y., Fan, J., Song, H., Liu, F., Yang, J.: Multi3: multi-templates siamese network with multi-peaks detection and multi-features refinement for target tracking in ultrasound image sequences. Physics in Medicine & Biology **67**(19), 195007 (2022)
23. Wulff, D., Hagenah, J., Ernst, F.: Landmark tracking in 4d ultrasound using generalized representation learning. International Journal of Computer Assisted Radiology and Surgery **18**(3), 493–500 (2023)

24. Wulff, D., Kuhlemann, I., Ernst, F., Schweikard, A., Ipsen, S.: Robust motion tracking of deformable targets in the liver using binary feature libraries in 4d ultrasound. Current Directions in Biomedical Engineering **5**(1), 601–604 (2019)
25. Zhao, C., Droste, R., Drukker, L., Papageorghiou, A.T., Noble, J.A.: Uspoint: Self-supervised interest point detection and description for ultrasound-probe motion estimation during fine-adjustment standard fetal plane finding. In: International Conference on Medical Image Computing and Computer-Assisted Intervention. pp. 104–114. Springer (2022)
26. Zheng, Y., Harley, A.W., Shen, B., Wetzstein, G., Guibas, L.J.: Pointodyssey: A large-scale synthetic dataset for long-term point tracking. In: Proceedings of the IEEE/CVF International Conference on Computer Vision. pp. 19855–19865 (2023)

Structure-aware World Model for Probe Guidance via Large-scale Self-supervised Pre-train

Haojun Jiang[1,2], Meng Li[2], Zhenguo Sun[2], Ning Jia[2], Yu Sun[2], Shaqi Luo[2], Shiji Song[1], and Gao Huang[1,2(✉)]

[1] Department of Automation, BNRist, Tsinghua University, Beijing, China
[2] Beijing Academy of Artificial Intelligence, Beijing, China
gaohuang@tsinghua.edu.cn

Abstract. The complex structure of the heart leads to significant challenges in echocardiography, especially in acquisition cardiac ultrasound images. Successful echocardiography requires a thorough understanding of the structures on the two-dimensional plane and the spatial relationships between planes in three-dimensional space. In this paper, we innovatively propose a large-scale self-supervised pre-training method to acquire a cardiac structure-aware world model. The core innovation lies in constructing a self-supervised task that requires structural inference by predicting masked structures on a 2D plane and imagining another plane based on pose transformation in 3D space. To support large-scale pre-training, we collected over 1.36 million echocardiograms from ten standard views, along with their 3D spatial poses. In the downstream probe guidance task, we demonstrate that our pre-trained model consistently reduces guidance errors across the ten most common standard views on the test set with 0.29 million samples from 74 routine clinical scans, indicating that structure-aware pre-training benefits the scanning.

Keywords: Echocardiography · World Model · Structural Understanding · Self-supervised Pre-train · Probe Guidance

1 Introduction

Cardiovascular diseases are the leading cause of death in worldwide [18,19]. Echocardiography is the most commonly used method in clinical practice to assess heart conditions. However, the structure of the heart is extremely complex. According to [12], up to seven anatomical structures need to be identified in a single plane, such as the Parasternal Long-axis Plane (Fig. 1 Left). Recognizing these anatomical structures is crucial for diagnosis, and understanding their

---

H. Jiang, M. Li and Z. Sun—These authors contributed equally to this work. This work was done while Haojun Jiang was an intern at Beijing Academy of Artificial Intelligence.

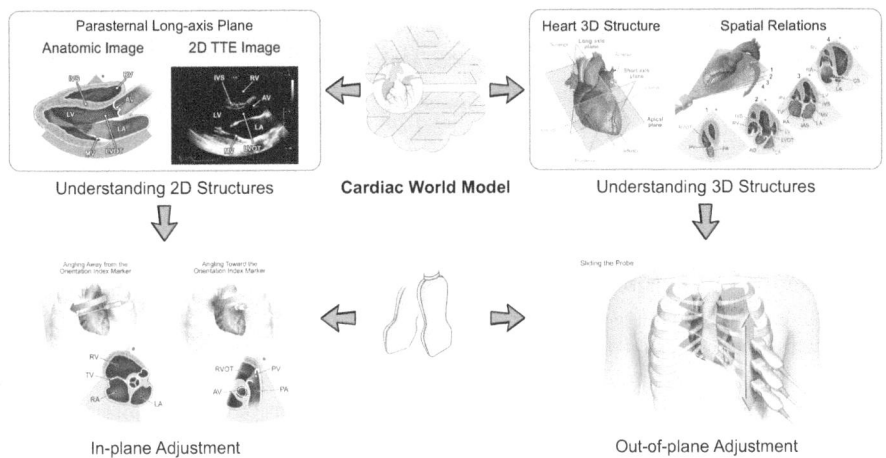

Fig. 1. Diagram illustrating the capabilities of a cardiac world model. We aim to develop a cardiac world model that can understand both two-dimensional and three-dimensional structures. **(Left)** The world model needs to recognize various structures in two-dimensional planes and understand their spatial relationships for in-plane probe adjustment. **(Right)** Understanding the three-dimensional structure of the heart, specifically the spatial relationships between different planes, is crucial for out-of-plane probe adjustment. The images used in the diagram are sourced from [12].

spatial relationships in a two-dimensional plane also helps the sonographer fine-tune the probe to obtain the best quality images. Additionally, up to 27 different planes need to be examined, requiring the sonographer to understand the spatial relationships between these planes in three-dimensional space and to finely adjust the ultrasound probe's position to reach the target location (Fig. 1 Right). Due to the aforementioned reasons, cardiac ultrasound examinations are extremely challenging. This also results in a long training period for ultrasound medical personnel, as they need to spend a lot of time familiarizing themselves with both 2D and 3D structures. Consequently, there is a significant talent shortage in this field, especially in regions with scarce medical resources, such as Africa.

With technological advancements [4,6,7,21–23], AI algorithms has shown great potential in improving the efficiency of echocardiography. For example, Ouyang et al. [14] proposed a video-based deep learning algorithm, *i.e.*, EchoNet-Dynamic, that can automatically make accurate assessments of cardiac function. More importantly, with the rise of large language models [2,16,17,20] and multi-modal learning [8,10,11,15], the interpretation of echocardiograms [3] has shown increasing improvement, demonstrating excellent performance in tasks such as pulmonary artery pressure estimation, left ventricular hypertrophy, heart failure, and left atrial enlargement. These AI-assisted diagnostic tools have demonstrated performance almost comparable to human experts. However, this comes with a prerequisite: the acquisition of high-quality echocardiograms. In regions with scarce medical resources, there are often no sonographers available to obtain high-quality echocardiograms. In such cases, the powerful capabilities of these

AI-assisted diagnostic tools cannot be fully utilized. Few works [5,9,13] have focused on how to use AI technology to assist inexperienced sonographers in accurately acquiring target planes. Recently, Jiang et al. [9] proposed a cardiac dreamer, which only focuses on supervised learning of the 3D-structure of the heart and serves as a "heart map" for the probe guidance task. This work demonstrates a potential AI-assisted scanning method that is expected to improve the scanning skills of novices.

According to the clinical experience of sonographers, understanding both the 2D and 3D structures is crucial for efficient scanning. For example, when you need to adjust the probe's viewing angle on a particular plane to capture specific anatomical structures, you must have a good understanding of the spatial positions of those anatomical structures on that plane (Fig.1 Left). Undoubtedly, when navigating between different planes, it is essential for sonographers to grasp the spatial relationships within the three-dimensional space (Fig.1 Right). Thus, in this paper, we propose a 2D-3D joint structure-aware pre-training framework to obtain a data-driven cardiac world model that benefits ultrasound scanning. Specifically, we require the world model to learn important spatial relationships in the following ways: (1) for understanding two-dimensional structures, we use a masking approach that requires the world model to predict features at adjacent positions in the two-dimensional plane; (2) for understanding three-dimensional structures, we provide information on the positional changes of two planes in 3D space, requiring the world model to predict the features of the target plane after the positional change. We further collected expert operational data on acquiring the most common ten standard planes from 364 routine clinical scans, resulting in 1.36 million sample pairs gathered by three certified sonographers, to enhance the model's learning of generalizable cardiac structure knowledge. Results on the downstream probe guidance task indicate that the proposed pre-training method learns useful knowledge for assisting in the acquisition of echocardiograms.

2 Method

In this section, we describe the proposed structure-aware pre-training framework, illustrated in Fig. 2. We first introduce the prior I-JEPA work [1], on which we based our method, in Section 2.1. Next, we discuss how we construct a pre-training framework that simultaneously learns 2D and 3D structural information by introducing three-dimensional spatial information in Section 2.2.

2.1 Preliminary

In the context of echocardiogram analysis, accurately understanding 2D structural information is fundamental for making correct diagnoses and conducting efficient scans. Recently, Assran et al. proposed a Joint-Embedding Predictive Architecture (I-JEPA) [1] to learn highly semantic image representation. The key idea for I-JEPA is learning the representation of images by predicting features of target blocks based on the non-overlapping context block and the positional embedding in the same image. This paradigm requires the model to understand

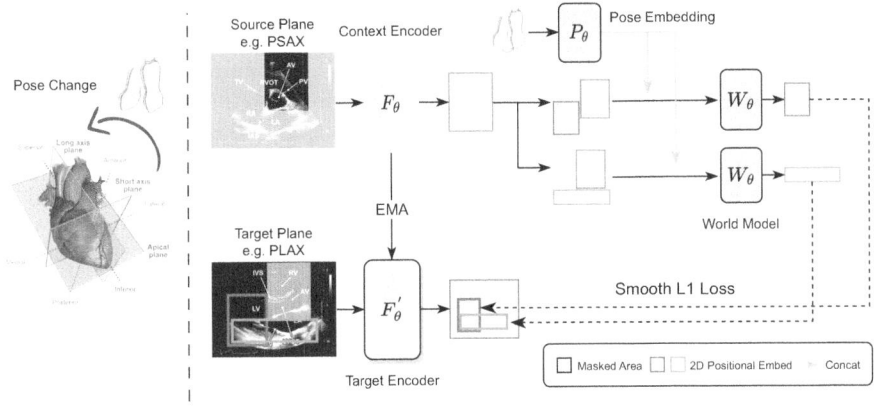

Fig. 2. Diagram illustrating the pre-training method and downstream task. The world model and encoder are required to predict features on the target plane based on the spatial relationships in both two-dimensional and three-dimensional spaces.

the spatial relationships of different semantic structures in the 2D plane. For example, if a context block contains the head of a dog, it is likely that the body of the dog will be located below the context block. For echocardiogram analysis, this paradigm also enables the model to learn the spatial relationships of fine structures in the two-dimensional plane. For instance, the left ventricle (LV) is located below the interventricular septum (IVS), as shown on the left side of Fig. 1. Therefore, it is highly suitable for modeling two-dimensional structural information in cardiac ultrasound images. Next, we briefly introduce the modeling and training method.

Targets. Specifically, the I-JEPA model employs a Vision Transformer [4]. Firstly, the input image $\mathbf{I} \in \mathbb{R}^{H \times W}$ is divided into N non-overlapping patches, which are further processed by the target encoder F_θ'. Then, we select a portion of the patches to form M target blocks, which may have overlapping regions. We denote the ground-truth target blocks' features as $\mathbf{Y}_i^t \in \mathbb{R}^{L_t \times C}, i \in \{1, 2, \cdots, M\}$.

Context and Prediction. For the context features, patches not belonging to the target blocks are randomly selected and input into the context encoder to obtain features $\mathbf{Z}_c \in \mathbb{R}^{L_c \times C}$. Subsequently, the predictor W_θ (world model) generates the features of target blocks based on the context features and positional embeddings which indicate the location of context and target blocks. We denote the predicted target blocks' feature as $\hat{\mathbf{Y}}_i^t \in \mathbb{R}^{L_t \times C}, i \in \{1, 2, \cdots, M\}$.

Loss. With the ground-truth and predicted features of target blocks, the model is optimized using the following loss:

$$\mathcal{L}_{total} = \frac{1}{M} \sum_{i=1}^{M} \sum_{j=1}^{L_t} \mathcal{L}_{\text{SmoothL1}}(\mathbf{Y}_{i,j}^t, \hat{\mathbf{Y}}_{i,j}^t). \tag{1}$$

2.2 2D-3D Joint Structure-aware Pre-training

Echocardiography involves acquiring high-quality echocardiogram and subsequently conducting analysis and diagnosis based on these images. However, previous researches [3,14] have primarily focused on understanding and analyzing the two-dimensional plane, neglecting how AI can assit in acquiring high-quality echocardiogram. While understanding the 2D structure of a plane can aid in scanning, especially when some features of the standard view are already visible, this alone is insufficient. Particularly when transitioning from one standard view to another, a deep understanding of the heart's 3D structure is essential. Therefore, we propose a 2D-3D joint structure-aware pre-training framework, as illustrated in Fig. 2. The core insight is predicting the visual features of structures at target locations based on given 2D and 3D positional conditions, thereby learning the mapping relationship between spatial positions and visual features. Next, we provide details of the modeling and training method.

Input. Given a source image $\mathbf{I}^s \in \mathbb{R}^{H \times W}$, we select a target image $\mathbf{I}^t \in \mathbb{R}^{H \times W}$ from the same individual's images. To ensure sufficient spatial pose variation between the two images, there must be an interval of at least 150 frames between their sequence numbers. Then, both images are divided into N non-overlapping patches $\mathbf{I}_p^s, \mathbf{I}_p^t \in \mathbb{R}^{N \times h \times w}$.

Context and Target. First, we randomly select a rectangular region from the patches of the source image $\mathbf{I}^s$ as the context information. These patches are then fed through the context encoder F_θ, resulting in the context feature $\mathbf{Z}^s$:

$$\mathbf{Z}^s = F_\theta(\mathbf{I}_p^s \odot \mathbf{B}^s), \quad \mathbf{Z}^s \in \mathbb{R}^{L_s \times C}, \tag{2}$$

where $\mathbf{B}^s \in \mathbb{R}^{N \times 1 \times 1}$ is a binary mask indicating the selected patches, L_s is the number of context patches, and C is the hidden dimension. Next, we select M non-overlapping regions on the target image as the target blocks, requiring the model to understand both the three-dimensional structure of the heart and the spatial relationships of heart structures in the two-dimensional plane. If we choose regions on the target image that have the same spatial position as the context block, the model only needs to understand the three-dimensional spatial relationships. The target features are obtained as follows:

$$\mathbf{Y}_i^t = F_\theta(\mathbf{I}_p^t) \odot \mathbf{B}_i^t, \quad \mathbf{Y}_i^t \in \mathbb{R}^{L_t \times C}, i \in \{1, 2, \cdots, M\}, \tag{3}$$

where $\mathbf{B}_i^t \in \mathbb{R}^{N \times 1}$ is a binary mask indicating the selected patches and L_t is the number of target patches.

Condition and Prediction. The three-dimensional spatial relationship between the source image and the target image is denoted as $\mathbf{a} \in \mathbb{R}^6$, which encapsulates the translation and rotation changes in the x, y, and z directions. This vector $\mathbf{a}$ is encoded by P_θ to obtain the pose embedding, denoted as $\mathbf{P} \in \mathbb{R}^{1 \times C}$. Then, the 2D positional embeddings indicating the location of the context

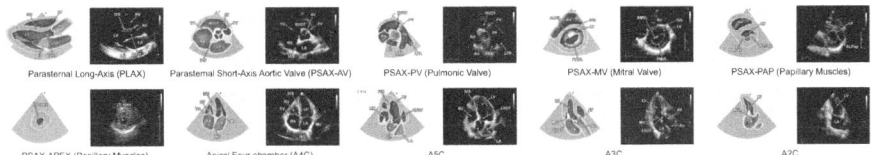

Fig. 3. Anatomic and 2D ultrasound images of ten standard planes. The cardiac images used in the diagram are sourced from [12].

and target block are denoted as $\mathbf{Q}^s \in \mathbb{R}^{L_s \times C}$ and $\mathbf{Q}_i^t \in \mathbb{R}^{L_t \times C}, i \in \{1, 2, \cdots, M\}$. Finally, the predicted features from the world model W_θ are obtained as follows:

$$\mathbf{Z}^{s'} = \mathbf{Z}^s + \mathbf{Q}^s, \tag{4}$$

$$\mathbf{Z}_i^{t'} = \mathbf{Z}_i^t + \mathbf{Q}_i^t, \tag{5}$$

$$\hat{\mathbf{Y}}_i^t = W_\theta(\text{concat}[\mathbf{Z}^{s'}, \mathbf{P}, \mathbf{Z}_i^{t'}]), \tag{6}$$

where $\mathbf{Z}_i^t \in \mathbb{R}^{L_t \times C}, i \in \{1, 2, \cdots, M\}$ is a set of learnable parameters representing the features to be predicted. These parameters interact with the context feature and condition information to generate the target feature. Then, the models are optimized according to the loss function defined in Eq. (1).

3 Experiments

3.1 Implementation Details

Dataset. In this paper, we collected data and conducted experiments on the ten most common standard planes [12], as shown in Fig. 3. The ultrasound images and scan data were acquired following the procedure described in [9]. Ultimately, we amassed data from 364 routine clinical scans, resulting in a total of 1.36 million image and 3D pose data pairs. The whole data collection process was approved and supervised by The University Science and Technology Ethics Committee. We split the dataset into 290 scans (1.07 million samples) for training and 74 scans (0.29 million samples) for testing. For pre-training, only the training set was utilized. Both the training and test sets were employed for the downstream probe guidance task. It is important to note that the individuals in the training and test sets are different to avoid information leakage and fairly validate the model's generalization performance.

Pre-training. The context and target encoders were implemented using ViT-Small/16, and the world model utilized a custom vision transformer with a depth of 6 layers and a hidden dimension of 384. The entire model was trained for 50 epochs with a batch size of 1024 on 8 Nvidia RTX-4090 GPUs. The training included a 7-epoch warmup period (starting learning rate is 1e-4), followed by a

Table 1. Evaluation of the probe guidance task. We report MAE results that represent probe guidance errors (lower is better) across ten standard planes.

Plane	Model	Translation (mm)			Rotation (degree)		
		x	y	z	rx	ry	rz
PLAX	Cardiac Dreamer [9]	8.66	8.14	5.63	6.60	5.42	8.23
	+ Our Pre-train	**8.39**	**8.02**	**5.53**	**6.46**	**5.34**	**7.89**
PSAX-AV	Cardiac Dreamer	7.26	6.63	4.51	5.28	6.26	7.43
	+ Our Pre-train	**7.06**	**6.57**	**4.34**	**5.28**	**6.03**	**7.18**
PSAX-PV	Cardiac Dreamer	7.59	6.58	4.71	5.47	5.67	8.54
	+ Our Pre-train	**7.49**	**6.56**	**4.66**	**5.46**	**5.52**	**8.21**
PSAX-MV	Cardiac Dreamer	7.81	6.42	4.89	6.68	5.87	9.11
	+ Our Pre-train	**7.51**	**6.42** (0.04 %)	**4.77**	**6.55**	**5.78**	**8.78**
PSAX-PAP	Cardiac Dreamer	7.18	6.07	4.43	6.35	5.39	8.53
	+ Our Pre-train	**6.92**	**5.97**	**4.35**	**6.11**	**5.33**	**8.42**
PSAX-APEX	Cardiac Dreamer	6.98	5.98	4.25	5.69	4.89	7.33
	+ Our Pre-train	**6.85**	**5.77**	**4.11**	**5.55**	**4.90** (0.07%)	**7.25**
A4C	Cardiac Dreamer	7.72	7.17	5.45	5.64	4.89	8.91
	+ Our Pre-train	**7.55**	**7.00**	**5.36**	**5.48**	**4.86**	**8.60**
A5C	Cardiac Dreamer	7.38	6.65	5.54	5.83	5.91	12.03
	+ Our Pre-train	**7.15**	**6.46**	**5.40**	**5.80**	**5.88**	**11.88**
A3C	Cardiac Dreamer	7.21	6.52	5.21	5.92	6.29	9.81
	+ Our Pre-train	**6.90**	**6.34**	**5.08**	**5.77**	**6.12**	**9.52**
A2C	Cardiac Dreamer	7.28	6.89	4.95	8.47	5.46	14.51
	+ Our Pre-train	**7.04**	**6.70**	**4.83**	**8.37**	**5.33**	**13.98**

learning rate of 5e-4, using a cosine scheduler with a final learning rate of 5e-7. The implementation details for generating the context block and target blocks, as well as the hyper-parameters, followed the procedures described in [1].

Downstream Task. For the probe guidance task, we adopted the framework and procedure proposed in [9]. The input for this task is an ultrasound image, and the output is the probe position adjustment needed to achieve a specific standard view. This task aims to assist junior ultrasound medical personnel in scanning, enhancing the success rate and quality of view acquisition. During fine-tuning, our pre-trained world model W_θ was loaded and optimized for 5 epochs with a batch size of 1024 on 8 Nvidia RTX-4090 GPUs. The learning rate was set to 1e-4, using a cosine scheduler with a final learning rate of 1e-6. The optimizer was set to AdamW.

Evaluation Metrics. The metric used for probe guidance task is the Mean Absolute Error (MAE) between the predicted and ground truth probe poses.

3.2 Results

Comparison with SOTA. To validate that the proposed structure-aware pre-training method benefits the acquisition of echocardiogram, we conducted comprehensive evaluations on the downstream probe guidance task. As shown in Table 1, the pre-trained model consistently achieved better or comparable results across all dimensions in the ten standard views. Notably, the highest observed improvement observed was up to 4.34%. The pre-trained model demonstrated

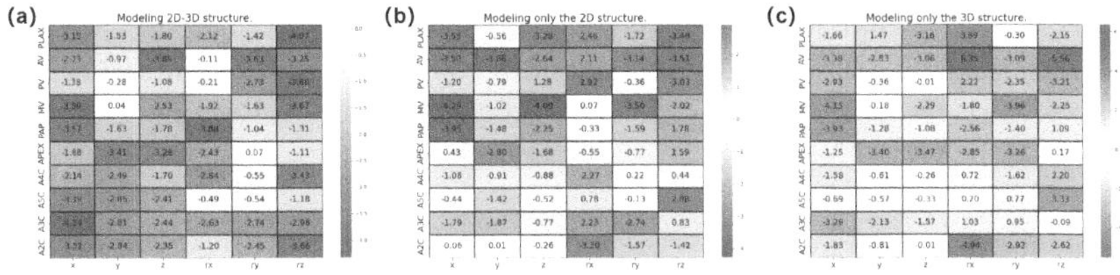

Fig. 4. Ablation of the pre-training objectives. The figure shows the relative change in MAE across six degrees of freedom for ten standard views, comparing different pre-training objectives with Cardiac Dreamer [9]. Smaller values indicate better performance. **(a)** Our proposed 2D-3D Joint Structure-aware pre-training. **(b, c)** Pre-training focused only on 2D or 3D structures.

slight weakness compared to the Cardiac Dreamer in only one dimension for the PSAX-MV and PSAX-APEX planes. Despite this minor shortfall, the overall performance indicates that the model has effectively learned valuable information about the 2D and 3D structures of the heart. This acquired knowledge enhances the precision of probe guidance during cardiac ultrasound scanning tasks, thereby potentially supporting less experienced sonographers in acquiring high-quality echocardiograms in the future.

Ablations. To demonstrate the importance of each component in our proposed joint 2D-3D modeling approach, we decoupled the 2D and 3D modeling, either focusing solely on 2D structure or 3D structure modeling. As shown in Fig. 4, our method achieves improvements in almost all dimensions, whereas using only 2D or 3D modeling results in poorer performance in rotation dimension. In summary, while either 2D or 3D modeling alone enhances the model's performance to some extent, combining both in joint pre-training achieves the best results. This conclusion aligns with practical experience as well. First, 3D modeling helps in understanding the 3D structure of the heart, while 2D modeling enables the model to more accurately identify anatomical landmarks on standard views, thereby providing crucial guidance for probe positioning adjustments.

4 Conclusion and Discussion

In this work, we propose a 2D-3D joint structure-aware pre-training framework to enhance the cardiac world model's understanding of spatial relationships within two-dimensional structures on a single view and the three-dimensional spatial relationships between different views. We innovatively designed a self-supervised learning task that predicts visual features based on both two-dimensional and three-dimensional spatial information. To support large-scale self-supervised pre-training, we collected over a million ultrasound image and 3D pose data pairs. After pre-training on the large-scale dataset, considerable improvement were observed in downstream probe guidance tasks across the ten standard views. In the future, we will attempt to: (1) validate our pre-trained model in more downstream tasks that require a comprehensive understanding of the heart's 2D and 3D structures; (2) validate our pre-trained model in real clinical settings, aiming to directly translate algorithmic improvements into enhanced medical outcomes or increased efficiency.

Acknowledgement. This work was supported in part by the National Key R&D Program of China (2021ZD0140407), the NSFC (62321005) and the Deng Feng Fund.

Disclosure of Interests. The authors have no competing interests to declare that are relevant to the content of this article.

References

1. Assran, M., Duval, Q., Misra, I., Bojanowski, P., Vincent, P., Rabbat, M., LeCun, Y., Ballas, N.: Self-supervised learning from images with a joint-embedding predictive architecture. In: Proceedings of the IEEE/CVF Conference on Computer Vision and Pattern Recognition. pp. 15619–15629 (2023)
2. Brown, T., Mann, B., Ryder, N., Subbiah, M., Kaplan, J.D., Dhariwal, P., Neelakantan, A., Shyam, P., Sastry, G., Askell, A., et al.: Language models are few-shot learners. Advances in neural information processing systems **33**, 1877–1901 (2020)
3. Christensen, M., Vukadinovic, M., Yuan, N., Ouyang, D.: Vision–language foundation model for echocardiogram interpretation. Nature Medicine pp. 1–8 (2024)
4. Dosovitskiy, A., Beyer, L., Kolesnikov, A., Weissenborn, D., Zhai, X., Unterthiner, T., Dehghani, M., Minderer, M., Heigold, G., Gelly, S., et al.: An image is worth 16x16 words: Transformers for image recognition at scale. arXiv preprint arXiv:2010.11929 (2020)
5. Droste, R., Drukker, L., Papageorghiou, A.T., Noble, J.A.: Automatic probe movement guidance for freehand obstetric ultrasound. In: Medical Image Computing and Computer Assisted Intervention–MICCAI 2020: 23rd International Conference, Lima, Peru, October 4–8, 2020, Proceedings, Part III 23. pp. 583–592. Springer (2020)
6. He, K., Zhang, X., Ren, S., Sun, J.: Deep residual learning for image recognition. In: Proceedings of the IEEE conference on computer vision and pattern recognition. pp. 770–778 (2016)
7. Huang, G., Liu, Z., Van Der Maaten, L., Weinberger, K.Q.: Densely connected convolutional networks. In: Proceedings of the IEEE conference on computer vision and pattern recognition. pp. 4700–4708 (2017)
8. Jiang, H., Lin, Y., Han, D., Song, S., Huang, G.: Pseudo-q: Generating pseudo language queries for visual grounding. In: Proceedings of the IEEE/CVF Conference on Computer Vision and Pattern Recognition. pp. 15513–15523 (2022)
9. Jiang, H., Sun, Z., Jia, N., Li, M., Sun, Y., Luo, S., Song, S., Huang, G.: Cardiac copilot: Automatic probe guidance for echocardiography with world model. arXiv preprint arXiv:2406.13165 (2024)
10. Jiang, H., Zhang, J., Huang, R., Ge, C., Ni, Z., Lu, J., Zhou, J., Song, S., Huang, G.: Cross-modal adapter for text-video retrieval. arXiv preprint arXiv:2211.09623 (2022)
11. Li, J., Selvaraju, R., Gotmare, A., Joty, S., Xiong, C., Hoi, S.C.H.: Align before fuse: Vision and language representation learning with momentum distillation. Advances in neural information processing systems **34**, 9694–9705 (2021)

12. Mitchell, C., Rahko, P.S., Blauwet, L.A., Canaday, B., Finstuen, J.A., Foster, M.C., Horton, K., Ogunyankin, K.O., Palma, R.A., Velazquez, E.J.: Guidelines for performing a comprehensive transthoracic echocardiographic examination in adults: recommendations from the american society of echocardiography. Journal of the American Society of Echocardiography **32**(1), 1–64 (2019)
13. Narang, A., Bae, R., Hong, H., Thomas, Y., Surette, S., Cadieu, C., Chaudhry, A., Martin, R.P., McCarthy, P.M., Rubenson, D.S., et al.: Utility of a deep-learning algorithm to guide novices to acquire echocardiograms for limited diagnostic use. JAMA cardiology **6**(6), 624–632 (2021)
14. Ouyang, D., He, B., Ghorbani, A., Yuan, N., Ebinger, J., Langlotz, C.P., Heidenreich, P.A., Harrington, R.A., Liang, D.H., Ashley, E.A., et al.: Video-based ai for beat-to-beat assessment of cardiac function. Nature **580**(7802), 252–256 (2020)
15. Radford, A., Kim, J.W., Hallacy, C., Ramesh, A., Goh, G., Agarwal, S., Sastry, G., Askell, A., Mishkin, P., Clark, J., et al.: Learning transferable visual models from natural language supervision. In: International conference on machine learning. pp. 8748–8763. PMLR (2021)
16. Radford, A., Narasimhan, K., Salimans, T., Sutskever, I., et al.: Improving language understanding by generative pre-training (2018)
17. Radford, A., Wu, J., Child, R., Luan, D., Amodei, D., Sutskever, I., et al.: Language models are unsupervised multitask learners. OpenAI blog **1**(8), 9 (2019)
18. Roth, G.A., Johnson, C., Abajobir, A., Abd-Allah, F., Abera, S.F., Abyu, G., Ahmed, M., Aksut, B., Alam, T., Alam, K., et al.: Global, regional, and national burden of cardiovascular diseases for 10 causes, 1990 to 2015. Journal of the American college of cardiology **70**(1), 1–25 (2017)
19. Song, P., Fang, Z., Wang, H., Cai, Y., Rahimi, K., Zhu, Y., Fowkes, F.G.R., Fowkes, F.J., Rudan, I.: Global and regional prevalence, burden, and risk factors for carotid atherosclerosis: a systematic review, meta-analysis, and modelling study. The Lancet Global Health **8**(5), e721–e729 (2020)
20. Thirunavukarasu, A.J., Ting, D.S.J., Elangovan, K., Gutierrez, L., Tan, T.F., Ting, D.S.W.: Large language models in medicine. Nature medicine **29**(8), 1930–1940 (2023)
21. Wang, Y., Chen, Z., Jiang, H., Song, S., Han, Y., Huang, G.: Adaptive focus for efficient video recognition. In: proceedings of the IEEE/CVF international conference on computer vision. pp. 16249–16258 (2021)
22. Yan, X., Jiang, Y., Wu, G., Chen, C., Huang, G., Li, X.: Multi-modal interaction control of ultrasound scanning robots with safe human guidance and contact recovery. arXiv preprint arXiv:2302.05685 (2023)
23. Yang, L., Jiang, H., Cai, R., Wang, Y., Song, S., Huang, G., Tian, Q.: Condensenet v2: Sparse feature reactivation for deep networks. In: Proceedings of the IEEE/CVF Conference on Computer Vision and Pattern Recognition. pp. 3569–3578 (2021)

An Evaluation of Low-Cost Hardware on 3D Ultrasound Reconstruction Accuracy

Étienne Léger[1()], Niki Najafi[2], Houssem-Eddine Gueziri[3], D. Louis Collins[1], and Marta Kersten-Oertel[2]

[1] Montréal Neuro, Montréal, Québec, Canada
etienne.leger@mail.concordia.ca
[2] Concordia University, Montréal, Québec, Canada
[3] TÉLUQ, Montréal, Québec, Canada

Abstract. The advances in consumer-grade hardware, such as optical trackers and portable ultrasound machines, has paved the way for the development of more cost-effective systems. In this paper, we aimed to assess the accuracy of low-cost tracking alternatives in the context of 3D freehand ultrasound (US) reconstruction. Specifically, we compared two low-cost tracking options: a depth camera and a low-end optical tracker, to an FDA approved high-end infrared optical tracking system. Additionally, we compared two US systems, a low-cost handheld US system with a high-resolution ultrasound mobile station. Each tracker and probe pair underwent 20 acquisitions in ideal conditions. An additional 20 acquisitions were made at 3 suboptimal tracker placements. These two experiments showed no statistically significant difference between probes and no difference between the low- and high-end optical trackers on accuracy of reconstructions. As a proof of principle, we performed volume-to-volume registration using the US reconstructions and found that low-cost probe and low-cost optical tracking is similar to using the standard high cost system. These findings suggest that low-cost hardware may offer a solution in the operating room or environments where commercial hardware systems are not available without compromising on the accuracy and usability of US image-guidance.

Keywords: Ultrasound Imaging · Low-cost Hardware · Image-guided Surgery

1 Introduction

Ultrasonography (US) is a low-powered imaging method often used in various clinical assessment and treatment settings. US provides cost-effective, accessible, and non-ionizing radiation imaging, which aligns with the World Health Organization's recommendation for primary diagnostics in resource-limited environments [23].

US systems are hand-held, operated by a single person, and offer diagnostic capabilities at significantly reduced costs compared to imaging modalities like Computed Tomography (CT) or Magnetic Resonance Imaging (MRI) [21]. These features make US a compelling choice for clinical applications in low and middle-income countries [21]. US has been employed in image-guided and minimally invasive surgery for knee arthroscopy [24], spine surgery [12], and neurosurgery [11], for biopsies [19], and tumour grading [20]. In low and middle-income countries, US has shown to improve surgical precision, reduce procedural invasiveness, and improve patient outcomes [17] in such areas as intrathecal anesthesia [1], catheterization in cardiovascular interventions [7], conservation breast surgery [22] and splenectomy [2]. Significant effort has been made to facilitate access to low-cost ultrasound navigation, e.g., for neurosurgery [14], prostate biopsy [9], anesthesia [1], catheterization in cardiovascular interventions [7], breast conservation surgery [22] and splenectomy [2] among other applications [17].

With the emergence of portable, low-cost US systems and consumer grade hardware components that can be used for spatial tracking, there is a need to determine the accuracy and usability of these systems. In this study, we evaluated the precision of US reconstruction with various hardware configurations spanning low and high price points. Specifically, we compared two US systems, and four tracking systems with the goal of quantifying and comparing the tracking accuracy and usability of reconstructions. We focus on the accuracy provided by off-the-shelf hardware components, without applying any further processing to improve the quality of reconstruction, calibration, or tracking. Our goal is to identify the limits of devices at different price points and evaluate their suitability for use in image-guided interventions.

2 Previous Work

A number of groups have looked at the impact of lower cost hardware on tracking and US reconstruction. Asselin *et al.* studied web-cam based tracking for clinical interventions and found that the web-cam based system had errors on the order of 20.0 mm and 4.1° and thus was not sufficiently accurate for computer assisted surgery or training [3]. Cenni *et al.* compared two tracking systems for freehand ultrasound reconstruction and found no differences in terms of reconstruction accuracy. However, details were not given as to the hardware [6]. Cai *et al.* developed a low-cost camera-based US tracking system for obstetric imaging and were able to obtain tracking error of less than 1 mm for position and 1° for orientation [5]. In similar work, Baba *et al.* developed a camera-based system for 3D US volume reconstruction and found that a pair of points 10 mm apart in the volume could be reconstructed with an average error of 0.7 mm [4]. In a previous study [13], we compared various tracking devices at a number of price points as well as a low-cost and a high cost US system and found on a set of 10 ultrasound acquisitions no significant difference between the probes and various optical trackers.

We expand on [13], augmenting the experiment with a with a larger dataset to derive more robust statistics, and add two new experiments. Unlike previous studies, we examine the impact of suboptimal probe position in relation to the tracking system, and assess the influence of reconstruction quality on the goodness of fit in volume-to-volume registration. The suboptimal placement analysis provides meaningful results that may be more indicative of what would typically be achieved in real-world conditions and the TRE of a volume-to-volume registration is a metric closer to the expected clinical use. This paper therefore expands on previous work by providing per axis robust and clinically applicable error estimates of US reconstruction giving insights necessary to build low-cost, accurate ultrasound-based surgical navigation tools.

3 Methodology

We performed experiments on an in-house constructed phantom. Ultrasound acquisitions were made using two ultrasound probes in combination with four tracking systems at various price points as shown in Table 1.

3.1 Experimental Setup

A specialized *wire phantom* was created to enable precise evaluation in the first two experiments. The phantom was constructed using Lego^{TM} bricks (accurate to within 0.04 mm [15]) and consisted of eight wires stretched tautly between the bricks (Fig. 1 left), forming a cuboid shape with precisely known dimensions (11.20 mm by 9.60 mm by 19.00 mm in x, y, and z dimensions respectively). The wires intersected at right angles, resulting in precisely known angles between line segments. This phantom was used to measure the distortion in the shape of the reconstructed volume as detailed in the next section. For the proof-of-principle experiment on volume-to-volume registration, the phantom described in [25] was built. Both phantoms were submerged in water at room temperature for both US acquisition and probe calibration, minimizing speed of sound issues.

For US acquisition, a custom marker that enabled tracking of the probes with both RGB and optical trackers was built [3,13] (Fig. 1, right). The marker was 3D printed with polylactic acid using a Raise 3D Pro2 printer (Raise 3D Technologies, Inc., Irvine, CA, USA) at 0.1 mm layer thickness. A shared location at the center of the structure was established as the marker's pivot for all tracking

Table 1. Hardware that was used in the experiments and their different price points.

Ultrasound Systems	
MicrUs MC4-2R20S-3 probe (TELEMED, Vilnius, Lithuania)	7,000 USD
BK3500 14L3 probe (BK Medical, Peabody, MA, USA)	250k USD
Tracking Systems	
ArUco markers [10] with RealSense RGB camera [10]	25 USD
RealSense D435 (Intel Corporation, Santa Clara, CA, USA)	300 USD
Optitrack V120:Duo (NaturalPoint Inc., Corvallis, OR, USA)	3,000 USD
Atracsys FusionTrack 500 (Atracsys LLC, Puidoux, Switzerland)	25k USD

techniques. This location coincided with the center of the ArUco marker and the central point of the reflective sphere positions. A mounting bracket to fix the marker on the US probe was also designed and 3D printed. Finally, a second marker was created to serve as a reference and was attached to the phantom. All trackers were co-located so that the axes of the tracking volume would match that of the phantom (see Fig. 1, center).

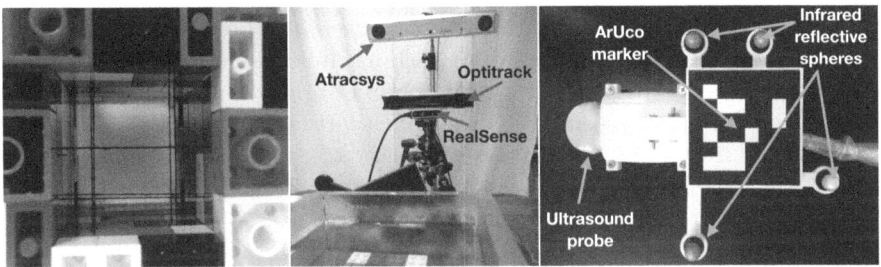

Fig. 1. Left to right: (1) custom built Lego phantom, (2) tracker set-up, (3) custom hybrid markers and probe attachment.

3.2 Data Acquisition and Analysis

Three datasets were collected using the experimental set-up and hardware.

Dimensional and Angular Distortion Per Probe: $D_{straight}$ consists of twenty sweeps of the wire phantom with each US probe. For each acquisition, tracking data were recorded simultaneously with all tracking systems. All sweeps were performed in a single linear motion along the z axis (view axis of the trackers), with the marker facing the view direction of the tracking devices (optimal position). Independent reconstructions were then computed from each sweep and hardware combination. A total of *20 acquisitions × 2 US probes × 4 tracking devices = 160 volumes* were reconstructed and further analyzed for both angular and dimensional distortions. For each volume reconstructed, the eight wires were manually segmented using 3D Slicer [8], and each line was derived through least-square fitting (see Fig. 2). The line intersections form the corners of the reconstructed cuboid and the coordinate points corresponding to these corners were then used in all further analysis. Two metrics were considered: (i) *the dimensional distortion (DD)*, corresponding to the distance between the points along each axis that form the cuboid, expressed as an absolute percentage difference from the nominal length, and (ii) *the angular distortion (AD)*, corresponding to the angles between the intersecting lines computed around each axis, expressed as an absolute difference in degrees from the nominal angle. For dimensional distortion, all four segments that were generated from the connections of points along that axis were averaged. Similarly, for angles, all eight angles corresponding to rotation around that axis were averaged.

Tracking Position Dependence: D_{tilt} was acquired with the Telemed probe and consisted of sweeps of the same wire phantom. The acquisition was done in the same linear motion as the first dataset, but with the probe positioned at varying angles from the facing direction of the tracking devices: 0° (optimal, facing tracker view axis), 10° off axis, 22.5° off axis and 45° off axis. Segmentation and analysis of the wires was performed the same way as for $D_{straight}$.

Volume-to-Volume Registration Accuracy: D_{Lego}, consisted of acquisitions of the *Lego* phantom from [25]. Three sweeps were acquired and independent reconstructions were then computed for each hardware combination (3 acquisitions × 2 probes × 4 trackers). For this proof-of-principle experiment, the 24 volumes were all registered independently to a virtual MRI of the Lego phantom generated from known geometry. For each reconstruction, the preoperative model was manually brought into rough alignment with the reconstruction using 3D Slicer [8]. Then the volume registration module was used to compute the registration transform with the Mattes Mutual Information (MMI) cost metric [16]. The target registration error (TRE) was computed using seven target points distributed across the Lego phantom. These points were located on the center of cylindrical protrusions on Lego blocks and were easily identifiable in both the model and the volume.

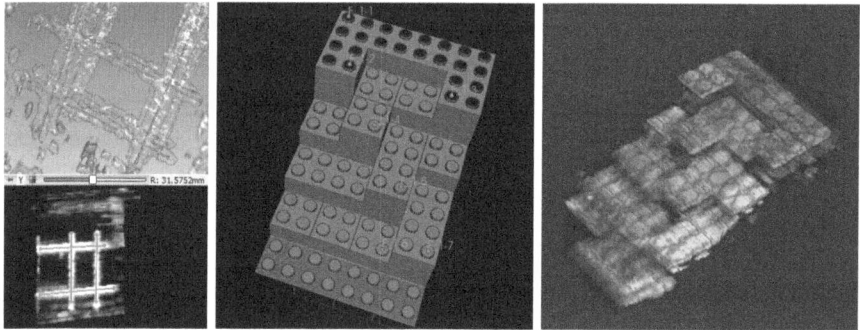

Fig. 2. Left: Segmentation of wire phantom (3D view at the top and US slice at the bottom); Center: Volume-to-volume phantom with seven landmarks used for TRE computation; Right: example ultrasound reconstruction of the volume-to-volume phantom.

4 Results

Dimensional and Angular Distortion: A two-way (probe, tracker) ANOVA showed no statistical difference between probes in terms of dimensional distortion for all axes. We did find a statistical difference in angular distortion for both the x-axis ($p < 0.04$) and z-axis ($p < 0.014$). In both cases, the angular distortion was higher with the BK probe (at +0.64° in x and +0.33° in z).

Acquisitions made using the Atracsys and Optitrack systems did not differ statistically ($p > 0.05$). The same is true for acquisitions made with the Aruco and D435, no statistical difference was found. However, acquisitions made with Aruco were significantly worse ($p < 0.05$) from those made with both Atracsys and Optitrack for both dimensional and angular distortions. Similarly, acquisitions made using D435 were significantly worse ($p < 0.05$) than those done using the Atracsys or Optitrack, except for dimensional distortion in x. The results for DD and AD per tracker are shown in Fig 3.

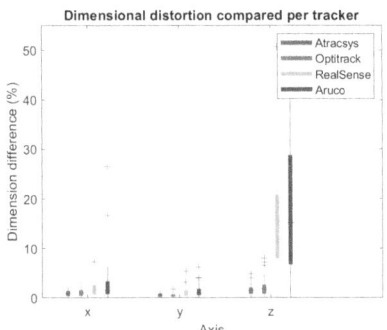
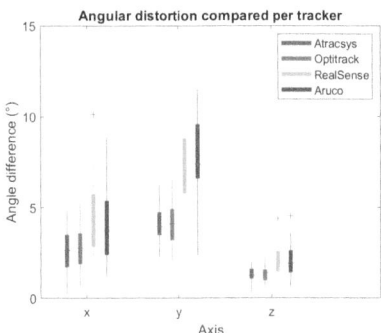

Fig. 3. Boxplots of dimensional (left) and angular (right) distortion in x, y and z axes per tracker. We grouped both US acquisitions as no statistical difference was found.

Tracker Positioning Dependence: Figure 4 shows results for the impact of varying line of sight angles from the probe to the trackers. We can observe the that error increases as viewing angle degrades, with a notably sharp increase between 0 and 10° off-axis. This trend is observed for all tracking systems, but the magnitude of the decline correlates negatively with system cost.

Volume-to-Volume Registration Accuracy: The TRE results for the dataset D_{Lego} are reported in Table 2. The TRE is smaller for the FusionTrack 500 and Optitrack in comparison to the Aruco and D435.

5 Discussion

While no significant difference was found in dimensional distortion between US probes, we found small ($< 1°$) but significant difference in angular distortion, but it is possible that this small difference could simply be due to factors such as image transfer latency. The results indicates that the low-cost ultrasound system may be a viable alternative to more expensive systems, without compromising on the accuracy of the US image-guidance.

The second experiment on the effect of using a misaligned tracker on quality of reconstruction reveals some important findings. As expected, the quality of

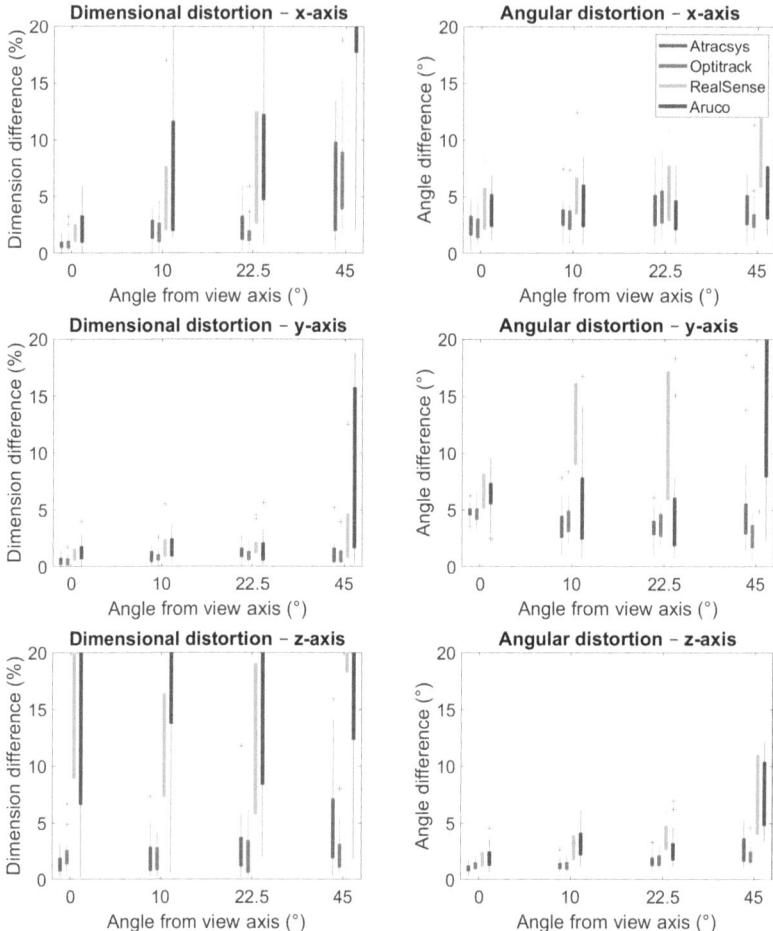

Fig. 4. Comparison per tracker on reconstructions acquired at different angles relative to the optimal tracking view direction. Top to bottom: x, y and z-axis; Left: Boxplots of dimensional distortion; Right: Boxplots of angular distortion. x is the axis angled relative to tracker view direction and z is the axis the sweeps were acquired along and the depth direction in the tracker coordinate frame.

reconstructions decreases as optimal view angle between tracker and probe does. This is true for all tracking systems, even the higher-end ones. For usable reconstructions, the markers should be kept facing the tracking system to within the 0-10° range. This finding offers valuable insights for clinical use. In the crowded and busy OR setting, with all its constraints, a misalignment in this range may be quite commonplace. Specific attention must be paid to ensuring that the camera, reference marker and probe marker are well aligned with each other. Failure to do so can result in erroneous or degraded guidance.

Table 2. Average TRE after volume-to-volume registration for each combination of hardware reported both independently in the three dimensions of space as well as overall, with associated standard deviations in parentheses.

Probe	Tracker	TRE x (mm)	TRE y (mm)	TRE z (mm)	RMS TRE (mm)
BK	FusionTrack 500	2.69 (2.69)	2.36 (1.33)	2.02 (2.30)	4.40 (2.31)
	V120:Duo	2.30 (1.27)	2.25 (1.40)	1.68 (1.47)	3.80 (1.79)
	D435	8.72 (6.17)	18.19 (13.18)	6.16 (5.10)	21.48 (14.39)
	ArUco	9.17 (5.97)	20.63 (13.14)	10.13 (6.69)	27.15 (9.92)
Telemed	FusionTrack 500	2.50 (2.41)	2.40 (1.40)	3.77 (3.39)	5.26 (2.83)
	V120:Duo	3.03 (3.38)	3.31 (3.23)	4.35 (4.57)	6.57 (2.58)
	D435	8.85 (7.13)	16.52 (13.56)	12.97 (10.59)	23.43 (12.41)
	ArUco	8.32 (7.20)	16.74 (13.34)	7.13 (7.39)	21.40 (11.49)

In line with what was previously reported [18], we found that image-based tracking, even when augmented with depth information, is an order of magnitude less accurate in the z axis than other axes. For volume-to-volume registration the results align with the results from the first experiments. It confirms that our results would apply to a real clinical use case such as US reconstruction for registration in surgical guidance. This study's findings could thus be used to inform hardware decisions.

In terms of limitations, the two probes compared have different central frequencies and geometries, which could have introduced a bias in the comparison. However, this bias would have favoured the BK3500, therefore this does not invalidate our findings and makes our conclusion stronger if anything.

6 Conclusion

Results obtained in this paper confirm those from previous studies exploring 3D freehand ultrasound reconstruction quality obtained with hardware at varying price points but on a larger dataset. Further, unlike previous studies, we explore the influence of poor tracker placement on reconstruction quality and found it is a major contributor to error, much more so than hardware cost. Finally, we validate real-world applicability of both of these experiments by comparing reconstructed volumes obtained on all sets of hardware to perform a typical surgical guidance scenario, that of intraop US to preop MRI volume-to-volume registration. This study highlights three key findings: (1) both low-end US probes and low-end optical trackers can be used for this application with negligible negative impact on usability of results; (2) 2D marker based tracking, even when augmented with a depth sensor, performs significantly worse than optical trackers and may be ill-suited for this application; (3) good placement of the tracking device relative to the surgical field is paramount to obtain usable reconstructions.

References

1. Abdelhamid, S.A., Mansour, M.A.: Ultrasound-guided intrathecal anesthesia: Does scanning help? Egyptian Journal of Anaesthesia **29**(4), 389–394 (2013)
2. Afuwape, O., Ogole, G., Ayandipo, O.: Splenectomy in a nigerian teaching hospital: A comparison of sonographic correlation with intra-operative findings in trauma. Journal of Emergencies, Trauma, and Shock **6**(3), 186 (2013)
3. Asselin, M., Lasso, A., Ungi, T., Fichtinger, G.: Towards webcam-based tracking for interventional navigation. In: Medical Imaging 2018: Image-Guided Procedures, Robotic Interventions, and Modeling. vol. 10576, pp. 534–543. SPIE (2018)
4. Baba, M.M., Mohamed, O.A., Awwad, F., Daoud, M.I.: A low-cost camera-based transducer tracking system for freehand three-dimensional ultrasound. In: 2016 14th IEEE International New Circuits and Systems Conference (NEWCAS). pp. 1–4. IEEE (2016)
5. Cai, Q., Peng, C., Prieto, J.C., Rosenbaum, A.J., Stringer, J.S., Jiang, X.: A low-cost camera-based ultrasound probe tracking system: Design and prototype. In: 2019 IEEE International Ultrasonics Symposium (IUS). pp. 997–999. IEEE (2019)
6. Cenni, F., Monari, D., Desloovere, K., Aertbeliën, E., Schless, S.H., Bruyninckx, H.: The reliability and validity of a clinical 3d freehand ultrasound system. Computer methods and programs in biomedicine **136**, 179–187 (2016)
7. Dharma, S., Kedev, S., Patel, T., Kiemeneij, F., Gilchrist, I.C.: A novel approach to reduce radial artery occlusion after transradial catheterization: postprocedural/prehemostasis intra-arterial nitroglycerin. Catheterization and Cardiovascular Interventions **85**(5), 818–825 (2015)
8. Fedorov, A., Beichel, R., Kalpathy-Cramer, J., Finet, J., Fillion-Robin, J.C., Pujol, S., Bauer, C., Jennings, D., Fennessy, F., Sonka, M., et al.: 3d slicer as an image computing platform for the quantitative imaging network. Magnetic resonance imaging **30**(9), 1323–1341 (2012)
9. Fichtinger, G., Mousavi, P., Ungi, T., Fenster, A., Abolmaesumi, P., Kronreif, G., Ruiz-Alzola, J., Ndoye, A., Diao, B., Kikinis, R.: Design of an ultrasound-navigated prostate cancer biopsy system for nationwide implementation in senegal. Journal of Imaging **7**(8), 154 (2021)
10. Garrido-Jurado, S., Muñoz-Salinas, R., Madrid-Cuevas, F., Marín-Jiménez, M.: Automatic generation and detection of highly reliable fiducial markers under occlusion. Pattern Recognition **47**(6), 2280–2292 (2014)
11. Gerard, I.J., Kersten-Oertel, M., Hall, J.A., Sirhan, D., Collins, D.L.: Brain shift in neuronavigation of brain tumors: an updated review of intra-operative ultrasound applications. Frontiers in Oncology **10**, 618837 (2021)
12. Gueziri, H.E., Santaguida, C., Collins, D.L.: The state-of-the-art in ultrasound-guided spine interventions. Medical Image Analysis **65**, 101769 (2020)
13. Léger, É., Gueziri, H.E., Collins, D.L., Popa, T., Kersten-Oertel, M.: Evaluation of low-cost hardware alternatives for 3d freehand ultrasound reconstruction in image-guided neurosurgery. In: Simplifying Medical Ultrasound: Second International Workshop, ASMUS 2021, Held in Conjunction with MICCAI 2021, Strasbourg, France, September 27, 2021, Proceedings 2. pp. 106–115. Springer (2021)
14. Léger, É., Horvath, S., Fillion-Robin, J.C., Allemang, D., Gerber, S., Juvekar, P., Torio, E., Kapur, T., Pieper, S., Pujol, S., et al.: Nousnav: A low-cost neuronavigation system for deployment in lower-resource settings. International Journal of Computer Assisted Radiology and Surgery **17**(9), 1745–1750 (2022)

15. Lemes, S.: Comparison of similar injection moulded parts by a coordinate measuring machine. SN Applied Sciences **1**(2), 193 (2019)
16. Mattes, D., Haynor, D.R., Vesselle, H., Lewellen, T.K., Eubank, W.: Pet-ct image registration in the chest using free-form deformations. IEEE transactions on medical imaging **22**(1), 120–128 (2003)
17. Navarro, S.M., Shaikh, H., Abdi, H., Keil, E.J., Odusanya, S., Stewart, K.A., Tuyishime, E., Mazingi, D., Tuttle, T.M.: Surgical applications of ultrasound use in low-and middle-income countries: a systematic review. Australasian Journal of Ultrasound in Medicine **25**(2), 80–97 (2022)
18. Popescu, D.C., Cernaianu, M.O., Ghenuche, P., Dumitrache, I.: An assessment on the accuracy of high precision 3d positioning using planar fiducial markers. 2017 21st International Conference on System Theory, Control and Computing (ICSTCC) pp. 471–476 (2017)
19. Pradipta, A.R., Tanei, T., Morimoto, K., Shimazu, K., Noguchi, S., Tanaka, K.: Emerging technologies for real-time intraoperative margin assessment in future breast-conserving surgery. Advanced Science **7**(9), 1901519 (2020)
20. Shao, J., Zheng, J., Zhang, B.: Deep convolutional neural networks for thyroid tumor grading using ultrasound b-mode images. The Journal of the Acoustical Society of America **148**(3), 1529–1535 (2020)
21. Stewart, K.A., Navarro, S.M., Kambala, S., Tan, G., Poondla, R., Lederman, S., Barbour, K., Lavy, C.: Trends in ultrasound use in low and middle income countries: a systematic review. International Journal of Maternal and Child Health and AIDS **9**(1), 103 (2020)
22. Vispute, T., Seenu, V., Parshad, R., Hari, S., Thulkar, S., Mathur, S., et al.: Comparison of resection margins and cosmetic outcome following intraoperative ultrasound-guided excision versus conventional palpation-guided breast conservation surgery in breast cancer: A randomized controlled trial. Indian journal of cancer **55**(4), 361–365 (2018)
23. Wittenberg, M.: Will ultrasound scanners replace the stethoscope? BMJ **348** (2014)
24. Wu, L., Jaiprakash, A., Pandey, A.K., Fontanarosa, D., Jonmohamadi, Y., Antico, M., Strydom, M., Razjigaev, A., Sasazawa, F., Roberts, J., et al.: Robotic and image-guided knee arthroscopy. In: Handbook of robotic and image-guided surgery, pp. 493–514. Elsevier (2020)
25. Xiao, Y., Yan, C.X.B., Drouin, S., De Nigris, D., Kochanowska, A., Collins, D.L.: User-friendly freehand ultrasound calibration using Lego bricks and automatic registration. International Journal of Computer Assisted Radiology and Surgery **11**(9), 1703–1711 (2016)

Learning to Match 2D Keypoints Across Preoperative MR and Intraoperative Ultrasound

Hassan Rasheed[1,3,4], Reuben Dorent[1], Maximilian Fehrentz[1,3], Tina Kapur[1], William M. Wells III[1,2], Alexandra Golby[1], Sarah Frisken[1], Julia A. Schnabel[3,4], and Nazim Haouchine[1(✉)]

[1] Harvard Medical School, Brigham and Women's Hospital, Boston, MA, USA
nhaouchine@bwh.harvard.edu
[2] Massachusetts Institute of Technology, Cambridge, MA, USA
[3] Technical University of Munich, Munich, Germany
[4] Helmholtz Center Munich, Munich, Germany

Abstract. We propose in this paper a texture-invariant 2D keypoints descriptor specifically designed for matching preoperative Magnetic Resonance (MR) images with intraoperative Ultrasound (US) images. We introduce a *matching-by-synthesis* strategy, where intraoperative US images are synthesized from MR images accounting for multiple MR modalities and intraoperative US variability. We build our training set by enforcing keypoints localization over all images then train a patient-specific descriptor network that learns texture-invariant discriminant features in a supervised contrastive manner, leading to robust keypoints descriptors. Our experiments on real cases with ground truth show the effectiveness of the proposed approach, outperforming the state-of-the-art methods and achieving 80.35% matching precision on average.

1 Introduction

Multimodal image matching is a fundamental problem that involves identifying and pairing similar features or patterns across images from different modalities, with significant appearance changes [11]. It has a wide range of applications in medical imaging, including image retrieval and classification [11,14], slice-to-volume alignment [7] and image registration [6,10,12,17,18]. When used during image-guided surgery, it can provide surgeons with complementary imaging information from various modalities, facilitating the identification of key anatomical and surgical structures for improved surgical outcomes. For instance, during neurosurgery, intraoperative Ultrasound (US) is often used in conjunction with preoperative Magnetic Resonance Imaging (MRI) to localize tumor boundaries that may have been shifted due to brain shift [8]. This allows surgeons to achieve maximally safe resection, which is positively correlated with a patient's chances of survival [9,20]. However, although affordable and real-time in comparison to intraoperative MRI, US images can be difficult to interpret [4], requiring image registration with preoperative MRI to disambiguate US images.

In this work, we focus on keypoint-based multi-modal methods, where correspondences between a relatively small set of keypoints extracted from both images are first identified before being matched. They typically rely on discriminative descriptors that can be matched under various imaging conditions allowing for robust matching. This area has been extensively studied [11] and some approaches have been successfully applied to medical images, in MRI with different weights, such as T1, T2, and proton density, or with angiographic retinal images [2]. However, these methods are limited to preoperative images where dissimilarities between modalities are relatively small. MR-US image matching is a non-trivial task due to the large dissimilarity between these two modalities [23]. Moreover, these modalities provide different textures, and volumetric information, operate at different spatial resolutions, and are corrupted by various sources of noise. In particular, MRI uses pulse sequences to obtain images with contrasts between soft tissue types, producing high-resolution 3D volumetric images, whereas US acquires partial and noisy images that echo back structures based on wave distances. Adapting such methods to MR-US images requires modeling the intraoperative texture gap related to US acquisitions. A texture-invariant feature descriptor can take several forms [11] focusing on temporal changes [22], structural changes [1] or appearance changes [3].

This work presents novel texture-invariant 2D keypoint descriptors designed explicitly for matching preoperative MR with intraoperative US images. We introduce a *matching-by-synthesis* strategy, where intraoperative US images are synthesized from a patient-specific MR image and then used to train a cross-modality descriptor network. This network is trained in a supervised contrastive manner to be agnostic to US texture changes and to be robust to speckle noise. Our approach does not require human-annotated key points or a large training dataset. Moreover, our method is interpretable since the matched and mismatched keypoints can be visualized. Our experiments on real cases with ground truth show the effectiveness of the proposed approach, outperforming the state-of-the-art methods.

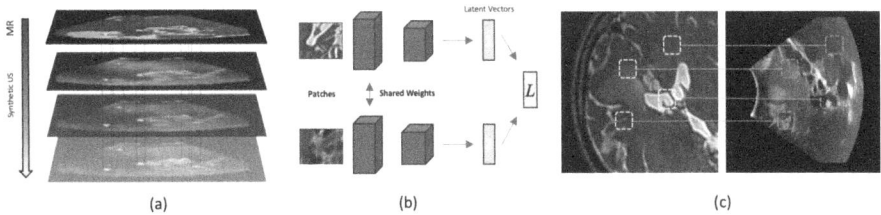

Fig. 1. Method overview: We rely on training images composed of one MR image and multiple synthesized US images, generated under different modes and noise levels (a). We train a Siamese network on image patches to learn similar and dissimilar features in a supervised contrastive manner (b). Applying this network to patches from each image leads a MR-US cross-modal matching (c).

2 Methods

2.1 Overview and Problem Setting

Let us assume a preoperative MR image $\mathbf{I}_{\text{MR}} \in \mathbb{R}^{H \times W \times D}$, an intraoperative US image $\mathbf{I}_{\text{US}} \in \mathbb{R}^{H \times W \times D}$, and a set of 2D points of interest $\mathbf{x} = \{x_i | i \in 1 \ldots n\} \in \mathbf{I}_{\text{MR}}$ and $\mathbf{y} = \{y_i | i \in 1 \ldots m\} \in \mathbf{I}_{\text{US}}$, independently detected on each image. We seek at finding a mapping $\pi : \{1, 2, \ldots, n\} \to \{1, 2, \ldots, m\}$ which maximizes the similarity function $\mathcal{M}$:

$$\underset{\pi \in \Pi(n)}{\arg\max} \mathcal{M}\big([\mathbf{d}(x_{\pi(i)})]_{i=1}^n, [\mathbf{d}(y_i)]_{i=1}^m\big) \tag{1}$$

where $\Pi(n)$ denotes all possible mappings and $\mathbf{d}$ is a 2D keypoint descriptor.

To build the cross-modality descriptor $\mathbf{d}$, we train a descriptor network on image patches by minimizing the sum of the loss for pairs of corresponding and non-corresponding patches in a supervised contrastive manner. Since this type of training requires a large number of paired images ($\mathbf{I}_{\text{MR}}, \mathbf{I}_{\text{US}}$) to efficiently mine positive and negative patches, we propose a *matching-by-synthesis* strategy, where intraoperative US images are synthesized from preoperative MR images using a generative network. We describe below how we build the cross-modality training dataset and train the 2D descriptor network (See Fig. 1).

2.2 Intraoperative Image Synthesis

To synthesize an intraoperative US image $\mathbf{I}_{\text{SynUS}}$ from a preoperative MR image $\mathbf{I}_{\text{MR}}$, we define a generative network $g(\cdot)$ so that $\mathbf{I}_{\text{SynUS}} = g(\mathbf{I}_{\text{MR}}, \widehat{\theta}_g, \gamma)$, with $\widehat{\theta}_g$ being the network pre-trained parameters and γ are a set of parameters to vary the texture of the generated image at inference. We rely on the multimodal hierarchical variational auto-encoder (MHVAE) proposed in [5], which is the current state-of-the-art for MR to iUS synthesis. MHVAE has the flexibility to handle incomplete sets of MR images as input and produces realistic US synthesis (See Fig. 2), allowing us to synthesise ultrasound for any combination of input modalities (T1, T2, FLAIR MRs). Moreover, this method uses a principled probabilistic fusion operation to create a common representation space between modalities and a hierarchical latent structure to represent global features with the coarsest latent variable while the finer variables capture local characteristics. Sampling is performed at each level of the hierarchy to perform synthesis. By varying γ, the set of sampling parameters, we can generate images US images with different speckles and content from any combination of input modalities (T1, T2, FLAIR MRs). This allows us to create a 1-to-many set of paired images $T = \{\mathbf{I}_{\text{MR}}, \mathbf{I}_{\text{SynUS}}^1, \ldots, \mathbf{I}_{\text{SynUS}}^p\}$ that will be used to build the training dataset. We generate 28 synthetic US images ($p = 28$) for each MR with the following combination: T1, T2, FLAIR, T1+T2, T1+FLAIR, T2+FLAIR, and T1+T2+FLAIR with 4 different sampling parameters.

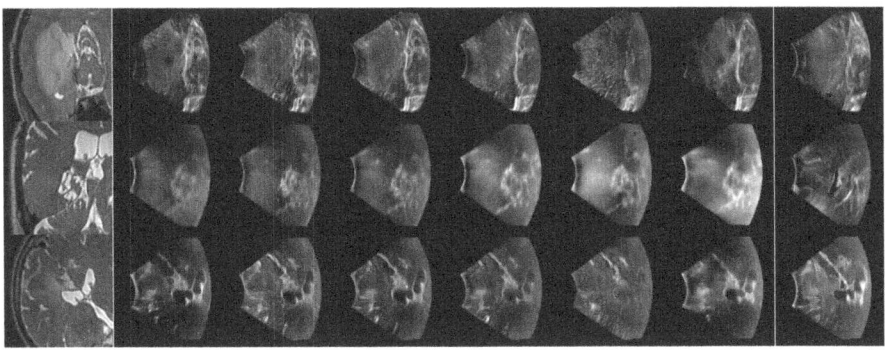

Fig. 2. Synthetic US image generations for three different T2 MR images (One case per row). The first column shows T2 MR; the middle columns show samples of synthetic US images generated using different combinations of T2, T1, and FLAIR with different speckles; the last column shows the ground truth US image.

2.3 Building the Training Dataset

As in [1], we chose to train our network on 2D patches, that we denote $\mathbf{p}$, extracted at keypoints locations, and standardized into $s \times s$ pixels. We use SuperPoint [3]. Note that other detectors could be considered as well. To collect a training set of positive patches, we first detect keypoints on the MR image $\mathbf{I}_{MR}$. We then iterate over the synthesized US images from $\{\mathbf{I}^i_{SynUS}\}^p_{i=1}$ and enforce SuperPoint to detect keypoints at the same location as keypoints from $\mathbf{I}_{MR}$. If a keypoint is detected at the same location (within a 5px margin) in at least 3 images, its location is likely to be a good candidate to learn. We then cluster keypoints within a 5px radius using the DBSCAN method. We normalize the patches with the grayscale mean and standard deviation of the entire training set. We choose a patch size of $s = 64$ pixel and extract 256 patches per slice while retaining about half after clustering.

This strategy allows us to keep only the most repeatable keypoints for training, discarding the ones that were detected only on one modality. Moreover, our network is trained to learn texture-invariance by enforcing keypoints locations over all sets of synthetic US images.

2.4 Learning Cross-Modal Feature Descriptor

Model Architecture and Loss Function. Given an image patch $\mathbf{p}$ around a detected keypoint, the objective is to build a descriptor $\mathbf{d}$ that retains structural similarity between modalities but is invariant to changes in textures. Following on related work, our descriptor network is a convolutional neural network $h(\cdot)$ with a relatively simple Siamese architecture so that $\mathbf{d} = h(\mathbf{p}, \theta_h)$, where θ_h are the network parameters. To train $h(\cdot)$, we consider corresponding and non-corresponding pairs of patches and use a *Triplet Loss* that learns the ideal embedding space for the patches. We propose to pair patch $\mathbf{p}^k_a \in \mathbf{I}_{MR}$ with multiple positive and negative patches $\mathbf{p}_p^k \in \mathbf{I}_{\text{SynUS}}$ and $\mathbf{p}_n^{k'} \in \mathbf{I}_{\text{SynUS}}$ respectively (with $k \neq k'$), enforcing the network to discard texture changes between modalities while learning content similarity. Formally, the loss is defined as:

$$L_{triplet}(\mathbf{d}_a^k, \mathbf{d}_p^k, \mathbf{d}_n^{k'}) = \sum_k \max\left(0, |\mathbf{d}_a^k - \mathbf{d}_p^k|^2 - |\mathbf{d}_a^l - \mathbf{d}_n^{k'}|^2 + C\right) \quad (2)$$

where $C = 1$ is the margin. We use hard mining during training, which was shown in [1] to be critical for descriptor performance. We select the negative samples from within the training batch that have the lowest loss, based on L_2 distance, against the current patch and use that for backpropagation. We use balanced batches of positive and negative pairs.

Training and Optimization Details. We train our model in 2D, pairing individual slices rather than the whole volume. This makes the learning scalable without loss of information, as most volume regions do not contain keypoints. We include all the slices in the training. We train one model per patient, in a patient-specific manner. This also allows us to maintain a batch with multiple patch pairs, which helps convergence. The training typically takes less than 30 mn on a single 10 GB GPU. For optimization, we use ADAM with a learning rate of 10^{-3} and a batch size of 256.

Run-Time Inference and Matching. At inference, we set the detection to $n = 200$ keypoints from the MR image. For the US image, rather than specifying an exact number of keypoints, m, we impose a limit of 1500 keypoints. We build the descriptors on each patch by running a feed-forward inference using one branch of the Siamese network. Our similarity function $\mathcal{M}$ takes the form of a K nearest neighbors (KNN) similarity search via Cosine-based representations, which we found empirically to perform better than an L_2 similarity. We use the standard criteria consisting of distance threshold, Lowe's ratio test, and matching uniqueness to filter out false negative matches.

3 Experimentations and Results

Data. We evaluate our method on a dataset of 7 cases where both pre-operative 3D T2-SPACE and pre-dural opening intraoperative US reconstructed from a tracked handheld 2D probe were acquired. We used the ReMIND dataset [13] where 3D T2-SPACE scans are registered with the pre-dural US. Images are resampled to an isotropic 0.5 mm resolution, padded for an in-plane matrix of $(192, 192)$, and normalized in $[-1, 1]$.

Metrics. Since paired data with ground truth is available for evaluation, we use keypoints locations (within a 4px radius) to evaluate our method. We report the following metrics: Matching Score (MSc.) as the ratio of ground truth correspondences over the number of detected keypoints of the whole pipeline and

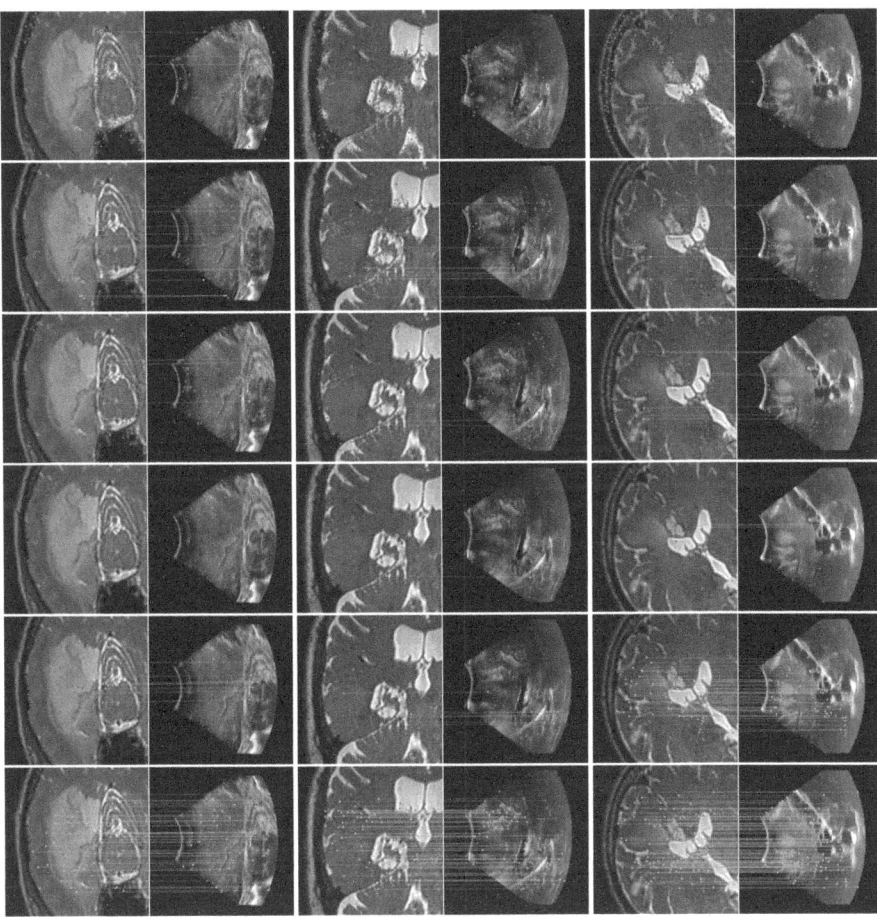

Fig. 3. Examples of matching on three cases, one per column (MR on left and US on right). From top to bottom: SIFT+Cosine, MIND+Cosine, SP+Cosine, SP+LG, Ours+LG, Ours+Cosine. Correct matches recovered by each method are shown in green lines and mismatched are shown with a red dot. (Color figure online)

Precision (Prec.) as the ratio of ground truth correspondences over the number of matched keypoints. We also report the number of matched points MP. Overall, our method achieves an average matching score of 26.62%, an average matching precision of 80.35%, and an average of 43.33 matched points.

Ablation Study and Evaluation. We first measure the impact of varying modalities during US synthesis on the matching performance by excluding and including T1 and Flair modalities. It can be observed in Table 1 that while the matching precision is only marginally impacted, using all modalities in the synthesis improves the matching scores by more than 12%. In addition, it increases

Table 1. Impact of modalities synthesis (Averages over ≈ 80 slices)

T2	T1	FLAIR	Prec. (%)	MSc. (%)	Avg MP	Area (%)
●	○	○	**85.64**	7.06	16.50	25.05
●	○	●	83.01	7.60	18.33	30.73
●	●	○	83.25	12.87	30.92	44.77
●	●	●	81.08	**20.32**	50.14	**55.11**

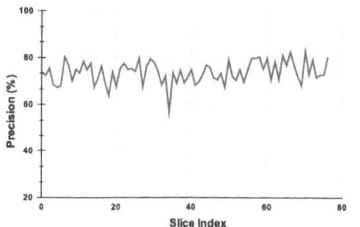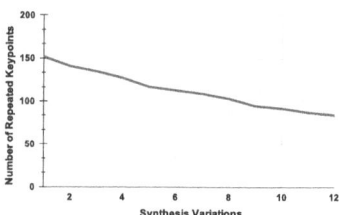

Fig. 4. Repeatability of matches over slices (left) and textures changes (right).

the number of matched points and the percentage of covered area. This can be explained by the fact that modalities complete each other when information is missing which highlights the benefits of using our synthesis strategy. We also measure the performance of the descriptor across slices, expressed as the average amount by which each matching precision per slice differs from the mean overall volume. We can observe from Fig. 4-left a quasi-constant trend line of matching precision over slices, with a low average standard deviation of 7.1%. Moreover, to measure the repeatability of the descriptor across multiple synthesis modes, we exclude 12 modes from the training set on which we test our model and calculate the number of repeated keypoints. The Fig. 4-right shows that more than 50% of the initially matched points are repeatedly found despite varying the synthesis modes highlighting the texture-invariance properties of the descriptor.

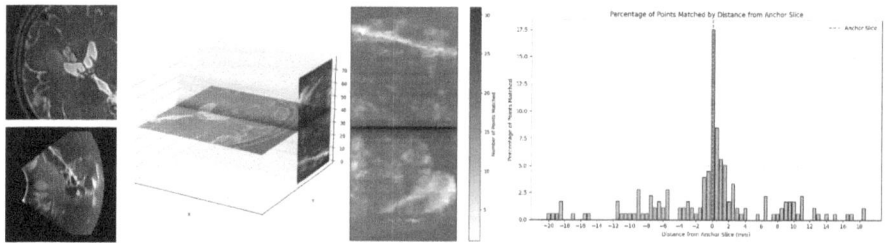

Fig. 5. MR slice #40 retrieved in US volume using descriptor matching.

Table 2. Validation on synthetic data and comparisons using real data.

Method	Case 1			Case 2			Case 3		
	Prec.	MSc.	MP	Prec.	MSc.	MP	Prec.	MSc.	MP
SIFT+Cosine	4.77	3.65	153.7	2.91	2.65	182.5	2.09	2.35	224.03
MIND+Cosine	5.15	5.15	200.0	4.44	4.44	200	4.66	4.66	200
SP+Cosine	4.58	3.45	150.8	2.76	1.58	144.83	3.82	2.80	147.58
SP+LG	55.31	10.92	25.28	13.06	1.38	13.60	17.99	2.29	16.34
Ours+LG	80.61	**20.86**	51.78	**76.92**	4.59	11.76	53.46	3.67	13.74
Ours+Cosine	**81.08**	20.32	50.14	73.42	**16.38**	44.64	**66.35**	**17.90**	53.96

We also perform a slice retrieval test to measure the discriminating properties of our method. We search for a target slice over the whole volume by matching $n = 200$ keypoints from the target MR slice with $m \times d$ keypoints of the whole US volume. Results reported in Fig. 5 show that our descriptor can successfully retrieve the target slice and discriminate it over other slices with an average 1.34 mm error within 20 slices and 2.48 mm error within 40 slices.

State-of-the-Art Comparison. To evaluate the performance of our model against existing image methods, we compared it to three approaches: SIFT [16], which remains the standard for keypoints matching, SuperPoint (SP) [3] built using a self-supervised learning approach and MIND [10], a modality-invariant descriptor for medical imaging, that although not designed for 1-to-1 keypoint matching, is extensively used for multimodal medical image registration through grid regularizing. We use SIFT and SP as keypoints detectors and descriptors, while we combine MIND with SP keypoints since it only provides a descriptor. We match these descriptors using both Cosine similarity and the deep neural network LightGlue (LG) [15] when possible (SP and Ours). Results reported in Table 2 and shown in Fig. 3 show that our approach outperforms these methods in terms of matching score, precision, and number of matched points. We only report results on three cases for readability reasons. Associating our descriptor with Cosine and LG reached similar performance depending on the metric.

4 Conclusion

We presented a novel multimodal image matching method between preoperative MR and intraoperative US images. Our matching-by-synthesis strategy, coupled with a patient-specific contrastive learning approach led to a texture-invariant descriptor, capable of matching 2D keypoints under different acquisition variations. Future work will extend the descriptor to 3D affine transformations and will integrate physics-based modelling [19,21] to account for elastic deformations and tissue resections, essential to achieve post-resection MR-US registration.

Acknowledgement. This work was supported by the National Institutes of Health grants R01EB032387, R01EB034223, R03EB033910, and K25EB035166.

References

1. Baruch, E.B., Keller, Y.: Joint detection and matching of feature points in multimodal images. IEEE Transactions on Pattern Analysis and Machine Intelligence **44**(10), 6585–6593 (2021)
2. Christy, D., Moses, C.J.: Retinal image registration feature descriptors-a survey. In: 2014 International Conference on Electronics and Communication Systems (ICECS). pp. 1–5. IEEE (2014)
3. DeTone, D., Malisiewicz, T., Rabinovich, A.: Superpoint: Self-supervised interest point detection and description. In: Proceedings of the IEEE conference on computer vision and pattern recognition workshops. pp. 224–236 (2018)
4. Dixon, L., Lim, A., Grech-Sollars, M., Nandi, D., Camp, S.: Intraoperative ultrasound in brain tumor surgery: a review and implementation guide. Neurosurgical Review **45**(4), 2503–2515 (2022)
5. Dorent, R., Haouchine, N., Kogl, F., Joutard, S., Juvekar, P., Torio, E., Golby, A.J., Ourselin, S., Frisken, S., Vercauteren, T., et al.: Unified brain mr-ultrasound synthesis using multi-modal hierarchical representations. In: International conference on medical image computing and computer-assisted intervention. pp. 448–458. Springer (2023)
6. Evan, M.Y., Wang, A.Q., Dalca, A.V., Sabuncu, M.R.: Keymorph: Robust multimodal affine registration via unsupervised keypoint detection. In: Medical Imaging with Deep Learning (2021)
7. Ferrante, E., Paragios, N.: Slice-to-volume medical image registration: A survey. Medical image analysis **39**, 101–123 (2017)
8. Gonzalez-Darder, J.M.: State of the Art of the Craniotomy in the Early Twenty-First Century and Future Development, pp. 421–427. Springer International Publishing, Cham (2019)
9. Haouchine, N., Juvekar, P., Nercessian, M., Wells III, W.M., Golby, A., Frisken, S.: Pose estimation and non-rigid registration for augmented reality during neurosurgery. IEEE Transactions on Biomedical Engineering **69**(4), 1310–1317 (2022)
10. Heinrich, M.P., Jenkinson, M., Bhushan, M., Matin, T., Gleeson, F.V., Brady, M., Schnabel, J.A.: Mind: Modality independent neighbourhood descriptor for multi-modal deformable registration. Medical image analysis **16**(7), 1423–1435 (2012)
11. Jiang, X., Ma, J., Xiao, G., Shao, Z., Guo, X.: A review of multimodal image matching: Methods and applications. Information Fusion **73**, 22–71 (2021)
12. Joutard, S., Dorent, R., Ourselin, S., Vercauteren, T., Modat, M.: Driving points prediction for abdominal probabilistic registration. In: International Workshop on Machine Learning in Medical Imaging. pp. 288–297. Springer (2022)
13. Juvekar, P., Dorent, R., Kögl, F., Torio, E., Barr, C., Rigolo, L., Galvin, C., Jowkar, N., Kazi, A., Haouchine, N., et al.: Remind: The brain resection multimodal imaging database. medRxiv (2023)
14. Kumar, A., Kim, J., Cai, W., Fulham, M., Feng, D.: Content-based medical image retrieval: a survey of applications to multidimensional and multimodality data. Journal of digital imaging **26**, 1025–1039 (2013)
15. Lindenberger, P., Sarlin, P.E. and Pollefeys, M.: Lightglue: Local feature matching at light speed. In: Proceedings of the IEEE/CVF International Conference on Computer Vision. pp. 17627–17638 (2023)

16. Lowe, D.G.: Distinctive image features from scale-invariant keypoints. International journal of computer vision **60**, 91–110 (2004)
17. Luo, J., Toews, M., Machado, I., Frisken, S., Zhang, M., Preiswerk, F., Sedghi, A., Ding, H., Pieper, S., Golland, P., Golby, A., Sugiyama, M., Wells III, W.M.: A feature-driven active framework for ultrasound-based brain shift compensation. In: MICCAI 2018. pp. 30–38 (2018)
18. Machado, I., Toews, M., Luo, J., Unadkat, P., Essayed, W., George, E., Teodoro, P., Carvalho, H., Martins, J., Golland, P., Pieper, S., Frisken, S., Golby, A., III, W.: Non-rigid registration of 3d ultrasound for neurosurgery using automatic feature detection and matching. International Journal of Computer Assisted Radiology and Surgery **13** (06 2018)
19. Paulus, C.J., Haouchine, N., Kong, S.H., Soares, R.V., Cazier, D., Cotin, S.: Handling topological changes during elastic registration: Application to augmented reality in laparoscopic surgery. International journal of computer assisted radiology and surgery **12**, 461–470 (2017)
20. Sanai, N., Polley, M.Y., McDermott, M.W., Parsa, A.T., Berger, M.S.: An extent of resection threshold for newly diagnosed glioblastomas: Clinical article. Journal of Neurosurgery JNS **115**(1), 3–8 (2011)
21. Talbot, H., Haouchine, N., Peterlik, I., Dequidt, J., Duriez, C., Delingette, H., Cotin, S.: Surgery Training, Planning and Guidance Using the SOFA Framework. In: Hege, H.C., Ropinski, T. (eds.) Eurographics 2015 - Dirk Bartz Prize. The Eurographics Association (2015). 10.2312/egm.20151028
22. Verdie, Y., Yi, K., Fua, P., Lepetit, V.: Tilde: A temporally invariant learned detector. In: Proceedings of the IEEE conference on computer vision and pattern recognition. pp. 5279–5288 (2015)
23. Wu, M., Goodman, N.: Multimodal Generative Models for Scalable Weakly-Supervised Learning. NeurIPS **31** (2018)

Automatic Facial Axes Standardization of 3D Fetal Ultrasound Images

Antonia Alomar[1(✉)], Ricardo Rubio[2,3], Laura Salort[1], Gerard Albaiges[4], Antoni Payà[2,3], Gemma Piella[1], and Federico Sukno[1]

[1] Department of Information and Communications Technologies, Universitat Pompeu Fabra, 122-140 Tànger, Barcelona, Spain
antoniaalomaradrover@gmail.com
[2] Department of Obstetrics and Gynecology, Hospital del Mar, 25-29 Passeig Marítim, Barcelona, Spain
[3] Department of Medicine and Life Sciences, Universitat Pompeu Fabra, 88 Doctor Aiguader, Barcelona, Spain
[4] Fetal Medicine Unit, Obstetrics Service, Department of Obstetrics, Gynecology and Reproductive Medicine, University Hospital Quirón Dexeus, Barcelona, Spain

Abstract. Craniofacial anomalies indicate early developmental disturbances and are usually linked to many genetic syndromes. Early diagnosis is critical, yet ultrasound (US) examinations often fail to identify these features. This study presents an AI-driven tool to assist clinicians in standardizing fetal facial axes/planes in 3D US, reducing sonographer workload and facilitating the facial evaluation. Our network, structured into three blocks-feature extractor, rotation and translation regression, and spatial transformer-processes three orthogonal 2D slices to estimate the necessary transformations for standardizing the facial planes in the 3D US. These transformations are applied to the original 3D US using a differentiable module (the spatial transformer block), yielding a standardized 3D US and the corresponding 2D facial standard planes. The dataset used consists of 1180 fetal facial 3D US images acquired between weeks 20 and 35 of gestation. Results show that our network considerably reduces inter-observer rotation variability in the test set, with a mean geodesic angle difference of $14.12° \pm 18.27°$ and an Euclidean angle error of $7.45° \pm 14.88°$. These findings demonstrate the network's ability to effectively standardize facial axes, crucial for consistent fetal facial assessments. In conclusion, the proposed network demonstrates potential for improving the consistency and accuracy of fetal facial assessments in clinical settings, facilitating early evaluation of craniofacial anomalies.

Keywords: 3D transformation · facial planes · fetal ultrasound

Supplementary Information The online version contains supplementary material available at https://doi.org/10.1007/978-3-031-73647-6_9.

1 Introduction

Craniofacial anomalies serve as indicators of developmental disturbances at early stages of life, encompassing a wide range of heterogeneous conditions associated with many genetic syndromes [1,13]. Estimates suggest that up to 40% of genetic syndromes produce alterations in the normal morphology of the face and the head. Although these associations have predominantly been identified in adult populations, there is increasing interest in early assessment [25]. Consequently, diagnostic efforts are moving towards prenatal and postnatal stages [4].

To evaluate the fetal development, 2D ultrasound (US) imaging is the standard procedure. Unfortunately, dysmorphology features are hard to identify in this way, due to the noisy nature of fetal US (low signal-to-noise ratio, fetal or probe movements, fetal position, and limbs in front of the face) [5]. Currently, 3D/4D US serves as a complement to 2D US. They prove to be particularly useful in diagnosing various fetal anomalies, especially those involving facial abnormalities, neural tube defects, and skeletal anomalies [8,18].

In this context, acquiring an US standard plane (SP) is crucial for performing an accurate fetal diagnosis, as the SP is used to measure and analyse biomarkers and abnormal features [20,22]. 3D US has the advantage of capturing multi-view planes allowing sonographers to manually select SPs from 3D US images or videos during prenatal exams. While this process is essential, it is also time-consuming and observer-dependent. This manual selection can be laborious and biased due to the extensive search space, the sonographer experience, and the variability of the fetus orientation [10,21].

In this study, we aim to reduce the sonographer's workload while enhancing the accuracy and interpretability of fetal facial SP detection. We propose an AI-driven tool designed to assist clinicians in standardizing the facial axes/planes in the 3D US. It aims to minimize variability across planes detection while mitigating the effects of clinician subjectivity in selecting accurate SPs for fetal facial assessment. Standardizing the fetal facial axes intends to facilitate the evaluation of facial biomarkers and biometric measurements to perform facial assessment. The proposed method consists in regressing the transformation necessary to standardize the sagittal, coronal and axial fetal facial axes, taking as input 3 orthogonal planes centered at the middle of the 3D US image. The novelty lies in that instead of combining the regression model with another task, such as the classification of the planes, we add a differentiable block that incorporates the image loss between estimated and ground truth (GT) planes as part of the minimization strategy. This helps the network learn the structures that should be present in the SPs. Additionally, the proposed algorithm offers the advantage of low computational cost and easy integration into in the echographer or in 3D Slicer as a built-in feature.

2 Related Work

Several methods have been proposed for automatically detecting 2D SPs in US images using deep learning. Usually, this task has been approached as an image classification problem, using convolutional neural networks (CNNs) or recurrent neural networks (RNNs) [2,3,14,26]. However, these methods only determine whether the acquired 2D slices are SPs, but do not inform on what correction shall be applied to them in case they are not SPs.

Another common strategy consists of regressing the plane parameters or transformation matrices to achieve the SP in the 3D US volume. For example, Feng et al. [9] proposed a constrained marginal space learning method that combines both 2D and 3D information for fetal face detection in 3D US. Nie et al. [19] introduced a deep belief network combined with a detection algorithm to provide a prior structural knowledge to the network. Li et al. [16] presented an iterative transformation network to detect SPs in 3D fetal US using a CNN that performs both plane classification and regression to estimate the transformation parameters. Di Vece et al. [6] improved the previous results obtained estimating the six-dimensional pose of arbitrary oriented US plane of the fetal brain with respect to a template normalized frame using a CNN regression network. Recently, reinforcement learning (RL) has shown great potential in addressing SP localization as a regression task [7,11,15,27]. Although RL approaches have achieved high performance, several issues remain to be addressed, such as the reliance of current studies on initial registration to ensure data orientation consistency, which can easily fail if the pre-registration process is unsuccessful. Moreover, unlike parameters regression models using a CNN, RL models simplify the problem of regressing the transformation parameters by considering a discrete action space and, in consequence, limiting the transformation that can be applied. To avoid dependence on pre-registration and ensure no limitations on the transformations that can be performed, we choose a classical yet effective parameters regression approach using a CNN. To help the network learn the structures that should be present in the SPs, we add a differentiable block that incorporates the image loss between estimated and GT planes as part of the minimization strategy. As a result, the number of parameters of the network is significantly reduced because no classification blocks are used.

3 Method

Data & Pre-processing: The dataset used consists of 1180 fetal facial 3D US images acquired between week 20 and 35 of gestation (26.56 ± 2.72) using a Voluson E8 RSA (BT-20) with a convex probe (4D-RAB6-D, 2–8 MHz) at two hospitals in Barcelona (Hospital de Mar and Hospital Universitari Dexeus) according to their Ethical Research Committee and the current legislation (Organic Law 15/1999). The study population comprises subjects from low-risk pregnancies, meaning without any pathology, or known family cases of craniofacial or syndromic pathologies, which were all carried to term. The data is divided into training, validation, and test sets, with 72%, 12%, and 16% of the data allocated to each set, respectively. To facilitate the use of deep learning, it is essential to standardize the input image size across the training, validation, and test sets. We implemented this through two steps: 1) down-sampling the 3D US image by a factor of two, to reduce the computational cost of the network; 2) symmetric zero-padding to the center of the 3D US to achieve a size of $U \in \mathbb{R}^{C \times H \times W \times D}$

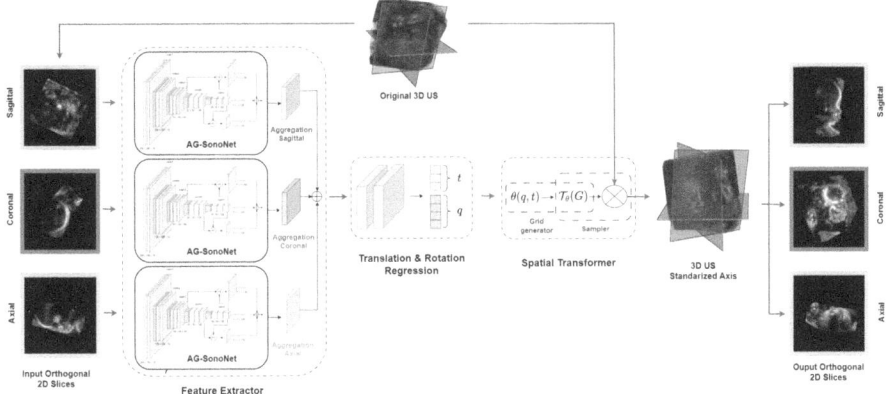

Fig. 1. Proposed architecture. The network is divided in three blocks: feature extractor, rotation and translation regression, and the spatial transformer block. The two first blocks extract the features and estimate the transformation necessary to obtain the standard facial axes/planes taking as input three orthogonal slices in arbitrary position. Then, the differentiable spatial transformer block applies the estimated transformation to the original 3D US to obtain the standardized 3D US and the 2D facial SPs.

where $H, W, D = 256$ are the height, width, and depth dimension and $C = 1$. The latter is performed to ensure that no information is cropped-out during rotation and translation. The 2D initial planes are defined by $I_0 = [I_s, I_c, I_a]$ with $I_s = U(1, \frac{H}{2}, :, :)$, $I_c = U(1, :, \frac{W}{2}, :)$ and $I_a = U(1, :, :, \frac{D}{2})$, corresponding to the sagittal, coronal, and axial planes, respectively.

Ground Truth Standard Planes: The facial GT SPs we are interested in locating are the axial, coronal and sagittal planes that define the canonical axes of the fetal face. They are obtained by minimizing the 3 orthogonal planes defined by 23 anatomical landmarks located by expert clinicians in the 3D US (see Appendix Fig.1) and following the recommendations from the international 3D focus group [17]. We constrain the planes' normal vectors $\vec{n_a}, \vec{n_c}$, and $\vec{n_s}$ to be orthonormal. The center of the planes $\vec{c} = (c_x, c_y, c_z)^T$ is defined as the intersection point of the 3 planes. The GT is obtained using custom code in 3D Slicer. The extracted normal vectors of the 3 orthogonal planes are used to compute the rotation matrix $R_{gt} \in \mathbb{R}^{3\times 3}$ needed to standardize the image axes to the estimated facial SPs. The GT rotation can be written as the change-of-basis matrix $S_{\mathbb{B}_1 \to \mathbb{B}_2}$ from $\mathbb{B}_1 \to \mathbb{B}_2$. In our case, $\mathbb{B}_1$ coordinates correspond to the canonical basis and $\mathbb{B}_2$ coordinates are the estimated normal vectors. Thus,

$$R_{gt} = S_{\mathbb{B}_1 \to \mathbb{B}_2} = \begin{pmatrix} \vec{n_s}^T \\ \vec{n_c}^T \\ \vec{n_a}^T \end{pmatrix} = \begin{bmatrix} r_{11} & r_{12} & r_{13} \\ r_{21} & r_{22} & r_{23} \\ r_{31} & r_{32} & r_{33} \end{bmatrix} \quad (1)$$

The rotation regression is performed in terms of quaternion representation for compactness, i.e., $\vec{q_{gt}} = (q_0, q_1, q_2, q_3)^T$. The conversion from rotation matrix to quaternion follows

$$\vec{q_{gt}} = \begin{pmatrix} q_0 \\ q_1 \\ q_2 \\ q_3 \end{pmatrix} = \begin{bmatrix} \frac{1}{2}\sqrt{1 + r_{11} - r_{22} - r_{33}} \\ \frac{r_{12}+r_{21}}{4q_0} \\ \frac{r_{13}+r_{31}}{4q_0} \\ \frac{r_{23}-r_{32}}{4q_0} \end{bmatrix} \quad (2)$$

The intersection/center of the planes is the GT translation $\vec{t_{gt}} = \vec{c} \in \mathbb{R}^3$. Then, the GT transformation matrix is

$$\theta_{gt} = \left(R_{gt}, \vec{t_{gt}}\right) = \begin{bmatrix} r_{11} & r_{12} & r_{13} & t_x \\ r_{21} & r_{22} & r_{23} & t_y \\ r_{31} & r_{32} & r_{33} & t_z \end{bmatrix} \in \mathbb{R}^{3 \times 4} \quad (3)$$

To ensure compatibility with the spatial transformer block, the translation is expressed in image relative size. Thus, each component of $\vec{t_{gt}}$ is in the range $[-1,1]$. The 2D GT sagittal, coronal and axial SPs are obtained as $I_{gt} = [I_s, I_c, I_a]$ where $I_s = V_{gt}(1, \frac{H}{2}, :, :)$, $I_c = V_{gt}(1, ; , \frac{W}{2}, :)$ and $I_a = V_{gt}(1, ;, ;, \frac{D}{2})$, and V_{gt} is the transformed US using θ_{gt}.

Feature Extractor Block: The inputs of the feature extractor block ($I_0 \in \mathbb{R}^{H \times W \times 3}$) are the 3 orthogonal planes located at the center of the 3D US image (sagittal, coronal and axial plane). Each branch uses the AG-SonoNet [23] as the backbone feature extractor, with the weights shared among the three branches. Then, each view has a specialized aggregation block that adds the attention information from multiple layers of the network to extract specialized features from each view. This information is concatenated and fed to the translation and rotation regression block.

Translation & Rotation Regression Block: It consists of two fully connected layers that convert the extracted features from the three orthogonal planes into the translation and rotation necessary to achieve the standardized axes/planes. The output is the regression vector $\vec{z} \in \mathbb{R}^7$. The first three positions correspond to the translation vector $\vec{t_{es}} \in \mathbb{R}^3$ where $\vec{t_{es}} = (t_x, t_y, t_z)^T$ with each component being in the range $[-h_{max}, h_{max}]$. The remaining 4 positions correspond to the quaternion representation of the rotation matrix $\vec{q_{es}} = (q_0, q_1, q_2, q_3)^T$ with each component being in the range $[-1, 1]$. To represent a valid rotation, $||\vec{q_{es}}||$ needs to be 1. To ensure that this condition is satisfied, a normalization layer was added after the last fully connected layer. Given $\vec{q_{es}}$, the estimated rotation can be expressed as:

$$R_{es} = \begin{bmatrix} 1 - 2(q_2^2 + q_3^2) & 2(q_1q_2 - q_0q_3) & 2(q_1q_3 + q_0q_2) \\ 2(q_1q_2 + q_0q_3) & 1 - 2(q_1^2 + q_3^2) & 2(q_2q_3 - q_0q_1) \\ 2(q_1q_3 - q_0q_2) & 2(q_2q_3 + q_0q_1) & 1 - 2(q_1^2 + q_2^2) \end{bmatrix} = \begin{bmatrix} r_{11} & r_{12} & r_{13} \\ r_{21} & r_{22} & r_{23} \\ r_{31} & r_{32} & r_{33} \end{bmatrix} \quad (4)$$

Spatial Transformer Block: It is a differentiable module capable of applying spatial transformations to the original 3D US image $U \in R^{H \times W \times D \times C}$, resulting in a new standardized 3D US image $V \in R^{H \times W \times D \times C}$ and facial 2D SPs. The spatial transformer uses a differentiable 3D bi-linear sampling as defined in [12]. Each output value for pixel i can be written as

$$V_i = \sum_n^H \sum_m^W \sum_l^D U_{n,m,l}^c \max(0, 1 - |x_i^s - m|) \max(0, 1 - |y_i^s - n|) \max(0, 1 - |z_i^s - l|) \quad (5)$$

where $(x_i^{inp}, y_i^{inp}, z_i^{inp})$ are the input coordinates that define the sampling points in the original 3D US U and U_{nml} is the value of U at location (n, m, l). The output coordinates $(x_i^{out}, y_i^{out}, z_i^{out})$ are defined to lie on a regular grid $G = G_i$ of pixels $G_i = (x_i^{out}, y_i^{out}, z_i^{out})$ and can be obtained by a 3D affine transformation:

$$\begin{pmatrix} x_i^{inp} \\ y_i^{inp} \\ z_i^{inp} \end{pmatrix} = \mathcal{T}_\theta(G) = \theta(\vec{q}, \vec{t}) \begin{pmatrix} x_i^{out} \\ y_i^{out} \\ z_i^{out} \\ 1 \end{pmatrix} = \begin{bmatrix} r_{11} & r_{12} & r_{13} & t_x \\ r_{21} & r_{22} & r_{23} & t_y \\ r_{31} & r_{32} & r_{33} & t_z \end{bmatrix} \begin{pmatrix} x_i^{out} \\ y_i^{out} \\ z_i^{out} \\ 1 \end{pmatrix} \quad (6)$$

$\theta(\vec{q}, \vec{t})$ is the 3D transformation matrix estimated. We use height, weight and depth normalized coordinates, such that $x_i, y_i, z_i \in [-1, 1]$. The 2D estimated SPs are obtained as $I_{es} = [I_s, I_c, I_a]$ where $I_s = V(1, \frac{H}{2}, :, :)$, $I_c = V(1, :, \frac{W}{2}, :)$ and $I_a = V(1, :, :, \frac{D}{2})$.

Cumulative Transformations & Initialization: At initialization time ($it = 0$), R_0 is a random rotation defined by the Euclidean angles $\alpha_x, \alpha_y, \alpha_z \in [-20, 20]$ degrees and $\vec{t_0} = (t_x, t_y, t_z)^T$ is random translation with each component being in the range $[-0.05, 0.05]$. To preserve image quality, we accumulate the transformations and perform a unique transformation to the input 3D image. If multiple steps of the network are applied, we define the transformations at step it as $R_{es}^{it} = R_{es}^{it-1} R_{es}$ and $\vec{t_{es}^{it}} = \vec{t_{es}^{it-1}} + \vec{t_{es}}$, whereas $R_{gt}^{it} = R_{es}^{-1} R_{gt}^{it-1}$ and $\vec{t_{gt}^{it}} = -(R_{es}^{it-1})^{-1} \vec{t_{es}} + (R_{es}^{it-1})^{-1} \vec{t_{gt}}$. Here, R_{es}, t_{es} correspond to the rotation and translation estimated by the CNN at the current iteration, whereas R_{es}^{it}, t_{es}^{it} denote the accumulated rotation and translation at iteration it. We found that 3 iterations are enough to improve performance by refining the SP estimates. However, there was no need to train the network in an iterative way.

Network Loss: It is defined as a combination of the mean absolute error (MAE) between the GT and estimated translation, the relative angle (SO3) between the GT and estimated rotation and the image loss between computed as the Frobenius norm of the difference between the GT and estimated SPs:

$$\mathcal{L} = \beta ||\vec{t_{es}} - \vec{t_{gt}}||_1 + \gamma \ acos(0.5 * (Tr(R_{es}(R_{gt})^T) - 1)) + ||I_{gt} - I_{es}||_1 \quad (7)$$

where Tr correspond to the trace, β and γ are the translation and rotation weights in the loss, I_{gt} and I_{es} are the 2D GT and estimated slices corresponding to the fetal facial sagittal, coronal and axial SPs.

4 Experiments

The proposed method is compared to the inter-observer variability obtained from 3 different observers placing landmarks on the 3D US images as described in González-Aranceta et al. [10], which are then used for estimating the planes as described in Sect. 3. Next, we compare to the state of the art method proposed by Li et al. [16]. For a fair comparison, the network used is their M1 baseline model with the addition of the differential spatial transformer model to be able to train with the image loss. The only task learned is the regression of $\vec{t}, \vec{q}$ using as input 3 orthogonal planes. The predicted SPs/axes are evaluated in the test set against the GT using the distance between the GT and the estimated translation, and the rotation angles between the GT and the estimated rotation. The image similarity of the planes is also measured using the peak to noise-ratio (PSNR) and structural similarity index (SSIM).

Table 1 summarizes the results obtained. The proposed method outperforms the state of the art method from Li et al. [16] and even challenges inter-observer variability, producing smaller angular errors although larger translation errors.

Table 1. Quantitative test set comparison of the 3D standard facial axes standardization. Metrics evaluated are the geodesic angle difference (SO3), mean Euclidean angle error (EA), mean absolute translation (Trans) error, SSIM, and PSNR for estimated 2D standard planes (SP). The arrows indicate if higher/lower values are better.

Method	SO3 (°) ↓	EA(°) ↓	Trans(mm) ↓	SSIM(%) ↑	PSNR(dB) ↑
Inter-observer	21.91 ± 34.38	10.35 ± 19.33	3.31 ± 2.46	0.73 ± 0.10	23.46 ± 7.90
Li et al. [16]	30.33 ± 36.34	17.32 ± 30.27	13.30 ± 12.99	**0.62 ± 0.08**	**17.90 ± 2.87**
Ours	**14.12 ± 18.27**	**7.45 ± 14.88**	**12.89 ± 6.07**	0.61 ± 0.07	16.98 ± 1.62

Table 2. Quantitative test set comparison per plane/axes. The rotation and translation are separated in plane/axes components.

Metric	Model	Sagittal	Axial	Coronal
Translation (mm)	Inter-observer	1.60 ± 1.74	1.94 ± 1.84	1.51 ± 1.40
	Li et al. [16]	**6.42 ± 8.89**	5.97 ± 8.41	7.14 ± 8.25
	Ours	7.26 ± 6.57	**5.78 ± 4.20**	**5.76 ± 4.78**
Rotation (°)	Inter-observer	11.35 ± 21.66	7.08 ± 9.60	12.63 ± 26.73
	Li et al. [16]	19.29 ± 33.21	10.88 ± 11.42	21.81 ± 34.12
	Ours	**8.70 ± 19.69**	**6.14 ± 6.73**	**7.49 ± 18.88**

5 Results and Discussion

Table 2 shows the translation and rotation Euclidean angles error obtained per SP/axes. It highlights that the coronal and sagittal planes are more challenging to locate in terms of rotation than the axial plane. Our approach reduces the inter-observer rotation error of the sagittal, axial and coronal planes. The translation error obtained is around 6mm per plane/axes, higher than the inter-observer error. Figure 2 shows some qualitative examples and comparisons between the GT 2D planes and the estimated by the proposed method. Despite a translation error per plane of approximately 6 mm in patient 2 and 3, the estimated plane closely approximates the GT plane.

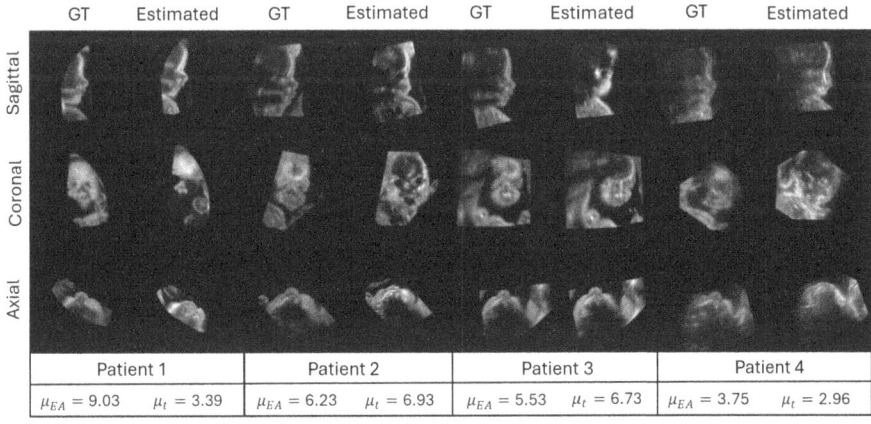

Fig. 2. Qualitative test set examples. Four examples of the estimated 2D planes using the proposed method, the mean Euclidean angle (μ_{EA}) in degrees and the mean translation (μ_t) error in mm obtained per plane compared to the GT.

Thus, the proposed network correctly learns the plane angles but its translation error is higher than the inter-observer error. This could be due to the high variability defining the planes localization, as multiple slices could closely resemble each other [24]. However, it could also be that the most informative planes for the network are not the ones defined as GT planes and it sacrifices translation accuracy for rotation accuracy. Although the translation errors obtained with the proposed network are larger than the inter-observer, the mean translation error per plane is around 6 mm. Moreover, rotation can be regarded more important than translation, as the aim is to standardize the facial axes. This allows the sonographer to examine the standardized fetal 3D facial US, where the fetal pose/US probe rotations are removed, facilitating the evaluation of the fetal face. Furthermore, the proposed network is able to reduce the rotation inter-observer variability. This can be highly beneficial to homogenize the facial analysis evaluation criteria and to reduce the reliance on clinician expertise while reducing the time burden of manually locating the planes.

6 Conclusions

We propose a network that estimates the transformation necessary to obtain the standard sagittal, coronal and axial facial US axes taking as input three 2D orthogonal planes. Evaluation on 184 US volumes shows that the network correctly standardizes the US 3D axes while reducing the rotation variability across observers. The method has the potential to be applied easily in a clinical setting due to its low computational cost. The standardization of the facial 3D US aims to facilitate the analysis of the facial biometric measurements to assess the presence of craniofacial abnormalities.

Acknowledgments. This work was partly supported by grants PID2020-114083GB-I00 and PRE2021-097544 funded by MICIU/AEI/10.13039/501100011033/ and under the ICREA Academia programme.

Disclosure of Interests. None of the authors have any competing interests.

References

1. Bartzela, T.N., Carels, C., Maltha, J.C.: Update on 13 syndromes affecting craniofacial and dental structures. Frontiers in Physiology **8** (12 2017). https://doi.org/10.3389/fphys.2017.01038
2. Baumgartner, C.F., et al.: SonoNet: Real-Time Detection and Localisation of Fetal Standard Scan Planes in Freehand Ultrasound. IEEE Transactions on Medical Imaging **36**, 2204–2215 (11 2017). https://doi.org/10.1109/TMI.2017.2712367
3. Chen, H., et al.: Ultrasound standard plane detection using a composite neural network framework. IEEE Transactions on Cybernetics **47**(6), 1576–1586 (2017). https://doi.org/10.1109/TCYB.2017.2685080
4. Chen, J., Kanekar, S.: Imaging of congenital craniofacial anomalies and syndromes. Clinics in Perinatology **49**, 771–790 (9 2022). https://doi.org/10.1016/j.clp.2022.04.005
5. Conner, S.N., Longman, R.E., Cahill, A.G.: The role of ultrasound in the diagnosis of fetal genetic syndromes. Best Practice & Research Clinical Obstetrics & Gynaecology **28**, 417–428 (4 2014). https://doi.org/10.1016/j.bpobgyn.2014.01.005
6. Di Vece, C., Lous, M.L., Dromey, B., Vasconcelos, F., David, A.L., Peebles, D., Stoyanov, D.: Ultrasound plane pose regression: Assessing generalized pose coordinates in the fetal brain. IEEE Transactions on Medical Robotics and Bionics **6**(1), 41–52 (2024). https://doi.org/10.1109/TMRB.2023.3328638
7. Dou, H., et al.: Agent with Warm Start and Active Termination for Plane Localization in 3D Ultrasound, pp. 290–298 (2019). https://doi.org/10.1007/978-3-030-32254-0_33
8. Dyson, R.L., et al.: Three-dimensional ultrasound in the evaluation of fetal anomalies. Ultrasound in Obstetrics & Gynecology **16**, 321–328 (9 2000). https://doi.org/10.1046/j.1469-0705.2000.00183.x
9. Feng, S., Zhou, S.K., Good, S., Comaniciu, D.: Automatic fetal face detection from ultrasound volumes via learning 3D and 2d information. pp. 2488–2495. IEEE (6 2009). https://doi.org/10.1109/CVPR.2009.5206527

10. González-Aranceta, N., Alomar, A., Rubio, R., Maya-Enero, S., Payá, A., Piella, G., Sukno, F.: Accuracy and repeatability of fetal facial measurements in 3D ultrasound: A longitudinal study. Early Human Development **193**, 106021 (6 2024). https://doi.org/10.1016/j.earlhumdev.2024.106021
11. Huang, Y., et al.: Searching Collaborative Agents for Multi-plane Localization in 3D Ultrasound, pp. 553–562 (2020). https://doi.org/10.1007/978-3-030-59716-0_53
12. Jaderberg, M., Simonyan, K., Zisserman, A., Kavukcuoglu, K.: Spatial transformer networks. In: Proceedings of the 28th International Conference on Neural Information Processing Systems - Volume 2. p. 2017-2025. NIPS'15, MIT Press, Cambridge, MA, USA (2015)
13. Junaid, M., Slack-Smith, L., Wong, K., Bourke, J., Baynam, G., Calache, H., Leonard, H.: Association between craniofacial anomalies, intellectual disability and autism spectrum disorder: Western australian population-based study. Pediatric Research **92**, 1795–1804 (12 2022). https://doi.org/10.1038/s41390-022-02024-9
14. Lei, B., Tan, E.L., Chen, S., Zhuo, L., Li, S., Ni, D., Wang, T.: Automatic recognition of fetal facial standard plane in ultrasound image via fisher vector. PLOS ONE **10**, e0121838 (5 2015). https://doi.org/10.1371/journal.pone.0121838
15. Li, K., Wang, J., Xu, Y., Qin, H., Liu, D., Liu, L., Meng, M.Q.H.: Autonomous navigation of an ultrasound probe towards standard scan planes with deep reinforcement learning. pp. 8302–8308. IEEE (5 2021). https://doi.org/10.1109/ICRA48506.2021.9561295
16. Li, Y., et al.: Standard Plane Detection in 3D Fetal Ultrasound Using an Iterative Transformation Network, pp. 392–400 (2018). https://doi.org/10.1007/978-3-030-00928-1_45
17. Merz, E., et al.: 3D imaging of the fetal face - recommendations from the international 3D focus group. Ultraschall in der Medizin - European Journal of Ultrasound **33**, 175–182 (4 2012). https://doi.org/10.1055/s-0031-1299378
18. Merz, E., Pashaj, S.: Advantages of 3D ultrasound in the assessment of fetal abnormalities. Journal of Perinatal Medicine **45** (1 2017). https://doi.org/10.1515/jpm-2016-0379
19. Nie, S., Yu, J., Chen, P., Wang, Y., Zhang, J.Q.: Automatic Detection of Standard Sagittal Plane in the First Trimester of Pregnancy Using 3-D Ultrasound Data. Ultrasound in Medicine & Biology **43**, 286–300 (1 2017). https://doi.org/10.1016/j.ultrasmedbio.2016.08.034
20. Salomon, L., et al.: Isuog practice guidelines: ultrasound assessment of fetal biometry and growth. Ultrasound in Obstetrics & Gynecology **53**, 715–723 (6 2019). https://doi.org/10.1002/uog.20272
21. Sarris, I., et al.: Intra- and interobserver variability in fetal ultrasound measurements. Ultrasound in Obstetrics & Gynecology **39**, 266–273 (3 2012). https://doi.org/10.1002/uog.10082
22. Sarris, I., et al.: Standardization of fetal ultrasound biometry measurements: improving the quality and consistency of measurements. Ultrasound in Obstetrics & Gynecology **38**, 681–687 (12 2011). https://doi.org/10.1002/uog.8997
23. Schlemper, J., Oktay, O., Schaap, M., Heinrich, M., Kainz, B., Glocker, B., Rueckert, D.: Attention gated networks: Learning to leverage salient regions in medical images. Medical Image Analysis **53**, 197–207 (2019). https://doi.org/10.1016/j.media.2019.01.012, https://www.sciencedirect.com/science/article/pii/S1361841518306133

24. Skelton, E., et al.: Towards automated extraction of 2d standard fetal head planes from 3D ultrasound acquisitions: A clinical evaluation and quality assessment comparison. Radiography **27**, 519–526 (5 2021). https://doi.org/10.1016/j.radi.2020.11.006
25. Tavares, A.L.P., Moody, S.A.: Advances in understanding the pathogenesis of craniofacial birth defects. Journal of Developmental Biology **10**, 27 (7 2022). https://doi.org/10.3390/jdb10030027
26. Zhen, C., et al.: Locating multiple standard planes in first-trimester ultrasound videos via the detection and scoring of key anatomical structures. Ultrasound in Medicine & Biology **49**, 2006–2016 (9 2023). https://doi.org/10.1016/j.ultrasmedbio.2023.05.005
27. Zou, Y., et al.: Agent with Tangent-Based Formulation and Anatomical Perception for Standard Plane Localization in 3D Ultrasound, pp. 300–309 (2022). https://doi.org/10.1007/978-3-031-16440-8_29

Segmentation

C-TRUS: A Novel Dataset and Initial Benchmark for Colon Wall Segmentation in Transabdominal Ultrasound

Ramona Leenings[1,2(✉)], Maximilian Konowski[2], Nils R. Winter[2], Jan Ernsting[2,4], Lukas Fisch[2], Carlotta Barkhau[2], Udo Dannlowski[2], Andreas Lügering[3], Xiaoyi Jiang[1], and Tim Hahn[2]

[1] Faculty of Mathematics and Computer Science, University of Münster, Münster, Germany
leenings@uni-muenster.de
[2] University of Münster, Institute of Translational Psychiatry, Münster, Germany
[3] Medizinisches Versorgungszentrum Portal 10, 48155 Münster, Germany
[4] Institute for Geoinformatics, University of Münster, Münster, Germany

Abstract. Examining the colon wall in transabdominal ultrasound images emerges as a promising, non-invasive approach for diagnosing and managing ulcerating colitis, a widespread inflammatory bowel disease affecting millions of people worldwide. However, due to its intricacies, this examination has thus far been confined to experts with specialized training. To the best of our knowledge, we are the first to evaluate automated colon wall segmentation using several advanced deep learning segmentation architectures in combination with established and specialized loss functions. To this end, we publish a new open-source dataset, named C-TRUS, including expert annotations for 827 transabdominal ultrasound images as well as image quality categorizations. Furthermore, we establish inter-observer variability, and find that colon wall segmentation is challenging even for medical experts, reaching a moderate average consensus Dice score of 0.6134. The best performing model is the Mask R-CNN architecture, achieving an average Dice score of 0.7249 across all image quality categories and a Dice score of 0.8218 on high quality images. We provide the C-TRUS dataset at https://github.com/wwu-mmll/c-trus.

Keywords: Transabdominal Ultrasound · Colon Wall · Segmentation

1 Introduction

Ulcerative colitis is a chronic inflammatory bowel disease affecting millions of people worldwide [13]. The disease activity is intermittent, with idiopathic periods of symptom exacerbation, followed by periodic intervals of symptom

---

X. Jiang and T. Hahn—These authors contributed equally.

improvement or remission [13]. Therefore, therapy and medication are fluid and must always be tailored to the current disease activity. Disease activity is currently assessed via endoscopic procedures such as colonoscopy or sigmoidoscopy. These modalities expose the patient to discomfort, anesthetic risks, potential complications and are restricted in accessibility. Recently, ultrasound of the colon wall has emerged as a reliable, non-invasive, and accessible alternative [2,10]. To this end, a computer-aided colon wall segmentation tool has the potential to facilitate clinical care routines. In this work, we are, to the best of our knowledge, the first to automate colon wall segmentation in ultrasound images of ulcerative colitis patients.

1.1 Related Work

In an earlier work, Pahl et al. trained a Gabor filter to pre-process ultrasound images to facilitate measurements of colon wall thickness [21]. We did not find any other prior studies that locate, segment or outline the colon wall in transabdominal ultrasound. Nevertheless, there are other anatomical structures within the abdomen for which ultrasound segmentation algorithms have been developed, including the kidneys and their substructures [4,5,12,22], the liver [7,27] and the bladder-sac [1].

In general, ultrasound artifacts, including motion blurring, weak boundaries, acoustic shadows, speckle noise, and a low signal-to-noise ratio, commonly exacerbate ultrasound segmentation tasks [8]. Therefore, a significant number of available segmentation models leverage geometrical constraints and/or shape information to guide and improve the segmentation result in ultrasound images [1,6,12,22,24,25]. In this work, we therefore implement and evaluate a shape-aware compound loss, penalizing predicted segmentation contours that deviate from the expected ground-truth colon wall shape.

1.2 Clinical Relevance

Due to the complexity, transabdominal ultrasound of the colon wall requires specialized medical training and expertise, which thus far is hindering wide-spread clinical application. An automated segmentation algorithm holds promise by reducing dependency on the operator's efficacy and experience, thereby contributing to better availability in clinical care routines and consistent outcomes in scientific investigations. However, due to the depth of the anatomical location, the small structure size and its similarity to surrounding tissue, segmenting the colon wall is challenging (see Fig. 1). Depending on the angle of the transducer the colon wall appears in several shapes. It presents as one or two (parallel) lines, arcs as well as several shape variations. In addition, an ultrasound image may depict more than one part of the colon wall, which makes it a multi-part segmentation problem and adds additional complexity.

1.3 Contributions

We contribute an open-source dataset of expert-annotated images for ultrasound colon wall segmentation. Further, we ground performance expectations for this segmentation task by quantifying label consistency among different experienced gastroenterologists. Finally, we conduct a benchmark using advanced segmentation architectures in combination with several prevalent loss functions, a Dice loss derivative specialized on medical segmentation tasks and a custom Shape-Aware Dice loss.

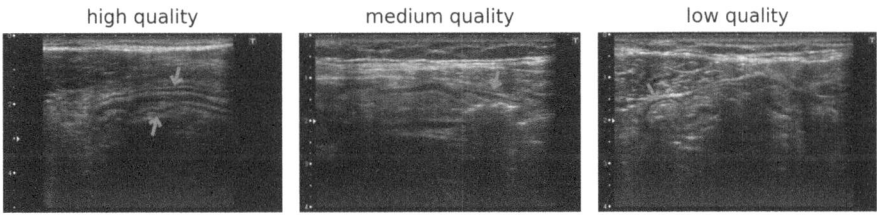

Fig. 1. Example ultrasound images depicting the colon wall with high, medium and low quality. Arrows point to instances of the colon wall.

2 Dataset

To advance research on colon wall segmentation, we provide a novel dataset of transabdominal ultrasound images from patients with ulcerating colitis. We name the dataset C-TRUS for **C**olon Wall Segmentation in **Tr**ansabdominal **U**ltrasound (https://github.com/wwu-mmll/c-trus).

2.1 Dataset Curation

The dataset was derived from clinical transabdominal ultrasound sequences, recorded with a Toshiba Xario General LCD from 13 patients with ulcerating colitis (mean age of 40.25 ± 15.37 years, 7 females). All identifying information was removed from the images. Image were extracted from the sequence every 5 s to avoid overly similar image content, resulting in 827 images of size 580×360 pixels, an average of 64 ± 28 images per patient.

Seven gastroenterological specialists were invited to manually annotate the colon wall in the images. To alleviate the workload and foster multi-perspective insight into the data structures, the 827 ultrasound images were divided among the medical experts. Each image received a ground truth label from one of the medical experts, mirroring the procedure utilized in clinical practice. The medical experts found the colon wall depicted in 507 of the 827 images (355 lines, 129 arcs and 23 variations). Additionally, as ultrasound images have varying quality due to factors such as machine settings, patient anatomy, and operator technique, the most experienced annotator subjectively rated each image with regard to image quality on a 3-step scale (low, medium, high) (see Fig. 1). This enables us to investigate the impact of image quality on manual or automated segmentation quality.

Table 1. Inter-observer variability evaluated on the annotations from experienced gastroenterological specialists.

Image Quality	Dice	Dice$_{\geq 0.50}$	Dice$_{\geq 0.75}$	Agreement	Disagreement
all	0.6134 ± 0.19	81.41%	23.72%	57.78%	21.85%
high	0.6035 ± 0.20	78.00%	20.00%	87.72%	11.40%
medium	0.6434 ± 0.18	88.64%	31.82%	77.19%	21.05%
low	0.5865 ± 0.23	83.33%	25.00%	12.12%	34.34%

2.2 Inter-observer Variability

We calculate inter-observer variability to quantify label consistency among different observers' interpretations. To this end, the most experienced expert categorized the image quality of 650 images extracted from ultrasound sequences of 8 additional patients (mean age 34.25 ± 15.36 years, 6 females). Subsequently, 20 images were selected for each quality category, maximizing diversity in image content and transabdominal view angles.

Each of the four most experienced medical experts independently labeled all 60 images. We treat each of the medical expert's annotations as a potential ground truth, i.e. we get six label comparisons for each of the 60 images, resulting in 360 comparisons for which we average the outcomes. We quantify the percentage of cases in which the annotators agree with a Dice score equal or above 0.5 or 0.75 (please refer to Sect. 3.3 for details on the metrics). Furthermore, we examine instances where both annotators detected the colon wall (Agreement), and cases where two annotators disagree about the presence of the colon wall (Disagreement). The resulting performance metrics are presented in Table 1.

On average, the expert's annotations show moderate spatial overlap (Dice score of 0.6134). The annotation masks overlap with a Dice score $_{\geq 0.50}$ in 4 of 5 cases, but with a Dice score $_{\geq 0.75}$ in only one of four cases. Notably, there are only minor changes to the Dice score across high-, medium- and low-quality images. While the medical experts agree on the presence of the colon wall on high-quality images in 87.72% of cases, they disagree on the presence or rather absence of the colon wall on every third image (34.34%) with low image quality. These findings underscore the dependency on image quality and the considerable difficulty of the segmentation task, imposed by the ambiguous structural context and the varying levels of confounding noise.

3 Methods and Experiments

We test established segmentation architectures and different loss functions to generate an initial benchmark for this intricate segmentation task.

3.1 Segmentation Architectures

Due to its efficacy in medical image segmentation tasks with small sample sizes, we evaluate the U-Net architecture [23] with the hyperparameters proposed by the nnU-Net [17]. We omit test time augmentation and apply minor deviations to adjust for ultrasound specifics (i.e. we change the training augmentations and avoid instance normalization), in the following indicated as U-Net^{nn}. Moreover, TMU-Net was included to assess the effectiveness of a more contemporary take on the U-Net's encoder-decoder architecture via hybrid transformer and CNN components, potentially enhancing segmentation quality through enriched feature representations [9]. Second, we test DeepLabv3+ and its Atrous Spatial Pyramid Pooling (ASPP) capable of capturing multi-scale context with a ResNet50 backbone, which has demonstrated superior performance in benchmarks of other abdominal ultrasound segmentation task [5,11]. Further, we include the transformer-based SegNext architecture [14], leveraging its parameter-efficient and effective convolution attention mechanism. In the same vein, the HiFormer architecture was incorporated into our benchmark, using a fusion of convolutional and hierarchical (Swin) transformer modules, adeptly merging multi-scale global and local features [16]. Finally, we rely on the Mask R-CNN architecture [15], specifically designed for instance segmentation tasks. We use a ResNet50 backbone to feed its Region Proposal Network (RPN) suggesting potential regions of interest (RoI). Utilizing a technique known as RoI Align, the ROIs are processed to yield fixed size feature maps, which are subsequently used to learn class labels, bounding box predictions and pixel-wise segmentation masks. Each model was selected to explore different approaches of local and global feature learning and their impacts on the task of ultrasound colon wall segmentation.

3.2 Loss Functions

Due to the large variations in image characteristics as well as the different segmentation contour shapes involved in colon wall segmentation, we evaluate different loss functions with regard to their effectiveness of capturing the nuances of this segmentation task. We evaluate the distribution-based Binary Cross Entropy (BCE) Loss, the region-based Dice loss as well as the Dice and BCE compound loss [18]. Further, we evaluate the Dice ++ loss, proposed by Yeung et al. [26] designed to prevent overconfident predictions in biomedical and clinical segmentation tasks, as a shape-agnostic measure of handling regions of uncertainty. The Dice loss is calibrated with a focal parameter that introduces exponential weight to over- and under-segmented regions.

As shape-awareness has led to superior performance in prior ultrasound segmentation tasks, we extend existing Fourier Descriptor loss functions [3,19] to handle multi-part segmentation masks and combine it with the Dice loss to form a compound loss evaluating both contour accuracy and spatial overlap. The colon wall shape is represented using the Elliptic Fourier Series coefficients of its boundary. These coefficients are able to represent different two dimensional contours in a low-dimensional, translation-, rotation- and scale-invariant manifold [20], and are thus able to accommodate the various geometrical forms, views and angles in which the colon wall may occur. As multiple parts of the colon wall may occur at different distinct locations in an ultrasound image, we assign each ground truth contour the prediction contour closest to its center of mass, as measured by the Euclidean distance. We then calculate the Euclidean distance between the normalized magnitudes $\hat{f}$ of the Elliptic Fourier Series coefficients a_n, b_n, c_n, d_n for a series of $N=10$ ellipses [20] for each ground truth contour and it's assigned predicted contour.

$$\mathcal{L}_{shape} = \mathcal{L}_{dice} + \frac{1}{G} \sum_{i=1}^{G} ||\hat{f}_{true,i} - \hat{f}_{p_{closest}}|| \tag{1}$$

where G is the number of ground truth contours.

3.3 Performance Evaluation

Within a five-fold cross-validation, we stratify the splits so that each of the training and test sets is balanced with regard to its ultrasound image quality distribution. In addition, different images from one patient may be similar or show salient anatomical peculiarities. Therefore, to avoid data leakage, images from one patient are restricted to exclusively be in either training or test set. We evaluate the performance of each of the architecture and loss combination on the test set predictions of all folds.

Particularly, we calculate the Dice score, Recall and Precision, and given the complexity of the task, the percentage of cases in which the predicted segmentation mask overlaps at least 0.50 or 0.75 with the ground truth segmentation mask ($Dice_{\geq 0.50}$ and $Dice_{\geq 0.75}$).

- $\text{Dice}_{\geq 0.50} = \frac{1}{N} \sum_{i=1}^{N} \mathbb{1}(Dice_i \geq 0.50)$
- $\text{Dice}_{\geq 0.75} = \frac{1}{N} \sum_{i=1}^{N} \mathbb{1}(Dice_i \geq 0.75)$

Here, $\mathbb{1}$ is an indicator function, returning 1 if the criterion defined in brackets holds, i.e. the Dice score of a particular segmentation mask is equal or above 0.50 or 0.75, respectively, and 0 otherwise.

All model architectures are implemented in PyTorch and trained for a maximum of 100 epochs for each cross validation fold, batch size of 8, using an Adam optimizer with exponentially decaying (gamma=0.95) individual learning rates (UNet^{nn}: 1e-04; DeepLabV3+: 1e-02; TMU-Net: 1e-04; SegNext: 4e-05, HiFormer: 1e-02, Mask R-CNN: 1e-04). Computational hardware included an AMD Ryzen 9 5950X @ 3.400GHz, 128 GB RAM and a NVIDIA GeForce RTX3090.

4 Results

Table 2 lists the cross-validation results. We chose the best loss function for each segmentation architecture by the maximum Dice score achieved across all quality categories. Among the tested architectures, DeepLabV3+, Mask R-CNN, and HiFormer demonstrated superior performance using the Dice and BCE compound loss, whereas U-Net[nn], TMU-Net, and SegNext optimized performance with Dice Shape Loss, Dice++ loss, and Dice loss, respectively. No architecture, with the exception of the U-Net, derives advantage from incorporating shape awareness in the loss function. This discrepancy may be attributed to the more sophisticated contextual encoding techniques implemented in the other architectures.

Table 2. Performance results of the best models for each segmentation architecture for high, medium, and low quality images, respectively. Best performing loss functions where DiceBCE for Mask R-CNN, DeepLabv3+ and HiFormer, Dice++ for TMU-Net, Dice for SegNext and Dice Shape for U-Net[nn].

Model	OVERALL					PER PATIENT		
	Dice	Recall	Precision	Dice$_{\geq 0.50}$	Dice$_{\geq 0.75}$	Dice	Dice$_{\geq 0.50}$	Dice$_{\geq 0.75}$
	All Images							
Mask R-CNN	**0.7249**	**0.7166**	**0.7835**	**86.39%**	**57.99%**	**0.6847**	**82.13%**	**52.58%**
U-Net[nn]	0.5195	0.6247	0.5119	59.17%	25.25%	0.4797	52.16%	20.93%
DeepLabV3+	0.5012	0.5884	0.5110	59.96%	16.77%	0.4615	54.13%	13.21%
HiFormer	0.4596	0.5810	0.4518	50.10%	6.88%	0.4386	45.06%	5.56%
TMU-Net	0.4201	0.4294	0.5341	44.40%	8.84%	0.3774	37.81%	6.51%
SegNext	0.4046	0.3725	0.5581	38.46%	0.59%	0.3883	37.54%	0.55%
	High Quality Images							
Mask R-CNN	**0.8218**	**0.8016**	**0.8647**	**94.67%**	**77.51%**	**0.7722**	**90.32%**	**67.51%**
U-Net[nn]	0.6603	0.7318	0.6467	82.25%	46.15%	0.5592	68.58%	35.57%
DeepLabV3+	0.6236	0.6914	0.6134	79.29%	31.36%	0.5284	67.85%	23.77%
HiFormer	0.5632	0.7106	0.5191	71.60%	13.02%	0.5075	57.03%	9.63%
TMU-Net	0.5458	0.5639	0.6284	62.13%	18.93%	0.5055	55.14%	12.54%
SegNext	0.4841	0.4466	0.6223	53.85%	0.00%	0.4557	52.72%	0.00%
	Medium Quality Images							
Mask R-CNN	**0.7046**	**0.7107**	**0.7597**	**86.53%**	**51.02%**	**0.7110**	**87.18%**	**54.54%**
U-Net[nn]	0.4790	0.6055	0.4653	50.61%	18.78%	0.4835	48.89%	19.20%
DeepLabV3+	0.4703	0.5769	0.4854	55.10%	10.20%	0.4644	52.99%	10.17%
HiFormer	0.4344	0.5492	0.4400	43.67%	3.67%	0.4424	43.89%	3.42%
TMU-Net	0.3987	0.4158	0.5199	41.63%	4.90%	0.3573	34.27%	4.12%
SegNext	0.3831	0.3467	0.5507	33.47%	0.82%	0.3853	36.47%	0.64%
	Low Quality Images							
Mask R-CNN	**0.6024**	**0.5773**	**0.6985**	**70.97%**	**40.86%**	**0.6073**	**71.93%**	**42.71%**
U-Net[nn]	0.3702	0.4806	0.3897	39.78%	4.30%	0.4050	48.03%	5.08%
DeepLabV3+	0.3602	0.4314	0.3928	37.63%	7.53%	0.3732	40.36%	8.65%
HiFormer	0.3400	0.4324	0.3623	28.42%	4.21%	0.3441	26.75%	2.63%
TMU-Net	0.2517	0.2254	0.4031	20.00%	1.05%	0.2282	16.38%	0.85%
SegNext	0.3169	0.3060	0.4611	23.66%	1.08%	0.3183	23.07%	1.92%

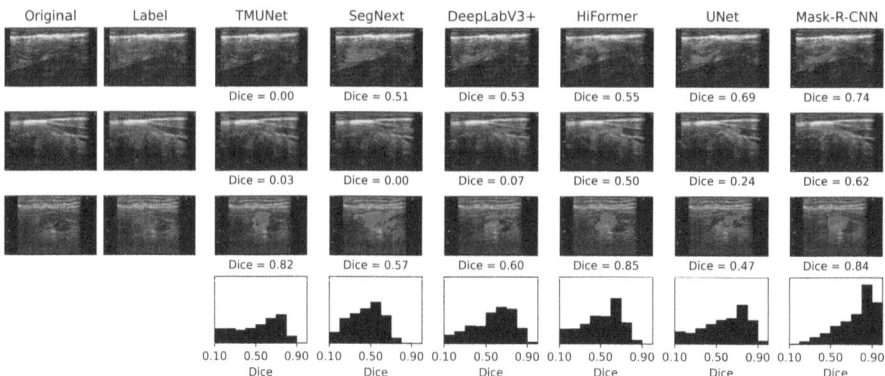

Fig. 2. *Top*: Example images (top) with annotation from medical experts (blue) and segmentation masks (orange) of the best model for each architecture, respectively. *Bottom*: Histogram of test set Dice Scores per model. (Color figure online)

Figure 2 depicts a qualitative comparison of the best models for each segmentation architecture. Notably, Mask R-CNN showed exceptional robustness across all quality levels, achieving an average Dice score of 0.7249. This performance distinctly surpassed that of the next best architecture, the U-Net^{nn}, which scored 0.5195 on average. We observe a decline in model performance with decreasing image quality, scaling from a Dice score of 0.8218 for high-quality images down to 0.6024 for low-quality images (Mask R-CNN). Evaluating model performance per-patient revealed a minor decrease in average performance. The best model (Mask R-CNN) achieved an average per-patient Dice score of 0.6847 compared to 0.7722 evaluated across all available images.

However, the highest-performing model (Mask R-CNN) maintained robust segmentation quality, with Dice scores above 0.75 in 78% (overall) and 68% (per person) cases of high-quality images, underlining its potential utility in clinical settings.

The distribution of Dice scores for all test predictions, as shown in Fig. 2, reflects the performance metrics and the architectural ranking. Precision and recall appear fairly balanced across all models and quality categories. The Mask R-CNN, TMU-Net, and SegNext models demonstrate greater precision than recall, while, in contrast, the other models-U-Net, DeepLabV3+, and HiFormer-show higher recall.

Compared to the inter-observer variability identified in this project (average Dice score of 0.6134), the performance of the Mask R-CNN indicates its ability to achieve human-level performance or better across all quality categories, efficiently handling the divergent labels provided by medical experts. In summary, the Mask R-CNN delivered the first benchmark performance for this complex segmentation task, demonstrating a promising direction for future research.

5 Conclusion

In this work, we introduced a novel ultrasound segmentation task accompanied by a novel open-source dataset of transabdominal ultrasound images with expert annotations of the colon wall. The results of our benchmark indicate that the instance segmentation approach of the Mask R-CNN architecture can achieve human-level performance, demonstrating superior robustness against noisy labels.

Our analysis of label agreement among specialized gastroenterologists highlights the segmentation task's complexity. The individual variability among experts emphasize the need for objectivity - an attribute that can be effectively achieved through automated segmentation. Moreover, model training might be enhanced by implementing strategies to increase consensus among labels. In the future, we would like to extend data collection efforts and include various different ultrasound devices to cope with different patient's anatomical particularities and machine-specific variance. Methodologically, we think that architectural extensions leveraging the temporal dynamic of ultrasound sequences could be a valuable complement to the existing instance segmentation approach.

Overall, automating colon wall segmentation from ultrasound data in patients with ulcerative colitis represents a valuable advancement as it provides a reliable and objective basis for developing tailored and effective treatment strategies for this debilitating condition.

Acknowledgments. We thank Dominik Bettenworth, Jürgen Büning, Marcel Foppe, Patrick König, Sebastian Küpper and Christian Maaser for sharing their invaluable domain expertise and providing annotations. This work was funded by the German Research Foundation (DFG grants HA7070/2-2, HA7070/3, and HA7070/4 to T.H.) and the Interdisciplinary Center for Clinical Research (IZKF) of the medical faculty of Münster (grants Dan3/012/17 to U.D. and MzH 3/020/20 to T.H.). X. Jiang was supported by the Deutsche Forschungsgemeinschaft (DFG) under Grant CRC 1450-431460824.

Disclosure of Interests. The authors have no competing interests to declare that are relevant to the content of this article.

References

1. Akkus, Z., Kim, B.H., Nayak, R., Gregory, A., Alizad, A., Fatemi, M.: Fully Automated Segmentation of Bladder Sac and Measurement of Detrusor Wall Thickness from Transabdominal Ultrasound Images. Sensors **20**(15), 4175 (2020). https://doi.org/10.3390/s20154175
2. Maaser et al., C.: Intestinal ultrasound for monitoring therapeutic response in patients with ulcerative colitis: results from the TRUST&UC study. Gut **69**(9), gutjnl–2019–319451 (2019). https://doi.org/10.1136/gutjnl-2019-319451
3. Erden et al., M.B.: FourierLoss: Shape-Aware loss function with fourier descriptors. arXiv (2023). https://doi.org/10.48550/arxiv.2309.12106

4. Yin et al., S.: Automatic kidney segmentation in ultrasound images using subsequent boundary distance regression and pixelwise classification networks. Medical Image Analysis **60**, 101602 (2020). https://doi.org/10.1016/j.media.2019.101602
5. Valente et al., S.: A comparative study of deep learning methods for multi-class semantic segmentation of 2D kidney ultrasound images. 2023 45th Annual International Conference of the IEEE Engineering in Medicine & Biology Society (EMBC) **00**, 1–4 (2023). https://doi.org/10.1109/embc40787.2023.10341170
6. Peng et al., T.: H-ProMed: Ultrasound image segmentation based on the evolutionary neural network and an improved principal curve. Pattern Recognition **131**, 108890 (2022). https://doi.org/10.1016/j.patcog.2022.108890
7. Ansari, M.Y., Yang, Y., Meher, P.K., Dakua, S.P.: Dense-PSP-UNet: A neural network for fast inference liver ultrasound segmentation. Computers in Biology and Medicine **153**, 106478 (2023). 10.1016/j.compbiomed.2022.106478
8. Avola, D., Cinque, L., Fagioli, A., Foresti, G., Mecca, A.: Ultrasound medical imaging techniques. ACM Computing Surveys (CSUR) **54**(3), 1–38 (2021). 10.1145/3447243
9. Azad, R., Heidari, M., Wu, Y., Merhof, D.: Contextual attention network: Transformer meets u-net. In: Lian, C., Cao, X., Rekik, I., Xu, X., Cui, Z. (eds.) Machine Learning in Medical Imaging. pp. 377–386. Springer Nature Switzerland, Cham (2022)
10. Bots, S., Nylund, K., Löwenberg, M., Gecse, K., D'Haens, G.: Intestinal ultrasound to assess disease activity in ulcerative colitis: development of a novel UC-Ultrasound Index. Journal of Crohn's and Colitis **15**(8), 1264–1271 (2021). 10.1093/ecco-jcc/jjab002
11. Chen, L., Papandreou, G., Schroff, F., Adam, H.: Rethinking atrous convolution for semantic image segmentation. arXiv (2017). https://doi.org/10.48550/arxiv.1706.05587
12. Daoud, M.I., Shtaiyat, A., Younes, H.A., Al-Najar, M.S., Alazrai, R.: Improved kidney outlining in ultrasound images by combining deep learning semantic segmentation with conventional active contour. 2023 10th International Conference on Electrical and Electronics Engineering (ICEEE) **00**, 74–78 (2023). https://doi.org/10.1109/iceee59925.2023.00021
13. Du, L., Ha, C.: Epidemiology and pathogenesis of ulcerative colitis. Gastroenterology Clinics of North America **49**(4), 643–654 (2020). 10.1016/j.gtc.2020.07.005
14. Guo, M., Lu, C., Hou, Q., Liu, Z., Cheng, M., Hu, S.: SegNeXt: Rethinking convolutional attention design for semantic segmentation. arXiv (2022). https://doi.org/10.48550/arxiv.2209.08575
15. He, K., Gkioxari, G., Dollár, P., Girshick, R.: Mask R-CNN. 2017 IEEE International Conference on Computer Vision (ICCV) pp. 2980–2988 (2017). https://doi.org/10.1109/iccv.2017.322
16. Heidari, M., Kazerouni, A., Soltany, M., Azad, R., Aghdam, E.K., Cohen-Adad, J., Merhof, D.: HiFormer: Hierarchical multi-scale representations using transformers for medical image segmentation. In: 2023 IEEE/CVF Winter Conference on Applications of Computer Vision (WACV). IEEE (2023)
17. Isensee, F., Jaeger, P.F., Kohl, S.A., Petersen, J., Maier-Hein, K.H.: nnu-net: A self-configuring method for deep learning-based biomedical image segmentation. Nature methods **18**(2), 203–211 (2021)
18. Jadon, S.: A survey of loss functions for semantic segmentation. In: IEEE Conference on Computational Intelligence in Bioinformatics and Computational Biology (CIBCB). arXiv (2020). https://doi.org/10.48550/arxiv.2006.14822

19. Jeon, Y.S., Yang, H., Feng, M.: FCSN: Global context aware segmentation by learning the fourier coefficients of objects in medical images. IEEE journal of biomedical and health informatics **PP**(99), 1–11 (2022). https://doi.org/10.1109/jbhi.2022.3225205
20. Kuhl, F.P., Giardina, C.R.: Elliptic Fourier features of a closed contour. Computer Graphics and Image Processing **18**(3), 236–258 (1982). 10.1016/0146-664x(82)90034-x
21. Pahl, C.: Performance observation of gabor filter for wall thickness measurement of human colon based on ultrasound image. International Journal of Information and Electronics Engineering **4**(2) (2014). https://doi.org/10.7763/ijiee.2014.v4.429
22. Ravishankar, H., Venkataramani, R., Thiruvenkadam, S., Sudhakar, P., Vaidya, V.: Learning and Incorporating Shape Models for Semantic Segmentation. Lecture Notes in Computer Science pp. 203–211 (2017). https://doi.org/10.1007/978-3-319-66182-7_24
23. Ronneberger, O., Fischer, P., Brox, T.: Convolutional networks for biomedical image segmentation. Lecture Notes in Computer Science pp. 234–241 (2015). https://doi.org/10.1007/978-3-319-24574-4_28
24. Song, Z., Liu, X., Gong, Y., Hao, T., Zeng, K.: A Two-Stage Framework for Kidney Segmentation in Ultrasound Images. Communications in Computer and Information Science pp. 60–74 (2023). https://doi.org/10.1007/978-981-99-5847-4_5
25. Wang, Y., Ge, X., Ma, H., Qi, S., Zhang, G., Yao, Y.: Deep learning in medical ultrasound image analysis: a review. IEEE Access **9**, 54310–54324 (2021). 10.1109/access.2021.3071301
26. Yeung, M., Rundo, L., Nan, Y., Sala, E., Schönlieb, C., Yang, G.: Calibrating the dice loss to handle neural network overconfidence for biomedical image segmentation. Journal of Digital Imaging pp. 1–14 (2022). https://doi.org/10.1007/s10278-022-00735-3
27. Zhang, J., Chen, Y., Liu, P.: Automatic recognition of standard liver sections based on vision-transformer. 2022 IEEE 16th International Conference on Anti-counterfeiting, Security, and Identification (ASID) **00**, 1–4 (2022). https://doi.org/10.1109/asid56930.2022.9995936

Label Dropout: Improved Deep Learning Echocardiography Segmentation Using Multiple Datasets with Domain Shift and Partial Labelling

Iman Islam[✉], Esther Puyol-Antón, Bram Ruijsink, Andrew J. Reader, and Andrew P. King

School of Biomedical Engineering and Imaging Sciences, King's College London, London, UK
iman.islam@kcl.ac.uk

Abstract. Echocardiography (echo) is the first imaging modality used when assessing cardiac function. The measurement of functional biomarkers from echo relies upon the segmentation of cardiac structures and deep learning models have been proposed to automate the segmentation process. However, in order to translate these tools to widespread clinical use it is important that the segmentation models are robust to a wide variety of images (e.g. acquired from different scanners, by operators with different levels of expertise etc.). To achieve this level of robustness it is necessary that the models are trained with multiple diverse datasets. A significant challenge faced when training with multiple diverse datasets is the variation in label presence, i.e. the combined data are often *partially-labelled*. Adaptations of the cross entropy loss function have been proposed to deal with partially labelled data. In this paper we show that training naively with such a loss function and multiple diverse datasets can lead to a form of shortcut learning, where the model associates label presence with domain characteristics, leading to a drop in performance. To address this problem, we propose a novel *label dropout* scheme to break the link between domain characteristics and the presence or absence of labels. We demonstrate that label dropout improves echo segmentation Dice score by 62% and 25% on two cardiac structures when training using multiple diverse partially labelled datasets.

Keywords: Partial labels · Segmentation · Echocardiography

1 Introduction

Echocardiography (echo) is the first imaging examination carried out when assessing cardiac function. Based on segmentations of the cardiac structures from echo images, useful biomarkers can be extracted to measure the function of the heart for diagnosis and treatment management. Deep learning models have been proposed to automate this segmentation process [2,5,7,8,10,13], but for clinical translation it is important that such models are robust to the wide variation in image characteristics that will be encountered in the real world (e.g. different scanners and operator levels of expertise etc.). In other applications, such as cardiac magnetic resonance, segmentation models have been trained using diverse data sources and shown to be robust to such variations [6]. In this work we aim to train a similarly robust model for echo segmentation.

One significant challenge that must be overcome when training with diverse datasets is the variation in label presence in the training data. For instance, a number of public datasets exist for training echo segmentation models but the manually defined labels present are different. A summary of these datasets can be found in Table 1. This means that the combination of these datasets will be *partially labelled*, i.e. not all structures will be labelled in all training samples.

Training naively with partially labelled datasets such as these can cause a conflict in the supervision due to structures being labelled as foreground in some samples and background in others. A number of methods have been proposed to deal with such data by modifying the loss function to deal with the conflict. For example, Petit et al. [9] proposed a loss function that summed the binary cross entropy (BCE) losses for each foreground class. For samples with missing ground truth labels, only the BCE terms with ground truth labels were computed. A related approach was proposed by Shi et al. [12]. Their work proposed a marginal loss, which was a modification of the categorical cross entropy (CCE) loss function, in which any missing label was merged with the background class. In these merged regions, the loss function essentially considered both the missing label and the background to be a correct prediction. Finally, Mariscal-Harana et al. [6] proposed the adaptive loss, which was similar in concept to the approach of Petit et al. [9], but removed the loss for the label not present in the ground truth from the CCE loss calculation.

In this work, we show for the first time through a series of qualitative and quantitative experiments that when training an echo segmentation model using a loss function designed for use with partially labelled data, a form of shortcut learning can occur which leads the model to associate image characteristics with label presence. This causes a significant drop in performance for the missing labels. We propose a novel approach to address this problem, called *label dropout*, which aims to break the link between image characteristics and label presence and hence prevent the shortcut learning. We demonstrate that label dropout significantly improves segmentation performance when training using multiple diverse partially labelled echo datasets.

2 Materials and Methods

Datasets: Three publicly available 2D echo datasets were exploited in this work (see Table 1). CAMUS and EchoNet Dynamic contain images at end diastole (ED) and end systole (ES) for each subject. Unity Imaging does not provide information at the subject level. Upon manual review, several of the Unity Imaging segmentations were discarded due to the left ventricular myocardium (LVM) being overlabelled into the right ventricular myocardium. Therefore, we utilised 400 mostly apical 2-chamber images out of the 1504 available. The extraneous information outside the echo cone in the Unity Imaging and EchoNet Dynamic images were removed before use in our experiments using an nnU-Net [4] model trained to segment the ultrasound cone. After pre-processing, all images were resized to 256×256.

Table 1. Summary of the three datasets used in this work showing the number of subjects, number of images, ground truth segmentation labels present and image views. LV = left ventricle, LVM = left ventricular myocardium, LA = left atrium, A2C = apical 2-chamber, A4C = apical 4-chamber.

	No. of subjects	No. of images	LV	LVM	LA	Image view(s)
CAMUS [5]	500	1000	✓	✓	✓	A2C + A4C
Unity Imaging [3]	-	400	✓	✓	✓	A2C
EchoNet Dynamic [7]	10024	20048	✓			A2C + A4C

Baseline Segmentation Models: A U-Net [11] was used as the baseline segmentation model. All models were trained using a stochastic gradient descent optimizer with a variable learning rate and a Nestorov momentum of 0.9 for 500 epochs. The initial learning rate and batch size was selected using a grid search and the model with the best foreground Dice score on the validation set was used for evaluation on the test set. Models were trained using two different loss functions. First, *standard loss* models were trained using a standard CCE loss function calculated over all classes including the background. Second, we trained *adaptive loss* models using the adaptive cross entropy loss proposed in [6]. This loss was implemented by removing the labels which are missing from the ground truth from the predicted segmentation, eliminating their contribution to the loss. Data augmentation was applied on the fly when training some models as specified in Sect. 3. The following augmentations were applied: scaling, rotation, Gaussian blur, brightness and contrast adjustment. The data were randomly split into 80%/10%/10% for the training, validation and test sets.

Label Dropout: As we will show in Sect. 3, a significant drop in performance of the adaptive loss model was observed when training with partially labelled datasets which have a domain shift between them. It was hypothesised that this was due to the model learning to associate domain specific characteristics with the presence of labels. Therefore, we propose the label dropout scheme, which aims to break the link between domain characteristics and the presence or absence of certain labels. In label dropout, we introduce a probability of a label being removed (i.e. set to background) from the ground truth mask of each sample during training. Each training sample is considered individually on the fly during training. Label dropout is applied only to partially labelled classes (i.e. those that are missing in some ground truth masks). In the case of there being multiple missing partially labelled classes, only one of them is dropped out, with an equal chance of each of them being chosen.

3 Experiments and Results

This section will detail a series of experiments which aim to illustrate the problem when training with multiple diverse partially labelled datasets, as well as the effectiveness of our proposed label dropout scheme in overcoming this problem.

Experiment 1 - The Need for Training with Multiple Diverse Datasets: We first illustrate the need to train echo segmentation models using multiple diverse datasets. In this experiment we trained left ventricle (LV) segmentation models with data augmentation using each of the datasets previously described in Sect. 2. Each model was evaluated on each of the three datasets. Figure 1 shows the test set Dice scores achieved for each evaluation. As can be seen, the models perform worse when tested on datasets they were not trained on. Therefore, training models using multiple diverse datasets is necessary to improve the generalisability of echo segmentation models.

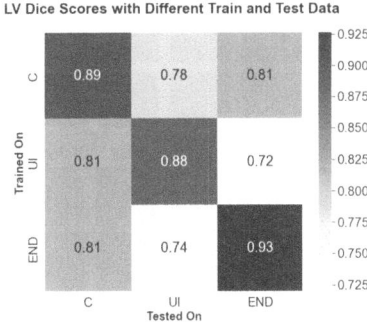

Fig. 1. Experiment 1: Test Dice scores achieved by training and evaluating intra-domain and cross-domain LV segmentation models using three different datasets. C = CAMUS [5], UI = Unity Imaging [3], END = EchoNet Dynamic [7].

Experiment 2 - Training Using a Combination of Three Diverse Partially Labelled Echo Datasets: The purpose of this experiment was to illustrate the problem of using the standard loss model when training with diverse partially labelled datasets and explore if using the adaptive loss model would lead to satisfactory results. We again used all three datasets in this experiment but this time combined them into a single training dataset. Therefore, the training dataset was partially labelled and highly diverse including various cone shapes and sizes, intensity inhomogeneities within the cones and differing contrasts.

Using these data, we trained three different models to segment the LV, LVM and LA: a standard loss model with augmentation and adaptive loss models with and without augmentation. Figure 2 shows a representative sample of the results for this experiment. The difference in quality between the model predictions for the LV, where ground truth masks were always available is minimal. However, the standard loss model completely fails to predict the LVM and LA in the EchoNet Dynamic dataset whilst predicting all three labels in the other datasets. This shows a form of shortcut learning in which the model has learnt to associate domain characteristics with label presence or absence, resulting in a model that only predicts labels which were present in the datasets' ground truths. Furthermore, contrary to expectations, the adaptive loss models do not produce accurate predictions for structures with missing labels. Even with augmentation, the predictions are less than satisfactory, particularly for the EchoNet Dynamic dataset. Data augmentation improved the results to some extent by providing a way to reduce the impacts of the domain shifts, however it did not completely overcome the impact of the shortcut learning.

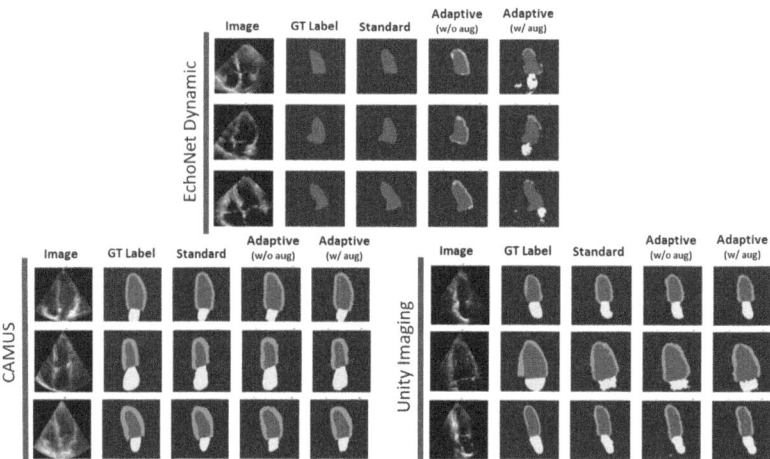

Fig. 2. Experiment 2: Example test results from the three datasets. From left to right: image, ground truth segmentation and model predictions using standard loss model, adaptive loss without augmentation and adaptive loss with augmentation.

Experiment 3 - Investigating the Adaptive Loss in a Controlled Experiment: The purpose of this experiment was to further investigate our hypothesis that domain shift has led to shortcut learning in the adaptive loss model. Here, we investigate the viability of the adaptive loss model in a controlled environment, with no domain shift between the differently labelled samples. To achieve this, ground truth labels were artificially removed from a subset of samples from the CAMUS dataset. Three models were trained and evaluated. The first was a benchmark model viewed as the best achievable performance with no partial labelling, using a standard loss. Then, a standard loss model and an adaptive loss model (both without augmentation) were trained with the LVM label artificially removed from 50% of the training data.

The test set results are shown in Fig. 3. The benchmark model, standard loss model and adaptive loss model achieved mean foreground Dice scores of 0.873 ± 0.05, 0.803 ± 0.06, and 0.863 ± 0.05 respectively. Therefore, in this controlled experiment, although the adaptive loss model was trained with missing labels, it performed comparably to the benchmark model. The standard loss model suffered a significant drop in performance due to the conflict in supervision information. The box plots in Fig. 3 show the breakdown of the Dice scores for each class, with the adaptive loss model achieving a significantly higher Dice score for the LVM compared to the standard loss model.

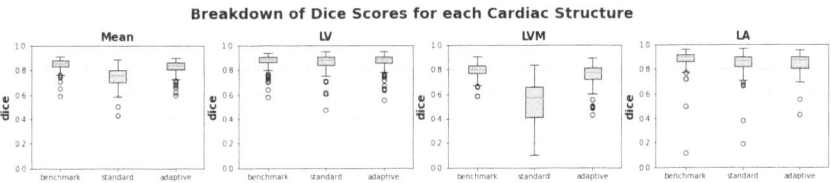

Fig. 3. Experiment 3: Test set results when training using only the CAMUS dataset with 50% of LVM labels removed. Box plots show Dice coefficients for each segmented structure and the overall mean. Green = benchmark, blue = standard, pink = adaptive. (Color figure online)

This experiment shows the viability of the adaptive loss as a solution to the problem of partial labelling. It also supports our hypothesis that the lack of improvement of the adaptive loss model in Experiment 2 was due to the domain shift between the datasets leading to a form of shortcut learning.

Experiment 4 - Label Dropout: Experiment 3 showed that the adaptive loss has the potential to deal with partially labelled training data, but it did not produce clinically acceptable segmentations in Experiment 2 when there were domain shifts between the differently labelled datasets. In this experiment, the utility of our proposed label dropout scheme in addressing this problem is explored. Two datasets were used in the first part of this experiment: CAMUS and Unity Imaging. The LA was artificially removed in all Unity Imaging ground truth masks in the training set to produce a combined training set with partial labels and a domain shift. Two types of model were trained: adaptive loss models with label dropout using the partially labelled data, and a benchmark model with a standard loss and fully labelled data, which represents the best achievable performance. For the label dropout model, different probabilities for label dropout ranging from 0.0 to 1.0 in steps of 0.1 were tested. This is the probability of the LA being dropped out from the ground-truth segmentation for each training pair during training. Augmentation was used for training all models in this experiment.

Figure 4 shows the test set results of this experiment. The plot clearly shows the improved performance when using the label dropout technique which persists across a range of dropout probabilities. Note that the 0% label dropout model is equivalent to the adaptive loss model without label dropout. The benchmark model and the 0% label dropout models achieved Dice scores of 0.83 and 0.71 respectively. The Dice scores of the adaptive loss models with label dropout were approximately 0.8. 100% label dropout means that the LA is never seen during training. Figure 4 shows how introducing label dropout, even with a very low probability of dropout at 10%, helps to break the link between domain characteristics and the presence of labels. In Fig. 4, sample model predictions from this experiment are also displayed. When there is no label dropout, the LA in the Unity Imaging dataset has a visibly worse segmentation compared to the adaptive loss model with 50% label dropout. This experiment shows that label dropout can improve model performance when training with diverse partially labelled datasets and a Wilcoxon Signed Rank Test confirms this with a p-value of <0.01. The Dice scores for the LV and LVM were similar for both models for each dataset.

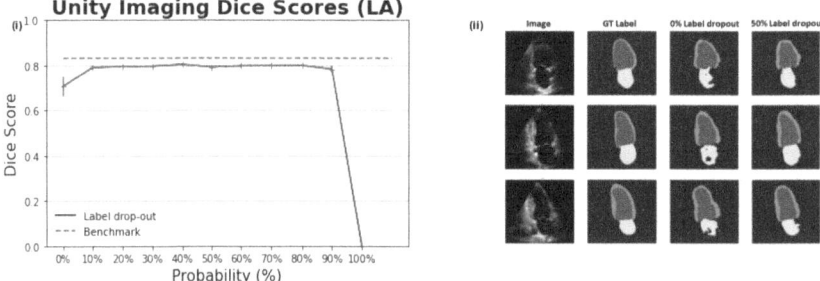

Fig. 4. Experiment 4: Label Dropout. (i) Test set Dice scores from models trained with different probabilities of label dropout on the LA for images from the Unity Imaging dataset. Models were trained three times with different random seeds and the error bars show the mean and standard deviation of the results. Benchmark was trained with a standard loss using fully labelled data. (ii) Sample results on the Unity Imaging dataset. From left to right: image, ground truth segmentation and model predictions without label dropout and with 50% label dropout.

As a final experiment, we repeated Experiment 2 but now using the combination of all three datasets using label dropout. Sample test set results are shown in Fig. 5. We see a visible improvement in the performance of the adaptive loss model when using label dropout, further supporting our hypothesis that a form of shortcut learning can negatively affect the performance of the adaptive loss when training using diverse partially labelled datasets.

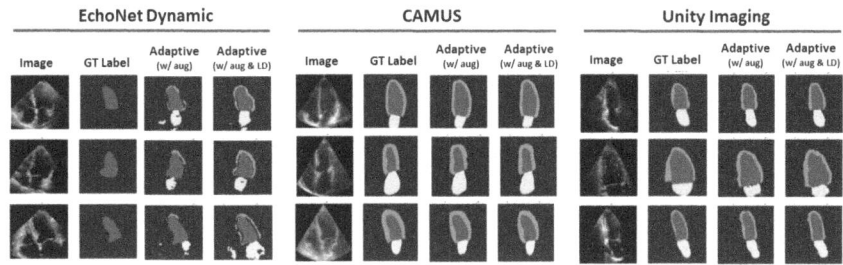

Fig. 5. Repetition of Experiment 2 with label dropout. Randomly selected test set results when training with all 3 datasets using label dropout (LD). From left to right: image, ground truth segmentation and model predictions using adaptive loss with augmentation and adaptive loss with augmentation and label dropout.

To quantify these improvements, the LVM and LA were manually segmented by a trained observer (and checked by a cardiologist) in a random sample of 20 images from EchoNet Dynamic test set and some key results are shown in Table 2. The LVM and LA Dice scores represent Dice increases of 0.199 and 0.136 (or 62% and 25%) respectively, supported by a Wilcoxon Signed Rank Test with a p-value of <0.05. Model predictions for 10 random images from these 20 are displayed in Supplementary Fig. 1.

Table 2. Mean test Dice scores over 20 random images from EchoNet Dynamic when trained on EchoNet Dynamic, CAMUS and Unity Imaging data. Dice scores are displayed for each of the three cardiac structures segmented by the adaptive loss model with and without label dropout. Aug = augmentation, LD = label dropout, LV = left ventricle, LVM = left ventricular myocardium, LA = left atrium.

	LV	LVM	LA
Adaptive (w/ aug)	0.892	0.319	0.553
Adaptive (w/ aug & LD)	0.910	0.518	0.689

4 Discussion and Conclusion

This paper has made two significant contributions: (i) we have highlighted for the first time that state-of-the-art approaches for dealing with partially labelled segmentation data can be negatively affected by a form of shortcut learning when trained with datasets featuring domain shift, (ii) we have proposed a new label dropout technique for dealing with this problem. For contribution (i), we note that the adaptive loss that we employed to deal with the partially labelled data was shown to work effectively in an experimental environment with no domain shift (Experiment 3) and has previously been shown to be effective when there was domain shift but no relationship between domain characteristics and label presence (e.g. occasionally missing LVM at ES in cine cardiac magnetic resonance [6]). Thus, we conclude that its poorer performance in Experiment 2 was due to the presence of such a relationship. For contribution (ii), label dropout was shown to improve model performance in Experiment 4. It is noticeable that the Dice score for the label dropout scheme plateaus when the label dropout is introduced. We speculate that this could be because, after a certain number of epochs, the model eventually sees all images with all labels.

We believe that this work is important for training robust segmentation models. When combining multiple diverse echocardiography segmentation datasets, the resulting training datasets are typically partially labelled and therefore this technique could allow the training of more generalisable models.

Further work will include investigating the impact of label dropout on different network architectures, such as transformers [1], as well as alternative strategies for dealing with partial labels, such as the marginal loss [12]. Furthermore, the label dropout technique will also be evaluated on datasets from different imaging modalities.

Acknowledgments. We would like to acknowledge funding from the EPSRC Centre for Doctoral Training in Medical Imaging (EP/L015226/1).

References

1. Cao, H., Wang, Y., Chen, J., Jiang, D., Zhang, X., Tian, Q., Wang, M.: Swin-Unet: Unet-like Pure Transformer for Medical Image Segmentation (May 2021), http://arxiv.org/abs/2105.05537, arXiv:2105.05537 [cs, eess]
2. Ghorbani, A., Ouyang, D., Abid, A., He, B., Chen, J.H., Harrington, R.A., Liang, D.H., Ashley, E.A., Zou, J.Y.: Deep learning interpretation of echocardiograms. npj Digital Medicine **3**(1), 10 (Jan 2020). https://doi.org/10.1038/s41746-019-0216-8, https://www.nature.com/articles/s41746-019-0216-8
3. Huang, Z., Sidhom, M.J., Wessler, B.S., Hughes, M.C.: Fix-A-Step: Semi-supervised Learning from Uncurated Unlabeled Data (May 2023), http://arxiv.org/abs/2208.11870, arXiv:2208.11870 [cs]
4. Isensee, F., Jaeger, P.F., Kohl, S.A.A., Petersen, J., Maier-Hein, K.H.: nnU-Net: a self-configuring method for deep learning-based biomedical image segmentation. Nature Methods **18**(2), 203–211 (Feb 2021). https://doi.org/10.1038/s41592-020-01008-z, http://www.nature.com/articles/s41592-020-01008-z
5. Leclerc, S., Smistad, E., Pedrosa, J., Ostvik, A., Cervenansky, F., Espinosa, F., Espeland, T., Berg, E.A.R., Jodoin, P.M., Grenier, T., Lartizien, C., Dhooge, J., Lovstakken, L., Bernard, O.: Deep Learning for Segmentation Using an Open Large-Scale Dataset in 2D Echocardiography. IEEE Transactions on Medical Imaging **38**(9), 2198–2210 (Sep 2019). https://doi.org/10.1109/TMI.2019.2900516, https://ieeexplore.ieee.org/document/8649738/

6. Mariscal-Harana, J., Asher, C., Vergani, V., Rizvi, M., Keehn, L., Kim, R.J., Judd, R.M., Petersen, S.E., Razavi, R., King, A.P., Ruijsink, B., Puyol-Antón, E.: An artificial intelligence tool for automated analysis of large-scale unstructured clinical cine cardiac magnetic resonance databases. European Heart Journal - Digital Health 4(5), 370–383 (Oct 2023). https://doi.org/10.1093/ehjdh/ztad044, https://academic.oup.com/ehjdh/article/4/5/370/7223886
7. Ouyang, D., He, B., Ghorbani, A., Yuan, N., Ebinger, J., Langlotz, C.P., Heidenreich, P.A., Harrington, R.A., Liang, D.H., Ashley, E.A., Zou, J.Y.: Video-based AI for beat-to-beat assessment of cardiac function. Nature **580**(7802), 252–256 (Apr 2020). https://doi.org/10.1038/s41586-020-2145-8, https://www.nature.com/articles/s41586-020-2145-8
8. Painchaud, N., Duchateau, N., Bernard, O., Jodoin, P.M.: Echocardiography Segmentation With Enforced Temporal Consistency. IEEE Transactions on Medical Imaging **41**(10), 2867–2878 (Oct 2022). https://doi.org/10.1109/TMI.2022.3173669, https://ieeexplore.ieee.org/document/9771186/
9. Petit, O., Thome, N., Charnoz, A., Hostettler, A., Soler, L.: Handling missing annotations for semantic segmentation with deep convnets. In: Deep Learning in Medical Image Analysis and Multimodal Learning for Clinical Decision Support: 4th International Workshop, DLMIA 2018, and 8th International Workshop, ML-CDS 2018, Held in Conjunction with MICCAI 2018, Granada, Spain, September 20, 2018, Proceedings 4. pp. 20–28. Springer (2018)
10. Puyol-Antón, E., Ruijsink, B., Sidhu, B.S., Gould, J., Porter, B., Elliott, M.K., Mehta, V., Gu, H., Xochicale, M., Gomez, A., Rinaldi, C.A., Cowie, M., Chowienczyk, P., Razavi, R., King, A.P.: AI-enabled Assessment of Cardiac Systolic and Diastolic Function from Echocardiography (Jul 2022), http://arxiv.org/abs/2203.11726, arXiv:2203.11726 [physics]
11. Ronneberger, O., Fischer, P., Brox, T.: U-Net: Convolutional Networks for Biomedical Image Segmentation (May 2015), http://arxiv.org/abs/1505.04597, arXiv:1505.04597 [cs]
12. Shi, G., Xiao, L., Chen, Y., Zhou, S.K.: Marginal loss and exclusion loss for partially supervised multi-organ segmentation. Medical Image Analysis **70**, 101979 (May 2021). https://doi.org/10.1016/j.media.2021.101979, https://linkinghub.elsevier.com/retrieve/pii/S1361841521000256
13. Tromp, J., Seekings, P.J., Hung, C.L., Iversen, M.B., Frost, M.J., Ouwerkerk, W., Jiang, Z., Eisenhaber, F., Goh, R.S.M., Zhao, H., Huang, W., Ling, L.H., Sim, D., Cozzone, P., Richards, A.M., Lee, H.K., Solomon, S.D., Lam, C.S.P., Ezekowitz, J.A.: Automated interpretation of systolic and diastolic function on the echocardiogram: a multicohort study. The Lancet Digital Health **4**(1), e46–e54 (Jan 2022). https://doi.org/10.1016/S2589-7500(21)00235-1, https://linkinghub.elsevier.com/retrieve/pii/S2589750021002351

Introducing Anatomical Constraints in Mitral Annulus Segmentation in Transesophageal Echocardiography

Børge Solli Andreassen[1]((✉)), Sarina Thomas[1], Anne H. Schistad Solberg[1], Eigil Samset[1,2], and David Völgyes[3]

[1] University of Oslo, 0316 Oslo, Norway
borgesan@ifi.uio.no
[2] GE Healthcare, 3183 Horten, Norway
[3] David Völgyes Consulting, 1481 Hagan, Norway

Abstract. The morphology of the mitral annulus plays an important role in diagnosing and treating mitral valve disorders. Automated segmentation has the promise to be time-saving and improve consistency in clinical practice. In the past years, segmentation has been dominated by methods based on deep learning. Deep learning-based segmentation methods have shown good results, but their consistency and robustness are still subjects of active research. In this work, we introduce a method that combines Graph Convolutional Networks with a 3D CNN model to integrate an anatomical shape template for the predictions. Our method leverages the feature extraction capability of CNN models to provide input features to the graph neural networks. The proposed method leverages strengths from a shape model approach with the strengths of deep learning. Further, we propose loss functions for the CNN designed to guide the graph model training. The CNN was trained with transfer learning, using a limited number of labeled transesophageal echocardiography volumes to adapt to the mitral annulus segmentation task. When comparing the segmentation of the mitral annulus achieved by the proposed method with the test set annotations, the method showed a high degree of accuracy, achieving a curve-to-curve error of 2.00 ± 0.81 mm and a relative perimeter error of $4.42\pm3.33\%$. Our results show that the proposed method is a promising new approach for introducing anatomical template structures in medical segmentation tasks.

Keywords: Echocardiography · Anatomical segmentation · Graph Neural Networks

1 Introduction

Minimally invasive Transesophageal echocardiography (TEE) is a diagnostic tool to assess the patients' heart function with ultrasound. TEE is particularly useful

---

Supplementary Information The online version contains supplementary material available at https://doi.org/10.1007/978-3-031-73647-6_12.

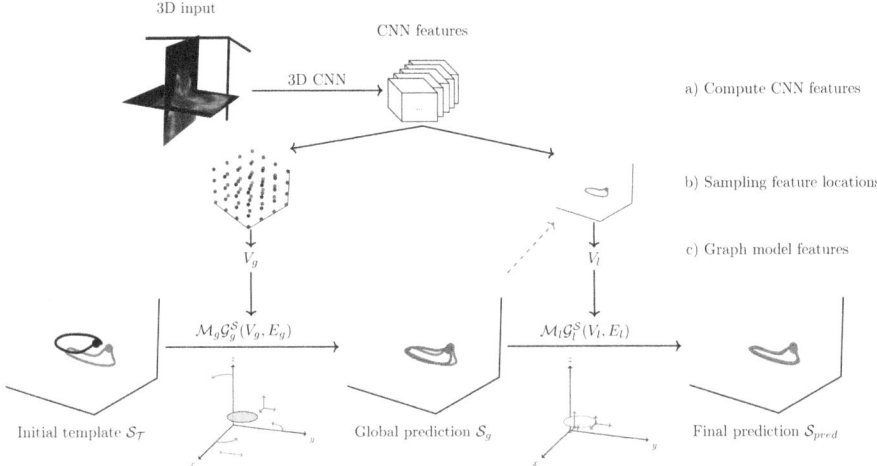

Fig. 1. Method overview: (a) Spatial features are calculated using the 3D CNN. (b) Global GCN samples each CNN feature channel in a uniform grid. Local GCN samples the CNN features at the global prediction coordinates, $\mathcal{S}_g$. (c) The sampled values are graph features of the respective GCNs. **Bottom:** Illustrates the GCNs stages. Orange curves are the target coordinates. **Left model:** The global GCN transforms the initial anatomical template (black) by predicting scaling, translation, and rotation. **Right model:** The local GCN iteratively updates each point of the global GCN output ($\mathcal{S}_g$), to the final prediction, $\mathcal{S}_{\text{pred}}$ (green). See Sect. 2.2 for details. **Notation:** Global GCN ($\mathcal{M}_g$), local GCN ($\mathcal{M}_l$), global graph ($\mathcal{G}_g$) and vertices (V_g), local graph ($\mathcal{G}_l$) and vertices (V_l), initial shape template ($\mathcal{S}_T$), global GCN output ($\mathcal{S}_g$), final prediction ($\mathcal{S}_{pred}$). E_g and E_l are learned adjacency matrices.

in evaluating the severity and type of mitral valve dysfunction and in identifying mitral valve diseases such as mitral stenosis, mitral regurgitation, and mitral valve prolapse. The two leaflets of the mitral valve are anchored to a fibrous ring called the mitral annulus. Quantifying the ring's geometry is an important step for diagnosis and pre-operative planning. Therefore, automating the segmentation of this structure has become an active field of research. However, the development of automatic methods is impeded by the lack of larger publicly available patient cohorts and TEE protocols being less standardized as compared to transthoracic echocardiography. Earlier work modeled the annulus as a simplified geometric D-shape [2], but the majority of more recent works are based on different deep learning approaches. Several works have been published on mitral valve [4,5,9,14] and annulus segmentations [1,21] but the accuracy of the different models is not directly comparable across datasets. Given its closed and unique ring-like structure, the annulus is well suited to be modeled with shape models or Graph Convolutional Networks (GCN) that can induce a geometric prior. Adding this additional shape prior can not only help the model to converge to the right location but also avoids outliers and is more robust to occlusion and noise compared to segmentation and regression-based approaches. Segmentation results need to be post-processed to obtain a corresponding contour model that can be adversely affected by prediction inaccuracies. Extracting corresponding landmarks directly allows for geometric modeling and shape statistics. However, conventional statistical shape models require alignment and dimension reduction steps and are sensitive to initialization. Adding CNNs in the shape optimization process can make annulus segmentation more robust towards this initialization and does not require any pre-processing steps except that the number of keypoints must be fixed and roughly align with each other.

This paper proposes a synergy between shape models and deep learning-based approaches by leveraging the advantages of both techniques. Our work is inspired by [6,13] that follows the global to local optimization paradigm of statistical shape models [8]. First, a global step applies a rigid transformation and scaling to the initial shape model, guiding the anatomical shape toward the target anatomy. Then, the local step deforms the individual points of the shape model to fit the specific volume anatomy.

Recent approaches for mitral valve or annulus segmentation are mainly centered around different types of U-Net segmentation [16,20] or point regression [1]. Graph neural networks can be seen as a powerful alternative whenever the number of keypoints for the model is fixed as demonstrated in [15,19]. Most related to our approach is the work from Ivantsits et al. [9]. They model the mitral valve with a volume encoder-decoder network that induces features into a GCN to deform a simplified geometric shape. In this work, we explore whether we can incorporate the global and local shape optimization process into the GCN instead of directly regressing the target keypoints.

The paper presents two major contributions to the field of transesophageal ultrasound analysis and interpretation:

- **Global to local graph neural network:** Our proposed method combines a 3D CNN with GCNs, inspired by the optimization process of statistical shape models. This method expands on previous work [6,13,17], by extending their approach from 2D to 3D.
- **Guidance by targeted feature distance maps:** We exploit prior information of specific anatomical landmarks, incorporating these as additional feature maps to guide the network.

2 Materials and Methods

2.1 Dataset

The dataset used in this retrospective study consists of anonymized transesophageal echocardiography images obtained using GE Vivid E9 and GE Vivid E95 scanners at several clinical sites, with labels generated using the GE AutoMVQ tool. The training set consists of a total of 74, a validation set of 18, and a test set of 19 DICOM files, where a patient-level split across the datasets was ensured. Systolic frames from these acquisitions were used, resulting in 459, 106, and 135 total frames in the training, validation, and test sets, respectively.

Our experiment used volumes in Cartesian coordinates with a resolution of [128, 128, 128], where each dimension corresponds to 90 mm. To reduce overfitting, we created multiple samples from each DICOM frame in the training set, applying slight coordinate system rotations before making voxel samples. The labels for each sample are a closed curve, consisting of 58 points in normalized 3D space, i.e., $y_i \in [0,1]^3$.

Our method employs an *anatomical shape template*, denoted $\mathcal{S}_\mathcal{T}$. This template encapsulates the anatomical shape by averaging all annulus labels in the training set, projected onto a common plane. The shape template is represented in the same way as the sample labels, i.e., as 58 points in $[0,1]^3$.

The primary goal of our approach was to enable the model to accurately predict the mitral annulus curve within a given image from 3D input data by utilizing this initial shape template as a reference.

2.2 Method Overview

Our proposed model architecture consists of three networks: one 3D CNN and two GCNs. The CNN was used to extract spatial features from the input volumes—which served as vertex feature inputs for the graph models, as shown in Fig. 1. The initial shape model, $\mathcal{S}_\mathcal{T}$—introduced in Sect. 2.1—is a constant fixture in the method. The graph networks update this initial shape model towards the final model prediction—as illustrated in Fig. 1 and described in the following paragraphs. For further insight, we refer to the source code on Zenodo (DOI: 10.5281/zenodo.13144112).

Graph Models: We denote the first GCN model as $\mathcal{M}_g$, the global graph model, which applies a global transformation matrix, T, to the static initial shape, $\mathcal{S}_\mathcal{T}$. Specifically, the model predicts seven values per sample—three rotations, three translations, and a scaling parameter—used to generate the [4, 4] transformation matrix, T. This transformation matrix is applied to the shape template in homogeneous coordinates, with shape [4, 58]. Finally, the transformed coordinates are converted back to Cartesian coordinates, with shape [3, 58]. We denote this transformation as transform(T, $\mathcal{S}_\mathcal{T}$), yielding the global prediction $\mathcal{S}_g$. The loss functions described in Sect. 2.3 describe how the model is optimized to output a coarse prediction of the anatomy.

The second GCN model, denoted $\mathcal{M}_l$ for the local graph model, updates the individual coordinates of the anatomical template—deforming it to align with the specific anatomy in the current volume. This local graph model can have one or more iteration layers, each applying a small deformation, i.e., $\Delta \mathcal{S}_i$ of shape [3, 58] represents the deformation applied at the i-th iteration. Specifically:

$$\mathcal{M}_g(\mathcal{G}_g^\mathcal{S}) = \text{transform}(T, \mathcal{S}_\mathcal{T}) = \mathcal{S}_g \text{ and } \mathcal{M}_l(\mathcal{G}_l^\mathcal{S}) = \mathcal{S}_{\text{pred}} = \mathcal{S}_g + \sum_i \Delta \mathcal{S}_i, \quad (1)$$

where the $\mathcal{G}$ denotes graphs with vertices and edges: $\mathcal{G}_g^\mathcal{S}(V_g, E_g)$ and $\mathcal{G}_l^\mathcal{S}(V_l, E_l)$, and $\Delta \mathcal{S}_i$ denotes a local deformation of the points in the shape. The bottom row of Fig. 1 illustrates these steps.

The vertex features, V_g and V_l, are sampled values from the 3D CNN feature channels in coordinates, $\mathcal{S}$, indicated by the superscript in $\mathcal{G}^\mathcal{S}$. The vertex features for the global graph model, V_g, are sampled from a uniform grid, $\mathcal{S}_{\text{grid}}$ of points in $[0, 1]^3$. Thereby, the global graph layer samples features from the entire feature space, in order to predict the transformation matrix, T. The features of the local graph model, V_l, are sampled in the spatial coordinates of the current prediction estimate: the first layer samples in $\mathcal{S}_g$, and subsequent iteration layers sample in the updated coordinates from the previous layer. The edges, E_g and E_l, are adjacency matrices controlling message passing between nodes in the graph. These adjacency matrices, representing the edges, are learnable parameters optimized during model training with no prior structure assumed.

The architectures of the two graph models are largely identical, using *GCN Blocks* with four stacked DeepGCN layers [12]. An important difference is the dimensionality of the transform produced by the two models, see Equation (1): The global graph model, $\mathcal{M}_g$, aggregates values across points in $\mathcal{S}_{\text{grid}}$, to output seven parameters for the transformation matrix. The local graph model, $\mathcal{M}_l$, iteratively updates the anatomical shape template by outputting coordinate adjustments for each point. The model can be configured with a single or multiple GCN Blocks that sample the feature maps at the current coordinates and iteratively update the coordinates for the next block. In the experiments and results reported in Sect. 3, the model was configured with three such local updates.

Feature Extraction: The backbone of both graph models is the feature extraction capacity of the 3D CNN. The CNN architecture is a U-Net style model with a 3D Resnet encoder [7]. Two of the CNN feature maps are directly optimized to predict distance maps similar to [10]: one for the distance to any point on the mitral annulus and the other for the distance to the aortic outlet, as detailed in Sect. 2.3. The GCNs receive two additional feature channels: the raw input volume values and the raw input masked by the predicted mitral annulus distance map. These channels provide the graph models direct access to both the raw input image and a filtered version that emphasizes the mitral valve.

Note one implementation change about the U-Net: predictions are generated from each scale of the decoder branch. These predictions are then rescaled to the highest resolution level and averaged. This structure aims to strike a balance between local high-resolution features and long-range features, providing meaningful and robust input to the graph layers.

Given the constraints of space, we direct readers to the foundational papers on U-Net [18] and GCN [11,12] for comprehensive details on the architecture of these subnetworks and to the source code on Zenodo.

2.3 Loss Functions and Metrics

Loss: While our proposed method consists of three subnetworks, it is designed to be end-to-end differentiable. The global and local graph layers yield output coordinates directly, enabling the use of a direct Euclidean distance loss function ($L2$) and an average curve-to-curve (C2C) loss.

As described in Sect. 2.2, we apply a spatial regression loss to two of the CNN feature maps to provide explicit guidance to the CNN optimization. Specifically, these are optimized to predict distance maps: one predicts the pointwise distance to the nearest point on the mitral annulus—highlighting the core structure to detect—and the other predicts the distance to the aortic outlet for each voxel—providing a reference point for the anatomical structure's rotation. We use a pointwise mean absolute error for this, with the distance map to the respective label data inversely weighted by their frequency to improve stability. These two CNN feature maps with a direct regression loss are passed as non-differentiable features to the GCNs. In contrast, the remaining CNN feature maps are differentiable features directly optimized through the GCNs.

Finally, as described in Sect. 2.2, we allow the GCNs to sample from both the raw input volume and the input volume after being masked by the distance feature map from the CNN. This approach provides the GCNs with both the original data and contextually enriched information.

The total loss for our method is:

$$Loss = \alpha_1 Regression^\gamma + \alpha_2 L2^\gamma_{global} + \alpha_3 L2^\gamma_{local} + \alpha_4 C2C^\gamma_{global} + \alpha_5 C2C^\gamma_{local},$$

where α_i weights adjust the balance and relative importance of each loss function, and $\gamma = 2$ applies a focal-loss-like exponent to reduce the relative contribution of converged losses more rapidly.

Metrics: As our main metric, the C2C distance measures the distance between two curves by averaging the shortest distances from each point on one curve to the nearest point on the other, in both directions. This metric is particularly suitable for evaluating the accuracy of the predicted mitral annulus shape as it provides a robust measure of the overall alignment between the predicted and ground truth shapes. We also report the relative perimeter error of the annulus.

3 Experiments and Results

All model training was conducted on a fixed training set, with convergence and metrics evaluated on a separate validation set. The test set was held out until the final model checkpoint was selected.

Transfer learning was employed for the encoder of the 3D CNN using a pre-trained Resnet3D model. As a data augmentation step, we dropped 20% of slices from the training volumes in three spatial dimensions for 50% of the samples. This augmentation aims to enhance robustness and promote graph node connectivity, even when parts of the valve are occluded or at the edge of the field of view.

During the development of the methodology, we tested a selection of hyperparameters, including learning rates, relative loss magnitudes, and the number of local graph layers. This iterative process helped fine-tune the model's performance and stability. The models were trained on a single NVIDIA Tesla A100 Ampere 40 GB.

Results: As shown in Table 1, the test set prediction results of our method were 2.00 ± 0.81 mm C2C error and a relative perimeter error of the annulus prediction of $4.42\pm3.33\%$. Table 1 also presents the results from the coarse prediction made by the global graph model, as well as comparisons with findings from related research efforts. Figure 2 shows some visual results on test set samples.

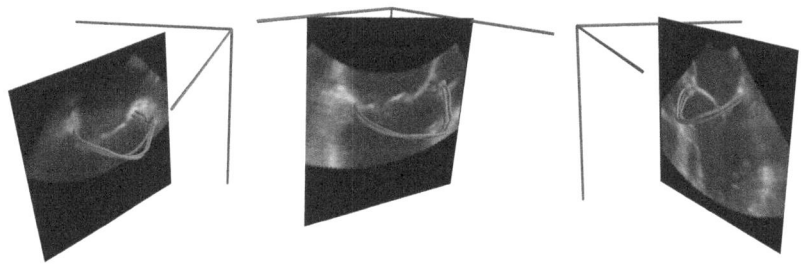

Fig. 2. Example results from three test set samples, showing the data from one cutplane in each sample. The color coding is the same as in Fig. 1: The labels are shown as an orange curve, and final predictions as the green curve. The purple curves show the output of the global GCN. The changes from the purple to the green curves show the adaptation from the transformed shape template to the final predictions.

Table 1. Experiment results for the mitral annulus localization and results from other work. The rightmost column shows the results of our work, while the second rightmost column shows the output of the global graph layer, i.e., the transformed shape template. Note that Carnahan reported absolute perimeter error.

	Carnahan [3]	Zhang et al. [21]	Andreassen et al. [1]	Proposed (global)	Proposed (final)
C2C error [mm]	2.7 ± 0.4	3.49 ± 2.21	1.82 ± 0.70	3.18 ± 1.33	2.00 ± 0.81
Relative perimeter error [%]	–	10 ± 16	5.8 ± 4.8	7.42 ± 4.16	4.42 ± 3.33

4 Discussion

Our results show that the proposed method is a promising step toward using deep neural networks in combination with anatomical shape templates. As shown in Table 1, the global graph model effectively transforms the initial template into a coarse prediction. Then, the local layer refines this coarse prediction, enhancing its accuracy. The fixed anatomical template simplifies the model training process by providing a consistent reference for all input images.

Our results outperform [3] and [21], however, comparing to the literature is not straightforward, as the size and quality of the TEE test sets vary among studies. It should be noted that all relevant studies have limited datasets. Compared to [1], which is evaluated on the same data, we achieve a lower perimeter error, however, a slightly higher C2C error. A notable benefit is that our proposed method does not require the mitral valve to be centered in the volume—unlike in [1], where this is a prerequisite.

Graph neural networks carry big potential in medical imaging, but their initialization and feeding them with meaningful feature maps can be a challenge. Our proposed method approaches this by having the CNN learn two distance maps (mitral annulus and aortic outlet) and providing the raw ultrasound feature map and its focused variant. These feature maps are somewhat handcrafted, but they are easy to generalize to other anatomical landmarks. In addition to injecting these anatomically relevant features, the remaining feature channels of the CNN are directly learned through end-to-end optimization via the GCN, allowing the method to learn and utilize other structures. Investigating the relative contributions of these engineered and learned feature maps remains future work.

The message passing through the graph edges enables both graph models to share information between the nodes in the model, mitigating the limited field of view of the CNN model. This makes the model more robust to the location of the annulus in the image.

The source code for this project is made openly available to enable benchmarking, encourage expansions, and facilitate future ablations of our method. Future studies could evaluate the impact of individual components of the method, assess the method on larger datasets as future TEE datasets become openly available, and expand the method by generalizing the curve template to a surface template.

4.1 Conclusion

In this paper, we propose an innovative approach that combines 3D CNNs with GNNs to estimate the mitral annulus geometry from TEE 3D images, mimicking the global-to-local refinement process of shape models. We further constrain some CNN feature maps by incorporating prior knowledge about anatomical landmarks while allowing the network to learn the remaining features independently. Additionally, we explore an occlusion-based augmentation method to enhance the model's robustness to occlusion. We believe our approach is straightforward to implement and easy to extend. A natural extension could be the detection of the mitral valve leaflets or other cardiac structures. Unlike other approaches that require initialization steps and may suffer from inaccuracies due to border occlusion and discontinuous segmentation masks, our method benefits from the naturally induced shape and anatomical priors.

Acknowledgement. The research presented in this paper has benefited from the Experimental Infrastructure for Exploration of Exascale Computing (eX3), which is financially supported by the Research Council of Norway under contract 270053.

References

1. Andreassen, B.S., Völgyes, D., Samset, E., Solberg, A.H.S.: Mitral annulus segmentation and anatomical orientation detection in tee images using periodic 3d cnn. IEEE Access **10**, 51472–51486 (2022). https://doi.org/10.1109/ACCESS.2022.3174059
2. Blanke, P., Dvir, D., Cheung, A., Ye, J., Levine, R.A., Precious, B., Berger, A., Stub, D., Hague, C., Murphy, D., Thompson, C., Munt, B., Moss, R., Boone, R., Wood, D., Pache, G., Webb, J., Leipsic, J.: A simplified d-shaped model of the mitral annulus to facilitate ct-based sizing before transcatheter mitral valve implantation. Journal of Cardiovascular Computed Tomography **8**(6), 459–467 (2014). https://doi.org/10.1016/j.jcct.2014.09.009
3. Carnahan, P.: Towards Patient Specific Mitral Valve Modelling via Dynamic 3D Transesophageal Echocardiography. Ph.D. thesis, The University of Western Ontario (2023), https://ir.lib.uwo.ca/etd/9885/, Electronic Thesis and Dissertation Repository
4. Carnahan, P., Moore, J., Bainbridge, D., Eskandari, M., Chen, E.C.S., Peters, T.M.: Deepmitral: Fully automatic 3d echocardiography segmentation for patient specific mitral valve modelling. In: de Bruijne, M., Cattin, P.C., Cotin, S., Padoy, N., Speidel, S., Zheng, Y., Essert, C. (eds.) Medical Image Computing and Computer Assisted Intervention – MICCAI 2021. pp. 459–468. Springer International Publishing, Cham (2021)
5. Chen, J., Li, H., He, G., Yao, F., Lai, L., Yao, J., Xie, L.: Automatic 3d mitral valve leaflet segmentation and validation of quantitative measurement. Biomedical Signal Processing and Control **79**, 104166 (2023). https://doi.org/10.1016/j.bspc.2022.104166
6. Fan, J., Liang, J., Liu, H., Huan, Z., Hou, Z.: Robust face alignment via adaptive attention-based graph convolutional network. Neural Computing and Applications **35**(20), 15129–15142 (2023)
7. Feichtenhofer, C., Fan, H., Malik, J., He, K.: Slowfast networks for video recognition. 2019 IEEE/CVF International Conference on Computer Vision (ICCV) pp. 6201–6210 (2018)
8. Heimann, T., Meinzer, H.P.: Statistical shape models for 3d medical image segmentation: A review. Medical Image Analysis **13**(4), 543–563 (2009). https://doi.org/10.1016/j.media.2009.05.004
9. Ivantsits, M., Pfahringer, B., Huellebrand, M., Walczak, L., Tautz, L., Nemchyna, O., Akansel, S., Kempfert, J., Sündermann, S., Hennemuth, A.: 3d mitral valve surface reconstruction from 3d tee via graph neural networks. In: Camara, O., Puyol-Antón, E., Qin, C., Sermesant, M., Suinesiaputra, A., Wang, S., Young, A. (eds.) Statistical Atlases and Computational Models of the Heart. Regular and CMRxMotion Challenge Papers. pp. 330–339. Springer Nature Switzerland, Cham (2022)
10. Jha, D., Riegler, M., Johansen, D., Halvorsen, P., Johansen, H.D.: DoubleU-Net: A Deep Convolutional Neural Network for Medical Image Segmentation. 2020 IEEE 33rd International Symposium on Computer-Based Medical Systems (CBMS) pp. 558–564 (2020). https://doi.org/10.1109/CBMS49503.2020.00111

11. Kipf, T.N., Welling, M.: Semi-supervised classification with graph convolutional networks. In: 5th International Conference on Learning Representations, ICLR 2017, Toulon, France, April 24-26, 2017, Conference Track Proceedings. OpenReview.net (2017), https://openreview.net/forum?id=SJU4ayYgl
12. Li, G., Müller, M., Thabet, A., Ghanem, B.: Deepgcns: Can gcns go as deep as cnns? In: The IEEE International Conference on Computer Vision (ICCV) (2019)
13. Li, W., Lu, Y., Zheng, K., Liao, H., Lin, C., Luo, J., Cheng, C.T., Xiao, J., Lu, L., Kuo, C.F., et al.: Structured landmark detection via topology-adapting deep graph learning. In: Computer Vision–ECCV 2020: 16th European Conference, Glasgow, UK, August 23–28, 2020, Proceedings, Part IX 16. pp. 266–283. Springer (2020)
14. Lopes, P., Van Herck, P., Verhoelst, E., Wirix-Speetjens, R., Sijbers, J., Bosmans, J., Vander Sloten, J.: Using particle systems for mitral valve segmentation from 3d transoesophageal echocardiography (3d toe) - a proof of concept. Computer Methods in Biomechanics and Biomedical Engineering: Imaging & Visualization **11**(1), 112–120 (2023). https://doi.org/10.1080/21681163.2022.2058416
15. Mokhtari, M., Mahdavi, M., Vaseli, H., Luong, C., Abolmaesumi, P., Tsang, T.S., Liao, R.: Echoglad: Hierarchical graph neural networks for left ventricle landmark detection on echocardiograms. In: Medical Image Computing and Computer Assisted Intervention – MICCAI 2023. pp. 227–237. Springer Nature Switzerland, Cham (2023)
16. Munafò, R., Saitta, S., Ingallina, G., Denti, P., Maisano, F., Agricola, E., Redaelli, A., Votta, E.: A deep learning-based fully automated pipeline for regurgitant mitral valve anatomy analysis from 3d echocardiography. IEEE Access **12**, 5295–5308 (2024). https://doi.org/10.1109/ACCESS.2024.3349698
17. Nguyen, L.Q., Li, Y., Wang, H., Dang, L.M., Song, H.K., Moon, H., et al.: Facial landmark detection with learnable connectivity graph convolutional network. IEEE Access **10**, 94354–94362 (2022)
18. Ronneberger, O., Fischer, P., Brox, T.: U-net: Convolutional networks for biomedical image segmentation. In: Medical Image Computing and Computer-Assisted Intervention – MICCAI 2015. pp. 234–241. Springer International Publishing, Cham (2015)
19. Thomas, S., Gilbert, A., Ben-Yosef, G.: Light-weight spatio-temporal graphs for segmentation and ejection fraction prediction in cardiac ultrasound. In: International Conference on Medical Image Computing and Computer-Assisted Intervention. pp. 380–390. Springer (2022). https://doi.org/10.1007/978-3-031-16440-8_37
20. Wifstad, S.V., Kildahl, H.A., Grenne, B., Holte, E., Hauge, S.W., Sæbø, S., Mekonnen, D., Nega, B., Haaverstad, R., Estensen, M.E., Dalen, H., Lovstakken, L.: Mitral valve segmentation and tracking from transthoracic echocardiography using deep learning. Ultrasound in Medicine & Biology (2024).https://doi.org/10.1016/j.ultrasmedbio.2023.12.023, https://www.sciencedirect.com/science/article/pii/S0301562923004179
21. Zhang, Y., Amadou, A.a., Voigt, I., Mihalef, V., Houle, H., John, M., Mansi, T., Liao, R.: A bottom-up approach for real-time mitral valve annulus modeling on 3d echo images. In: Medical Image Computing and Computer Assisted Intervention– MICCAI 2020: 23rd International Conference, Lima, Peru, October 4–8, 2020, Proceedings, Part VI 23. pp. 458–467. Springer (2020)

Interactive Segmentation Model for Placenta Segmentation from 3D Ultrasound Images

Hao Li[1(✉)], Baris Oguz[2], Gabriel Arenas[2], Xing Yao[1], Jiacheng Wang[1], Alison Pouch[2], Brett Byram[1], Nadav Schwartz[2], and Ipek Oguz[1]

[1] Vanderbilt University, Nashville, USA
`hao.li.1@vanderbilt.edu`
[2] University of Pennsylvania, Philadelphia, USA

Abstract. Placenta volume measurement from 3D ultrasound images is critical for predicting pregnancy outcomes, and manual annotation is the gold standard. However, such manual annotation is expensive and time consuming. Automated segmentation algorithms can often successfully segment the placenta, but these methods may not consistently produce robust segmentations suitable for practical use. Recently, inspired by the Segment Anything Model (SAM), deep learning-based interactive segmentation models have been widely applied in the medical imaging domain. These models produce a segmentation from visual prompts provided to indicate the target region, which may offer a feasible solution for practical use. However, none of these models are specifically designed for interactively segmenting 3D ultrasound images, which remain challenging due to the inherent noise of this modality. In this paper, we evaluate publicly available state-of-the-art 3D interactive segmentation models in contrast to a human-in-the-loop approach for the placenta segmentation task. The Dice score, normalized surface Dice, averaged symmetric surface distance, and 95-percent Hausdorff distance are used as evaluation metrics. We consider a Dice score of 0.95 a successful segmentation. Our results indicate that the human-in-the-loop segmentation model reaches this standard. Moreover, we assess the efficiency of the human-in-the-loop model as a function of the amount of prompts. Our results demonstrate that the human-in-the-loop model is both effective and efficient for interactive placenta segmentation. The code is available at https://github.com/MedICL-VU/PRISM-placenta.

Keywords: Interactive segmentation · Scribbles · Deep learning · Placenta segmentation · 3D Ultrasound (3DUS) image

1 Introduction

Placenta volume measurement from 3D ultrasound (3DUS) images is associated with fetal size [23] and adverse pregnancy outcomes, such as preeclampsia

[21,25] and intrauterine growth restriction [1], which contribute to perinatal morbidity and mortality. Manual annotations of the placenta are considered the gold standard in practice to ensure precise measurements. However, obtaining annotations is time-consuming, subjective, and requires expert knowledge. In contrast, fully automated algorithms using multi-atlas segmentation techniques have been developed to segment the placenta [18]. In more recent years, deep learning-based automated approaches have demonstrated state-of-the-art performance as the leading method for placenta segmentation. This includes applications in 2D placenta segmentation from ultrasound videos [4,22] and in 3D volume segmentation [13–15,17,20,24,34]. Despite their advancements, the relatively large standard deviations of these automated segmentation methods indicate that they may not consistently deliver high performance in every case, especially in poor quality images with high levels of noise or artifacts. Robust segmentation of the placenta remains challenging due to unclear boundaries in 3DUS images [30], especially during the early pregnancy when the placenta and uterine tissue are less distinct. Additionally, uterine contractions can cause significant anatomical variations [3]. This issue is further complicated by the weak contrast and inherent noise in 3DUS images, as well as shadow [32] and attenuation artifacts common in posterior placentas.

An interactive segmentation method could serve as a potential alternative for addressing these variabilities and improving the robustness of placenta segmentation. Practical uses of such a method would include facilitating annotation of large datasets for training automated models, as well as segmenting challenging images where automated methods may fail. Early work in this direction includes the VOCAL platform from GE-Healthcare, which involves interpolation between manually labeled slices, a random-walker algorithm [26], as well as a manually initialized multi-atlas label fusion method [19]. More recently, the deep learning-based interactive segmentation method, Segment Anything Model (SAM) [6], has shown generalizability and ability to produce precise segmentation and has been widely adopted in the medical domain [2,5,10,11,16,28], including for US applications [12,27,33]. These models either adapt pretrained weights from SAM or they are trained from scratch for the medical imaging domain. These SAM-based models require users to provide prompts, such as points [2,5,10–12,27–29], boxes [11,16,33], scribbles [11,31], and masks [2,11,28] for interactions.

However, a robust interactive segmentation model should be both _effective and efficient_ in responding to user prompts with minimal interactions. Unfortunately, even with such interactions, these current studies designed for US applications may not always provide consistent, robust segmentation for practical use. Moreover, 2D interactive models might not be as efficient for 3D images, which may require visual prompts within each slice. Even if prompts can be propagated accurately between slices to reduce user burden, a 2D model also cannot capture depth information as effectively as 3D models, which may limit the segmentation performance. Currently, there is no 3D interactive model designed for placenta segmentation that meets these goals for effectiveness and efficiency.

The current publicly available 3D interactive segmentation models aim to achieve robust performance by adapting pretrained weights from SAM [5,10] and incorporating a human-in-the-loop design for iterative corrections [11,28].

Among these methods, PRISM [11] stands out as it achieves human-level performance, making it an effective interactive segmentation model suitable for practical applications. Unlike other models, PRISM supports a wide range of prompt types, allowing for precise segmentation adjustments until user expectations are met. However, PRISM was not originally designed for placenta segmentation or for 3DUS data, and its effectiveness in this application remains untested.

In this paper, we evaluate the publicly available state-of-the-art 3D interactive segmentation models [5,10,28], in contrast to the human-in-the-loop PRISM algorithm [11] for placenta segmentation from 3DUS images. We focus on both effectiveness and efficiency, as our goal is to identify a model suitable for practical use. We consider a Dice score of 0.95 as a bar for success, since an effective interactive model should produce segmentations that closely match the information provided in user prompts. This is conservative given previous reports of inter-rater variability in the 0.85–0.90 range for manual segmentations [34]. Our comprehensive experiments show PRISM [11] has superior performance and reaches the success bar within only a few iterations. Our findings confirm that PRISM is effective and efficient, making it suitable for practical use.

2 Materials and Methods

2.1 Datasets

3D ultrasound volume datasets (n = 124) were acquired from women at 11–14 weeks of gestation using GE Voluson E8 ultrasound machines. The dimensions of the raw images ranged from $245 \times 265 \times 173$ to $714 \times 726 \times 488$ voxels, with a mean isotropic resolution of 0.49 ± 0.04 mm. The training set consisted of 100 subjects with 25 used for validation, and the remaining 24 were used for testing (14 anterior/10 posterior). We resampled all images to a 1 mm isotropic resolution, performed intensity clipping based on the 0.5^{th} and 99.5^{th} percentiles of the foreground, and applied Z-score normalization based on foreground voxels. Random zoom and intensity shift were used as data augmentations.

2.2 Interactive Segmentation Model

We adopt PRISM [11], a human-in-the-loop approach 3D interactive segmentation model (Fig. 1(a)), for the 3DUS placenta segmentation task. For each image, along with visual prompts, image and prompt encoders are used to produce respective embeddings. Specifically, the image encoder is a hybrid model that combines parallel convolutional and transformer paths [8], and the prompt encoder contains several embedding layers. These embeddings interact through self- and cross-attention mechanisms before being fed into a CNN-based decoder to generate the segmentation.

As a human-in-the-loop design, PRISM employs iterative learning to achieve improvements through successive iterations. To mimic human behavior in our experiments, the positive and negative visual prompts are generated from false

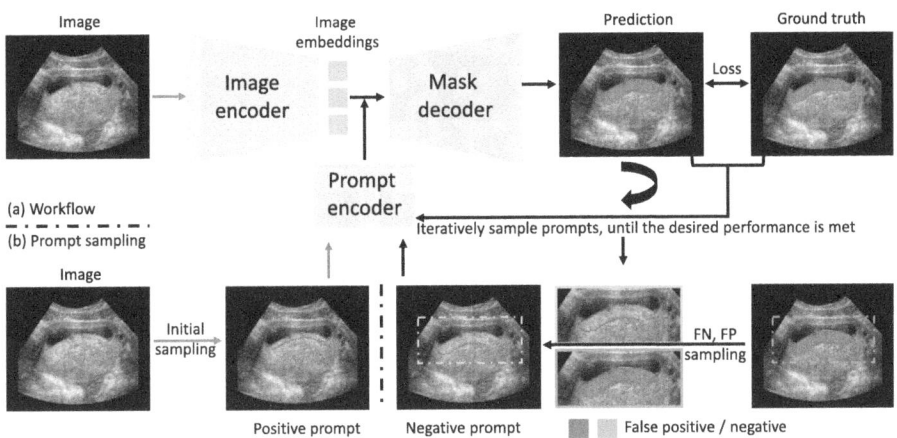

Fig. 1. (a) The 3D interactive segmentation model (PRISM [11]), illustrated in 2D. (b) Prompt sampling for positive (left) and negative prompts (right). To mimic human behavior, we sample prompts from the FN and FP regions of the current segmentation at each iteration. The initial sampling only has positive prompts.

negatives (FN) and false positives (FP) of the segmentation result at the previous iteration, respectively. For the initial sampling (Fig. 1(b), left), only false negatives are considered, and the positive prompts are used to indicate the target region. We use a constant number of iterations (n = 11) for all subjects for training and inference in our experiments. However, in practice, this number would vary between subjects, as the user would stop when the segmentation result meets their expectation.

2.3 Visual Prompt Generation

PRISM can take various visual prompts as additional input along the input image, including points, boxes, scribbles, and masks. Initially, the mask is set to zeros. For subsequent iterations, the output from the last iteration is used as the mask prompt. We generate other different visual prompts to indicate the target region as follows:

Point: At both initial and subsequent iterations, point prompts are randomly sampled with uniform distribution from the FN and FP regions.

Box: The 3D bounding box is determined based on the ground truth and represented as two points. It is only sampled at the initial iteration.

Centerline Scribble: Scribble generation follows the ScribblePrompt [31]. As depicted in Fig. 2 top row, the first step involves identifying the centerline, which is the skeleton of a binary mask (e.g., the FN region for the current iteration). Next, a random binary mask is created to divide the centerline into separate, smaller parts. Lastly, the curvature and thickness of scribbles are modified using a random deformation field and Gaussian filtering.

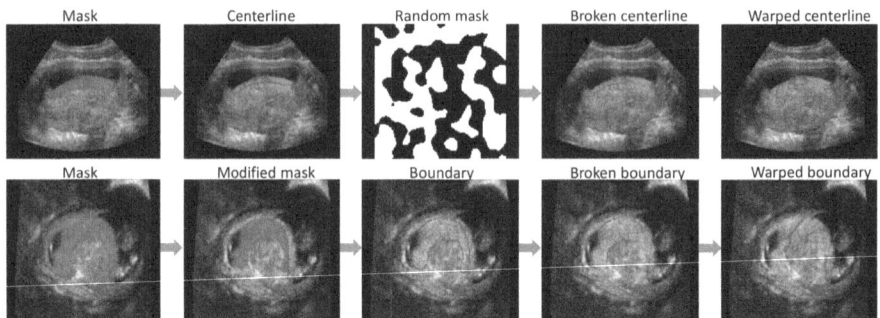

Fig. 2. Top: Centerline scribble generated from a longitudinal slice. Bottom: Boundary scribble generated from a transverse view. The binary mask can be derived from either FP or FN masks to generate negative and positive scribbles, respectively.

Boundary Scribble: As shown in Fig. 2 bottom row, the modified binary mask is created from the original binary mask by applying a Gaussian blur and then thresholding with a random number between its minimum and maximum values. Next, the boundary of this modified mask is extracted. The methods used to generate broken and warped boundaries are same as in centerline generation.

These positive and negative scribbles are generated in a 2D manner from the slices of 3D binary FN and FP masks, respectively. We run the scribble generation algorithm (which may result in multiple broken scribbles as described above) once per FN/FP region, excluding small (<100 voxels) FN/FP regions.

We note that box prompts provide a strong prior but they are often inadequate to correct FP and FN regions. Conversely, points are highly flexible and widely used for their simplicity and efficiency. Finally, drawing scribbles is practical and often favored as an extension of point prompts, as they encode more information about user intentions. With these visual prompts, PRISM could handle different applications at various difficulty levels.

2.4 Implementation Details

The training details and loss functions for PRISM follow [11]. We initially divided the data into training, validation, and testing with ratios of 0.6, 0.2, and 0.2, respectively. To assess the impact of varying training data ratios, we reduced the training ratio to 0.4 and 0.2, transferring the corresponding subjects (0.2 and 0.4) to the testing set. The subjects in the validation set remained unchanged. The Dice, normalized surface Dice (NSD) with 1 mm as tolerance [7], average symmetric surface distance (ASD), and 95% Hausdorff distance (HD95) are used as evaluation metrics, where distance are reported in mm. The study was conducted on an NVIDIA A6000.

2.5 Compared Methods

We compare PRISM performance to other interactive state-of-the-art methods, including model adaptation methods [5,10] and iterative methods for corrections

Table 1. $Dice/NSD$ results comparison. Bold indicates best performance.

	Prompt	Methods	Anterior	Posterior	Overall
	–	Automated [24]	90.46/80.72	89.42/75.75	90.03/78.65
Interactive	10 points/slice	SAM [6]	46.44/14.29	43.32/14.78	45.14/14.49
	1 point/volume	3DSAM-adapter [5]	84.57/70.34	85.97/68.58	85.15/69.61
	1 point/volume	ProMISe [10]	85.55/71.57	83.91/67.15	84.87/69.73
	1 point/volume	SAM-Med3D [28]	53.26/22.29	53.28/28.09	62.12/28.03
	1 point/volume	SAM-Med3D-turbo	89.51/76.22	88.59/73.32	89.13/75.01
	1 point/volume	PRISM [11]	87.04/72.43	88.55/73.40	87.66/72.83
	*	PRISM	**97.35/99.68**	**97.01/99.44**	**97.15/99.54**

* uses 1 point and 1 3D box per volume, as well as 2D warped centerline scribbles.

[28]. The pretrained weights of SAM are utilized for model adaptation methods [5,10]. The number of iterations is set to 11 to obtain the final segmentation using iterative methods for both training and inference [28]. We retrained the models with the hyperparameters using the official code for each, except for SAM, which was used only for inference. The prompt settings also follow their respective codes. The interactive segmentation methods show variability based on different prompts [9], and all results were produced using fixed seeds to control for randomness. We also compare the performance with a state-of-the-art fully automated placenta segmentation method [24].

3 Results

Quantitative Analysis. The quantitative results are presented in Table 1, where Dice and NSD are used as evaluation metrics. The automated method [24] can produce accurate placenta segmentation, with mean Dice scores slightly above 0.9. Interactive segmentation models tend to perform less effectively when using just one point prompt per volume, as all Dice scores for these methods are below 0.9. We note that, using a pretrained model (SAM-Med3D-turbo) significantly improves the accuracy of SAM-Med3D by leveraging the large dataset for pretraining. Among the methods using a single point prompt, PRISM outperforms these interactive models except the pretrained SAM-Med3D-turbo. PRISM achieves human-level performance when 2D scribble prompts are used, similar to the performance in non-ultrasound applications described in [11]. The performance is slightly lower for posterior placentas, which is expected since these are harder to image and often contain shadowing artifacts and poorer contrast.

Qualitative Analysis. The qualitative results are shown in Fig. 3. Local defects are observed in all compared methods, except for PRISM with scribbles (PRISM* in Fig. 3), which produces the result closest to the ground truth.

Comparison of Scribble Types. Next, we compare the different scribble settings for PRISM in Table 2. Specifically, we explore performance variations by

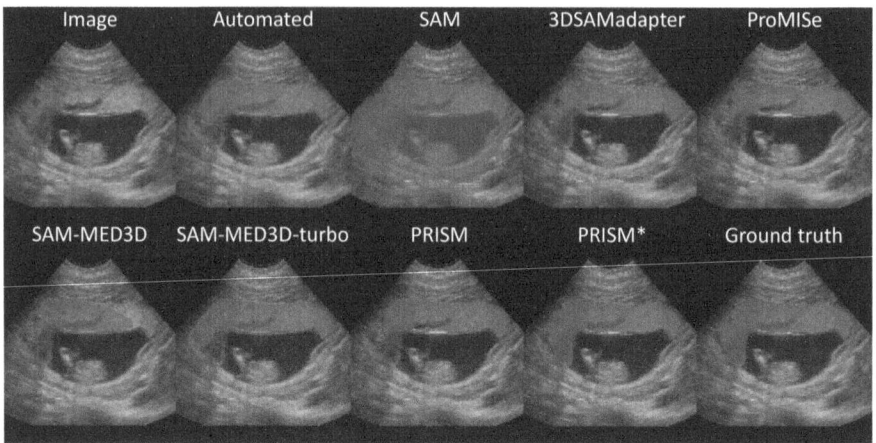

Fig. 3. Qualitative segmentation results. While several of the compared methods achieve reasonable performance, PRISM with scribbles (PRISM*) matches the ground truth most closely.

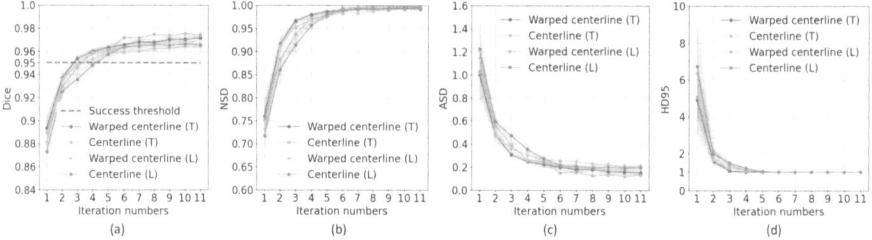

Fig. 4. PRISM segmentation performance with different scribbles across iterations. (a) Dice, (b) NSD, (c) ASD, (d) HD95. The mean values (lines) and 95% confidence intervals (shades) are shown. T and L denote transverse and longitudinal views, respectively.

labeling scribbles on either longitudinal (Fig. 2 (top)) or transverse (Fig. 2 (bottom)) slices. In addition, we compare scribbles generated using the centerline, warped centerline, boundary, and warped boundary methods from Fig. 2.

We observe that generally, centerline scribbles are more effective than boundary scribbles, and generating them in the transverse slice achieves higher performance than in the longitudinal view.

We note that the centerline and boundary scribbles are perfect representations of the associated FN/FP region, whereas the warped variants introduce noise and randomness and are more representative of realistic human behavior. The warped variants also contain fewer points per scribble. Despite these two disadvantages, the performance of the various scribble types are comparable, which suggests that PRISM is effective even with fewer and imperfect prompts. Even though it provides a slight performance boost, requiring an exact scribble

Table 2. Comparison of different scribble types for PRISM, presented as $Dice/NSD$. Bold indicates best performance. 2.3.

View	Methods	Anterior	Posterior	Overall
Longitudinal	Centerline	**96.33/99.01**	**96.87/99.58**	**96.56/99.25**
	Warped centerline	96.24/98.85	96.64/99.25	96.41/99.02
	Boundary	95.51/97.95	96.10/98.98	95.75/98.38
	Warped boundary	96.18/99.16	96.54/99.40	96.33/99.26
Transverse	Centerline	**97.41/99.75**	**97.31/99.70**	**97.55/99.82**
	Warped centerline	97.35/99.68	97.01/99.44	97.15/99.54
	Boundary	96.05/98.85	96.48/99.21	96.22/99.00
	Warped boundary	96.88/99.47	97.29/99.77	97.04/99.59

Table 3. Sparse sampling results are presented as $Dice/NSD/ASD/HD95$. We report both the performance on the whole 3D volume, as well as on just the slices with annotations. 'Freq.' indicates prompt frequency, i.e., every 2 and 5 slices.

$Freq.$	Entire volume	Annotated slices only
1	97.15/99.8/0.15/1.00	–
2	96.71/99.2/0.19/1.00	97.09/99.9/0.02/0.00
5	95.28/96.1/0.32/1.23	96.64/99.6/0.02/0.13

is not a desirable approach in practice. Instead, the warped scribbles require less effort to generate and closely mimic human behavior.

Iterative Analysis. Next, we investigate the performance as a function of number of iterations (Fig. 4). Regardless of the scribble type, the effectiveness of PRISM is significantly improved in the early iterations. The warped centerline reaches the 0.95 Dice score, which we consider indicative of a successful segmentation, by the third iteration.

Sparse Sampling. The results presented so far require scribbles to be generated for each 2D slice, which lowers the efficiency. Here, we investigate the performance of sparser scribbles by only generating them on a subset of slices.

Table 3 and Fig. 5-a show the results with scribbles in every 2 and every 5 transverse slices. Compared to dense sampling, there is a slight decrease in performance, but it still reaches the 0.95 Dice bar. We also report the performance on only the slices with scribbles. Table 3 shows that the results are slightly better in these annotated slices compared to the rest of the volume. Exploring strategies for either propagating the sparse prompts prior to the segmentation, or propagating the segmentation from the annotated slices to the other slices remains as future work. Figure 5-b shows the ratio of scribble voxels to placenta volume for each setting. We observe that the required prompt voxels quickly

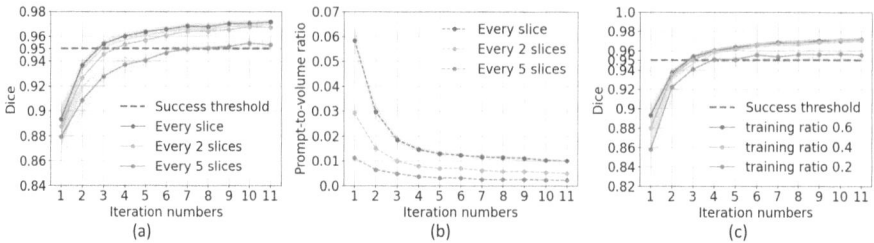

Fig. 5. (a) Dice per iteration for sparse sampling. (b) Prompt-to-volume ratio at each iteration for sparse sampling. The prompt-to-volume ratio is the ratio of the total number of scribble voxels to the number of placenta voxels in the ground truth. (c) Dice score on different training set size, without changing the test set.

goes down after the first few iterations. Overall, we conclude that PRISM can produce robust segmentations with even sparsely labeled scribbles.

Smaller Training Dataset. Finally, we explore the robustness of the model to smaller training datasets. The training data ratio in the experiments presented so far was set at 0.6, and here we reduce it to 0.4 and 0.2. The test subjects remain the same for a fair comparison. The results are presented in Fig. 5-c. Despite having fewer training images, PRISM can maintain similar performance and reach 0.95 Dice in just a few iterations, showing its effectiveness and efficiency.

4 Conclusion

In this study, we present a comprehensive evaluation of deep learning-based 3D interactive segmentation models for placenta segmentation, specifically focusing on the effectiveness and efficiency of PRISM in terms of segmentation quality and the effort required to generate prompts. With scribbles and a few iterative corrections, PRISM can produce segmentations that reach human-level performance. The results show both effectiveness and efficiency in responding to scribbles. Future work will involve a pretrained model to further improve efficiency, as well as extension to data from later stages of pregnancy when the placenta may not be fully captured within the 3D ultrasound volume.

Acknowledgments. This work was supported, in part, by NIH grants R01-HD109739, R01-HL156034, U01-HD087180, and R03-HD069742, as well as by the Penn Presbyterian George L. and Emily McMichael Harrison Fund for Research in Obstetrics and Gynecology.

References

1. Biswas, S., Ghosh, S.: Gross morphological changes of placentas associated with intrauterine growth restriction of fetuses: a case control study. Early human development **84**(6), 357–362 (2008)
2. Cheng, J., Ye, J., Deng, Z., Chen, J., Li, T., Wang, H., Su, Y., Huang, Z., Chen, J., Jiang, L., Sun, H., He, J., Zhang, S., Zhu, M., Qiao, Y.: Sam-med2d. arXiv:2308.16184 (2023)
3. Fiorentino, M.C., Villani, F.P., Di Cosmo, M., Frontoni, E., Moccia, S.: A review on deep-learning algorithms for fetal ultrasound-image analysis. MedIA (2023)
4. Gleed, A.D., Chen, Q., Jackman, J., Mishra, D., Chandramohan, V., Self, A., Bhatnagar, S., Papageorghiou, A.T., Noble, J.A.: Automatic image guidance for assessment of placenta location in ultrasound video sweeps. Ultrasound in Medicine & Biology **49**(1), 106–121 (2023)
5. Gong, S., Zhong, Y., Ma, W., Li, J., Wang, Z., Zhang, J., Heng, P.A., Dou, Q.: 3dsam-adapter: Holistic adaptation of sam from 2d to 3d for promptable medical image segmentation. arXiv:2306.13465 (2023)
6. Kirillov, A., Mintun, E., Ravi, N., Mao, H., Rolland, C., Gustafson, L., Xiao, T., Whitehead, S., Berg, A., Lo, W.Y., Dollar, P., Girshick, R.: Segment anything. In: ICCV (2023)
7. Kiser, K.J., Barman, A., Stieb, S., Fuller, C.D., Giancardo, L.: Novel autosegmentation spatial similarity metrics capture the time required to correct segmentations better than traditional metrics in a thoracic cavity segmentation workflow. Journal of Digital Imaging **34**, 541–553 (2021)
8. Li, H., Hu, D., Liu, H., Wang, J., Oguz, I.: Cats: complementary cnn and transformer encoders for segmentation. In: IEEE ISBI. pp. 1–5. IEEE (2022)
9. Li, H., Liu, H., Hu, D., Wang, J., Oguz, I.: Assessing test-time variability for interactive 3d medical image segmentation with diverse point prompts. arXiv (2023)
10. Li, H., Liu, H., Hu, D., Wang, J., Oguz, I.: Promise: Prompt-driven 3d medical image segmentation using pretrained image foundation models. arXiv (2023)
11. Li, H., Liu, H., Hu, D., Wang, J., Oguz, I.: Prism: A promptable and robust interactive segmentation model with visual prompts. arXiv:2404.15028 (2024)
12. Lin, X., Xiang, Y., Zhang, L., Yang, X., Yan, Z., Yu, L.: Samus: Adapting segment anything model for clinically-friendly and generalizable ultrasound image segmentation. arXiv:2309.06824 (2023)
13. Looney, P., Stevenson, G.N., Nicolaides, K.H., Plasencia, W., Molloholli, M., Natsis, S., Collins, S.L.: Automatic 3d ultrasound segmentation of the first trimester placenta using deep learning. In: IEEE ISBI. pp. 279–282. IEEE (2017)
14. Looney, P., Stevenson, G.N., Nicolaides, K.H., Plasencia, W., Molloholli, M., Natsis, S., Collins, S.L.: Fully automated, real-time 3d ultrasound segmentation to estimate first trimester placental volume using deep learning. JCI insight (2018)
15. Looney, P., Yin, Y., Collins, S.L., Nicolaides, K.H., Plasencia, W., Molloholli, M., Natsis, S., Stevenson, G.N.: Fully automated 3d ultrasound segmentation of the placenta, amniotic fluid, and fetus for early pregnancy assessment. IEEE transactions on ultrasonics, ferroelectrics, and frequency control **68**(6), 2038–2047 (2021)
16. Ma, J., He, Y., Li, F., Han, L., You, C., Wang, B.: Segment anything in medical images. Nature Communications **15**(1), 654 (2024)
17. Oguz, B.U., Wang, J., Yushkevich, N., Pouch, A., Gee, J., Yushkevich, P.A., Schwartz, N., Oguz, I.: Combining deep learning and multi-atlas label fusion for automated placenta segmentation from 3dus. In: PIPPI workshop. Springer (2018)

18. Oguz, I., Pouch, A.M., Yushkevich, N., Wang, H., Gee, J.C., Schwartz, N., Yushkevich, P.A.: Automated placenta segmentation from 3d ultrasound images. PIPPI (2016)
19. Oguz, I., Yushkevich, N., Pouch, A., Oguz, B.U., Wang, J., Parameshwaran, S., Gee, J., Yushkevich, P.A., Schwartz, N.: Minimally interactive placenta segmentation from three-dimensional ultrasound images. Journal of Medical Imaging (2020)
20. Pouch, A.M., Yushkevich, P.A., Aly, A.H., Woltersom, A.H., Okon, E., Aly, A.H., Yushkevich, N., Parameshwaran, S., Wang, J., Oguz, B., Gee, C.J., Oguz, I., Schwartz, N.: Automated meshing of anatomical shapes for deformable medial modeling: Application to the placenta in 3d ultrasound. In: IEEE ISBI (2020)
21. Redman, C.W., Sargent, I.L.: Latest advances in understanding preeclampsia. Science **308**(5728), 1592–1594 (2005)
22. Schilpzand, M., Neff, C., van Dillen, J., van Ginneken, B., Heskes, T., de Korte, C., van den Heuvel, T.: Automatic placenta localization from ultrasound imaging in a resource-limited setting using a predefined ultrasound acquisition protocol and deep learning. Ultrasound in Medicine & Biology **48**(4), 663–674 (2022)
23. Schwartz, N., Wang, E., Parry, S.: Two-dimensional sonographic placental measurements in the prediction of small-for-gestational-age infants. Ultrasound in obstetrics & gynecology **40**(6), 674–679 (2012)
24. Schwartz, N., Oguz, I., Wang, J., Pouch, A., Yushkevich, N., Parameshwaran, S., Gee, J., Yushkevich, P., Oguz, B.: Fully automated placental volume quantification from 3d ultrasound for prediction of small-for-gestational-age infants. Journal of Ultrasound in Medicine **41**(6), 1509–1524 (2022)
25. Schwartz, N., Sammel, M.D., Leite, R., Parry, S.: First-trimester placental ultrasound and maternal serum markers as predictors of small-for-gestational-age infants. American journal of obstetrics and gynecology **211**(3), 253–e1 (2014)
26. Stevenson, G.N., Collins, S.L., Ding, J., Impey, L., Noble, J.A.: 3-d ultrasound segmentation of the placenta using the random walker algorithm: Reliability and agreement. Ultrasound in Medicine & Biology **41**(12), 3182–3193 (2015)
27. Tu, Z., Gu, L., Wang, X., Jiang, B.: Ultrasound sam adapter: Adapting sam for breast lesion segmentation in ultrasound images. arXiv:2404.14837 (2024)
28. Wang, H., Guo, S., Ye, J., Deng, Z., Cheng, J., Li, T., Chen, J., Su, Y., Huang, Z., Shen, Y., et al.: Sam-med3d. arXiv:2310.15161 (2023)
29. Wang, J., Li, H., Hu, D., Tao, Y.K., Oguz, I.: Novel oct mosaicking pipeline with feature-and pixel-based registration. arXiv:2311.13052 (2023)
30. Wang, Y., Ge, X., Ma, H., Qi, S., Zhang, G., Yao, Y.: Deep learning in medical ultrasound image analysis: a review. IEEE Access **9**, 54310–54324 (2021)
31. Wong, H.E., Rakic, M., Guttag, J., Dalca, A.V.: Scribbleprompt: Fast and flexible interactive segmentation for any medical image. arXiv:2312.07381 (2023)
32. Xu, X., Sanford, T., Turkbey, B., Xu, S., Wood, B.J., Yan, P.: Shadow-consistent semi-supervised learning for prostate ultrasound segmentation. IEEE TMI (2021)
33. Yao, X., Liu, H., Hu, D., Lu, D., Lou, A., Li, H., Deng, R., Arenas, G., Oguz, B., Schwartz, N., Byram, B., Oguz, I.: False negative/positive control for sam on noisy medical images. In: Medical Imaging 2024: Image Processing. SPIE (2024)
34. Zimmer, V.A., Gomez, A., Skelton, E., Wright, R., Wheeler, G., Deng, S., Ghavami, N., Lloyd, K., Matthew, J., Kainz, B., Rueckert, D., Hajnal, J., Schnabel, J.: Placenta segmentation in ultrasound imaging: Addressing sources of uncertainty and limited field-of-view. Medical image analysis **83**, 102639 (2023)

Enhanced Uncertainty Estimation in Ultrasound Image Segmentation with MSU-Net

Rohini Banerjee[✉], Cecilia G. Morales, and Artur Dubrawski

Auton Lab, Carnegie Mellon University, Pittsburgh, PA 15213, USA
{rohinib,cgmorale,awd}@andrew.cmu.edu

Abstract. Efficient intravascular access in trauma and critical care significantly impacts patient outcomes. However, the availability of skilled medical personnel in austere environments is often limited. Despite advances in autonomous needle insertion, inaccuracies in vessel segmentation predictions pose risks. Understanding the uncertainty of predictive models in ultrasound imaging is crucial for assessing their reliability. We introduce MSU-Net, a novel multistage approach for training an ensemble of U-Nets to yield ultrasound image segmentation maps. We demonstrate substantial improvements, 27.7% over a single Monte Carlo U-Net, enhancing uncertainty evaluations, model transparency, and trustworthiness. By identifying areas where the model is highly confident, MSU-Net helps to better interpret anatomical details and improve the understanding of vessel locations.

Keywords: Uncertainty Quantification · Ultrasound Image Segmentation · Trustworthy and Interpretable Medical AI

1 Introduction

Trauma, the leading cause of death among young individuals in the U.S. [24], often results in blood loss, which requires rapid fluid resuscitation for vital organ oxygenation. In austere settings, accessing timely medical care can be challenging due to limited access, dangerous conditions, time constraints, or the absence of medical infrastructure. Autonomous robotic systems can assist in intravenous fluid administration when medical experts are unavailable, providing support in emergencies. These systems can also guide non-experts in accurate performance of phlebotomy tasks, empowering them to contribute effectively in dire medical situations.

Ultrasound imaging is widely used for locating vessels due to its affordability, speed, safety, and portability, unlike CT or MRI imaging that use ionizing

---

R. Banerjee and C. G. Morales—These authors contributed equally to this work.

Supplementary Information The online version contains supplementary material available at https://doi.org/10.1007/978-3-031-73647-6_14.

radiation [8]. Despite advancements in autonomous needle insertion into blood vessels [8], a critical challenge persists: inaccurate vessel predictions can lead to severe consequences. For example, incorrectly predicting two adjacent vessels as a single one could lead to laceration of the vessel wall and cause hemorrhage upon needle insertion [17]. Both medical personnel and automated tools need to assess the certainty of their estimates of vessel location and structure to mitigate this risk [16]. Building a model that communicates its uncertainty becomes essential to help users focus their attention and actions on where the model is confident, such as guiding needle insertion accurately within vessel segments. Our contributions include: (1) introducing MSU-Net, a novel Multistaged Monte Carlo U-Net, demonstrating significant advancements in uncertainty quantification; (2) the first known improvement in uncertainty estimation for ultrasound images.

2 Related Works

2.1 Uncertainty Quantification in Deep Learning

Uncertainty quantification is vital for assessing Artificial Intelligence (AI) model reliability. Traditionally, the frequentist approach relies on a single point estimate of network weights and uses class likelihoods as confidence measures. However, these likelihoods often overestimate accuracy [10], and the popular metric used to quantify confidence, expected calibration error, has been criticized for bias and inconsistency [9]. This motivates the need for alternative approaches to accurately quantify model uncertainty.

Predictive uncertainty includes aleatoric and epistemic components [7]. Aleatoric uncertainty accounts for inherent noise in observations, while epistemic uncertainty arises from limited training data and model parameter uncertainty. Recent advancements in Bayesian inference and Bayesian neural networks have provided robust frameworks to quantify both forms of uncertainty by estimating posterior distributions over model weights. Gal and Ghahramani [6] introduced Monte Carlo (MC) dropout for Bayesian inference in deep learning, using dropout for stochastic forward passes to approximate Bayesian variational inference. Bayesian approximation using MC dropout has been extensively applied: Kendall and Gal [12] developed Bayesian SegNet for scene understanding, while Dechesne and Lassalle [3] used it in U-Net for high-accuracy image segmentation. Yet, single-model architectures are now supplanted by model ensembles due to difficulties in capturing inherent variability.

2.2 Multistage Neural Network Ensembles

Ensembling multiple models offers various strategies to encourage diversity and accuracy. Techniques such as bagging [2], stacking [26], and boosting [5] achieve diversity. While non-Bayesian deep ensembles improve uncertainty estimation over single models [15], they are limited by naïve aggregation strategies such as simple or weighted averaging or majority vote [27]. Yang et al. [28] improves traditional ensembles by using a secondary neural network to adaptively assign weights, leveraging the flexibility and non-linear modeling of neural networks.

Lai et al. [14] designed a multistage reliability-based neural network ensemble learning approach to discriminate good from poor creditors. Similarly, Yin and Hu [29] designed Paw-Net, a two-stage ensemble for semantic segmentation, which achieves higher Intersection-over-Union (IoU) scores by integrating outputs of multiple U-Nets specialized in different classes. Our MSU-Net architecture builds on these methods by overproducing candidate U-Nets, selecting them based on decorrelation, and combining their outputs using a Monte Carlo U-Net approach for precise segmentation.

3 Methods

3.1 Monte Carlo U-Net (MCU-Net)

We introduce stochasticity into our inference process by incorporating dropout layers into the decoder of our chosen U-Net architecture as in MCU-Net [21]. MCU-Net is henceforth referred to as our baseline model. We approximate Bayesian inference by conducting T forward passes, MC samples, of the U-Net during testing. Our empirical results show no significant improvement beyond $T = 30$. Our model outputs both logits and logit variances to use for segmentation and epistemic uncertainty maps, with $[\widehat{p}_t, \widehat{\sigma}_t^2] = f^{\widehat{\omega}_t}(x)$ representing the t-th forward pass of MCU-Net with learned weights $\widehat{\omega}_t$. Given sigmoid activation, $\boldsymbol{\sigma}_{\text{SIG}}$, the ensemble prediction is aggregated by averaging individual model outputs, $\boldsymbol{\sigma}_{\text{SIG}}(\widehat{p}_t)$, across all T samples. Similarly, the raw epistemic uncertainty map is obtained by averaging logit variances across all MC samples and the aleatoric uncertainty map is computed as in [21].

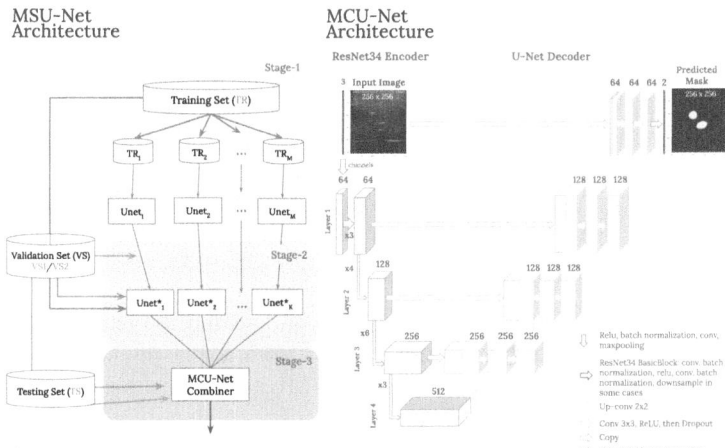

Fig. 1. Proposed MSU-Net architecture. U-Nets are trained on bootstrap samples and validated on VS1. Decorrelated ensemble members are chosen using VS2.

3.2 Multistage U-Net (MSU-Net)

The MSU-Net architecture, illustrated in Fig. 1, has three main stages: (1) ensembling, (2) candidate selection, and (3) combining. In stage 1, we train multiple models, or *candidates*, using bootstrapping. This is achieved by repeatedly sampling the training dataset with replacement to generate M training subsets, each of size n_{TR}. We train $M = 15$ bootstrapped models [15] and optimize hyperparameters, such as training epochs, using the VS1 validation set. Early stopping is applied to each candidate to prevent model overfitting.

In stage 2, we select K candidates to form a diverse and efficient ensemble, aiming to minimizing correlation and reduce computational cost. Using the decorrelation maximization method from [14], as shown in Section 7.1 of the supplementary material, we compute the Brier score loss matrix from models $f_1^{\widehat{\omega}_1}, f_2^{\widehat{\omega}_2}, \cdots, f_M^{\widehat{\omega}_M}$ on a validation set VS2 within a specified region of interest (ROI) selected to address class imbalance as shown in Fig. 2. We calculate the mean, variance, and covariance of the Brier scores to build the correlation matrix R, which shows the correlation between each pair of models. The matrix R is represented in block form for each candidate model $f_i^{\widehat{\omega}_i}$ as

$$R \xrightarrow{\text{extract principle submatrix}} \begin{bmatrix} R_{-i} & r_i \\ r_i^T & 1 \end{bmatrix} \quad (1)$$

where R_{-i} is the principle submatrix of R resulting from deleting the ith row and ith column. Subsequently, we compute the plural-correlation coefficient [19]

$$\rho_i^2 = r_i^T R_{-i}^{-1} r_i \quad (2)$$

by which candidate $f_i^{\widehat{\omega}_i}$ is kept if $\rho_i^2 \leq \theta$ for some threshold θ, else discarded, in order to build our final ensemble. Empirical trials testing θ thresholds indicate that $K = 3$ performs almost equally as well as $K = 15$, suggesting that minimal additional training will suffice for our new architecture.

In stage 3, we train a final MCU-Net combiner taking ensemble member outputs as inputs and outputting segmentation maps. We compute the segmentation and uncertainty maps of MSU-Net analogous to MCU-Net.

4 Experiments

Dataset and Training. We used an ultrasound scanning system described by Morales et al. [18] to scan the CAE Blue Phantom anthropomorphic gel model simulating femoral vessels. Equipped with a 5MHz linear transducer, the system can scan up to 5 cm in depth, producing 2D transverse ultrasound images. Expert clinicians annotated these images using the Computer Vision Annotating Tool (CVAT) [22], followed by cropping and resizing to 256 × 256 pixels. The dataset was split into training (1392 images), validation (907 images), and testing (856 images). The validation set was further randomly split into two disjoint sets, VS1 and VS2.

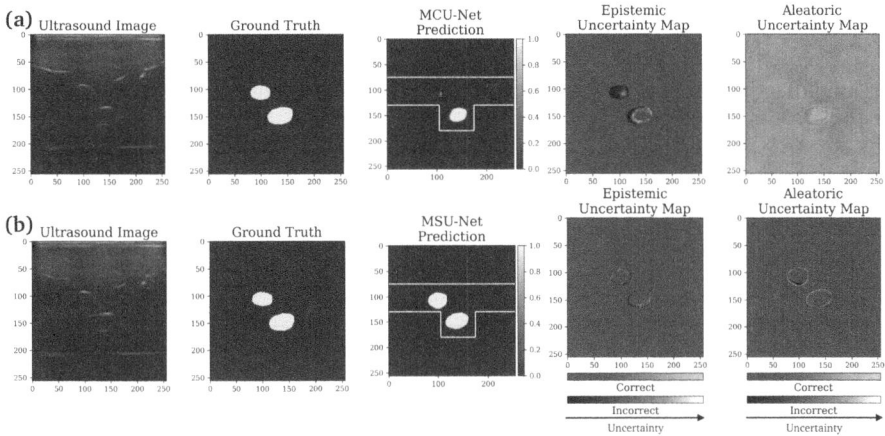

Fig. 2. Qualitative uncertainty maps for (a) MCU-Net and (b) MSU-Net. Darker colors show lower uncertainty; lighter colors show higher. Evaluations are confined to the white-outlined region of interest (ROI) to address class imbalance. (Color figure online)

For image segmentation, we used U-Net with a ResNet34 backbone in Pytorch, using the Segmentation Models library [11] pretrained on ImageNet, and trained on NVIDIA RTX A6000 GPUs. MC Dropout was integrated by adding dropout layers after each ReLU activation in the decoder [12,13], with drop rates of 0.4 and 0.5 empirically tested to maintain performance. MSU-Net incorporated bagging for ensembling and the plural-correlation coefficient as a correlation metric. Training involved a batch size of 8, Adam optimizer with a learning rate of 0.0001, and a combined Dice and Cross Entropy loss function.

Distribution Divergence Estimation. Model quality depends on accurately reflecting uncertainty: low for correct predictions and high for incorrect ones, improving calibration and user trust [23]. We use the Rényi divergence (RD) statistic, a generalization of Kullback-Leibler (KL) divergence, to measure dissimilarity between two probability distributions p and q. RD quantifies the compression gain achievable by mixing two codes, p and q [4].

We use a nonparametric estimator of RD that is conditionally L_2-consistent using only k-nearest-neighbor statistics to reduce computational effort [20]. For i.i.d. samples $X_{1:n_0} = (X_1, \cdots, X_{n_0})$ from a distribution with density p and $Y_{1:n_1} = (Y_1, \cdots, Y_{n_1})$ from a distribution with density q, $\rho_k(i)$ denotes the k-th nearest neighbor of observation X_i in $X_{1:n_0}$ and $v_k(i)$ the k-th nearest neighbor of X_i in $Y_{1:n_1}$. With $B_{k,\alpha} = \frac{\Gamma(k)^2}{\Gamma(k-\alpha+1)\Gamma(k+\alpha-1)}$ where $\Gamma(x) = (x-1)!$, we can estimate RD by:

$$\widehat{R}_\alpha(p\,\|\,q) = \frac{1}{\alpha-1} \ln\left(n_0^{-1} \sum_{i=1}^{n_0} \left(\frac{(n_0-1)\rho_k(i)}{n_1 v_k(i)}\right)^{1-\alpha} B_{k,\alpha} \right) \quad (3)$$

We use the estimated RD to measure the ability of a model to distinguish correct (p) from incorrect predictions (q). We conduct permutation testing to assess deterministicity and bootstrapping to obtain confidence intervals for the results. Nearest neighbor estimators are sensitive to perturbations in the underlying distribution, and hence their limited variance cannot be consistently estimated by a naïve Efron-type bootstrap [1]. Since this behavior may result in a non-negligible positive bias in bootstrap estimates, we instead apply a direct M-out-of-N (MooN) type bootstrap [25] for this metric, shown in Algorithm 1.

Algorithm 1. M-out-of-N bootstrapping

1: **Input:** Distributions p, q. Degree of undersampling, $\gamma \in (0, 1]$.
2: **Output:** Bootstrap estimates of nonparametric Rényi divergence statistic
3: $n_0, n_1 \leftarrow |p|, |q|$
4: $\alpha_n \leftarrow \frac{n_0}{n_1}$
5: $N^* \leftarrow \lfloor (n_0 + n_1)^\gamma + \frac{1}{2} \rfloor$
6: $n_0^* \leftarrow \lfloor \frac{\alpha_n}{1+\alpha_n} N^* + \frac{1}{2} \rfloor$
7: $n_1^* \leftarrow N^* - n_0^*$
8: samples $\leftarrow$ []
9: **for** i in range 1000 **do**
10:    boot_p $\leftarrow$ resample(p, n_samples=n_0^*) with replacement
11:    boot_q $\leftarrow$ resample(q, n_samples=n_1^*) with replacement
12:    samples $\stackrel{+}{=}$ [$\widehat{R}_{\alpha=0.85}$(boot_p, boot_q)]
13: **end for**
14: **return** samples
---

5 Results and Discussion

We evaluate MSU-Net using quantitative and qualitative metrics averaged over the predefined ROI. Figure 3 displays model uncertainty distributions on the test set. We use kernel density estimation with a Gaussian kernel and optimal bandwidth via Silverman's rule of thumb to visualize difference in means between correct ($\widehat{\mu}_{corr}$) and incorrect ($\widehat{\mu}_{incorr}$) prediction uncertainty distributions over 100,000 samples, denoted as $\Delta\widehat{\mu}$. To quantify separation between these distributions with RD, we select $k = 4$ for k-nearest neighbors and $\alpha = 0.85$ for numerical stability and interpretability [20]. We perform $B = 1000$ permutations and bootstrapped samples. For MooN-type bootstrap, $\gamma = 0.8$ is selected to maintain the largest proportion of original data while achieving the closest coverage probability of 0.95 for 95% confidence intervals. Our final results are displayed in Table 1.

Figure 4a shows training behavior for both models. MSU-Net shows a more stable convergence and consistently outperforms MCU-Net during validation performed after each epoch. MSU-Net achieves 27.7% better mean Dice Score

Table 1. Model quality in ROI. Arrows show direction of better performance.

	$\widehat{\mu}_{corr}$	$\widehat{\mu}_{incorr}$	$\Delta\widehat{\mu}(\uparrow)$	$\widehat{R}_\alpha(corr \| incorr)(\uparrow)$	95% CI on $\widehat{R}_\alpha$	p-val($\downarrow$)
MCU-Net	7.230	11.229	3.999	0.429	[0.426, 0.453]	0.003
MSU-Net	20.783	33.876	**13.093**	**0.638**	[0.603, 0.667]	0.003

Table 2. Model performance in ROI on test dataset.

	Mean DSC($\uparrow$)	Specificity($\uparrow$)	Sensitivity($\uparrow$)	FPR($\downarrow$)	FNR($\downarrow$)
MCU-Net	0.648	**0.998**	0.673	**0.002**	0.327
MSU-Net	**0.925**	0.996	**0.890**	0.004	**0.110**

Coefficient (DSC) and a significant improvement in sensitivity and false negative rate scores at alpha level 0.05, while other metrics remain similar. We additionally utilize precision-recall curves, seen in Fig. 4b, which are resilient to unbalanced classes since they only focus on positive class predictions. Performance results are displayed in Table 2.

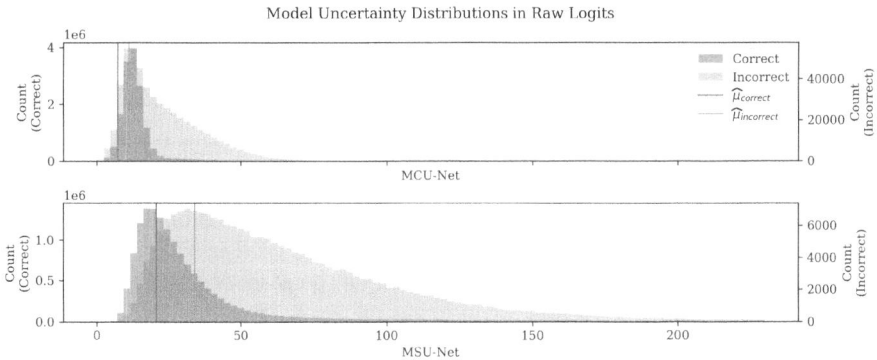

Fig. 3. Epistemic uncertainty distributions for correct (blue) and incorrect (orange) predictions for MCU-Net (top) and MSU-Net (bottom). Our approach yields a markedly better differentiation of correct and incorrect predictions. (Color figure online)

Permutation tests for MCU-Net and MSU-Net, p-val ≤ 0.003 for both, indicate that the observed separation between correct and incorrect predictions is statistically significant. Yet, at the 95% confidence level, we see no overlap between their confidence intervals, showing that the ability of MSU-Net to distinguish correct from incorrect predictions is significantly better than that of MCU-Net.

Qualitative uncertainty maps [3] visually validate our findings and capture local variations in model performance. MCU-Net exhibits indiscriminately low epistemic uncertainty in large patches where the model fails to segment a vessel and is highly sensitive to noise in the background class as shown by high aleatoric uncertainty outside of the vessels in Fig. 2. In contrast, MSU-Net provides more interpretable uncertainty values, demonstrating increased epistemic uncertainty for semantically challenging pixels at the bottom of vessels and decreased epistemic uncertainty for clearer vessel tops. Furthermore, MSU-Net excels by capturing the intrinsic variability in vessel shapes. This is evident from the increased aleatoric uncertainty around vessel walls, reflecting the diverse vessel structures inherent to each individual or model.

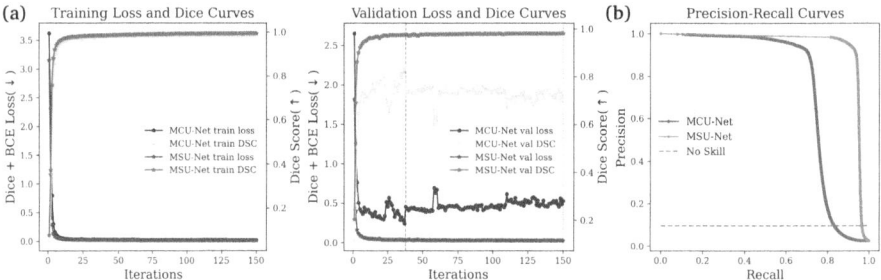

Fig. 4. (a) Training (left) and validation (right) curves for MCU-Net and MSU-Net. Early stopping delineated by gray lines. (b) Precision-recall curves. (Color figure online)

MSU-Net generally outperforms MCU-Net. Although it performs marginally worse at specificity and false positive rates (FPR), the precision-recall curves from Fig. 4b indicate that MSU-Net achieves an average precision score of 0.936, which is 18% higher than MCU-Net's score of 0.755, compared to the baseline score of 0.09 for a 'no-skill' classifier. As such, at the same level of recall, MSU-Net correctly classifies a greater proportion of pixels that are actually vessels than MCU-Net. Crucially, MSU-Net achieves a considerably lower false negative rate (FNR) than MCU-Net. In this context, not recognizing a real vessel can have more severe consequences for a critically injured person than mistakenly identifying a vessel that isn't actually there. MSU-Net improves credibility not only through higher quality results, but also through more accurate results while avoiding potentially disastrous deficiencies of predictive modeling in the context of medical image segmentation. Additionally, we conduct a preliminary ablation study, as shown in supplementary material Section 7.2, observing clear improvements when using a multistage approach over a bagging deep ensemble.

6 Conclusion

Our proposed multistage learning ensemble framework, MSU-Net, significantly improves uncertainty quantification and accuracy in femoral vessel segmentation in ultrasound images, outperforming traditional Monte Carlo U-Nets. The integration of bagging and decorrelation techniques ensures that the ensemble models are diverse and robust. Our results indicate a 27.7% improvement in the mean Dice Score, with better sensitivity and lower false negative rates, increasing transparency and trustworthiness. These advancements are achieved despite minimal additional training, making it a valuable tool for guiding autonomous systems and assisting non-experts in high-stakes medical environments. MSU-Net's differentiation between correct and incorrect predictions, measured by Rényi divergence and observed in qualitative uncertainty maps, highlights its ability to identify and address segmentation errors. Future research will focus on refining ensemble selection and validating our findings on live animal and human data, extending beyond the current phantom data and binary segmentation context.

Acknowledgments. Authors thank Nico Zevallos for gathering experiment data. This work was partially supported by the U.S. Dept. of Defense contracts W81XWH-19-C0083 and W81XWH-19-C0101.

Disclosure of Interests. The authors have no competing interests to declare that are relevant to the content of this article.

References

1. Abadie, A., Imbens, G.W.: On the failure of the bootstrap for matching estimators. Econometrica **76**(6), 1537–1557 (2008). https://doi.org/10.3982/ECTA6474, https://onlinelibrary.wiley.com/doi/abs/10.3982/ECTA6474
2. Breiman, L.: Bagging predictors. Machine Learning **24**(2), 123–140 (1996). https://doi.org/10.1007/BF00058655, https://doi.org/10.1007/BF00058655
3. Dechesne, C., Lassalle, P., Lefèvre, S.: Bayesian u-net: Estimating uncertainty in semantic segmentation of earth observation images. Remote Sensing **13**(19) (2021). https://doi.org/10.3390/rs13193836, https://www.mdpi.com/2072-4292/13/19/3836
4. van Erven, T., Harremoes, P.: Rényi divergence and kullback-leibler divergence. IEEE Transactions on Information Theory **60**(7), 3797-3820 (2014). https://doi.org/10.1109/tit.2014.2320500, http://dx.doi.org/10.1109/TIT.2014.2320500
5. Freund, Y., Schapire, R.E.: A short introduction to boosting (1999), https://api.semanticscholar.org/CorpusID:9621074
6. Gal, Y., Ghahramani, Z.: Dropout as a bayesian approximation: Representing model uncertainty in deep learning (2016)
7. Ghoshal, B., Tucker, A., Sanghera, B., Lup Wong, W.: Estimating uncertainty in deep learning for reporting confidence to clinicians in medical image segmentation and diseases detection. Computational Intelligence **37**(2), 701–734 (2021). https://doi.org/10.1111/coin.12411, https://onlinelibrary.wiley.com/doi/abs/10.1111/coin.12411
8. Goel, R., Morales, C.G., Singh, M., Dubrawski, A., Galeotti, J.M., Choset, H.: Motion-aware needle segmentation in ultrasound images. https://api.semanticscholar.org/CorpusID:265660400
9. Gruber, S.G., Buettner, F.: Better uncertainty calibration via proper scores for classification and beyond (2024)

10. Guo, C., Pleiss, G., Sun, Y., Weinberger, K.Q.: On calibration of modern neural networks. In: Proceedings of the 34th International Conference on Machine Learning - Volume 70. p. 1321-1330. ICML'17, JMLR.org (2017)
11. Iakubovskii, P.: Segmentation models pytorch. https://github.com/qubvel/segmentation_models.pytorch (2019)
12. Kendall, A., Badrinarayanan, V., Cipolla, R.: Bayesian segnet: Model uncertainty in deep convolutional encoder-decoder architectures for scene understanding (2016)
13. Kim, B.J., Choi, H., Jang, H., Lee, D., Kim, S.W.: How to use dropout correctly on residual networks with batch normalization (2023)
14. Lai, K.K., Yu, L., Wang, S., Zhou, L.: Credit risk analysis using a reliability-based neural network ensemble model. In: Kollias, S., Stafylopatis, A., Duch, W., Oja, E. (eds.) Artificial Neural Networks – ICANN 2006. pp. 682–690. Springer Berlin Heidelberg, Berlin, Heidelberg (2006)
15. Lakshminarayanan, B., Pritzel, A., Blundell, C.: Simple and scalable predictive uncertainty estimation using deep ensembles (2017)
16. Morales, C.G., Chen, H., Yao, J., Dubrawski, A.: 3d ultrasound reconstruction and visualization tool. In: New Evolutions in Surgical Robotics: Embracing Multi-modal Imaging Guidance, Intelligence, and Bio-inspired Mechanisms. International Conference on Robotics and Automation (ICRA), London, UK (June 2 2023)
17. Morales, C.G., Srikanth, D., Good, J.H., Dufendach, K.A., Dubrawski, A.: Bifurcation identification for ultrasound-driven robotic cannulation. International Conference on Intelligent Robots and Systems (IROS), Abu Dhabi (2024)
18. Morales, C.G., Yao, J., Rane, T., Edman, R., Choset, H., Dubrawski, A.: Reslicing Ultrasound Images for Data Augmentation and Vessel Reconstruction. 2023 IEEE International Conference on Robotics and Automation (ICRA) pp. 2710–2716 (2023), https://www.semanticscholar.org/paper/Reslicing-Ultrasound-Images-for-Data-Augmentation-Morales-Yao/cb3e8ae71dc3c189442427093b9124f35e373790
19. O'Neill, B.: Multiple linear regression and correlation: A geometric analysis (2021)
20. Poczos, B., Schneider, J.: On the estimation of α-divergences. In: Gordon, G., Dunson, D., Dudík, M. (eds.) Proceedings of the Fourteenth International Conference on Artificial Intelligence and Statistics. Proceedings of Machine Learning Research, vol. 15, pp. 609–617. PMLR, Fort Lauderdale, FL, USA (11–13 Apr 2011), https://proceedings.mlr.press/v15/poczos11a.html
21. Seedat, N.: Mcu-net: A framework towards uncertainty representations for decision support system patient referrals in healthcare contexts. CoRR **abs/2007.03995** (2020), https://arxiv.org/abs/2007.03995
22. Sekachev, B., Manovich, N., Zhiltsov, M., Zhavoronkov, A., Kalinin, D., Hoff, B., TOsmanov, Kruchinin, D., Zankevich, A., DmitriySidnev, Markelov, M., Johannes222, Chenuet, M., a andre, telenachos, Melnikov, A., Kim, J., Ilouz, L., Glazov, N., Priya4607, Tehrani, R., Jeong, S., Skubriev, V., Yonekura, S., vugia truong, zliang7, lizhming, Truong, T.: opencv/cvat: v1.1.0 (Aug 2020). https://doi.org/10.5281/zenodo.4009388, https://doi.org/10.5281/zenodo.4009388
23. Shamsi, A., Asgharnezhad, H., Tajally, A., Nahavandi, S., Leung, H.: An uncertainty-aware loss function for training neural networks with calibrated predictions (2023)
24. Wallace, H., Regunath, H.: Fluid resuscitation. StatPearls [Internet] (jan 2024), https://www.ncbi.nlm.nih.gov/books/NBK534791/

25. Walsh, C., Jentsch, C.: Nearest neighbor matching: M-out-of-n bootstrapping without bias correction vs. the naive bootstrap. Econometrics and Statistics (2023). https://doi.org/10.1016/j.ecosta.2023.04.005, https://www.sciencedirect.com/science/article/pii/S245230622300031X
26. Wolpert, D.H.: Stacked generalization. Neural Networks **5**(2), 241–259 (1992). https://doi.org/10.1016/S0893-6080(05)80023-1, https://www.sciencedirect.com/science/article/pii/S0893608005800231
27. Yang, S., Browne, A.: Neural network ensembles: combining multiple models for enhanced performance using a multistage approach. Expert Systems **21**(5), 279–288 (2004). https://doi.org/10.1111/j.1468-0394.2004.00285.x, https://onlinelibrary.wiley.com/doi/abs/10.1111/j.1468-0394.2004.00285.x
28. Yang, S., Browne, A., Picton, P.: Multistage neural network ensembles. vol. 2364, pp. 91–97 (06 2002). https://doi.org/10.1007/3-540-45428-4_9
29. Yin, B., Hu, Q., Zhu, Y., Zhao, C., Zhou, K.: Paw-net: Stacking ensemble deep learning for segmenting scanning electron microscopy images of fine-grained shale samples. Computers and Geosciences **168**, 105218 (2022). https://doi.org/10.1016/j.cageo.2022.105218, https://www.sciencedirect.com/science/article/pii/S0098300422001674

Classification and Detection

Multi-site Class-Incremental Learning with Weighted Experts in Echocardiography

Kit M. Bransby[1,2(✉)], Woo-Jin Cho Kim[1], Jorge Oliveira[1], Alex Thorley[1], Arian Beqiri[1], Alberto Gomez[1], and Agisilaos Chartsias[1]

[1] Ultromics Ltd., Oxford, UK
agis.chartsias@ultromics.com
[2] Queen Mary University of London, London, UK
k.m.bransby@qmul.ac.uk

Abstract. Building an echocardiography view classifier that maintains performance in real-life cases requires diverse multi-site data, and frequent updates with newly available data to mitigate model drift. Simply fine-tuning on new datasets results in "catastrophic forgetting", and cannot adapt to variations of view labels between sites. Alternatively, collecting all data on a single server and re-training may not be feasible as data sharing agreements may restrict image transfer, or datasets may only become available at different times. Furthermore, time and cost associated with re-training grows with every new dataset. We propose a class-incremental learning method which learns an expert network for each dataset, and combines all expert networks with a score fusion model. The influence of "unqualified experts" is minimised by weighting each contribution with a learnt in-distribution score. These weights promote transparency as the contribution of each expert is known during inference. Instead of using the original images, we use learned features from each dataset, which are easier to share and raise fewer licensing and privacy concerns. We validate our work on six datasets from multiple sites, demonstrating significant reductions in training time while improving view classification performance.

Keywords: class-incremental learning · multi-site learning · echocardiography

1 Introduction

Echocardiography (echo) view classification is often a necessary first step in automated image interpretation and analysis, as different tasks may require different views as input [19]. Several deep learning methods have been proposed to this end [10,14,19,22] demonstrating excellent performance. To generalise and maintain performance in real-life cases, view classifiers need to be trained on a diverse multi-site dataset to accommodate varying acquisition, demographic,

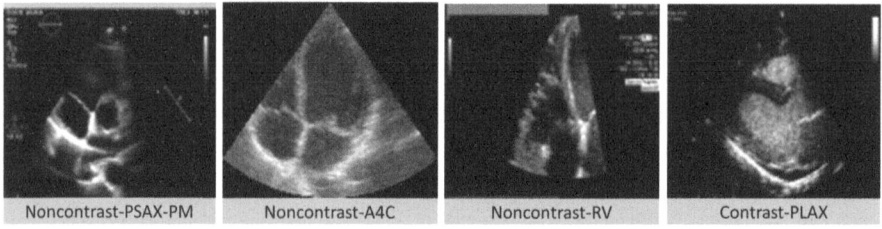

Fig. 1. Examples of different views from WASE, CAMUS, Medstar, StG datasets.

and clinical parameters. However, these parameters may change over time, e.g. with machine upgrades, modification of protocols, or changes in demographics. Such changes require updating the classifier with newly available data to mitigate model drift [17]. Naive approaches like fine-tuning on a new dataset may result in "catastrophic forgetting" [15], in which previous knowledge is forgotten at the expense of the new information. Retaining previous knowledge while learning on new data is the goal of incremental-learning [20].

Furthermore, newly available data (e.g. from sites with different protocols) may have different sets of view labels. Labels can be characterised as "base", "novel", or "overlapping", depending on whether they are present in the original data, the new data, or both. The goal of class-incremental learning (CIL) [20] is to learn to classify the increasing label set over time. A straightforward solution is to retrain using all data combined. However, this is not always feasible as data sharing agreements may limit access or transfer outside the acquisition site; or different datasets may be available at different times. In addition, retraining a classifier when a new dataset becomes available is inefficient as the total training time and cost grows considerably with the number and size of datasets.

A common approach for CIL is to use a single model, and update parts or all of the weights using knowledge distillation [4,12,16] or weight regularisation [1,9]. Others learn additional parameters with dynamic architecture changes [18,21,24], or by duplicating the model for novel data and pruning [25]. Wu et al. [23] expand on this by duplicating and fine-tuning a base model for each new dataset, resulting in set of expert model branches, each specialised on a single dataset. They combine the output logits of the independently trained branches using a learnt score fusion (SF) network that enables knowledge transfer between base and novel classes. This leverages shared information between representations in different branches, but is sensitive to one branch contributing ineffective information to another branch. We term this the "unqualified expert" problem and may happen when there are differences in data distributions, caused for instance by different label sets, patient demographics or scanner manufacturers. As a result view predictions for out-of-distribution (o.o.d.) images can be incorrect, but also highly confident.

In this paper we address the problem of building an echo view classifier model with multiple datasets from different sites (see Fig. 1) that are not simultaneously available and have different, overlapping sets of labels. To this end, we build upon [23], and mitigate the "unqualified expert" problem by weighing the contribution of each branch by a learnt in-distribution (i.d.) score. This minimises the influence of logits which are o.o.d. for a given input image, while maximising the i.d. logits. Our weighting improves transparency as the contribution of each model is known during inference, indicating the similarity between input data and different training sets. Our method has the benefit of using learnt features as input rather than images, which provides a simple workaround in cases where licensing prevents image sharing but not sharing of byproduct features.

Contributions: We apply CIL to echo view classification and propose a new i.d. score weighting that improves performance by minimising the influence of "unqualified experts" and promotes transparency. We validate our method on six datasets from multiple sites, demonstrating improved view classification without needing to transfer images out of remote servers. By bypassing the need for retraining with all data, the cumulative training time and cost is reduced with further reductions achieved through more incremental steps.

2 Method

2.1 Problem Setting

Given a dataset $D = \{(x_i, y_i)\}_{i=1}^{N}$, where x_i represents an ultrasound image and y_i denotes the corresponding ground truth view label, the objective of view classification is to learn an image encoder ϕ and linear classifier $W \in \mathbb{R}^{k \times |\mathcal{Y}|}$, where $\mathcal{Y}$ is the set of labels in D and k is the size of the image features. The view label is learnt by minimising the cross entropy loss between y and the label prediction $\hat{y} = \sigma(\phi(x)W)$ where $\sigma(\cdot)$ is a softmax function.

We first train a base model $\mathcal{M}_b = \{\phi_b, W_{bb}\}$ on a large dataset $\mathcal{D}_b$ with label set $\mathcal{Y}_b$ of base classes. We consider t incremental steps $n \in \{n1, n2, .., nt\}$ each with a dataset $\mathcal{D}_n$ and label set $\mathcal{Y}_n$. There can be varying degrees of intersection between base classes $\mathcal{Y}_b$ and the new label set $\mathcal{Y}_n$. For instance, there may be novel classes not present in the base classes ($\mathcal{Y}_n \cap \mathcal{Y}_b = \emptyset$) or overlapping classes ($\mathcal{Y}_b \cap \mathcal{Y}_n \neq \emptyset$). Our goal is to accurately predict all classes, regardless of whether they are introduced in an incremental step, are novel, base, or overlapping.

Simply combining base and incremental datasets into a single set and retraining $\mathcal{M}_b$ from scratch is not ideal due to cost, time, and restrictive data licensing as motivated in Sect. 1. Similarly, naively fine-tuning $\mathcal{M}_b$ on successive incremental datasets $\mathcal{D}_{n1}, \mathcal{D}_{n2}, .., \mathcal{D}_{nt}$ is difficult due to the changing size of the label set, and ultimately results in catastrophic forgetting of the base classes $\mathcal{Y}_b$.

2.2 Score Fusion

We follow Wu et al. [23] where $\mathcal{M}_b$ is cloned and fine-tuned for each incremental dataset $\mathcal{D}_n$, yielding $t + 1$ expert models $\{\mathcal{M}_b, \mathcal{M}_{n1}, .., \mathcal{M}_{nt}\}$[1]. This approach

---

[1] We unfreeze all layers instead of freezing the first two convolutional blocks as in [23], which we find improves performance.

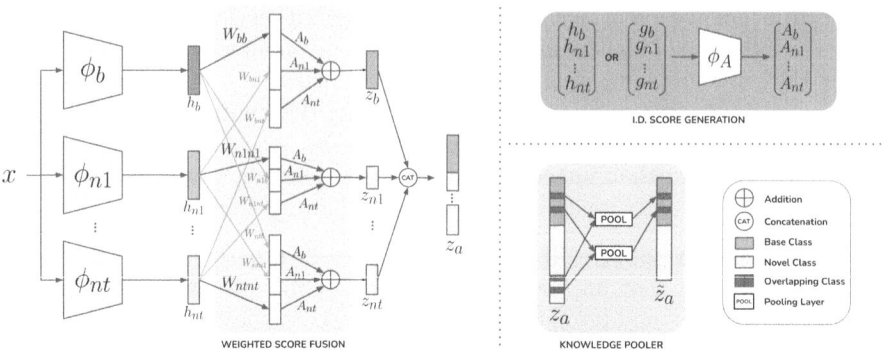

Fig. 2. Network architecture: predictions from expert branches are re-weighted by an in-distribution score to minimise the influence of unqualified experts.

mitigates the problem of forgetting by retaining all weights; however, it introduces a new challenge of selecting or combining experts during inference.

This is addressed with SF [23] that allows an expert to make a logit prediction on its label set as well as the label sets of other experts. This allows for knowledge sharing between branches and is useful for overlapping classes or shared semantics. Specifically, the weights of an expert $\{\phi_d, W_{dd}\}$, where $d \in \{b, n1, .., nt\}$, are frozen and used to compute a logit score $z_{dd} = h_d W_{dd}$ for its label set $\mathcal{Y}_d$ using feature vector $h_d \in \mathbb{R}^k$ and the weight W_{dd}. To compute logit predictions on label sets of other experts $\mathcal{Y}_{d'}$, each expert learns an additional set of weights $W_{dd'}$ for all $d' \in \{b, n1, .., nt\}, d \neq d'$. On each branch, we compute the final logits z_d by summing the logits contributed by each expert as follows:

$$z_d = \sum_{d'=b,n1,..,nt} h_d W_{dd'} \qquad (1)$$

The logits from each branch are concatenated to give z_a. As overlapping classes may be present between incremental steps, a logit for the same class may appear several times in z_a. We follow [23] with a "knowledge pooler" to obtain final logits $\tilde{z}_a$ by maxpooling the overlapping classes (See Fig. 2). This enables information sharing between experts, however some experts may have significant differences in knowledge and contribute unhelpful information that deteriorates performance. In the next section, we address the "unqualified expert" problem.

2.3 Weighted Score Fusion

Given an input image, we compute an i.d. score to weigh each expert's logits such that the influence of unqualified o.o.d experts is minimised and the influence of i.d. experts is maximised. We do so by learning an attention-like weighting vector $A \in \mathbb{R}^{|d|}$ using a feed-forward network ϕ_A consisting of 3 linear layers, the first two with ReLU activation and the last with a softmax.

Table 1. Frequency of view labels in training, validation and test sets.

View	Contrast	Train				Validation				Internal Test				External Test	
		Wase	Camus	Mstr	StG	Wase	Camus	Mstr	StG	Wase	Camus	Mstr	StG	Mahi	UoC
A2C	✓	0	0	0	1182	0	0	0	132	0	0	0	116	845	36
A3C	✓	0	0	0	1208	0	0	0	137	0	0	0	119	429	23
A4C	✓	0	0	0	1218	0	0	0	138	0	0	0	119	726	58
PLAX	✓	0	0	0	923	0	0	0	125	0	0	0	86	6	4
A2C	✗	4361	407	886	0	559	79	87	0	559	48	136	0	716	944
A3C	✗	4012	0	900	0	501	0	87	0	492	0	108	0	679	493
A4C	✗	6474	407	1668	0	811	42	166	0	801	48	202	0	825	1806
A5C	✗	1127	0	355	0	127	0	40	0	138	0	44	0	147	145
PLAX	✗	4661	0	1176	0	614	0	125	0	566	0	138	0	929	1072
PLAX-AV	✗	1480	0	223	0	190	0	24	0	185	0	23	0	306	113
PSAX-AV	✗	3936	0	448	0	488	0	44	0	515	0	60	0	597	612
PSAX-PM	✗	3351	0	755	0	420	0	93	0	435	0	80	0	310	543
RV	✗	0	0	462	0	0	0	72	0	0	0	60	0	60	318
SC	✗	0	0	589	0	0	0	72	0	0	0	62	0	482	328
SC-IVC	✗	0	0	398	0	0	0	47	0	0	0	49	0	242	275
Total		29402	814	7860	4531	3710	84	849	532	3691	96	962	440	7299	6700

We propose two strategies to learn A: (1) attention-weighted score fusion (attn-wSF) where the concatenated feature vectors of all experts $h \in \mathbb{R}^{k|d|}$ are used as input to ϕ_A; and (2) neural mean discrepancy weighted score fusion (nmd-wSF), which uses the neural mean discrepancy (nmd) [3] as input. Nmd is an out-of-distribution metric which measures the discrepancy between neural means of an input image and the average neural mean of the i.d. training set. The neural mean is calculated by averaging output activations of the convolutional layers. Like with attn-wSF, we compute a nmd vector g_d for each expert and concatenate them to $g \in \mathbb{R}^{p|d|}$ where p is the size of the nmd vector.

Similar to Eq. 1, we compute the final logits for each branch as follows:

$$z_d = \sum_{d'=b,n1,\ldots,nt} h_d W_{dd'} A_d \qquad (2)$$

2.4 Multi-site Training

Assuming that the incremental datasets are acquired at different medical sites, which often impose data sharing restrictions, we propose a multi-site training paradigm, which does not require transferring the image data. For every step, the view classifier is cloned, transferred into the remote server, and fine-tuned on dataset $\mathcal{D}_n$. We then make five forward passes of the fine-tuned classifier $\mathcal{M}_n$ on randomly augmented data from $\mathcal{D}_n$ to generate five different g and h vectors for each example. We then transfer these vectors back to the local server, which are used as input to train the weighted score fusion network.

Table 2. Quantitative Results for Internal Test Set (WASE, CAMUS, Medstar, StG datasets). Best results in bold, and second best underlined

Experiment	#Experts	Data Transfer	WASE		CAMUS		Medstar		StG		Average	
			Acc	F1	Acc	F1	Acc	F1	Acc	F1	Acc	F1
Fine-Tuning (Constant)	1	None	0.0	0.0	0.0	0.0	0.0	0.0	83.9	83.7	7.0	3.9
Fine-Tuning (Expand)	1	None	1.9	3.1	0.0	0.0	3.9	4.3	85.5	87.2	9.3	4.8
Single Expert (WASE)	1	None	**94.5**	**94.5**	76.0	80.9	65.1	58.7	0.0	0.0	68.6	60.2
Single Expert (CAMUS)	1	None	24.4	15.8	**95.8**	**95.8**	25.3	16.1	0.0	0.0	22.6	13.8
Single Expert (Medstar)	1	None	80.6	83.0	69.8	76.2	80.0	79.5	0.0	0.0	74.2	72.0
Single Expert (StG)	1	None	0.0	0.0	0.0	0.0	0.0	0.0	**94.1**	**94.1**	6.6	3.4
Max Logit [6]	4	None	62.5	71.3	84.4	89.4	63.1	68.4	71.4	81.0	63.8	69.3
MSP [7]	4	None	56.1	61.9	92.7	94.2	45.0	49.2	59.8	72.0	55.0	58.6
Confidence Routing [23]	4	None	63.4	68.6	92.7	94.2	46.7	50.8	51.8	66.0	59.9	63.4
SF [23]	4	Features	93.9	94.0	89.6	90.4	80.3	80.0	92.7	93.6	91.2	91.1
attn-wSF (ours)	4	Features	<u>94.1</u>	94.3	**95.8**	**95.8**	<u>81.4</u>	<u>80.9</u>	<u>93.9</u>	<u>94.0</u>	<u>91.8</u>	<u>91.7</u>
nmd-wSF (ours)	4	Features	**94.5**	<u>94.4</u>	<u>94.8</u>	<u>95.3</u>	80.8	80.5	**94.1**	**94.1**	**91.9**	**91.9**
Combine & Retrain (oracle)	1	Images	<u>94.1</u>	94.2	**95.8**	**95.8**	**82.1**	**82.1**	90.2	90.5	91.6	91.5

3 Experiments and Results

3.1 Datasets

As base dataset $\mathcal{D}_b$, we use WASE-Normals (WASE) [2], a large multi-site proprietary dataset of 2,009 healthy volunteers acquired at 18 sites from 15 countries. We also use three incremental datasets: (1) CAMUS [11], a public dataset acquired from 500 patients at University Hospital of St Etienne, half of which are considered at pathological risk; (2) Medstar WASE-Covid (Medstar) [8], a multi-site proprietary database of 870 patients with COVID-19 at 13 sites from 9 countries; 3) St George's (StG), a proprietary stress echo dataset of 420 patients some with coronary artery disease. We validate our method on an internal test set sampled from the four datasets and an independent external test set from two proprietary datasets: (1) Mazankowski Alberta Heart Institute (MAHI) consisting of 250 patients undergoing chemotherapy with cardiotoxic drugs; (2) University of Chicago (UoC) consisting of 391 patients with cardiomyopathy.

We extract images from 15 echo view labels and artificially decrease the overlap between datasets by removing non-contrast examples from StG and contrast examples from Medstar. As shown in Table 1, the resulting datasets have different label sets with varying degrees of overlap. Each dataset is split into train (80%), validation (10%) and test (10%) sets at a patient level. A single random frame (112×112) was sampled from each echo video. The final dataset has 42,622 train, 5,175 validation, 5,189 internal test, and 13,999 external test frames.

3.2 Implementation and Training

View classifiers use ResNet18 [5] architecture and were trained for 200 epochs on a NVIDIA GeForce RTX 2080Ti with cross-entropy loss, Adam optimiser,

Table 3. Quantitative Results for External Test Set (MAHI, UoC datasets). Best results in bold, and second best underlined

Experiment	# Experts	Data Transfer	MAHI		UoC		Average	
			Acc	F1	Acc	F1	Acc	F1
Fine-Tuning (Constant)	1	None	12.8	10.3	0.7	0.1	7.0	3.9
Fine-Tuning (Expand)	1	None	17.1	13.3	3.8	4.9	10.7	8.2
Single Expert (WASE)	1	None	55.9	45.5	72.9	67.8	64.1	55.1
Single Expert (CAMUS)	1	None	13.1	6.6	32.0	20.4	22.2	13.4
Single Expert (Medstar)	1	None	56.9	51.4	79.0	79.1	69.0	64.1
Single Expert (StG)	1	None	11.2	8.0	0.1	0.0	6.1	3.6
Max Logit [6]	4	None	43.2	44.0	61.2	68.6	51.8	54.7
MSP [7]	4	None	34.4	35.4	55.4	61.6	44.5	46.9
Confidence Routing [23]	4	None	38.2	39.4	57.1	63.2	47.3	49.7
SF [23]	4	Features	<u>72.0</u>	68.3	81.6	80.8	76.6	74.2
attn-wSF (ours)	4	Features	**72.5**	**69.6**	<u>82.6</u>	<u>82.1</u>	**77.4**	**75.6**
nmd-wSF (ours)	4	Features	71.6	<u>69.5</u>	79.8	79.5	75.5	74.3
Combine & Retrain (oracle)	1	Images	71.4	69.0	**82.7**	**82.7**	<u>76.8</u>	<u>75.1</u>

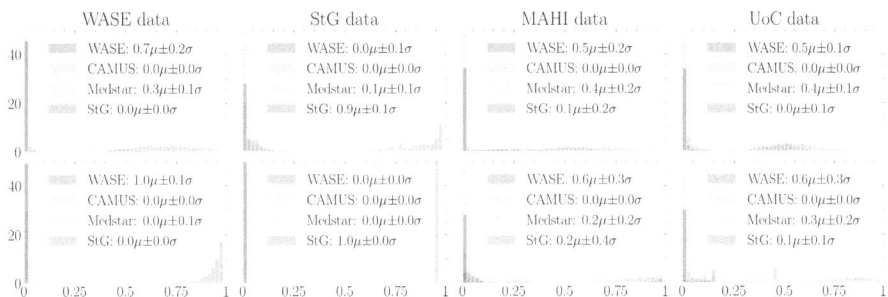

Fig. 3. Distribution of attention scores across a selection of test sets using attn-wSF (top row) and nmd-wSF (bottom row). Note when using nmd, the attention scores are pushed towards 0 and 1 which may reduce generalisability

batch size of 64, and learning rate of 1e−3. The score fusion networks were trained for 50 epochs with the same settings. Weights from the epoch with the highest validation accuracy were saved. Hyperparameters were tuned on a held-out validation set. We evaluate classification performance using accuracy and F1-score metrics. Our method is implemented in PyTorch, and the code is available here: https://github.com/kitbransby/class-incremental-learning-echo.

3.3 Comparison to Existing Methods and Ablation Study

We validate our method on an internal test set (WASE, CAMUS, Medstar, StG) to measure performance on incremental datasets seen during training, and an

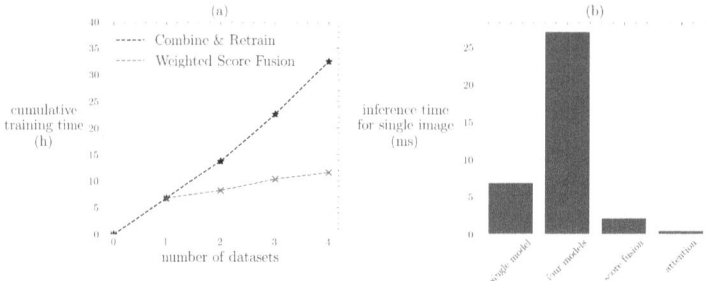

Fig. 4. Efficiency analysis: Cumulative training time (a) and inference time (b).

external set (MAHI, UoC) of data not seen during training to measure generalisability. Results are presented in Tables 2 and 3, respectively.

We demonstrate that naively fine-tuning a classifier on successive datasets results in "catastrophic forgetting". We test two configurations, one where the classifier head is replaced at every step, and a second that expands to accommodate novel classes [13]. These do not require data transfers and perform well on the final dataset (StG) but forget learning from previous data. We also explore other methods that do not require data transfer such as using a single expert and find they perform well on i.d. data but do not generalise well on o.o.d data.

Our primary comparison is to the training oracle where the model is retrained with all data combined at each incremental step. This method is preferred given unlimited compute, time constraints and data access, which are not typically available. On average our method outperforms the oracle on both the internal and external sets, including four out of six individual datasets.

In addition, we ablate our weighting method, demonstrating that attn-wSF and nmd-wSF lead to an improvement in performance when compared to SF [23]. We find that nmd-wSF performs best on the internal test set, however, attn-wSF generalises better to the external test set. We theorise that nmd vectors for each dataset are quite distinct, therefore the i.d. scores are pushed towards 0 and 1 during training (see Fig. 3). When presented with datasets from the external test set the attention mechanism deteriorates as it considers the input image o.o.d. for all experts.

Finally, we compare different confidence-based methods that select the best prediction from multiple experts, these include: (1) Max Logit [6] that selects the max logit for each class; (2) MSP [7], that selects the max softmax for each class; (3) Confidence Routing [23] that selects the expert with the highest softmax probability, and uses its softmax prediction as the final prediction. All such approaches perform poorly, perhaps as classifiers are optimised to be overconfident leading to predictions which are uncorrelated with confidence measures.

Figure 4 shows that our wSF methods reduce the cumulative training time, and this grows significantly with the number of datasets. Our attention-based weighting module has minimal computational overhead. While inference time is larger when using multiple experts, this can be reduced with parallelisation.

4 Conclusion

Echo view classifiers require training on diverse multi-site data, and frequent updates with newly acquired data to avoid model drift. We address the problem of updating such a model using multiple datasets with partly overlapping label sets that are from different sites and may not be simultaneously available. We propose attn-wSF and nmd-wSF, two CIL methods that train and combine predictions from multiple experts models with a learnt i.d. weighting which minimises the influence of o.o.d predictions from "unqualified experts". Our results demonstrate improved view classification with significantly reduced cumulative training time and without needing to transfer images out of remote servers. We aim to extend our wSF methods by training multiple experts within a single branch, which would reduce the memory requirements and inference time.

References

1. Aljundi, R., Babiloni, F., Elhoseiny, M., Rohrbach, M., Tuytelaars, T.: Memory aware synapses: Learning what (not) to forget. In: Proceedings of the European conference on computer vision (ECCV). pp. 139–154 (2018)
2. Asch, F.M., Banchs, J., Price, R., Rigolin, V., Thomas, J.D., Weissman, N.J., Lang, R.M.: Need for a global definition of normative echo values—rationale and design of the world alliance of societies of echocardiography normal values study (wase). Journal of the American Society of Echocardiography **32**(1), 157–162 (2019)
3. Dong, X., Guo, J., Li, A., Ting, W.T., Liu, C., Kung, H.: Neural mean discrepancy for efficient out-of-distribution detection. In: Proceedings of the IEEE/CVF Conference on Computer Vision and Pattern Recognition. pp. 19217–19227 (2022)
4. Douillard, A., Cord, M., Ollion, C., Robert, T., Valle, E.: Podnet: Pooled outputs distillation for small-tasks incremental learning. In: Computer vision–ECCV 2020: 16th European conference, Glasgow, UK, August 23–28, 2020, proceedings, part XX 16. pp. 86–102. Springer (2020)
5. He, K., Zhang, X., Ren, S., Sun, J.: Deep residual learning for image recognition. In: Proceedings of the IEEE conference on computer vision and pattern recognition. pp. 770–778 (2016)
6. Hendrycks, D., Basart, S., Mazeika, M., Zou, A., Kwon, J., Mostajabi, M., Steinhardt, J., Song, D.: Scaling out-of-distribution detection for real-world settings. In: International Conference on Machine Learning. pp. 8759–8773. PMLR (2022)
7. Hendrycks, D., Gimpel, K.: A baseline for detecting misclassified and out-of-distribution examples in neural networks. In: International Conference on Learning Representations (2016)
8. Karagodin, I., Singulane, C.C., Woodward, G.M., Xie, M., Tucay, E.S., Rodrigues, A.C.T., Vasquez-Ortiz, Z.Y., Alizadehasl, A., Monaghan, M.J., Salazar, B.A.O., et al.: Echocardiographic correlates of in-hospital death in patients with acute covid-19 infection: the world alliance societies of echocardiography (wase-covid) study. Journal of the American Society of Echocardiography **34**(8), 819–830 (2021)
9. Kirkpatrick, J., Pascanu, R., Rabinowitz, N., Veness, J., Desjardins, G., Rusu, A.A., Milan, K., Quan, J., Ramalho, T., Grabska-Barwinska, A., et al.: Overcoming catastrophic forgetting in neural networks. Proceedings of the national academy of sciences **114**(13), 3521–3526 (2017)

10. Kusunose, K., Haga, A., Inoue, M., Fukuda, D., Yamada, H., Sata, M.: Clinically feasible and accurate view classification of echocardiographic images using deep learning. Biomolecules **10**(5), 665 (2020)
11. Leclerc, S., Smistad, E., Pedrosa, J., Østvik, A., Cervenansky, F., Espinosa, F., Espeland, T., Berg, E.A.R., Jodoin, P.M., Grenier, T., et al.: Deep learning for segmentation using an open large-scale dataset in 2d echocardiography. IEEE transactions on medical imaging **38**(9), 2198–2210 (2019)
12. Li, Z., Hoiem, D.: Learning without forgetting. IEEE transactions on pattern analysis and machine intelligence **40**(12), 2935–2947 (2017)
13. Lomonaco, V., Maltoni, D.: Core50: a new dataset and benchmark for continuous object recognition. In: Conference on robot learning. pp. 17–26. PMLR (2017)
14. Madani, A., Arnaout, R., Mofrad, M., Arnaout, R.: Fast and accurate view classification of echocardiograms using deep learning. NPJ digital medicine **1**(1), 6 (2018)
15. McCloskey, M., Cohen, N.J.: Catastrophic interference in connectionist networks: The sequential learning problem. In: Psychology of learning and motivation, vol. 24, pp. 109–165. Elsevier (1989)
16. Rebuffi, S.A., Kolesnikov, A., Sperl, G., Lampert, C.H.: icarl: Incremental classifier and representation learning. In: Proceedings of the IEEE conference on Computer Vision and Pattern Recognition. pp. 2001–2010 (2017)
17. Sahiner, B., Chen, W., Samala, R.K., Petrick, N.: Data drift in medical machine learning: implications and potential remedies. The British Journal of Radiology **96**(1150), 20220878 (2023)
18. Tao, X., Chang, X., Hong, X., Wei, X., Gong, Y.: Topology-preserving class-incremental learning. In: Computer Vision–ECCV 2020: 16th European Conference, Glasgow, UK, August 23–28, 2020, Proceedings, Part XIX 16. pp. 254–270. Springer (2020)
19. Vaseli, H., Liao, Z., Abdi, A.H., Girgis, H., Behnami, D., Luong, C., Dezaki, F.T., Dhungel, N., Rohling, R., Gin, K., et al.: Designing lightweight deep learning models for echocardiography view classification. In: Medical Imaging 2019: Image-Guided Procedures, Robotic Interventions, and Modeling. vol. 10951, pp. 93–99. SPIE (2019)
20. Van de Ven, G.M., Tuytelaars, T., Tolias, A.S.: Three types of incremental learning. Nature Machine Intelligence **4**(12), 1185–1197 (2022)
21. Wang, F.Y., Zhou, D.W., Ye, H.J., Zhan, D.C.: Foster: Feature boosting and compression for class-incremental learning. In: European conference on computer vision. pp. 398–414. Springer (2022)
22. Wegner, F.K., Benesch Vidal, M.L., Niehues, P., Willy, K., Radke, R.M., Garthe, P.D., Eckardt, L., Baumgartner, H., Diller, G.P., Orwat, S.: Accuracy of deep learning echocardiographic view classification in patients with congenital or structural heart disease: importance of specific datasets. Journal of Clinical Medicine **11**(3), 690 (2022)
23. Wu, T.Y., Swaminathan, G., Li, Z., Ravichandran, A., Vasconcelos, N., Bhotika, R., Soatto, S.: Class-incremental learning with strong pre-trained models. In: Proceedings of the IEEE/CVF Conference on Computer Vision and Pattern Recognition. pp. 9601–9610 (2022)
24. Yan, S., Xie, J., He, X.: Der: Dynamically expandable representation for class incremental learning. In: Proceedings of the IEEE/CVF conference on computer vision and pattern recognition. pp. 3014–3023 (2021)
25. Yoon, J., Yang, E., Lee, J., Hwang, S.J.: Lifelong learning with dynamically expandable networks. In: International Conference on Learning Representations (ICLR) (2017)

Masked Autoencoders for Medical Ultrasound Videos Using ROI-Aware Masking

Ádám Szijártó[1(✉)], Bálint Magyar[2], Thomas Á. Szeier[3], Máté Tolvaj[1], Alexandra Fábián[1], Bálint K. Lakatos[1], Zsuzsanna Ladányi[1], Zsolt Bagyura[1], Béla Merkely[1], Attila Kovács[1], and Márton Tokodi[1]

[1] Heart and Vascular Center, Semmelweis University, Budapest, Hungary
sz.adam1996@gmail.com, tokmarton@gmail.com
[2] Faculty of Information Technology and Bionics, Pázmány Péter Catholic University, Budapest, Hungary
[3] Budapest, Hungary

Abstract. In routine clinical practice, a vast amount of data is generated, including myriads of ultrasound recordings. However, their annotation and interpretation are labor-intensive; thus, a method that can incorporate this unlabeled data into deep learning pipelines would be highly beneficial. Video masked autoencoders (VideoMAE) are state-of-the-art pre-training techniques and have performed exceptionally well in various computer vision tasks. Accordingly, we hypothesized that a VideoMAE pre-trained on a large unlabeled dataset of ultrasound recordings could also perform well in a downstream task following supervised training on a smaller but labeled dataset. Nevertheless, we found that the conventional masking strategy of the VideoMAE pipeline may perform sub-optimally in the specific domain of ultrasound videos. Motivated by this, we proposed a novel region of interest (ROI)-aware masking method that considers the specific characteristics of this domain. We demonstrated that applying our method instead of the conventional masking strategy significantly improves the VideoMAE's performance in clinically relevant downstream tasks, even when we reduced the labeled training dataset to one-tenth of its original sample size. The source code for this paper is available at https://github.com/szadam96/ROI-aware-masking.

Keywords: Ultrasound videos · Self-supervised learning · Video masked autoencoder

---

T. Á. Szeier—Independent Researcher.

Project no. RRF-2.3.1-21-2022-00004 (MILAB) has been implemented with the support provided by the European Union. TKP2021-NVA-12 has been implemented with the support provided by the Ministry of Innovation and Technology of Hungary from the National Research, Development, and Innovation Fund, financed under the TKP2021-NVA funding scheme. Dr Kovács has received grant support from the National Research, Development, and Innovation Office (NKFIH) of Hungary (FK 142573) and is supported by the János Bolyai Research Scholarship of the Hungarian Academy of Sciences.

© The Author(s), under exclusive license to Springer Nature Switzerland AG 2025
A. Gomez et al. (Eds.): ASMUS 2024, LNCS 15186, pp. 167–176, 2025.
https://doi.org/10.1007/978-3-031-73647-6_16

1 Introduction

Data annotation in the medical domain is time-consuming and requires specific knowledge, resulting in the limited availability of labeled data. Simultaneously, in routine clinical practice, imaging modalities such as ultrasound generate a vast amount of data without explicit labels or annotations, alongside labeled data originally intended for specific tasks but also potentially useful for other purposes. Such data can be potentially utilized in pre-training aimed at learning the underlying data distribution, thereby facilitating the development of models for various downstream tasks.

In recent years, several methods have been introduced to learn useful representations from unlabeled data [5]. Among these methods, masked autoencoders (MAE) stand out as efficient and scalable unsupervised approaches, even outperforming supervised pre-training methods [9]. When these techniques are applied to ultrasound videos, two key domain-specific aspects should be considered: the temporal information encompassed by the recordings and the distinct shape of the region of interest (ROI).

Accordingly, we proposed a novel masking strategy called ROI-aware masking for VideoMAEs, which takes into consideration the position and shape of the ROI, leading to reduced reconstruction error during pre-training on ultrasound videos. Using the proposed ROI-aware masking strategy, we pre-trained a VideoMAE on a large dataset of over 29,000 unlabeled cardiac ultrasound (i.e., echocardiographic) videos and fine-tuned it on a publicly available dataset (comprising over 2,900 labeled training echocardiographic videos) to perform two downstream tasks: predicting left ventricular ejection fraction (LVEF) and the primary diagnosis. Last, we also evaluated the impact of gradually reducing the sample size of the labeled training dataset on performance in these downstream tasks.

2 Related Work

Over the past years, self-supervised pre-training techniques have gained increasing popularity and have been successfully incorporated into many natural language processing pipelines [3,7]. Recently, these techniques have also been applied more and more frequently in computer vision, with contrastive representation learning being one of the most popular methods [4,8,10]. However, many of the self-supervised pre-training techniques are very resource-intensive as they require the simultaneous training of two models. Moreover, large batch sizes are also required to fully harness their true potential, which can be problematic for high-dimensional inputs like videos. MAEs [9], with their asymmetric encoder-decoder architecture, offer a different method for self-supervised learning. Unlike convolution-based autoencoders, MAEs take full advantage of patch embedding that transformers use. Inspired by MAE, VideoMAE is a masked video pre-training framework that introduced tube masking, enabling the model to learn temporally consistent representations during pre-training [16]. Recently, VideoMAEv2 was published [17], which improved upon the design of VideoMAE by adding a second mask for the decoder, thereby reducing the resources required for pre-training while preserving performance.

Contrastive representation learning has also been utilized for ultrasound videos. Holste et al. [11] proposed a self-supervised contrastive learning approach (EchoCLR) tailored to cardiac ultrasound (i.e., echocardiographic) videos that leverages distinct videos of the same patient as positive pairs. Chen et al. [6] introduced an ultrasound semi-supervised contrastive learning method (USCL) that adopts a sample pair generation method to enrich the features involved in a single step of contrastive optimization. Basu et al. [2] proposed an efficient unsupervised contrastive learning framework that exploits both intra-video and cross-video negatives through a hardness-sensitive negative mining curriculum. Zhang et al. [18] proposed a hierarchical contrastive learning (HiCo) method to improve the transferability of the ultrasound video model pre-training. Liu et al. [12] used pure convolution operations instead of the ViT structure in the MAE encoder to develop the Efficient Decoupled Masked Autoencoder (EDMAE) for view classification in pediatric echocardiography.

3 Methods

3.1 Previous Masking Strategies

In VideoMAE [16], the input videos $I \in \mathbb{R}^{T \times C \times H \times W}$ are transformed into a token sequence using cube embedding $S = \Phi(I)$. Then, a binary masking map $\mathbb{M}_e$ is generated on the sequence using a custom tube masking strategy to mask certain parts. The unmasked tokens $S^u = \{S_i\}_{i \in \neg \mathbb{M}_e}$ are used to generate a latent representation of the input $Z = \Phi_{enc}(S^u)$. This encoded representation is then combined with the learnable masking tokens A, and the decoder is tasked with reconstructing the masked tokens in the pixel space as $\hat{I} = \Phi_{dec}(Z, A)$.

VideoMAEv2 introduced the concept of dual masking [17]. By applying a mask to the decoder as well, the computational cost could be significantly reduced during pre-training, while performance remained comparable to the single masking method. A new mask $\mathbb{M}_d$ is calculated (with $\mathbb{M}_d \subset \mathbb{M}_e$), which is then used to limit the number of learnable tokens fed to the decoder $\Phi_{dec}(Z, A^m)$, where $A^m = \{A_i\}_{i \in \mathbb{M}_d}$.

3.2 Challenges in Ultrasound Video Processing

In a typical medical ultrasound video, only a fraction (typically less than 50%) of pixels in each frame displays the actual ultrasound image, whereas the remaining displays textual information and technical markers that are useful for the medical professionals performing the ultrasound examination but are considered noise for the deep learning algorithms. By cropping each frame using a rectangular bounding box, we can discard some of these irrelevant pixels. However, due to the sector shape of the ROI in cardiac ultrasound (i.e., echocardiographic) videos, a significant portion (on average about 42% in our dataset) will still hold no valuable information (Fig. 1).

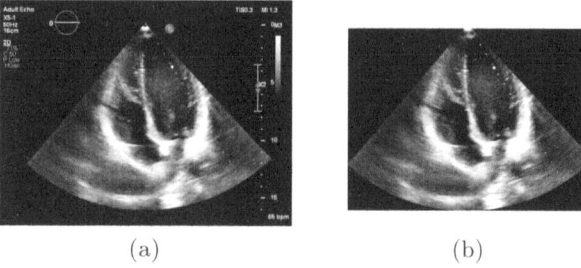

(a) (b)

Fig. 1. (a) The original frame of an example echocardiographic video, and (b) the same frame after cropping using a rectangular bounding box.

VideoMAE with tube masking has been shown to be highly effective on large-scale datasets of natural videos. However, we found it to exhibit substantially worse performance when applied to echocardiographic videos with a sector-shaped ROI.

3.3 ROI-Aware Masking

To overcome the challenge detailed above, we propose a novel ROI-aware masking strategy that considers the shape and location of the ROI.

As described later in Sect. 4.2, a binary segmentation mask $I_s \in \mathbb{R}^{HxW}$ can be created around the ROI. As the ROI is static across all frames of the given video, we can stack the mask along the temporal dimension to map the same binary mask to each input frame. Cube embedding is then applied to this stacked mask, resulting in a token masking map $\mathbb{M}_s$ that masks the embedded patches outside the segmentation mask. Using this new map we can define the encoder ($\hat{\mathbb{M}}_e$) and decoder masks ($\hat{\mathbb{M}}_d$) as follows:

$$\hat{\mathbb{M}}_e = \mathbb{M}_e \cup \neg \mathbb{M}_s \tag{1}$$

$$\hat{\mathbb{M}}_d = \mathbb{M}_e \cap \mathbb{M}_s \tag{2}$$

where $\mathbb{M}_e$ is the tube mask described in [16]. Equation (1) ensures that no unmasked tokens outside the ROI are used by the encoder, whereas Eq. (2) ensures that the learnable tokens fed to the decoder are limited to the remaining unmasked parts of the ROI. Figure 2 shows how the encoder and decoder masking maps are generated using the binary segmentation mask of the ROI. This way, the encoder is forced to learn the representation of the entire ROI, while the decoder is only tasked with reconstructing the relevant parts of the frames.

Additionally, the ROI mask is also applied to the encoder during downstream training. This is a crucial step as the model has never been exposed to tokens outside the ROI in the pre-training phase, so supplying such tokens to the model during the supervised training phase could potentially diminish its performance.

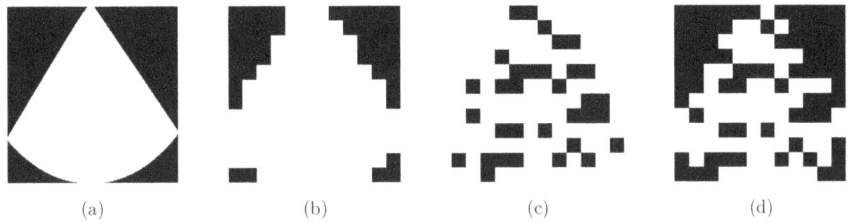

Fig. 2. (a) The binary segmentation mask generated for each frame of an example echocardiographic video (I_s). (b) The same binary segmentation mask downsampled to the resolution of the cube embedding ($\mathbb{M}_s$). (c) The encoder mask generated from the downsampled segmentation mask using the conventional tube masking method ($\hat{\mathbb{M}}_e$). (d) The decoder mask generated by intersecting the encoder mask with the downsampled segmentation mask ($\hat{\mathbb{M}}_d$).

4 Experiments

Using our novel ROI-aware masking method, we pre-trained a VideoMAE on a large dataset of unlabeled 2D apical 4-chamber (A4C) view echocardiographic videos. We then fine-tuned it on a smaller publicly available labeled dataset of similar videos for two downstream tasks: (1) predicting LVEF - the most commonly measured echocardiographic parameter of LV systolic function, and (2) assigning a primary diagnosis (healthy, athlete, heart failure with reduced LVEF, aortic valve disease, or mitral valve disease) to each video. We evaluated the proposed ROI-aware masking in comparison with simple tube masking both quantitatively (reconstruction loss – mean squared error [MSE]; performance in the downstream tasks – mean absolute error [MAE], coefficient of determination [R^2], and accuracy) and qualitatively by visually inspecting the reconstructed frames. In this section, we describe the datasets, the steps of our custom pre-processing pipeline, and the hardware and software environment used in our experiments.

4.1 Datasets

In our experiments, we used two separate datasets comprising 2D A4C echocardiographic videos in Digital Imaging and Communications in Medicine (DICOM) file format. Transthoracic echocardiography is usually performed using a phased array transducer, allowing the echocardiographer to visualize the heart even from small intercostal spaces. As a result of utilizing a phased array transducer, the ultrasound machine visualizes the heart in a sector-shaped ROI at the center of the screen while displaying technical markers, information regarding the imaging settings and the patient, and the electrocardiogram signal outside the ROI. Further details of the two datasets are provided in the subsections below.

Unlabeled Dataset. For pre-training, we used 29,424 unlabeled A4C videos (as DICOM files) from 15,533 transthoracic echocardiographic studies that belong to individuals representing the patient population referred to transthoracic echocardiographic examinations at the Heart and Vascular Center of Semmelweis University between 2006 and 2023.

Labeled Dataset. In the fine-tuning phase (i.e., downstream tasks), we used the publicly available RVENet dataset [13,15]. This dataset originally comprised 3,583 A4C view videos (in DICOM file format) from 944 transthoracic echocardiographic studies of health volunteers and patients with a wide variety of cardiac diseases. Nevertheless, we only used the videos with 3D echocardiography-derived LVEF values available (n = 3,523) and the videos of patients within one of the five abovementioned primary diagnosis categories (n = 2,545) in the two downstream tasks, respectively. These subsets of videos were split into training, validation, and testing sets in an approximately 70:10:20 ratio at the study level. We also performed a series of experiments by progressively decreasing the sample size of the training set in 10% steps while leaving the validation and testing sets unchanged.

4.2 Preprocessing

From the DICOM files of the two datasets, we extracted all frames of the videos and cropped them using the bounding box of the sector-shaped ROI. Next, we created a binary mask by tracking the frame-to-frame changes of each pixel's intensity value in the given video and denoting pixels changing their intensity values with <5 or fewer times than 10% of the total number of frames with black, whereas all the other pixels with white. To avoid the presence of multiple disjoint white patches in the binary mask, we kept only the contour with the largest area, to which we fitted a convex hull. Then, the bounding box enclosing all white pixels was used to crop the binary mask and each frame of the corresponding video.

Given that echocardiographic videos may substantially differ in length and contain different numbers of cardiac cycles, we split each video into sequences of images containing frames from exactly one cardiac cycle using a transformer we trained previously to identify end-systolic frames as proposed by Reynaud and coworkers [14]. From each of the sequences (i.e., cardiac cycles), we sampled 16 frames. Finally, the frames were resized to 192×192 pixels, and min-max scaling was applied to their pixel intensity values.

4.3 Experimental Setup

The code for the experiments was implemented in Python 3.9 with PyTorch 2.0 as the deep learning framework. Models were trained on two NVIDIA RTX3090 graphics processing units. ViViT-b 16×2 [1] was used for the encoder's backend.

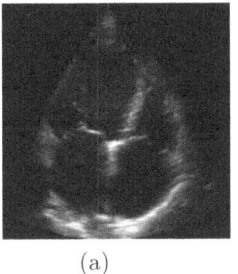 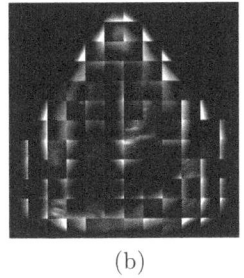 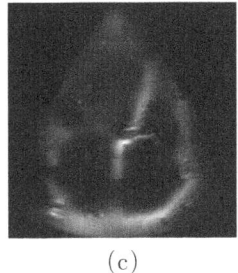

(a) (b) (c)

Fig. 3. (a) The original frame of an example echocardiographic video (b) and the same frame reconstructed using the conventional tube masking method and (c) the proposed ROI-aware masking method.

A masking ratio of 75% was used for pre-training. Pre-training involved training for 100 epochs with a batch size of 2×25, and the weights from the epoch with the lowest validation loss were chosen as the final model. In the subsequent fine-tuning phase (i.e., downstream task), the model was trained for 40 epochs with a batch size of 2×8.

In both the pre-training and fine-tuning phases, the Adam optimizer was used with a cosine annealing learning rate scheduler. Temporally consistent video augmentations were also applied during training in both phases: random cropping along the spatial dimension was used, preserving no less than 90% of the original frames, as well as random rotation with no more than $15°$ in either direction.

5 Results

5.1 Pre-training

When we compared our novel ROI-aware masking method with the conventional tube masking in terms of reconstruction loss, we found that the former outperformed the latter method by a large margin (MSE: 0.001 vs. 0.472).

As shown in Fig. 3, our method was able to capture the more granular structure of the heart seen in the original frame, whereas the model trained with tube masking focused on correctly identifying and reconstructing the edges of the ROI and learned only the local black-to-white gradients. These findings confirmed that by allowing tokens consisting of irrelevant pixels to be fed into the encoder and reconstructed by the decoder, a considerable amount of resources is wasted on learning the representation of such tokens.

5.2 Downstream Tasks

In both downstream tasks, the proposed ROI-aware masking method outperformed the conventional VideoMAE pipeline and a pipeline in which no pre-training was applied (Table 1). Furthermore, the performance dropped only

Table 1. Performance achieved in the downstream tasks using the different pre-training methods.

Method	Predicting LVEF (regression)		Predicting primary diagnosis (classification)
	MAE↓	**R²↑**	**Accuracy↑**
No pre-training	6.20	0.41	0.59
Tube masking	5.93	0.45	0.43
ROI-aware masking	**4.37**	**0.72**	**0.82**
ROI-aware masking (enc. frozen)	4.68	0.69	0.81

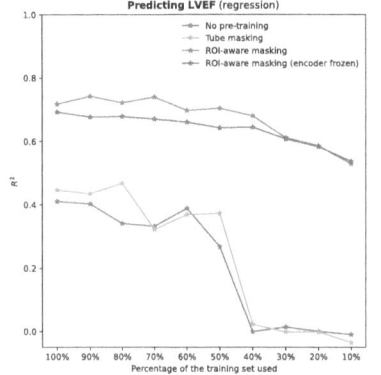
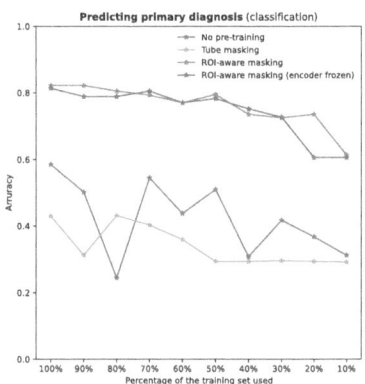

Fig. 4. The effect of progressively reducing the sample size of the labeled training set on the model's performance.

slightly when the regression head's weights were optimized during the fine-tuning phase while the encoder's weights were frozen (Table 1).

When we analyzed how progressively reducing the sample size of the labeled training set affects the model's performance, we observed that the performance of the model pre-trained using the ROI-aware masking method decreased only slowly in parallel with the decrease in the sample size (Fig. 4). On the other hand, the decrease in the performance of the other two models was more prominent, with a notable drop when the labeled training set was reduced to less than 50% of its original size.

6 Limitations

Although the results achieved using our novel ROI-aware masking method are promising, there are also some limitations that should be acknowledged. First, our preprocessing pipeline was specifically tailored to processing A4C echocardiographic videos. Second, we hypothesized that we could achieve the best results in the downstream task if we ensured that the unlabeled pre-training data was as similar to the labeled data as possible (i.e., by sampling cardiac cycles from the videos). Last, including other views or types of ultrasound videos in the pre-training dataset could substantially increase its size, which could potentially lead to improved model performance. On the other hand, increasing the diversity of the unlabeled pre-training dataset may also increase differences between the unlabeled and labeled datasets, potentially diminishing performance.

7 Conclusion

In this study, we demonstrated that pre-training VideoMAEs using the conventional tube masking method was ineffective in echocardiographic videos. Therefore, built on the concept of VideoMAEv2, we proposed a novel ROI-aware masking method that applies encoder and decoder masking maps that take into account the location and shape of the ROI. We demonstrated that this novel masking method outperforms previous techniques even if only a limited amount of labeled training data is available in the downstream task.

Although we tested the proposed method only in echocardiographic videos, it has a great potential for generalization to other domains (e.g., other medical or even non-medical videos) in which a substantial portion of pixels of the input frames do not carry useful information with respect to the deep learning task.

References

1. Arnab, A., Dehghani, M., Heigold, G., Sun, C., Lučić, M., Schmid, C.: Vivit: A video vision transformer. In: Proceedings of the IEEE/CVF international conference on computer vision. pp. 6836–6846 (2021)
2. Basu, S., Singla, S., Gupta, M., Rana, P., Gupta, P., Arora, C.: Unsupervised contrastive learning of image representations from ultrasound videos with hard negative mining. In: International Conference on Medical Image Computing and Computer-Assisted Intervention. pp. 423–433. Springer (2022)
3. Brown, T., Mann, B., Ryder, N., Subbiah, M., Kaplan, J.D., Dhariwal, P., Neelakantan, A., Shyam, P., Sastry, G., Askell, A., et al.: Language models are few-shot learners. Advances in neural information processing systems **33**, 1877–1901 (2020)
4. Chen, T., Kornblith, S., Norouzi, M., Hinton, G.: A simple framework for contrastive learning of visual representations. In: International conference on machine learning. pp. 1597–1607. PMLR (2020)
5. Chen, Y., Mancini, M., Zhu, X., Akata, Z.: Semi-supervised and unsupervised deep visual learning: A survey. IEEE transactions on pattern analysis and machine intelligence (2022)
6. Chen, Y., Zhang, C., Liu, L., Feng, C., Dong, C., Luo, Y., Wan, X.: Uscl: pretraining deep ultrasound image diagnosis model through video contrastive representation learning. In: Medical Image Computing and Computer Assisted Intervention–MICCAI 2021: 24th International Conference, Strasbourg, France, September 27–October 1, 2021, Proceedings, Part VIII 24. pp. 627–637. Springer (2021)

7. Devlin, J., Chang, M.W., Lee, K., Toutanova, K.: Bert: Pre-training of deep bidirectional transformers for language understanding. arXiv preprint arXiv:1810.04805 (2018)
8. Diba, A., Sharma, V., Safdari, R., Lotfi, D., Sarfraz, S., Stiefelhagen, R., Van Gool, L.: Vi2clr: Video and image for visual contrastive learning of representation. In: Proceedings of the IEEE/CVF international conference on computer vision. pp. 1502–1512 (2021)
9. He, K., Chen, X., Xie, S., Li, Y., Dollár, P., Girshick, R.: Masked autoencoders are scalable vision learners. In: Proceedings of the IEEE/CVF conference on computer vision and pattern recognition. pp. 16000–16009 (2022)
10. He, K., Fan, H., Wu, Y., Xie, S., Girshick, R.: Momentum contrast for unsupervised visual representation learning. In: Proceedings of the IEEE/CVF conference on computer vision and pattern recognition. pp. 9729–9738 (2020)
11. Holste, G., Oikonomou, E.K., Mortazavi, B., Wang, Z., Khera, R.: Efficient deep learning-based automated diagnosis from echocardiography with contrastive self-supervised learning. Commun. Med. (Lond.) **4**(1), 133 (2024)
12. Liu, Y., Han, X., Liang, T., Dong, B., Yuan, J., Hu, M., Liu, Q., Chen, J., Li, Q., Zhang, Y.: Edmae: An efficient decoupled masked autoencoder for standard view identification in pediatric echocardiography. Biomedical Signal Processing and Control **86**, 105280 (2023)
13. Magyar, B., Tokodi, M., Soós, A., Tolvaj, M., Lakatos, B.K., Fábián, A., Surkova, E., Merkely, B., Kovács, A., Horváth, A.: Rvenet: A large echocardiographic dataset for the deep learning-based assessment of right ventricular function. In: European Conference on Computer Vision. pp. 569–583. Springer (2022)
14. Reynaud, H., Vlontzos, A., Hou, B., Beqiri, A., Leeson, P., Kainz, B.: Ultrasound video transformers for cardiac ejection fraction estimation. In: Medical Image Computing and Computer Assisted Intervention–MICCAI 2021: 24th International Conference, Strasbourg, France, September 27–October 1, 2021, Proceedings, Part VI 24. pp. 495–505. Springer (2021)
15. Tokodi, M., Magyar, B., Soós, A., Takeuchi, M., Tolvaj, M., Lakatos, B.K., Kitano, T., Nabeshima, Y., Fábián, A., Szigeti, M.B., Horváth, A., Merkely, B., Kovács, A.: Deep learning-based prediction of right ventricular ejection fraction using 2d echocardiograms. JACC: Cardiovascular Imaging **16**(8), 1005–1018 (2023)
16. Tong, Z., Song, Y., Wang, J., Wang, L.: Videomae: Masked autoencoders are data-efficient learners for self-supervised video pre-training. Advances in neural information processing systems **35**, 10078–10093 (2022)
17. Wang, L., Huang, B., Zhao, Z., Tong, Z., He, Y., Wang, Y., Wang, Y., Qiao, Y.: Videomae v2: Scaling video masked autoencoders with dual masking. In: Proceedings of the IEEE/CVF Conference on Computer Vision and Pattern Recognition. pp. 14549–14560 (2023)
18. Zhang, C., Chen, Y., Liu, L., Liu, Q., Zhou, X.: Hico: Hierarchical contrastive learning for ultrasound video model pretraining. In: Proceedings of the Asian Conference on Computer Vision. pp. 229–246 (2022)

Uncertainty-Based Multi-modal Learning for Myocardial Infarction Diagnosis Using Echocardiography and Electrocardiograms

Yingyu Yang[1](✉), Marie Rocher[2], Pamela Moceri[2], and Maxime Sermesant[1]

[1] Centre Inria d'Université Côte d'Azur, Sophia Antipolis, France
yingyu.yang@inria.fr
[2] CHU de Nice - Hôpital Pasteur, Nice, France

Abstract. Medical devices used in cardiac diagnostics typically capture only one aspect of heart function. For instance, 2D B-mode echocardiography reveals the heart's anatomy and mechanical changes, while an electrocardiogram (ECG) records the heart's electrical activity from various positions. These examinations, essential for diagnosing cardiac diseases, are usually performed sequentially rather than simultaneously, providing complementary information for the final diagnosis. Recently, the integration of multi-modal information in AI research for healthcare has gained popularity, aiming for more robust diagnostic outcomes. However, the scarcity of publicly available multi-modal data for cardiac disease diagnosis poses a significant challenge to multi-modal learning and evaluation. In this study, we propose an uncertainty-based deep learning framework that utilizes unpaired data from different modalities to improve the diagnosis of myocardial infarction (MI) using both echocardiography and ECG data. Specifically, we trained two unimodal classification models incorporating uncertainty using public single-modal datasets. We then performed multi-modal classification using uncertainty-based decision fusion on a paired dataset, without the need for transfer learning or retraining. Our experiments demonstrated that uncertainty-based multi-modal decision fusion outperforms conventional fusion strategies by 4% in accuracy and unimodal models by 7% in accuracy. This approach is both flexible and data-efficient, making uncertainty-based multi-modal fusion a sustainable and strong solution for both unpaired and paired multi-modal classification.

Keywords: Multi-modal classification · Echocardiography · Electrocardiogram

1 Introduction

Clinicians usually combine information from different examinations and measurements to make clinical decisions. However, most current AI research for healthcare simply considers one single modality, which does not profit from the complex and heterogeneous information that one can observe from patients using different imaging modalities, sensor devices, biochemical tests, etc. Multi-modal machine learning, which seeks to model the interactions between different modalities, brings opportunities for improving the prevention, diagnosis and therapy in AI-enabled healthcare [1–4].

One challenge in biomedical multi-modal learning is to determine how to fuse information from different medical modalities for downstream tasks. Depending on when the fusion occurs, one can distinguish: early fusion and late fusion respectively. Early fusion combines the raw modality or extracted features at the input level according to certain fusion approaches, such as concatenation, multiplicative interaction [5], polynomial fusion [6], tensor fusion [7,8], etc. Late fusion aggregates the prediction outputs of different modalities at the decision level (e.g. using majority voting, weighted voting etc.) to generate a final decision. Early fusion usually demands paired multi-modality data to explore detailed interaction strategies, while late fusion only need single modality outputs, thus being less demanding for paired data.

In this study, we focus on detecting myocardial infarction (MI) using both echocardiography (ECHO) and eletrocardiogram (ECG) data. Researchers have explored different multi-modal approaches for MI detection, such as combining ECG with demographic features [9], using images and clinical data together [10]. Very few have investigated the combination of ECHO and ECG, while ECHO and ECG can reveal different diagnosis characteristics of MI respectively [11]. In addition, with very limited paired multi-modal data by hand, we concentrate on how to improve the late fusion strategy which can leverage on the most confident modality.

The contribution of this paper is twofold. Firstly, we have adapted a trustworthy method to fuse decisions from different modalities by considering the uncertainty of each prediction. The proposed fusion strategy is efficient and flexible, capable of fully utilising public single-modal datasets and performing test-time multi-modal fusion when paired multi-modal samples are available. Secondly, our experiments on multi-modal myocardial infarction detection using both ECHO and ECG demonstrate superior performance compared to single-modal detection or conventional fusion methods. This suggests the potential of combining ECHO and ECG for robust cardiac diagnosis.

2 Method

We first introduce how to quantify the uncertainty for unimodal classification using evidential deep learning [12]. In the second part, we present test-time multi-modal fusion strategy that takes into account the uncertainty from each modality.

2.1 Evidential Deep Learning for Unimodal Classification

Uncertainty and the Theory of Evidence. Evidential deep learning (EDL) quantifies the class probabilities and overall uncertainty in a unified theoretical framework [12]. Considering a K classification problem, it introduces an idea of evidence e_k, which represents a measure of the amount of support for k^{th} class category collected from data input. Using the evidence, the belief of possible class label assignments b_k and an overall uncertainty mass u can be obtained through

$$b_k = \frac{e_k}{S} \text{ and } u = \frac{K}{S}, S = \sum_{i=1}^{K}(e_i + 1) \qquad (1)$$

The sum of the $K+1$ mass values is one, i.e. $u + \sum_{k=1}^{K} b_k = 1$. Actually, EDL associates the belief of possible class label assignments (subjective opinion) with the parameters of a Dirichlet Distribution [13], i.e. $\alpha_k = e_k + 1$, including the belief that the truth label is equally likely (i.e., "I do not know" for uncertainty quantification).

The Dirichlet distribution is parameterised by K parameters $\alpha = [\alpha_1, ..., \alpha_K]$. Its probability density function (pdf) is given by

$$D(\mathbf{p}|\alpha) = \begin{cases} \frac{1}{B(\alpha)} \prod_{i=1}^{K} p_i^{\alpha_i - 1} & \text{for } \mathbf{p} \in \mathcal{S}_K, \\ 0 & \text{otherwise}, \end{cases} \qquad (2)$$

where $\mathcal{S}_K$ represents the K-dimensional unit simplex $\mathcal{S}_K = \{\mathbf{p}| \sum_{i=1}^{K} p_i = 1 \text{ and } 0 \leq p_1, ..., p_k \leq 1\}$, and $B(\alpha)$ is the K-dimensional multinomial beta function. Given an opinion, the expected probability $\hat{p}_k$ for the k_{th} class category is the mean of the corresponding distribution, $\hat{p}_k = \frac{\alpha_k}{S}$.

The above relationship reveals that the higher the evidence e_k for k^{th} class is observed, the greater the class belief b_k and the corresponding Dirichlet parameter α_k will be. Similarly, when the total evidence observed from the input data is small, i.e. $\sum e_k$ is closer to 0 and $\alpha_k, k = 1, ..K$ are closer to 1, the uncertainty of the prediction becomes higher.

Learning to Form Opinions. Evidential deep learning replaces the last *softmax* activation in neural network classifiers with non-negative activation, such as *ReLU*. The output of this final activation layer is taken as the evidence vector. It forms class belief masses and constitutes the parameters for the estimated Dirichlet distribution (illustrated in the upper right part of Fig. 1).

We assume that y_i is a one-hot vector of ground truth classification label for input data x_i. The cross-entropy loss is usually used in conventional neural network classifiers:

$$\mathcal{L}^{CE} = -\sum_{i=1}^{N} \sum_{j=1}^{K} y_{ij} \log(p_{ij}), \qquad (3)$$

where p_{ij} is the predicted probability for sample x_i belonging to class j. Under the theory of evidence and Dirichlet distribution assumption, we can compute the Bayes risk of cross-entropy loss function as

$$\mathcal{L}_i^{UC} = \int [\sum_{j=1}^{K} -y_{ij} \log(p_{ij})] \frac{1}{B(\alpha_i)} \prod_{j=1}^{K} p_{ij}^{\alpha_{ij}-1} d\mathbf{p}_i = \sum_{j=1}^{K} y_{ij}(\psi(S_i) - \psi(\alpha_{ij})), \qquad (4)$$

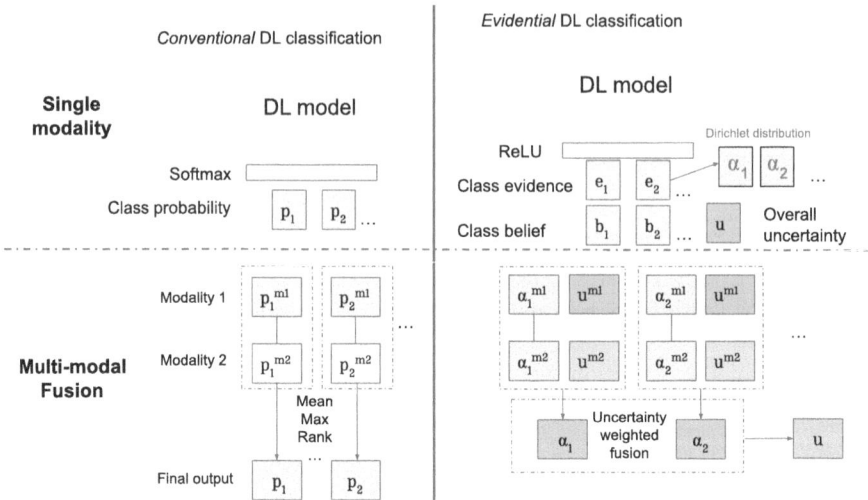

Fig. 1. Comparison of conventional fusion strategies and uncertainty based fusion.

where $\psi(\cdot)$ represents the *digamma* function.

The minimisation of the above loss does not guarantee that less evidence will be generated when the model predicts incorrect labels. To guide the network into learning zero total evidence for uncertain samples, a regularisation term is introduced. This term deploys a Kullback-Leibler divergence term to penalise the predictive Dirichlet distribution to be close to $D(\mathbf{p}|\mathbf{1})$.

$$KL[D(\mathbf{p}_i|\tilde{\alpha}_i)||D(\mathbf{p}_i|\mathbf{1})] = \log(\frac{\Gamma(\sum_{k=1}^{K}\tilde{\alpha}_{ik})}{\Gamma(K)\prod_{k=1}^{K}\Gamma(\tilde{\alpha}_{ik})}) + \sum_{k=1}^{K}(\tilde{\alpha}_{ik}-1)[\psi(\tilde{\alpha}_{ik}) - \psi(\sum_{k=1}^{K}\tilde{\alpha}_{ij})], \quad (5)$$

where $\Gamma(\cdot)$ represents the *gamma* function and $\mathbf{1}$ refers to a K-dim vector of all ones.

Thus, the final loss function for evidential deep learning neural networks reads:

$$\mathcal{L} = \sum_{i=1}^{N}\mathcal{L}_i^{UC} + \lambda_t \sum_{i=1}^{N} KL[D(\mathbf{p}_i|\tilde{\alpha}_i)||D(\mathbf{p}_i|\mathbf{1})], \quad (6)$$

where $\lambda_t = \min(1, t/T) \in [0,1]$ is a balancing coefficient for regularisation and t represents the current training epoch.

2.2 Multi-modal Fusion with Uncertainty

Considering two independent sets of evidence values $\{e_k^1\}_{k=1}^{K}$ and $\{e_k^2\}_{k=1}^{K}$, the corresponding parameters of Dirichlet distribution are $\{\alpha_k^1 = e_k^1 + 1\}_{k=1}^{K}$ and $\{\alpha_k^2 = e_k^2 + 1\}_{k=1}^{K}$. We propose to fuse opinions from all modalities through uncertainty-weighted fusion (illustrated in the lower right part of Fig. 1):

$$\alpha_k = (1-u^1)\alpha_k^1 + (1-u^2)\alpha_k^2, u = \frac{K}{\sum \alpha_k} \qquad (7)$$

3 Experiments and Results

3.1 Datasets

Two independent datasets of ECHO and ECG are involved in this study:

- HMC-QU dataset [14]: contains 130 long-axis 2-chamber view sequences (68 with MI) and 162 long-axis 4-chamber view sequences (93 with MI).
- PTB-XL dataset [15]: contains 12-lead ECG data (with 7185 samples of healthy controls and 2955 samples with 100%-certain MI).

In addition, a small number of paired ECHO and ECG data were collected retrospectively from Nice University hospital (CHU-Nice). This dataset contains data from 56 patients, with 56 paired data of ECG and 4-chamber view ECHO, along with 50 paired data of ECG and 2-chamber view ECHO. Detailed dataset information is listed in Table 1.

Table 1. Dataset statistics. *2ch: 2 chambers view, 4ch: 4 chambers view.*

Dataset	Modality	MI	non-MI	Total
HMC-QU	ECHO 2ch	68	62	130
HMC-QU	ECHO 4ch	93	69	162
PTB-XL	ECG 12-lead	2955	7185	10140
CHU-Nice	ECHO(2ch) + ECG	33	17	50
CHU-Nice	ECHO(4ch) + ECG	36	20	56

3.2 Experiments

We first extracted interpretable features from ECHO data in HMC-QU dataset and from ECG data in PTB-XL dataset (refer to Fig. 2(a)). For ECHO data, we used a motion tracking model [16] to predict the temporal motion of 10 key points around the myocardium (refer to Fig. 2(b)). From the temporal motion trace, we constructed a 40-dimension vector which composed of mean and standard deviation of the 10 key points along x- and y-axis. For ECG data, we followed the work [17] to decompose single-heartbeat ECG signal into 5 sub-components and used the predicted 21 parameters to constitute a 21×12-dimension vector as ECG features. We trained single modality models with 10-fold cross validation for ECG data (PTB-XL) and 5-fold cross validation for ECHO data (HMC-QU)

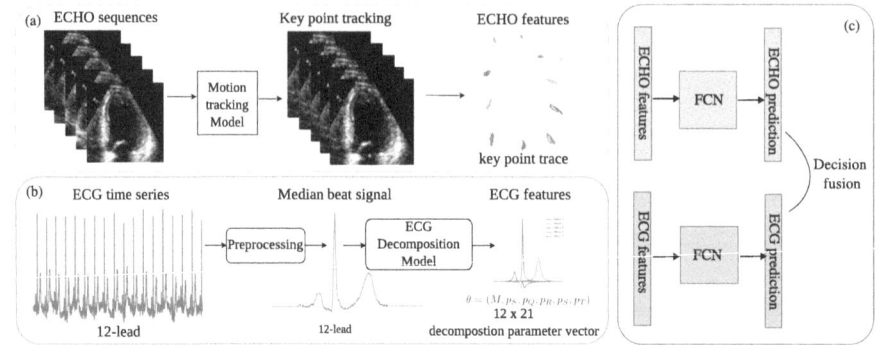

Fig. 2. ECHO and ECG feature extraction pipeline.

using a 4-layer fully connected network (FCN) respectively. The baseline single modality model without uncertainty (w/o UC) was trained using cross-entropy loss (Eq. 3) and the uncertainty model (w UC) with Eq. 6.

For models without uncertainty (w/o UC), we assumed that the output of FCN after Sigmoid function was p_c^k and the prediction class was $\bar{y}^k$, where $c \in \{0, 1\}$ refers to class and $k \in \{0, 1\}$ refers to modality. The MI class was set to label 1. The following fusion strategies were included in our study:

- Max fusion: $p_c = \max\{p_c^k, k = 1, ..., K\}$, $\bar{y} = \arg\max_c p_c$;
- Mean fusion: $p_c = \text{mean}\{p_c^k, k = 1, ..., K\}$, $\bar{y} = \arg\max_c p_c$;
- Rank fusion: $\bar{y} = (\sum_k \bar{y}^k) \geq 1$;
- Multiply fusion: $p_c = \prod_k p_c^k$, $\bar{y} = \arg\max_c p_c$.

The multi-modal fusion with uncertainty was performed according to Eq. 7.

3.3 Implementation

The uncertainty model for ECHO and ECG were trained using the following hyper-parameters:

- ECG: learning rate 0.01, batch size 512, total epochs 200, $T = 10$ for λ_t;
- ECHO: learning rate 0.0001, batch size 8, total epochs 200, $T = 50$ for λ_t.

We chose the model with the best validation loss during training.

3.4 Results

First, we present the cross validation results on HMC-QU and PTB-XL dataset in Table 2 and Table 3. Although evidential deep learning (EDL) model demonstrated reduced performance compared with model trained using standard cross-entropy loss, its performance was comparable when using mixed 2-chamber

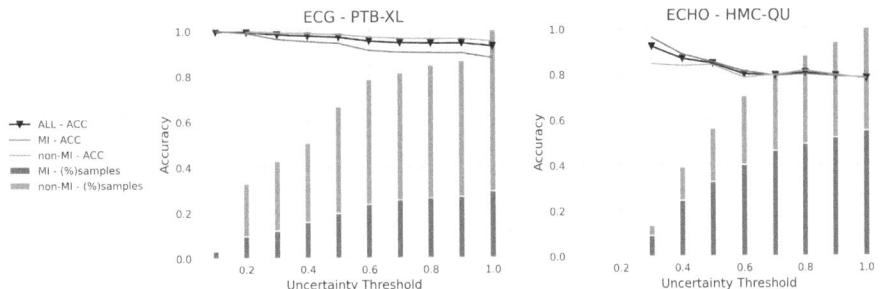

Fig. 3. The change of prediction accuracy with respect to uncertainty threshold on PTB-XL ECG dataset and HMC-QU ECHO dataset (2CH/4CH mixed). Bar plots represent the percentage of samples kept under varying uncertainty thresholds.

and 4-chamber (2CH/4CH mixed) views together (292 samples in total). We obtained a similar observation on ECG classification using uncertainty-based loss. Figure 3 shows how the test accuracy changes when EDL only keeps predictions under varying uncertainty thresholds. Notably, on both datasets, the accuracy increased as the uncertainty threshold decreased, which reflected the effectiveness of uncertainty quantification predicted by the model.

Table 2. ECHO classification: 5-fold CV results on HMC-QU dataset. w/o UC: without uncertainty, w UC: with uncertainty.

Method	View	Accuracy	Sensitivity	Specificity
KNN [14]	2CH	0.75	0.72	0.77
Ours (w/o UC)	2CH	**0.78**	**0.74**	0.82
Ours (w UC)	2CH	0.72	0.59	**0.85**
Random Forest [14]	4CH	**0.86**	**0.84**	**0.85**
Ours (w/o UC)	4CH	0.81	0.82	0.80
Ours (w UC)	4CH	0.82	0.83	0.81
Ours (w/o UC)	2CH + 4CH (mixed)	0.78	0.78	0.79
Ours (w UC)	2CH + 4CH (mixed)	0.78	0.78	0.78

We show the test-time multi-modal fusion evaluation on the CHU-Nice dataset in Table 4. The performance of conventional fusion (upper part) was limited by the best performing modality, in our case, by the ECHO modality. The mean fusion strategy outperformed the other conventional methods, with a slight improvement in sensitivity but significant reduction in specificity due to the erroneous output of the ECG prediction. In the lower part of Table 4, we observe that uncertainty-based fusion improved largely the prediction accuracy compared to single modalities with uncertainty (by 7%). In addition, this approach well combined the advantages of each modality: higher sensitivity than

Table 3. ECG classification: 10-fold CV results on PTB-XL dataset. *w/o UC: without uncertainty, w UC: with uncertainty.*

Method	Lead	Accuracy	Sensitivity	Specificity
SVM [17]	12-lead	0.96	0.93	0.96
Ours (w/o UC)	12-lead	0.95	0.89	0.97
Ours (w UC)	12-lead	0.93	0.88	0.95

Table 4. Evaluation on CHU-Nice dataset (with 2-chamber view and 4-chamber view mixed together, in total 106 paired samples). *w/o UC: without uncertainty, w UC: with uncertainty.*

Method	Modality	Accuracy	Sensitivity	Specificity
Ours (w/o UC)	ECG	0.69	0.84	0.43
Ours (w/o UC)	ECHO	**0.75**	0.75	**0.76**
Max Fusion	ECG + ECHO	0.73	0.81	0.57
Mean fusion	ECG + ECHO	**0.75**	0.86	0.54
Rank fusion	ECG + ECHO	0.73	**0.96**	0.30
Multiply fusion	ECG + ECHO	0.68	0.87	0.32
Ours (w UC)	ECG	0.72	**0.86**	0.48
Ours (w UC)	ECHO	0.71	0.68	**0.76**
Uncertain fusion	ECG + ECHO	**0.79**	0.83	0.73

single ECHO output and higher specificity than single ECG output, with only a slight decrease compared with the best value of single modality outputs. As evidenced by the fusion results, uncertainty-based fusion generated multi-modal prediction according to the most trustworthy modality, therefore improving the final prediction of diagnosis.

4 Conclusion

In this study, we explored various multi-modal late fusion strategies and found that uncertainty-based fusion outperformed conventional methods, improving classification accuracy by 4%. This approach, utilizing single-modality evidential deep learning, assessed the uncertainty of each modality's prediction to prioritize the most reliable input for the final decision. Additionally, it required no sampling steps and was straightforward to implement with deep learning techniques. The test-time fusion setting maximized the use of large public single-modality datasets while preserving valuable paired multi-modal data for evaluation. Despite promising preliminary results, several limitations demand further investigation. First, we need to quantify the impact of error propagation through feature extraction on downstream classification tasks. Second, the uncertainty predicted within the evidential framework is not fully calibrated, necessitating the incorporation of uncertainty calibration for both modalities before fusion.

Acknowledgements. This work has been supported by the French government through the National Research Agency (ANR) Investments in the Future with 3IA Côte d'Azur (ANR-19-P3IA-0002) and by Inria PhD funding. The authors are grateful to the OPAL infrastructure from Université Côte d'Azur for providing resources and support.

References

1. Acosta, J.N., Falcone, G.J., Rajpurkar, P., Topol, E.J.: Multimodal biomedical ai. Nature Medicine 28(9), 1773–1784 (2022)
2. Soto, J.T., Weston Hughes, J., Sanchez, P.A., Perez, M., Ouyang, D., Ashley, E.A.: Multimodal deep learning enhances diagnostic precision in left ventricular hypertrophy. European Heart Journal-Digital Health 3(3), 380–389 (2022)
3. Goto, S., Solanki, D., John, J.E., Yagi, R., Homilius, M., Ichihara, G., Katsumata, Y., Gaggin, H.K., Itabashi, Y., MacRae, C.A., et al.: Multinational federated learning approach to train ecg and echocardiogram models for hypertrophic cardiomyopathy detection. Circulation 146(10), 755–769 (2022)
4. Puyol-Antón, E., Sidhu, B.S., Gould, J., Porter, B., Elliott, M.K., Mehta, V., Rinaldi, C.A., King, A.P.: A multimodal deep learning model for cardiac resynchronisation therapy response prediction. Medical Image Analysis 79, 102465 (2022)
5. Jayakumar, S.M., Czarnecki, W.M., Menick, J., Schwarz, J., Rae, J., Osindero, S., Teh, Y.W., Harley, T., Pascanu, R.: Multiplicative interactions and where to find them (2020)
6. Kefalas, T., Vougioukas, K., Panagakis, Y., Petridis, S., Kossaifi, J., Pantic, M.: Speech-driven facial animation using polynomial fusion of features. In: ICASSP 2020-2020 IEEE International Conference on Acoustics, Speech and Signal Processing (ICASSP). pp. 3487–3491. IEEE (2020)
7. Zadeh, A., Chen, M., Poria, S., Cambria, E., Morency, L.P.: Tensor fusion network for multimodal sentiment analysis. In: Proceedings of the 2017 Conference on Empirical Methods in Natural Language Processing. Association for Computational Linguistics, Copenhagen, Denmark (Sep 2017)
8. Hou, M., Tang, J., Zhang, J., Kong, W., Zhao, Q.: Deep Multimodal Multilinear Fusion with High-order Polynomial Pooling. In: Wallach, H., Larochelle, H., Beygelzimer, A., Alché-Buc, F., Fox, E., Garnett, R. (eds.) Advances in Neural Information Processing Systems. vol. 32. Curran Associates, Inc. (2019)
9. Xiao, R., Ding, C., Hu, X., Clifford, G.D., Wright, D.W., Shah, A.J., Al-Zaiti, S., Zègre-Hemsey, J.K.: Integrating multimodal information in machine learning for classifying acute myocardial infarction. Physiological Measurement 44(4), 044002 (2023)
10. Sharma, R., Eick, C.F., Tsekos, N.V.: Sm2n2: A stacked architecture for multimodal data and its application to myocardial infarction detection. In: Statistical Atlases and Computational Models of the Heart. M&Ms and EMIDEC Challenges: 11th International Workshop, STACOM 2020, Held in Conjunction with MICCAI 2020, Lima, Peru, October 4, 2020, Revised Selected Papers 11. pp. 342–350. Springer (2021)

11. Thygesen, K., Alpert, J.S., Jaffe, A.S., Chaitman, B.R., Bax, J.J., Morrow, D.A., White, H.D., Group, E.S.D.: Fourth universal definition of myocardial infarction (2018). European Heart Journal 40(3), 237–269 (08 2018)
12. Sensoy, M., Kaplan, L., Kandemir, M.: Evidential deep learning to quantify classification uncertainty. Advances in neural information processing systems 31 (2018)
13. Jsang, A.: Subjective Logic: A formalism for reasoning under uncertainty. Springer Publishing Company, Incorporated (2018)
14. Degerli, A., Kiranyaz, S., Hamid, T., Mazhar, R., Gabbouj, M.: Early myocardial infarction detection over multi-view echocardiography. Biomedical Signal Processing and Control 87, 105448 (2024)
15. Wagner, P., Strodthoff, N., Bousseljot, R.D., Kreiseler, D., Lunze, F.I., Samek, W., Schaeffter, T.: Ptb-xl, a large publicly available electrocardiography dataset. Scientific data 7(1), 154 (2020)
16. Yang, Y., Sermesant, M.: Unsupervised polyaffine transformation learning for echocardiography motion estimation. In: International Conference on Functional Imaging and Modeling of the Heart. pp. 384–393. Springer (2023)
17. Yang, Y., Rocher, M., Moceri, P., Sermesant, M.: Explainable electrocardiogram analysis with wave decomposition: Application to myocardial infarction detection. In: International Workshop on Statistical Atlases and Computational Models of the Heart. pp. 221–232. Springer (2022)

Fetal Ultrasound Video Representation Learning Using Contrastive Rubik's Cube Recovery

Kangning Zhang[1(✉)], Jianbo Jiao[1,2], and J. Alison Noble[1]

[1] Department of Engineering Science, University of Oxford, Oxford, UK
kangning.zhang@eng.ox.ac.uk
[2] School of Computer Science, University of Birmingham, Birmingham, UK

Abstract. Contrastive learning (CL), which relies on the contrast between positive and negative pairs, has become the leading paradigm in self-supervised learning. In this paper, we propose a self-supervised learning framework, the feature-level Contrastive Rubik's Cube Recovery (CRCR). CRCR creates contrastive sub-cube pairs from ultrasound video, which capture local spatio-temporal ultrasound features, unlike traditional CL methods which are spatial and work at the global frame level. This approach learns a representation with both intra- and inter-feature contrast to provide strong local feature discrimination. The proposed method is validated on two fetal ultrasound video tasks. Extensive experiments demonstrate that our approach is effective for learning representations that transfer to both in-domain (second-trimester) and cross-domain (first-trimester) clinical downstream classification tasks. In particular, CRCR outperforms four state-of-the-art contrastive learning-based methods on the in-domain task by 3.8%, 2.0%, 1.9% and 1.1%, with each improvement being statistically significant.

Keywords: Ultrasound · Self-supervised · Contrastive Learning

1 Introduction

Ultrasound (US), due to its safety and portability, has become one of the most common medical imaging techniques for fetal health monitoring in prenatal care [1,20]. However, human annotation of fetal US images and videos could be expensive, and sometimes infeasible to obtain. Self-supervised learning (SSL) has been applied to US analysis to achieve promising results in US diagnostic tasks using a small amount of labelled data [18]. Most prior works focus on pretext tasks applied to US images, aiming to learn representations through spatial transformations [3,7,12,27]. As US scanning may include a video recording of the

Supplementary Information The online version contains supplementary material available at https://doi.org/10.1007/978-3-031-73647-6_18.

US scan, some recent works explore SSL for the entire video instead of video frames, to learn both spatial and temporal representations. Jiao et al. propose a joint reasoning approach to learn representations from both order correction and geometric transformation [10]. As contrastive learning (CL) has become one of the leading paradigms of SSL [4], Chen et al. propose the US semi-supervised contrastive learning (USCL) method [5] and Zhang et al. design the hierarchical contrastive (HiCo) learning method [26] for US video, which currently provides state-of-the-art performance.

Most existing US video pre-training methods generate contrastive pairs using video-level data augmentations [5,7,26]. Two main types of augmentations are spatio-temporal transformations (e.g. cropping, shuffling) and colour transformations (e.g. solarization) [17]. Normally, augmented views from the same video are referred to as positive pairs, and samples from different videos are referred to as negative pairs. CL learns global representation by relying on the representation invariant of positive pairs [4]. However, given the fact that fetal US videos often share a global spatial pattern with significant local variations, we are motivated to explore the use of local contrastive pairs generated from sub-cubes of US videos for local representation learning.

In this paper, we address this issue by proposing a SSL framework Feature-level Contrastive Rubik's Cube Recovery (CRCR) for US video representation learning. We introduce Rubik's cube recovery (RCR) [29] and cube reconstruction [13], which are pretext tasks designed to learn spatio-temporal context by image restoration, as effective tools to provide strong spatio-temporal distortions and create contrastive pairs from sub-cubes of US video. Unlike recent methods DiRA [8] and Swin UNETR [19], which leverage other pretext-tasks to CL frameworks by directly combining the training objectives of each pretext task. Our method, motivated by [22], provides a novel approach to generate both inter- and intra-feature contrastive pairs based on the introduced pretext tasks. Here, inter-feature pairs include sub-cubes from distinct US videos, and intra-feature pairs include distinct distorted sub-cubes from the same US video. We hypothesise that our approach could provide stronger local discrimination and enhance local representation learning.

In summary, our main contributions are as follows: 1) We propose a SSL framework, called feature-level Contrastive Rubik's Cube Recovery (CRCR) for fetal ultrasound video, which is customized to combine contrastive learning with Rubik's cube recovery and cube reconstruction; 2) We introduce an approach to generate local contrastive pairs from sub-cubes of US video, which facilitate discriminative and consistent local representation learning; 3) We empirically compare the effect of using feature-level pretext tasks and stronger feature extractor (i.e. 3D Swin Transformer) to enhance feature learning; 4) The proposed method CRCR consistently outperforms several existing SSL methods on both in-domain and cross-domain US clinical downstream tasks, showing its effectiveness and generalisability.

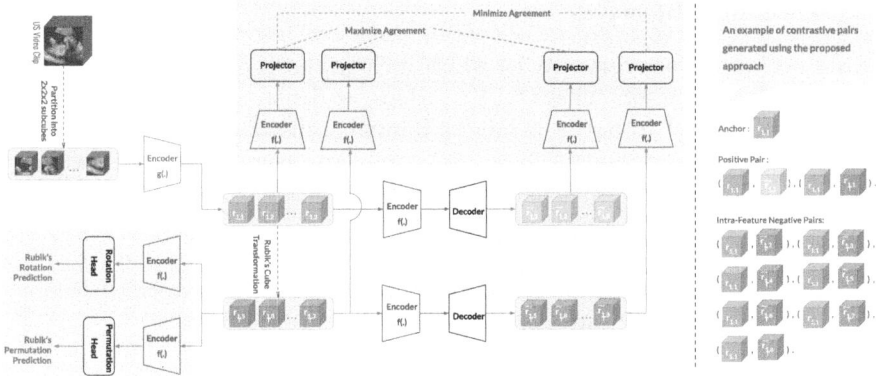

Fig. 1. The pipeline of the proposed Contrastive Rubik's Cube Recovery (CRCR) framework, consisting of three pretext tasks: contrastive learning (the blue block), cube reconstruction (the   block), and Rubik's Cube recovery (the   block). An example of our proposed local contrastive pair generation approach is demonstrated with a given anchor. (Color figure online)

2 Methods

2.1 CRCR Framework

Suppose $x_i \in \mathcal{X} \subset \mathbb{R}^{1 \times H \times W \times K}$ is a video clip in an US video dataset, where 1 represents the grey-scale property of US and H, W and K denotes the height, width, number of frames in the video clip, respectively.

The overall framework of our method is illustrated in Fig. 1, which consists of two encoders $g(.)$ and $f(.)$, one projection head $h(.)$ for contrastive learning, two MLP head $r(.)$ and $p(.)$ for Rubik's cube recovery task and one decoder $d(.)$ for the cube reconstruction task.

Different from the normal CL paradigm [4], CRCR introduces two novel designs for effective local representation learning. Firstly, we perform pretext tasks on the feature level instead of the video level, and secondly, we proposed an approach to generate local contrastive pairs from sub-cubes of US video. Since the quality of US videos is always affected by the extensive presence of speckle noises and acoustic shaded [11], whereas low-level information (i.e. boundaries) and local noise could be discarded at the encoder features. It is worth considering operating pretext tasks at the feature level instead of the video level to learn stronger and meaningful representations. As shown in Fig. 1, an input US video clip x_i is firstly partitioned into $2 \times 2 \times 2$ sub-cubes $\{x_{i,j}\}_{j=1}^{8}$, following the partition of Rubik's cube. The sub-cubes of US video along with its position embedding are then sent into the encoder $g(.)$ to get sub-cubes of US features $\{r_{i,j}\}_{j=1}^{8}$. Distortions (Rubik's cube transformation and reconstruction) are operated on the obtained features. Local contrastive pairs are generated from sub-cube of US features with the designed distortions, as in Sect. 2.2.

2.2 Training Objectives

Rubik's Cube Recovery. RCR, which includes both rotation and permutation, are operated on sub-cubes $\{r_{i,j}\}_{j=1}^{8}$. Here, we define the set of permutations $\mathcal{P} = \{p_1, p_2, ..., p_K\}$ to have the largest Hamming distance for sub-cubes shuffling and the set of rotations $\mathcal{R} = \{r_1, r_2, ..., r_M\}$ to ensure either a horizontal or vertical flip for each sub-cube, maximising the distortion. $P_k \sim \mathcal{P}$ and $R_{m,j} \sim \mathcal{R}$ are sampled. The transformed sub-cubes are denoted as $\{r_{i,j}^T\}_{j=1}^{8}$, with position embedding updated to aligned with P_k. The predicted results l_j and $\{g_{m,j}\}_{j=1}^{8}$ are obtained from the rotation and permutation heads, respectively. RCR loss is calculated as the sum of rotation and permutation loss as follows:

$$L_{RCR} = -\{\sum_{k=1}^{K} p_k \log l_k + \sum_{j=1}^{8}\sum_{m=1}^{M} r_{m,j} \log g_{m,j}\}. \quad (1)$$

Cube Reconstruction. Cube reconstruction is operated on the sub-cubes $\{r_{i,j}\}_{j=1}^{8}$ and $\{r_{i,j}^T\}_{j=1}^{8}$, with the latter's position embedding updated. The obtained reconstructions are denoted as $\{\tilde{r}_{i,j}\}_{i=1}^{8}$ and $\{\tilde{r}_{i,j}^T\}_{i=1}^{8}$, with the latter's position embedding updated. The reconstruction loss is calculated as follows:

$$L_{Reconst.} = \alpha_1 \times \sum_{j=1}^{8} MSE(\tilde{r}_{i,j}, r_{i,j}) + \alpha_2 \times \sum_{j=1}^{8} MSE(\tilde{r}_{i,j}^T, r_{i,j}^T). \quad (2)$$

Contrastive Learning. With the assumption that US videos share a global spatial pattern with local divergence, we propose generating local contrastive pairs using sub-cubes of US videos, instead of global pairs using the entire video.

Normally, CL considers different US videos as negative pairs, which might result in the high similarity between negative pairs (i.e. videos from the same scan or performing the same measurement task) and potentially mislead representation learning [5]. The proposed approach is designed to generate two sets of strongly discriminative negative samples $I^{-} = \{I_{intra}^{-}, I_{inter}^{-}\}$ by introducing the aforementioned pretext tasks as effective distortion tools. We assume that rotating and shuffling the cube would cause severe spatial and temporal distortion, resulting in the loss of both spatial and temporal information and leading to poor-quality reconstruction. A Local positive samples set, I^{+}, is generated with appropriate similarities. For a given anchor sub-cube $r_{i,j}$, the local contrastive pairs generated from the proposed approach consist of:

- **Positive sample** $I^{+} = \{r_{i,j}^T, \tilde{r}_{i,j}\}$: rotated and reconstructed views of anchor
- **Intra-feature negative samples** $I_{intra}^{-} = \{\tilde{r}_{i,j}^T, ..., \tilde{r}_{i,j}^T\}$: distorted sub-cubes from the remaining sub-cubes within the same video
- **Inter-feature negative samples** $I_{inter}^{-} = \{\tilde{r}_{k,l}^T\}_{k=1\ne i, l=1}^{N, 8}$: distorted sub-cubes from different videos

Those two sets of negative samples enable the model to learn representations from different perspectives. Inter-feature negative pairs enhance instance discrimination, while intra-feature negative pairs provide local contextual information. Referred to [4,25], we adapt NT-Xent for our contrastive loss function, which is calculated as follows:

$$L_{CLR} = -\sum_{j=1}^{8}\sum_{i^+\in I^+} \log \frac{\exp(\varphi(r_{i,j}, i^+)/\tau)}{\sum_{i^-\in I^-}\exp(\varphi(r_{i,j}, i^-)/\tau)} \quad (3)$$

$$= -\sum_{j=1}^{8}\sum_{i^+\in I^+} \{\varphi(r_{i,j}, i^+)/\tau - \log\sum_{i^-\in I^-}\exp(\varphi(r_{i,j}, i^-)/\tau)\}$$

where τ and $\varphi(.)$ denote the temperature parameter and the pairwise cosine similarity function, respectively.

Overall Loss Function. The overall learning target is a weighted combination of Rubik's cube recovery loss, reconstruction loss, and contrastive loss,

$$L_{CRCR} = \alpha \times L_{Rubik} + \beta \times L_{Reconst.} + \eta \times L_{CLR}. \quad (4)$$

A grid-search hyperparameter optimization was performed which estimated the optimal values of $\alpha = \eta = 1, \beta = 0.5$.

2.3 Stronger Feature Extractor

We propose to replace the traditional convolutional neural network with a stronger feature extractor. 3D Swin Transformer [14,23], as an effective transformer-based backbone, is considered. In 3D patch partition module, we take a sub-cube of size $\frac{T}{2} \times \frac{H}{2} \times \frac{W}{2}$ as the basic processing unit, which align with the partition of a Rubik's cube. A linear embedding is then applied to project the feature into a C-dimensional space and a positional embedding, which would be updated with the applied permutations, is added to retain sub-cube's positional information. The subsequent training stages follow the implementation described in [23].

2.4 Implementation Details

Both 3D ResNet-18 [9] and 3D Swin Transformers [23] are utilized as the backbone networks for the proposed self-supervised learning method. ResNet-18 is chosen based on prior work [5,28], while Swin Transformer is chosen for its strong feature extraction capability. We return each sub-cube to its embedded position before passing it to 3D ResNet encoders to include positional information.

For SSL pretraining, we employ an AdamW optimizer [15] to be consistent with [19]. Both networks are trained with a momentum of 0.9, a warm-up cosine scheduler of 500 iterations and a mini-batch of 32 for 40 epochs. After parameter tuning, an initial learning rate of 1×10^{-3} is used with decay of 0.1 for every 25K iterations for 3D ResNet-18 and an initial learning rate of 1×10^{-3} is used with decay of 0.01 for every 45K iteration for 3D Swin Transformer. All models are implemented with PyTorch [16], with our methods taking around 180 h to run on a single NVIDIA Titan V GPU.

For transfer learning, we fine-tune the combined encoder $f(g(.))$ along with an attached classifier head. For the standard plane detection task, networks are trained with SGD optimizer with momentum of 0.9 and mini-batch of 16 for 70 epochs. An initial learning rate of 0.01 is used with 0.1 decay at epochs 30 and 55. For first-trimester anatomies recognition, networks are trained with SGD optimizer with momentum 0.9 and mini-batch 16 for 200 epochs. An initial learning rate of 0.1 is used with a decay of 0.1 at epochs 150.

3 Results

3.1 Ultrasound Data

Our experiments are based on a large-scale fetal Ultrasound (US) video dataset [6]. Full-length routine fetal ultrasound videos are recorded and sampled at the rate of 30 Hz using a commercial Voluson E8 version BT18 ultrasound machine. We consider a subset of the entire dataset for pre-training, in which only scan recordings of the second trimester (gestational age of 18–22 weeks) are considered. The pre-training dataset consists of a total number of 70,661 video clips (each of length 32, with 2,261,179 frames in total) from 719 US scan recordings. 135 s-trimester scans are selected for three-fold cross-validation on the standard plane detection task, which consists of 15,384 labelled frames. A subset of first-trimester scans is used for cross-domain anatomy recognition task, which consists of 55,871 frames with 5 anatomy categories. All frames were central cropped to remove the fan shape and resized to 224×224 pixels.

3.2 Transfer Learning on Standard Plane Detection

Task Description. We evaluate the pre-trained representation by transferring it to the in-domain second-trimester standard plane detection task. Similar to [2], 14 classes are considered, which include four *cardiac* views, three-vessel and trachea (3VT), four-chamber (4CH), right ventricular outflow tract (RVOT), and left ventricular outflow tract (LVOT), two *brain* views, transventricular (BrainTv.) and transcerebellum (BrainTc.), two *spine* views, coronal (SpineCor.) and sagittal (SpineSag.), abdominal, femur, kidneys, lips, profile and background class. Precision, recall and F1-scores as used as the evaluation metrics.

Results. Table 1 shows a quantitative comparison of fine-tuning performance on the standard plane detection task. The table indicates that CRCR generally outperforms four state-of-the-art CL-based methods, i.e. SimCLR [4], DiRA [8],

USCL [5], and HiCo [26], by 3.8%, 1.9%, 2.0% and 1.1%, respectively, in F-1 score with the 3D ResNet backbone. Additionally, CRCR improves the performance of SimCLR and Swin UNETR by 3.7% and 1.9%, when using 3D Swin Transformer as the backbone. These improvements are statistically significant using the Wilcoxon signed-rank test [21], validating the effectiveness of our proposed method. In particular, CRCR performs better with 3D Swin Transformer as the backbone network, demonstrating the benefit of utilising a stronger feature extractor to enhance feature learning. Supp. Table 1 shows the F1-score for each class, in which CRCR owns the best performance in the majority of classes. The improvement is particularly notable for *cardiac* views, which share a global heart perspective but each has a local focus on specific structures, making them difficult to distinguish even for experts. This finding is in line with our assumption that by contrasting local contrastive pairs, the proposed method can learn semantically meaningful information from these local areas.

Table 1. Quantitative comparison of downstream task performance (mean ± std.[%]) on second-trimester standard plane detection task and first-trimester anatomy recognition task. *Rand. Init.* indicates the 3D ResNet18 trained from scratch, and [‡] denotes the use of 3D Swin Transformer as backbone network. The best results for each backbone network are marked in **bold**. P-values are calculated between our CRCR results and the previous top-1 result for each backbone network. Any $p < 0.05$ represents a statistically significant improvement and is highlighted in green.

Pretrain Method	Standard Plane Detection			Anatomy Recognition		
	Precision	Recall	F1	Precision	Recall	F1
Rand. Init.	69.3 ± 1.6	58.8 ± 3.1	59.1 ± 3.1	80.8 ± 3.2	78.4 ± 0.7	81.1 ± 0.5
RCR [29]	70.0 ± 0.8	66.3 ± 3.5	66.4 ± 2.3	89.2 ± 1.4	88.6 ± 1.6	89.5 ± 1.7
SimCLR [4]	70.9 ± 0.5	68.9 ± 1.7	68.7 ± 1.2	95.5 ± 0.5	94.7 ± 0.3	94.8 ± 0.8
DiRA [8]	72.0 ± 2.5	70.4 ± 2.3	70.6 ± 2.3	95.7 ± 1.4	95.3 ± 1.3	95.1 ± 1.2
USCL [5]	71.6 ± 1.1	70.2 ± 1.5	70.5 ± 0.9	95.9 ± 0.7	95.2 ± 0.8	95.3 ± 1.5
HiCo [26]	72.3 ± 1.7	71.7 ± 1.9	71.4 ± 2.0	96.3 ± 0.3	95.7 ± 0.7	95.8 ± 0.9
CRCR (ours)	**73.1 ± 2.3**	**72.6 ± 2.7**	**72.5 ± 2.2**	**96.8 ± 1.2**	**96.1 ± 1.4**	**96.2 ± 1.8**
P-value	0.048	0.021	0.010	0.018	0.027	0.035
SimCLR [4][‡]	72.8 ± 0.8	70.7 ± 1.2	70.7 ± 1.6	95.9 ± 1.3	95.3 ± 0.8	95.1 ± 1.5
SwinUNETR [19][‡]	73.6 ± 1.2	73.2 ± 3.5	72.5 ± 2.1	96.7 ± 2.7	96.9 ± 2.4	96.5 ± 2.3
CRCR (ours)[‡]	**74.9 ± 2.5**	**74.8 ± 3.0**	**74.4 ± 2.6**	**97.1 ± 2.3**	**97.1 ± 1.6**	**97.2 ± 1.3**
P-value	0.003	0.001	<0.001	0.042	0.062	0.009

3.3 Transfer Learning on First-Trimester Anatomy Recognition

Task Description. We explore the generalisability of the pre-trained representation to a cross-domain first-trimester anatomy recognition task. Similar to [24], five key anatomy categories are considered, which include crown rump length (CRL), nuchal translucency (NT), biparietal diameter (BPD), 3D-mode (3D) and other (BK) for first-trimester fetal biometry measurements.

Results. Table 1 demonstrates quantitative results of fine-tuning performance on the first-trimester anatomy recognition task. From the results, we observe that our proposed method achieves the best performance among all the compared methods with both 3D ResNet and 3D Swin Transformer as backbone networks. Most improvements are statistically significant with paired t-tests. This task of anatomical recognition could be challenging due to the small fetal size in the first trimester. While the compared CL-based methods focus on global representation learning, CRCR leans local patterns through local contrastive pairs, which could be valuable when the clinical region-of-interest is small. Among the compared methods, USCL and HiCo, which are designed specifically for US videos, perform better than those designed for general computer vision. Supp. Table 2 shows the F1-score for each anatomy category, in which CRCR achieves the highest F1 scores in all categories. This finding demonstrates the effectiveness and generalisability of our proposed method CRCR on first-trimester US video.

3.4 Ablation Study

Efficacy of Self-supervised Objectives. We perform an empirical study on pre-training with different combinations of self-supervised objectives used in CRCR loss. Results are shown in Table 2. An improvement could be seen by adding pretext tasks, with the combination of contrastive learning and Rubik's cube recovery task as the best-performing pairing. These results indicate that three selected tasks harmonize with each other and the proposed collaborative learning methods enhance representation learning and downstream performance.

Table 2. Ablation studies on the effectiveness of each self-supervised objective and the effectiveness of performing pretext tasks at the feature level. Experiments are fine-tuned using 3D ResNet for the standard plane detection task.

L_{CLR}	L_{Rubik}	L_{Rec}	Feature-level			Video-level		
			Precision	Recall	F1-score	Precision	Recall	F1-score
✓			71.2	69.4	69.5	70.9	68.9	68.7
	✓		70.4	66.7	66.4	70.0	66.3	66.4
		✓	70.3	66.1	65.8	69.8	64.2	64.5
	✓	✓	70.9	69.0	68.5	70.6	68.5	68.1
✓	✓		72.3	71.1	70.9	71.4	69.7	69.8
✓		✓	71.8	70.5	70.3	71.0	69.5	69.1
✓	✓	✓	**73.1**	**72.6**	**72.0**	**72.4**	**71.1**	**71.3**

Efficacy of Feature-Level Pretext Task. We investigate how performing pretext tasks at the feature-level impacts representation learning compared to the video level. As illustrated in Table 2, performing pretext tasks at video level degrades the performance of the standard plane detection task to feature level. This aligns with our hypothesis that performing pretext tasks at the feature level enables the model to be less sensitive to superficial changes and focus more on informative regions, as local noise and irrelevant features could be discarded through encoder optimization.

4 Conclusion

In this paper, we present a novel self-supervised learning method named feature-level Contrastive Rubik's Cube Recovery (CRCR) for local representation learning of fetal US video. The proposed method leverages the advantages of contrastive learning with Rubik's cube recovery task and cube reconstruction task. A local contrastive pair generation approach is introduced to contrast sub-cube pairs from US video. Through extensive experiments, it is demonstrated that CRCR achieves state-of-the-art performance on both second-trimester standard plane detection task and first-trimester anatomy recognition task and significantly improves the quality of learnt representation in pre-training for both in-domain and cross-domain downstream tasks. In the future, the proposed approach can be potentially applied to other medical imaging modalities.

Acknowledgement. The authors would like to thank the support from the ERC Project PULSE ERC-ADG-2015 694581 and the EPSRC Center for Doctoral Training in Health Data Science (EP/S02428X/1). Jianbo Jiao is supported by the Royal Society Short Industry Fellowship (SIF\R1\231009).

References

1. Abramowicz, J.S.: Benefits and risks of ultrasound in pregnancy. In: Seminars in perinatology. vol. 37, pp. 295–300. Elsevier (2013)
2. Baumgartner, C.F., Kamnitsas, K., Matthew, J., Fletcher, T.P., Smith, S., Koch, L.M., Kainz, B., Rueckert, D.: Sononet: real-time detection and localisation of fetal standard scan planes in freehand ultrasound. IEEE transactions on medical imaging **36**(11), 2204–2215 (2017)
3. Chen, L., Bentley, P., Mori, K., Misawa, K., Fujiwara, M., Rueckert, D.: Self-supervised learning for medical image analysis using image context restoration. Medical image analysis **58**, 101539 (2019)
4. Chen, T., Kornblith, S., Norouzi, M., Hinton, G.: A simple framework for contrastive learning of visual representations. arXiv preprint arXiv:2002.05709 (2020)
5. Chen, Y., Zhang, C., Liu, L., Feng, C., Dong, C., Luo, Y., Wan, X.: Uscl: pretraining deep ultrasound image diagnosis model through video contrastive representation learning. In: Medical Image Computing and Computer Assisted Intervention–MICCAI 2021: 24th International Conference, Strasbourg, France, September 27–October 1, 2021, Proceedings, Part VIII 24. pp. 627–637. Springer (2021)

6. Drukker, L., Sharma, H., Droste, R., Alsharid, M., Chatelain, P., Noble, J.A., Papageorghiou, A.T.: Transforming obstetric ultrasound into data science using eye tracking, voice recording, transducer motion and ultrasound video. Scientific Reports **11**(1), 14109 (2021)
7. Fu, Z., Jiao, J., Yasrab, R., Drukker, L., Papageorghiou, A.T., Noble, J.A.: Anatomy-aware contrastive representation learning for fetal ultrasound. In: European Conference on Computer Vision. pp. 422–436. Springer (2022)
8. Haghighi, F., Taher, M.R.H., Gotway, M.B., Liang, J.: Dira: Discriminative, restorative, and adversarial learning for self-supervised medical image analysis. In: Proceedings of the IEEE/CVF Conference on Computer Vision and Pattern Recognition. pp. 20824–20834 (2022)
9. He, K., Zhang, X., Ren, S., Sun, J.: Deep residual learning for image recognition. In: CVPR (2016)
10. Jiao, J., Droste, R., Drukker, L., Papageorghiou, A.T., Noble, J.A.: Self-supervised representation learning for ultrasound video. In: 2020 IEEE 17th international symposium on biomedical imaging (ISBI). pp. 1847–1850. IEEE (2020)
11. Li, H., Fang, J., Liu, S., Liang, X., Yang, X., Mai, Z., Van, M.T., Wang, T., Chen, Z., Ni, D.: Cr-unet: A composite network for ovary and follicle segmentation in ultrasound images. IEEE journal of biomedical and health informatics **24**(4), 974–983 (2019)
12. Liu, H., Liu, J., Hou, S., Tao, T., Han, J.: Perception consistency ultrasound image super-resolution via self-supervised cyclegan. Neural Computing and Applications pp. 1–11 (2023)
13. Liu, X., Zhang, F., Hou, Z., Mian, L., Wang, Z., Zhang, J., Tang, J.: Self-supervised learning: Generative or contrastive. IEEE transactions on knowledge and data engineering **35**(1), 857–876 (2021)
14. Liu, Z., Lin, Y., Cao, Y., Hu, H., Wei, Y., Zhang, Z., Lin, S., Guo, B.: Swin transformer: Hierarchical vision transformer using shifted windows. In: Proceedings of the IEEE/CVF international conference on computer vision. pp. 10012–10022 (2021)
15. Loshchilov, I., Hutter, F.: Decoupled weight decay regularization. arXiv preprint arXiv:1711.05101 (2017)
16. Paszke, A., Gross, S., Massa, F., Lerer, A., Bradbury, J., Chanan, G., Killeen, T., Lin, Z., Gimelshein, N., Antiga, L., et al.: Pytorch: An imperative style, high-performance deep learning library. Advances in neural information processing systems **32** (2019)
17. Rani, V., Nabi, S.T., Kumar, M., Mittal, A., Kumar, K.: Self-supervised learning: A succinct review. Archives of Computational Methods in Engineering **30**(4), 2761–2775 (2023)
18. Shurrab, S., Duwairi, R.: Self-supervised learning methods and applications in medical imaging analysis: A survey. PeerJ Computer Science **8**, e1045 (2022)
19. Tang, Y., Yang, D., Li, W., Roth, H.R., Landman, B., Xu, D., Nath, V., Hatamizadeh, A.: Self-supervised pre-training of swin transformers for 3d medical image analysis. In: Proceedings of the IEEE/CVF conference on computer vision and pattern recognition. pp. 20730–20740 (2022)
20. Whitworth, M., Bricker, L., Mullan, C.: Ultrasound for fetal assessment in early pregnancy. Cochrane database of systematic reviews (7) (2015)
21. Woolson, R.F.: Wilcoxon signed-rank test. Encyclopedia of Biostatistics **8** (2005)
22. Xie, E., Ding, J., Wang, W., Zhan, X., Xu, H., Sun, P., Li, Z., Luo, P.: Detco: Unsupervised contrastive learning for object detection. In: Proceedings of the IEEE/CVF international conference on computer vision. pp. 8392–8401 (2021)

23. Yang, Y.Q., Guo, Y.X., Xiong, J.Y., Liu, Y., Pan, H., Wang, P.S., Tong, X., Guo, B.: Swin3d: A pretrained transformer backbone for 3d indoor scene understanding. arXiv preprint arXiv:2304.06906 (2023)
24. Yasrab, R., Fu, Z., Zhao, H., Lee, L.H., Sharma, H., Drukker, L., Papageorgiou, A.T., Noble, J.A.: A machine learning method for automated description and workflow analysis of first trimester ultrasound scans. IEEE Transactions on Medical Imaging **42**(5), 1301–1313 (2022)
25. You, Y., Chen, T., Sui, Y., Chen, T., Wang, Z., Shen, Y.: Graph contrastive learning with augmentations. Advances in neural information processing systems **33**, 5812–5823 (2020)
26. Zhang, C., Chen, Y., Liu, L., Liu, Q., Zhou, X.: Hico: hierarchical contrastive learning for ultrasound video model pretraining. In: Proceedings of the Asian Conference on Computer Vision. pp. 229–246 (2022)
27. Zhang, J., He, Q., Xiao, Y., Zheng, H., Wang, C., Luo, J.: Ultrasound image reconstruction from plane wave radio-frequency data by self-supervised deep neural network. Medical Image Analysis **70**, 102018 (2021)
28. Zhu, J., Li, Y., Hu, Y., Ma, K., Zhou, S.K., Zheng, Y.: Rubik's cube+: A self-supervised feature learning framework for 3d medical image analysis. Medical image analysis **64**, 101746 (2020)
29. Zhuang, X., Li, Y., Hu, Y., Ma, K., Yang, Y., Zheng, Y.: Self-supervised feature learning for 3d medical images by playing a rubik's cube. In: Medical Image Computing and Computer Assisted Intervention–MICCAI 2019: 22nd International Conference, Shenzhen, China, October 13–17, 2019, Proceedings, Part IV 22. pp. 420–428. Springer (2019)

LoRIS - Weakly-Supervised Anomaly Detection for Ultrasound Images

Marco Colussi[1](✉), Dragan Ahmetovic[1], Gabriele Civitarese[1], Claudio Bettini[1], Aiman Solyman[1], Roberta Gualtierotti[2,3], Flora Peyvandi[2,3], and Sergio Mascetti[1]

[1] Department of Computer Science, Università degli Studi di Milano, Via Celoria, 18, 20133 Milan, Italy
marco.colussi@unimi.it
[2] Department of Pathophysiology and Transplantation, Università degli Studi di Milano, Via Pace, 9, 20122 Milan, Italy
[3] Fondazione IRCCS Ca' Granda Ospedale Maggiore Policlinico, Angelo Bianchi Bonomi Hemophilia and Thrombosis Center, Via Pace, 9, 20122 Milan, Italy

Abstract. This paper presents **LoRIS** (Localized Reconstruction-by-Inpainting with Single-mask), a novel weakly-supervised anomaly detection technique designed to identify knee joint recess distension in musculoskeletal ultrasound images, which are noisy and unbalanced (as distended cases are rarer). In this context, supervised techniques require a high number of annotated images of both classes (distended and nondistended). On the other hand, we show that existing unsupervised anomaly detection techniques, which can be trained with images from a single class, are ineffective and often unable to correctly localize the anomaly. To overcome these issues, **LoRIS** is trained with nondistended images only and uses the recess bounding box as location prior to guide the reconstruction. Experimental results show that **LoRIS** outperforms state-of-the-art unsupervised anomaly detection techniques. When compared to a state-of-the-art fully supervised solution, **LoRIS** presents similar performance but has two key advantages: during training it requires images from a single class only, and it also outputs the recess segmentation, without the need for segmentation annotations.

Keywords: Anomaly detection · Weak-supervision · Ultrasound imaging

1 Introduction

For patients with hemophilia, joint bleeding is a common complication. If not treated promptly, it can lead to synovial hyperplasia, osteochondral damage, and hemophilic arthropathy [9]. Ultrasound (US) imaging is emerging as a practical approach for detecting bleeding in the joint recess [22]. In order to support medical practitioners in the diagnosis process, Computer-Aided Diagnosis (CAD) systems based on US images have been extensively researched [10]. Specifically, to support the diagnosis of joint bleeding, prior works have proposed techniques to detect joint recess distention caused by joint bleeding. The proposed solutions are based on binary classification [27] and multi-task learning (combining classification and detection) [3]. In these works, the task of distinguishing between distended and non-distended recesses is addressed with supervised classification. In addition to classification, segmentation is also of utmost importance in medical imaging, as it facilitates the identification of structures or regions of interest, hence enabling visual guidance for professionals [2]. A major problem of these solutions is the reliance on labeled images, which are scarce, imbalanced between the two classes (distended cases are rarer than non-distended ones), and have a high annotation cost.

In the literature, a common approach to tackle these types of problems is unsupervised anomaly detection [26], in which the model is trained only using normal data samples and is used to identify anomalous samples deviating from the learned distribution. Several solutions have been proposed for unsupervised anomaly detection: reconstruction by inpainting [30], conditional GANs [1], patch-based memory banks [24], synthesizing anomaly samples [16,29], and normalizing flows [8]. Other works propose specific solutions tackling the problems of medical imaging: normalizing reconstruction error with uncertainty [18] or through patch-interpolation [25]. These techniques provide both an overall anomaly score and, often, a pixel-level anomaly map that can be used for anomaly segmentation. However, as we show in this paper, these techniques are ineffective in the specific domain considered in this paper.

To address the ineffectiveness of unsupervised anomaly detection techniques, we propose a solution inspired by weakly supervised segmentation approaches that have been extensively researched in the segmentation domain, where acquiring the segmentation masks is not always feasible [5]. These approaches rely on *weak* labels that contain partial information compared to the labels used in the supervised approach. In particular, previous works suggest that the use of a *location prior*, in the form of the bounding box of the element of interest, can effectively mitigate the cost of annotation while still providing high accuracy in semantic segmentation [14], referring image segmentation [6], and in medical image segmentation [12,17]. However, to the best of our knowledge, these approaches have never been applied in the field of anomaly detection.

In this paper, we present **LoRIS** (Localized Reconstruction-by-Inpainting with a Single mask), a weakly supervised anomaly detection approach that uses the joint recess bounding box as prior knowledge during the inpainting. We also propose *Directional Distance* (DD), a new image similarity deviation metric that yields better anomaly segmentation results than existing metrics, like Multi-Scale Gradient Magnitude Similarity Deviation (MSGMSD) [28]. Experimental results, conducted on a dataset of 483 images, show that **LoRIS** is more accurate in detecting recess distention when using MSGMSD (image-level AUROC 0.78), outperforming state-of-the-art unsupervised techniques and providing similar results as a previous approach specifically designed for this problem [3]. Instead, considering the segmentation problem, **LoRIS** provides better results when adopting DD (Dice score of 0.35), outperforming the existing unsupervised techniques. To summarize, our main contributions are:

- We propose **LoRIS**, the first weakly supervised anomaly detection and segmentation technique for ultrasound images.
- We demonstrate, through a comprehensive evaluation and an ablation study, that a) state-of-the-art unsupervised anomaly detection approaches are ineffective in this domain, and that b) **LoRIS** is effective and also provides similar performance as a supervised solution. The advantages over the supervised solution are that **LoRIS** can be trained with images of a single class and also produces recess segmentation.
- We show an effective solution to automatically compute the location prior, hence achieving a fully automated detection pipeline at inference time.

2 Methodology

After defining the problem (Sect. 2.1), we describe the two main steps of **LoRIS**: *localized reconstruction* (Sect. 2.2) and *anomaly detection* (Sect. 2.3). Finally, Sect. 2.4 describes how to automatically compute the location prior.

2.1 Problem Formulation

Hemophilia is a rare disease and its management has improved dramatically in the last decade for two reasons. First, the use of ultrasound imaging emerged as a practical solution for the detection of recess joint distention, caused by joint bleeding [19]. A second factor is the increased availability of replacement treatments (coagulation factor VIII and factor IX) and non-replacement treatments [20]. This has led to a reduction in the number of acute bleeding episodes, including intra-articular bleeding [7], which is otherwise a common cause of recess distention. Since in this paper we consider a cohort of patients treated with these drugs, images of distended recesses are rarer than non-distended ones. For this reason, we propose to frame the problem as an anomaly detection task in which a distended recess represents the anomalous case.

Specifically, we address the problem of detecting the distension of the subquadricipital recess (SQR), which is the main recess of the knee joint. Our approach uses images of the longitudinal US scan of the knee joint, which are commonly used to diagnose SQR distention by medical practitioners [19].

2.2 Localized Reconstruction

The *localized reconstruction module* takes in input an image of the longitudinal US scan of the knee joint and the recess bounding box location prior (see Fig. 1). The module first inpaints the area in the image defined by the location prior with a black rectangle. Then, it reconstructs the inpainted area using a specifically trained network. One advantage of reconstructing the detected recess area only is that this solution avoids reconstructing areas that are of no interest for the given problem and that, due to noise and high inter-patient variability, can be reconstructed imprecisely also for physiological (non-pathological) images.

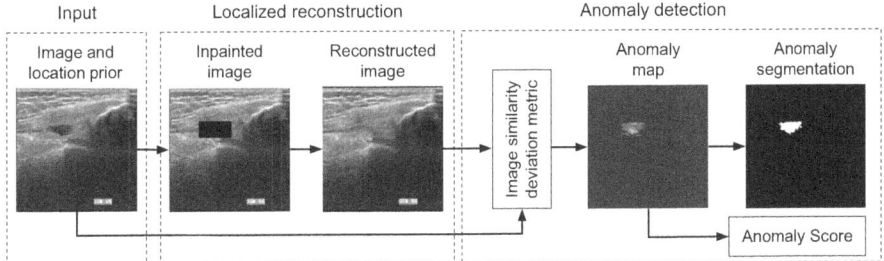

Fig. 1. LoRIS procedure schema

The network used is a U-Net [23], trained on a single class (images with non-distended recess) to reconstruct the inpainted image while focusing solely on the masked region. This is achieved through skip connections, directly propagating the information from low-level layers to the higher ones, facilitating the reconstruction process by preserving fine details, and maintaining contextual information from the original input. Consistently with previous works [30], we trained the network with the sum of three different losses:

$$L_{tot} = L_{MSGMS}(I, I_r) + L_{SSIM}(I, I_r) + L_2(I, I_r)$$

where L_{MSGMS} is the Multi-Scale Gradient Magnitude Similarity loss, L_{SSIM} indicates the structural similarity index loss and the pixel-wise loss L_2 between the original image I and the reconstructed one I_r.

At inference time, image reconstruction is achieved in a single iteration that reconstructs the entire masked area. This is in contrast with the approach of using multiple masks, adopted by existing reconstruction-by-inpainting techniques, that iteratively mask and reconstruct portions of the image, finally joining all the reconstructed areas to obtain the entire reconstructed image [30]. The problem with the multiple-masks approach is that, during its iterations, only a portion of the recess could be masked at a time, hence resulting in the image being precisely reconstructed even when the recess is distended. Instead, by using a single mask, the entire recess is inpainted, so it is more likely that it will be reconstructed as non-distended also in distended images, hence revealing the anomaly.

2.3 Anomaly Detection

At inference time, **LoRIS** runs the localized reconstruction module to obtain the reconstructed image. Then, an *anomaly map* is computed, indicating an anomaly score for each pixel of the original image, using an image similarity deviation metric (see Fig. 1). An overall anomaly score is computed at image level by average pooling the pixel-wise anomaly scores of the anomaly map. The anomaly is segmented by first selecting the set of pixels in the anomaly map whose value is above a threshold that maximizes the dice score (as in [16]) and then by applying a post-processing step using morphological closing, followed by opening with kernel $3x3$.

In this paper, we propose a novel image similarity deviation metric called **directional difference** (DD) that is based on the following observation: a distended recess appears in a US image as a thick dark area, whereas a non-distended recess appears as a thin dark line on a lighter background. If an image containing a distended recess is provided in input, we expect the reconstruction to produce an image that resembles a non-distended recess, with the recess bounding box containing lighter pixels, on average, than the original image. The DD metric measures the increase of light intensity for the pixels in the reconstructed image with respect to the original one, ignoring the pixels where the light intensity actually decreases. Formally:

$$DD(p, p_r) = \max((p_r - p), 0)$$

where p_r is the intensity of a pixel in the reconstructed image and p is the intensity of the corresponding pixel in the original image.

We experimented **LoRIS** also considering alternative image similarity deviation metrics. Some of them are derived from the existing literature on similarity deviation between images, including Gradient Magnitude Similarity Deviation (GMSD), and Multi-Scale Gradient Magnitude Similarity Deviation (MSGMSD) [31]. We also experimented with similarity scoring functions between images by computing their dual, such as the Structural Similarity Index (SSIM). Among all these image similarity deviation metrics, **LoRIS** obtained the best results with MSGMSD in terms of image-wise and pixel-wise accuracy, while best Dice score was obtained using **DD**.

2.4 Automatic Detection of the Recess Bounding Box

LoRIS requires the recess bounding box as location prior both at training and inference time. The use of (manually annotated) bounding box priors limits the real-world applicability of the proposed approach. To address this issue, we further propose the use of object detection for automatically annotating the bounding box location priors, thus achieving a fully automated pipeline (from image acquisition to anomaly prediction). Note that, also in this case, the object detection has to be trained on non-distended images only to maintain the applicability of the approach in the anomaly detection setting.

3 Experimental Evaluation

This section describes the experimental methodology (Sect. 3.1), the experimental results in terms of anomaly detection and segmentation performance (Sect. 3.2), and the impact of automatic location prior detection (Sect. 3.3).

3.1 Experimental Methodology

We used the same dataset as in [3], containing 483 US images of the knee recess, 123 of which are distended, according to the annotation of a physician who is an expert US reader in this specific field. The same physician also annotated the images with the recess bounding box (the location prior) and the recess segmentation, which is used to compute pixel-wise segmentation accuracy. The images are divided into 5 folds using patient-based splits, thus ensuring that no images of the same patient are simultaneously in the training and test folds. Due to this, the exact number of images in each fold can vary. Approximately, each fold contains 308, 78, and 97 images for the training, validation, and test sets, respectively. Note that the images of distended recesses in the training and validation sets are ignored for the training of the proposed anomaly detection technique. Therefore, for each fold, we use approximately 226, 63, and 97 images in the training, validation, and test sets, respectively.

For what concerns the model training, for each fold, the U-net model was trained for 1000 epochs with an early-stopping criterion of 50 epochs on the validation loss, a learning rate of 0.0001 with Adam optimizer [13], and a batch size of 4. Parameters were selected empirically. We ran the experiments on a Ubuntu Server with a partitioned NVIDIA A100 GPU, 42Gb of RAM, and an AMD EPYC 8-core CPU. The code is publicly available[1].

To assess the accuracy of the anomaly detection, we consider metrics commonly used in the state-of-the-art: Image-level AUROC (I-AUROC) and Pixel-level AUROC (P-AUROC). Additionally, we employ the Dice score as it more accurately evaluates the anomaly segmentation accuracy [4].

3.2 Anomaly Detection and Segmentation Results

Table 1 compares **LoRIS** with state-of-the-art unsupervised anomaly detection approaches and a previously proposed supervised technique [3]. Considering the unsupervised techniques, recent ones (PatchCore [24], Simplenet [16] and Cflow [8]) yield the best results, with PatchCore having an I-AUROC of 0.701 and a P-AUROC of 0.871. However, unsupervised techniques have a Dice score lower than 0.2, showing that they do not obtain a relevant segmentation of the anomalous region. This is also exemplified in Fig. 2 that shows, for three sample images, the segmentation results of various techniques. As shown in the figure, the unsupervised techniques fail in most of the cases to detect the recess area, and, even when they do, they do not approximate the recess accurately. The *multi-task* supervised technique [3] achieves a higher I-AUROC value of 0.780 but it cannot compute the recess segmentation.

Table 1 also shows the results of two variants of **LoRIS**, when using MSGMSD (**LoRIS+MSGMSD**) and DD (**LoRIS+DD**) as image similarity deviation metrics. The former achieves the best performance in terms of image-level AUROC (0.783) when compared with all other techniques, including *multi-task*. It also outperforms all other unsupervised techniques in terms

---
[1] https://github.com/warpcut/LoRIS

Table 1. Anomaly detection and segmentation results

Model	Setting	I-AUROC	P-AUROC	Dice
RIAD [30]	Unsupervised	0.583 ± 0.083	0.682 ± 0.016	0.051 ± 0.017
InTrans [21]	Unsupervised	0.581 ± 0.053	0.574 ± 0.033	0.028 ± 0.009
Ganomaly [1]	Unsupervised	0.573 ± 0.035	-	-
FAIR [15]	Unsupervised	0.544 ± 0.035	0.668 ± 0.021	0.102 ± 0.012
Cflow [8]	Unsupervised	0.645 ± 0.125	0.864 ± 0.011	0.124 ± 0.049
Draem [29]	Unsupervised	0.547 ± 0.066	0.626 ± 0.041	0.033 ± 0.007
UAE [18]	Unsupervised	0.621 ± 0.068	0.699 ± 0.014	0.061 ± 0.018
Simplenet [16]	Unsupervised	0.68 ± 0.104	0.818 ± 0.01	0.144 ± 0.047
PatchCore [24]	Unsupervised	0.701 ± 0.090	0.871 ± 0.009	0.193 ± 0.066
Multi-task [3]	Supervised	0.780 ± 0.050	-	-
LoRIS+MSGMSD	Weakly-supervised	**0.783 ± 0.050**	**0.932 ± 0.018**	0.263 ± 0.042
LoRIS+DD	Weakly-supervised	0.750 ± 0.100	0.746 ± 0.047	**0.353 ± 0.034**

of pixel-level AUROC (0.932). Taking into account the segmentation ability, **LoRIS+DD** achieves the best results, with a Dice score of 0.353. However, we note that the Dice score is still relatively low, indicating that accurate anomaly segmentation in this domain is particularly challenging. This observation is also supported by the results obtained using UAE [18] which, despite being designed for medical imaging, yields poor results (AUROC of 0.699 and dice of 0.061). Nevertheless, as shown in Fig. 2, while segmentation is not extremely accurate, it approximates the actual recess shape well.

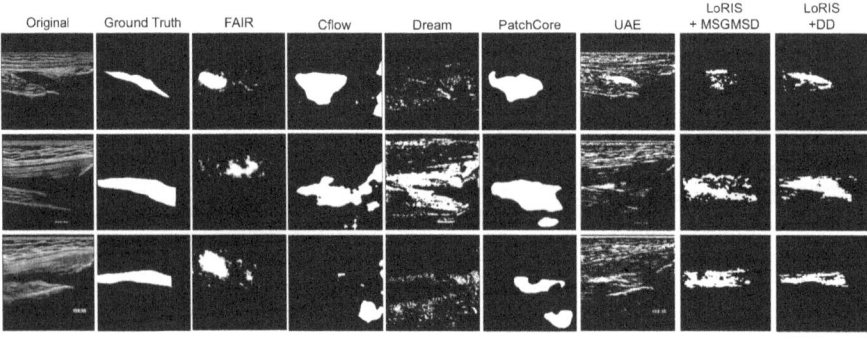

Fig. 2. Comparison of the anomaly segmentations generated by different techniques

3.3 Automated Detection of the Recess Bounding Box

For the automated detection of the bounding box location prior, we examine two object detection approaches, Yolo (V5) [11] and Co-DETR [32]. We trained the two models on the non-distended images in the training set and measured the performance of **LoRIS+MSGMSD** with the location prior automatically computed by the trained object detection model at test time.

As shown in Table 2, YOLO fails to achieve results comparable to the upper baseline represented by the Ground Truth (GT) annotations. Indeed, there is a significant drop in performance: -4.4% in I-AUROC, -5.4% in P-AUROC and -6.2 in Dice score. Instead, using CoDETR, shown to perform better in several domains [32], the results remain comparable with those obtained with GT: -0.7% in I-AUROC, -2.2% in P-AUROC and -2.3% in Dice score.

Table 2. Performances of the object detection algorithms and their impact.

	precision	map@50	mAP@75	I-AUROC	P-AUROC	Dice
GT	-	-	-	0.783 ± 0.050	0.932 ± 0.018	0.263 ± 0.042
Yolo-V5	0.954 ± 0.044	0.796 ± 0.052	0.254 ± 0.063	0.773 ± 0.038	0.872 ± 0.033	0.223 ± 0.030
CoDETR	1.0 ± 0.0	0.9 ± 0.035	0.41 ± 0.066	0.776 ± 0.029	0.910 ± 0.038	0.240 ± 0.031

4 Conclusions

The approach proposed in this paper is the first anomaly detection technique to use a location prior and to adopt the reconstruction-by-inpainting approach on US images, which are noisy and have high variability. Experimental results show that the technique can separate normal images from anomalous ones better than state-of-the-art unsupervised approaches, achieving results comparable to a fully supervised approach proposed previously [3], when **LoRIS+MSGMSD** is used. Instead, **LoRIS+DD** yields the best results for the purpose of anomaly segmentation.

Furthermore, **LoRIS** has two additional benefits with respect to the supervised approach. First, it is trained using non-anomalous data only, and therefore it is more suitable to the target problem domain in which anomalous data is scarce. Second, it provides more anatomically reasonable anomaly segmentations, only requiring the recess bounding box as a location prior. We also show that this information can be obtained using a state-of-the-art object detection technique, achieving results comparable to the use of the manually annotated data and thus achieving a fully automated SQR distension detection pipeline.

As a future work, we will experiment different image similarity deviation metrics for different tasks: **MSGMSD** can be used to achieve a better SQR distension detection accuracy, while **DD** can be used to compute more accurate anomaly segmentation. We will also investigate the possibility of using the bounding box location prior in existing anomaly detection techniques, for example for delimiting the areas targeted with synthetic anomalies in Draem [29]. Finally, we will integrate the location prior detection to form an end-to-end solution, and we will explore how our anomaly detection approach performs on other medical imaging sources as well as other application domains.

Acknowledgments. This research is partially supported by the MUSA (Multilayered Urban Sustainability Action) and by the FAIR (Future Artificial Intelligence Research) projects both funded by the NextGeneration EU program. It is also partially supported by the Italian Ministry of Health - Bando Ricerca Corrente. The Hemostasis & Thrombosis Unit of the Fondazione IRCCS Ca' Granda Ospedale Maggiore Policlinico is member of the European Reference Network on Rare Haematological Diseases EuroBloodNet-Project ID No 101157011. ERN-EuroBloodNet is partly co-funded by the European Union within the framework of the Fourth EU Health Programme.

Disclosure of Interests. The authors have no competing interests to declare that are relevant to the content of this article.

References

1. Akcay, S., Atapour-Abarghouei, A., Breckon, T.P.: Ganomaly: Semi-supervised anomaly detection via adversarial training. In: Asian Conference on Computer Vision. Springer (2019)
2. Asgari Taghanaki, S., Abhishek, K., Cohen, J.P., Cohen-Adad, J., Hamarneh, G.: Deep semantic segmentation of natural and medical images: a review. Artificial Intelligence Review **54**, 137–178 (2021)
3. Colussi, M., Civitarese, G., Ahmetovic, D., Bettini, C., Gualtierotti, R., Peyvandi, F., Mascetti, S.: Ultrasound detection of subquadricipital recess distension. Intelligent Systems with Applications (2023)
4. Eelbode, T., Bertels, J., Berman, M., Vandermeulen, D., Maes, F., Bisschops, R., Blaschko, M.B.: Optimization for medical image segmentation: theory and practice when evaluating with dice score or jaccard index. IEEE Transactions on Medical Imaging **39**(11), 3679–3690 (2020)
5. El Jurdi, R., Petitjean, C., Honeine, P., Cheplygina, V., Abdallah, F.: High-level prior-based loss functions for medical image segmentation: A survey. Computer Vision and Image Understanding **210**, 103248 (2021)
6. Feng, G., Zhang, L., Hu, Z., Lu, H.: Learning from box annotations for referring image segmentation. IEEE Transactions on Neural Networks and Learning Systems (2022)
7. Gualtierotti, R., Solimeno, L.P., Peyvandi, F.: Hemophilic arthropathy: current knowledge and future perspectives. Journal of Thrombosis and Haemostasis (2021)
8. Gudovskiy, D., Ishizaka, S., Kozuka, K.: Cflow-ad: Real-time unsupervised anomaly detection with localization via conditional normalizing flows. In: IEEE/CVF Winter Conference on Applications of Computer Vision (2022)
9. Hilgartner, M.W.: Current treatment of hemophilic arthropathy. Current opinion in pediatrics **14**(1), 46–49 (2002)
10. Huang, Q., Zhang, F., Li, X.: Machine learning in ultrasound computer-aided diagnostic systems: a survey. BioMed research international **2018** (2018)

11. Jocher, G., Chaurasia, A., Stoken, A., Borovec, J., NanoCode012, Kwon, Y., TaoXie, Fang, J., imyhxy, Michael, K., Lorna, V, A., Montes, D., Nadar, J., Laughing, tkianai, yxNONG, Skalski, P., Wang, Z., Hogan, A., Fati, C., Mammana, L., AlexWang1900, Patel, D., Yiwei, D., You, F., Hajek, J., Diaconu, L., Minh, M.T.: ultralytics/yolov5: v6.1 (Feb 2022). https://doi.org/10.5281/zenodo.6222936
12. Kervadec, H., Dolz, J., Wang, S., Granger, E., Ayed, I.B.: Bounding boxes for weakly supervised segmentation: Global constraints get close to full supervision. In: Medical imaging with deep learning. pp. 365–381. PMLR (2020)
13. Kingma, D.P., Ba, J.: Adam: A method for stochastic optimization. arXiv preprint arXiv:1412.6980 (2014)
14. Kulharia, V., Chandra, S., Agrawal, A., Torr, P., Tyagi, A.: Box2seg: Attention weighted loss and discriminative feature learning for weakly supervised segmentation. In: European Conference on Computer Vision. pp. 290–308. Springer (2020)
15. Liu, T., Li, B., Du, X., Jiang, B., Geng, L., Wang, F., Zhao, Z.: Fair: Frequency-aware image restoration for industrial visual anomaly detection. arXiv preprint arXiv:2309.07068 (2023)
16. Liu, Z., Zhou, Y., Xu, Y., Wang, Z.: Simplenet: A simple network for image anomaly detection and localization. In: Proceedings of the IEEE/CVF Conference on Computer Vision and Pattern Recognition. pp. 20402–20411 (2023)
17. Ma, J., He, Y., Li, F., Han, L., You, C., Wang, B.: Segment anything in medical images. Nature Communications **15**(1), 654 (2024)
18. Mao, Y., Xue, F.F., Wang, R., Zhang, J., Zheng, W.S., Liu, H.: Abnormality detection in chest x-ray images using uncertainty prediction autoencoders. In: Medical Image Computing and Computer Assisted Intervention–MICCAI 2020: 23rd International Conference, Lima, Peru, October 4–8, 2020, Proceedings, Part VI 23. pp. 529–538. Springer (2020)
19. Martinoli, C., Alberighi, O.D.C., Di Minno, G., Graziano, E., Molinari, A.C., Pasta, G., Russo, G., Santagostino, E., Tagliaferri, A., Tagliafico, A., Morfini, M.: Development and definition of a simplified scanning procedure and scoring method for haemophilia early arthropathy detection with ultrasound (head-us). Thrombosis and haemostasis **109**(6), 1170–1179 (2013)
20. Peyvandi, F., Garagiola, I., Biguzzi, E.: Advances in the treatment of bleeding disorders. Journal of Thrombosis and Haemostasis **14**(11), 2095–2106 (2016)
21. Pirnay, J., Chai, K.: Inpainting transformer for anomaly detection. In: International Conference on Image Analysis and Processing. pp. 394–406. Springer (2022)
22. Plut, D., Kotnik, B.F., Zupan, I.P., Kljucevsek, D., Vidmar, G., Snoj, Z., Martinoli, C., Salapura, V.: Diagnostic accuracy of haemophilia early arthropathy detection with ultrasound (head-us): a comparative magnetic resonance imaging (mri) study. Radiology and oncology **53**(2), 178–186 (2019)
23. Ronneberger, O., Fischer, P., Brox, T.: U-net: Convolutional networks for biomedical image segmentation. In: Medical Image Computing and Computer-Assisted Intervention. Springer (2015)
24. Roth, K., Pemula, L., Zepeda, J., Schölkopf, B., Brox, T., Gehler, P.: Towards total recall in industrial anomaly detection. In: Proceedings of the IEEE/CVF Conference on Computer Vision and Pattern Recognition. pp. 14318–14328 (2022)
25. Tan, J., Hou, B., Day, T., Simpson, J., Rueckert, D., Kainz, B.: Detecting outliers with poisson image interpolation. In: Medical Image Computing and Computer Assisted Intervention–MICCAI 2021: 24th International Conference, Strasbourg, France, September 27–October 1, 2021, Proceedings, Part V 24. pp. 581–591. Springer (2021)

26. Tschuchnig, M.E., Gadermayr, M.: Anomaly detection in medical imaging-a mini review. In: International Data Science Conference. Springer (2022)
27. Tyrrell, P., Blanchette, V., Mendez, M., Paniukov, D., Brand, B., Zak, M., Roth, J.: Detection of joint effusions in pediatric patients with hemophilia using artificial intelligence-assisted ultrasound scanning; early insights from the development of a self-management tool. Res Pract Thromb Haemost **5** (2021)
28. Xue, W., Zhang, L., Mou, X., Bovik, A.C.: Gradient magnitude similarity deviation: A highly efficient perceptual image quality index. IEEE transactions on image processing **23**(2), 684-695 (2014)
29. Zavrtanik, V., Kristan, M., Skočaj, D.: Draem-a discriminatively trained reconstruction embedding for surface anomaly detection. In: Proceedings of the IEEE/CVF International Conference on Computer Vision. pp. 8330–8339 (2021)
30. Zavrtanik, V., Kristan, M., Skočaj, D.: Reconstruction by inpainting for visual anomaly detection. Pattern Recognition **112**, 107706 (2021)
31. Zhang, B., Sander, P.V., Bermak, A.: Gradient magnitude similarity deviation on multiple scales for color image quality assessment. In: International Conference on Acoustics, Speech and Signal Processing. pp. 1253–1257. IEEE (2017)
32. Zong, Z., Song, G., Liu, Y.: Detrs with collaborative hybrid assignments training. In: Proceedings of the IEEE/CVF international conference on computer vision. pp. 6748–6758 (2023)

Unsupervised Detection of Fetal Brain Anomalies Using Denoising Diffusion Models

Markus Ditlev Sjøgren Olsen[1], Jakob Ambsdorf[2,4], Manxi Lin[1], Caroline Taksøe-Vester[3], Morten Bo Søndergaard Svendsen[1], Anders Nymark Christensen[1], Mads Nielsen[2,4], Martin Grønnebæk Tolsgaard[3], Aasa Feragen[1,4(✉)], and Paraskevas Pegios[1,4]

[1] Technical University of Denmark, Kongens Lyngby, Denmark
{afhar,ppar}@dtu.dk
[2] University of Copenhagen, Copenhagen, Denmark
[3] CAMES, Rigshospitalet, Copenhagen, Denmark
[4] Pioneer Centre for AI, Copenhagen, Denmark

Abstract. Congenital malformations of the brain are among the most common fetal abnormalities that impact fetal development. Previous anomaly detection methods on ultrasound images are based on supervised learning, rely on manual annotations, and risk missing underrepresented categories. In this work, we frame fetal brain anomaly detection as an *unsupervised* task using diffusion models. To this end, we employ an inpainting-based Noise Agnostic Anomaly Detection approach that identifies the abnormality using diffusion-reconstructed fetal brain images from multiple noise levels. Our approach only requires normal fetal brain ultrasound images for training, addressing the limited availability of abnormal data. Our experiments on a real-world *clinical dataset* show the potential of using unsupervised methods for fetal brain anomaly detection. Additionally, we comprehensively evaluate how different noise types affect diffusion models in the fetal anomaly detection domain.

Keywords: Anomaly Detection · Diffusion Models · Fetal Ultrasound

1 Introduction

Congenital malformations of the brain are among the most common fetal developmental abnormalities, and their detection from ultrasound images is an important part of the mid-trimester fetal anomaly scan performed routinely around the world [24]. Detecting fetal brain anomalies using machine learning is challenging, as variations in image quality and probe position cause large variations in normal images [16], while abnormal images may differ only in small details [20], giving poor separability of the two distributions. Further, the distribution of

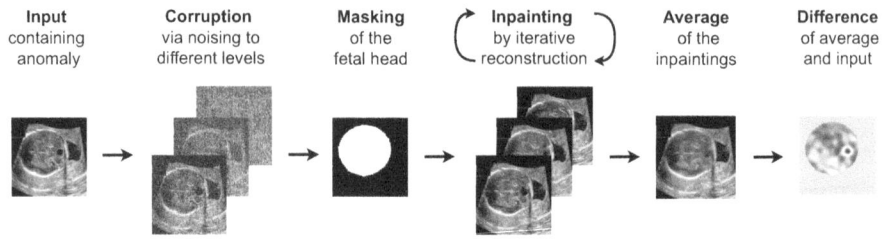

Fig. 1. Overview of iNAAD for unsupervised detection of fetal brain anomalies.

possible malformations is long-tailed, with many rare variations, and therefore little per-class training data.

Existing approaches [15,31,32] have demonstrated the feasibility of *supervised* detection of fetal brain anomalies. However, these methods (i) require labels for the individual malformations, sometimes down to anatomical details [15], (ii) are bound to the detection of a closed set of frequent anomalies from the training data. To overcome these limitations, we present a proof-of-concept for the *unsupervised* detection of fetal brain anomalies based on Denoising Diffusion Probabilistic Models [10] (DDPMs). Specifically, we adapt existing reconstruction-based methods [8,30] to build an inpainting-based Noise Agnostic Anomaly Detection (iNAAD) framework, involving averaging over reconstructions from multiple noise levels as in [8] and inpainting the fetal anatomy (see Fig. 1). To the best of our knowledge, no prior work has investigated unsupervised detection methods for fetal brain anomalies. Our approach requires access only to ultrasound images of normal fetal brains during training, which are more readily available than abnormal cases. In summary, we contribute 1) the first extensive evaluation of different noise types in DDPMs for the fetal ultrasound setting, 2) a diffusion-based algorithm iNAAD for unsupervised anomaly detection evaluated on a clinical dataset with a wide range of common fetal brain anomalies.

2 Related Work

Detecting developmental malformations from ultrasound images is a key goal of mid-trimester scans. Proposed methods include using biometry parameters from anatomical structures [25,27,29] or identifying expected normal structures [13] in fetal brains. The success of these methods, however, depends on auxiliary detection models. Other approaches [31,32] focus on directly predicting abnormal brains using standard supervised binary classification methods. In [15], a multi-task framework is used to classify nine types of abnormalities and detect sub-features with bounding boxes. Yet, these methods are constrained to detecting only the most common malformations and require extensive data collection and preprocessing. In this work, we frame the task of fetal brain anomaly detection as an unsupervised problem by leveraging a large clinical dataset of normal fetal brain images without assuming prior knowledge of specific anomaly types.

Detecting fetal brain anomalies can be approached as an out-of-distribution (OOD) task, utilizing only in-distribution (ID) images of normal anatomy during training [33]. Such methods, however, come with challenges of their own. Likelihood-based methods are prone to miscalibration [21,26] and adversarial attacks [6]. Reconstruction-based methods, including VAE-based [3], compare inputs to their reconstructions, assuming more accurate results for ID samples. The success of DDPMs [10] opened up new opportunities in medical anomaly detection, by tailoring noise types [7,12,30] or using classifier guidance [5] in weakly supervised methods [14,28]. In fetal ultrasound, DDPMs have been successfully used for fetal brain image generation [11], and counterfactual explanations [23]. In [20], a dual-conditional DDPM that requires ID subclass information of different heart views both during training and inference is proposed for OOD detection of other anatomies from ID heart views in ultrasound videos. In our work, we present a multi-reconstruction algorithm using unconditional DDPMs [10] for unsupervised OOD detection of fetal brain anomalies based on [8], integrating an inpainting step [19] to limit reconstruction changes in fetal brain and extensively evaluating different noise types [12] for the fetal ultrasound setting.

3 Method

3.1 Learning Distribution of Normal Brain Images with DDPMs

We model the distribution of ID brain images $\mathcal{P}_{ID}$ using DDPMs [10], enabling the generation and reconstruction of normal brain images. DDPMs consist of two processes: In the forward process, the image distribution is converted into a pre-defined noise distribution by adding noise $\epsilon \sim \mathcal{P}$ over T steps. while in the reverse process, images can be generated by progressively denoising them.

Formally, given a noise scheduler β_t which controls the magnitude of noise added at step t, $\alpha_t := 1 - \beta_t$ and $\bar{\alpha}_t := \prod_{s=1}^{t} \alpha_s$, the forward process is defined,

$$x_t = x_0 \sqrt{\bar{\alpha}_t} + \sqrt{1 - \bar{\alpha}_t}\epsilon, \epsilon \sim \mathcal{P} \quad (1)$$

where ϵ represents noise from a pre-defined distribution $\mathcal{P}$ and $0 \leq t \leq T$ denotes the level of noise degradation. When t is low, a significant amount of information from the original image is retained. No information is assumed to remain at $t = T$ and x_T appears similar to pure noise. The reverse process consists of a Markov chain that iteratively removes noise using a denoiser $\epsilon_\theta(x_t, t)$,

$$x_{t-1} = \frac{1}{\sqrt{\alpha_t}}\left(x_t - \frac{1-\alpha_t}{\sqrt{1-\bar{\alpha}_t}}\epsilon_\theta(x_t,t)\right) + \beta_t \epsilon, \epsilon \sim \mathcal{P} \quad (2)$$

We train a neural network ϵ_θ to estimate the noise for a given image x_t and then compare it to the actual noise $\epsilon \sim \mathcal{P}$ with the following objective,

$$\theta^* = \arg\min_\theta \mathbb{E}_{x_0 \sim \mathcal{P}_{ID}, t \sim \mathcal{U}(0,T)} \|\epsilon - \epsilon_\theta(x_t, t)\|^2 \quad (3)$$

where x_t follows the forward process in Eq. (1) and θ are learnable parameters.

In practice, $\mathcal{P}$ is typically a Gaussian distribution. However, recent studies [7,12,22,30] have shown that alternative noise distributions can significantly impact and improve medical anomaly detection tasks. In this paper, we assess the effect of three distinct noise distributions, namely Gaussian [10], Simplex [30], and Pyramid [7], on denoising diffusion models for fetal brain anomaly detection.

3.2 iNAAD: Inpainting-Based Noise Agnostic Anomaly Detection

Following [8,28,30], we adopt a reconstruction-based anomaly detection approach, aiming to reconstruct input images x_0 using DPPMs trained on normal, anomaly-free, fetal ultrasound scans. Specifically, we apply the forward process to corrupt x_0 to x_s, for a fixed $1 \leq s \leq T$, and then retrieve the reconstructed image from x_s by the reverse process. Hyperparameter s controls the level of noise degradation. Given the image x_{t-1} at step $t-1$ in the forward process, we denote its corresponding reconstruction with the same steps in the reverse process as $\bar{x}_{t-1}$. The altered content between the input image and its reconstruction can therefore be interpreted as an anomaly indicator. To quantify these anomalies, we present the iNAAD algorithm, which is outlined in Algorithm 1.

Inspired by [19], we constrain the reconstruction within the region of interest, i.e., the fetal brain in the image with inpainting. In particular, we apply a binary mask m obtained with a pre-trained segmentation model [18] to ignore all the variations beyond the fetal brain. Given a pre-defined noise distribution $\mathcal{P}$ and a trained denoiser ϵ_θ, we define the inpainted reconstruction $\hat{x}_{t-1}$ by,

$$\begin{aligned} x_{t-1} &= x_0 \sqrt{\bar{\alpha}_t} + \sqrt{1-\bar{\alpha}_t}\epsilon \\ \bar{x}_{t-1} &= \tfrac{1}{\sqrt{\alpha_t}}\left(x_t - \tfrac{1-\alpha_t}{\sqrt{1-\bar{\alpha}_t}}\epsilon_\theta(x_t,t)\right) + \beta_t\epsilon \\ \hat{x}_{t-1} &= m \odot x_{t-1} + (1-m) \odot \bar{x}_{t-1} \end{aligned} \quad (4)$$

During the forward process, the information content of x_0 is controlled by the noise level s. Similar to [8], we aggregate reconstructions obtained by degrading x_0 with a range of multiple noise levels $s \in S$. By reconstructing all corrupted versions of x_0 and averaging these reconstructions, we obtain a final reconstructed image $\bar{x}$ that integrates information from all reconstructed versions while reducing noise from individual reverse processes [8].

Finally, for detecting abnormalities, the choice of the similarity metric between x_0 and $\bar{x}$ is essential. We observed that the similarity metrics such as LPIPS, used in [8], were not effective for distinguishing abnormal from normal fetal images. Despite exploring other semantic similarity metrics [4] we empirically chose to utilize the standard pixel-based Structural Similarity Index (SSIM) which proved more effective for our task.

iNAAD requires only normal fetal brain ultrasound images for training. It identifies abnormalities by aggregating diffusion-reconstructed fetal brain images from various noise levels, incorporating an inpainting step to limit reconstruction changes in the fetal brain. The proposed method is summarised in Algorithm 1.

4 Experiments and Results

Dataset. We constructed our dataset using a pre-trained standard plane classifier [17] to extract images from the Danish national fetal ultrasound screening database. This includes a large set of ID images for developing DDPMs and OOD images for validation and testing. For the ID images, we sampled 221,177 mid-trimester images from unique patients, identifying 14,268 brain images. From 43,297 images with central nervous system malformations, we identified 3557 brain images and randomly sampled one per patient, resulting in 492 OOD images. Finally, we divided a split of 13568/250/250 ID images for train/validation/test, keeping 200 for external ID testing, and a split of 250/242 of OOD images for validation/test.

Algorithm 1. iNAAD for unsupervised fetal brain anomaly detection.

Input: original x_0, binary mask m, noise distribution $\mathcal{P}$, model ϵ_θ, noise levels S
Output: average reconstructed image $\bar{x}$, similarity metric between x_0 and $\bar{x}$
for s in S **do**
    Define time step $t := s$
    Corrupt original image x_0 up to noise level t by sampling from $\mathcal{P}$ (Eq. 1)
    for t to 1 **do**
        Get inpainted reconstruction $\hat{x}_{t-1}$ using mask m and model ϵ_θ (Eq. 4)
    end for
end for
return $\bar{x} = \frac{1}{|S|}\sum_{s\in\{S\}}\hat{x}_{0,s}$ and $similarity\_metric(x_0, \bar{x})$

Models and Implementation. We implement and evaluate the effect of three noise distributions in the fetal ultrasound setting: Gaussian [10], Pyramid [7], and Simplex [30]. These distributions range from least (Gaussian) to most correlated (Simplex), with the latter designed to enable multi-scale image reconstruction by varying perturbations across different regions. Following original implementations, we define Gaussian as $\epsilon \sim \mathcal{N}(\mu = 0, \sigma^2 = 1)$, Pyramid as $\epsilon \sim \sum_{i=1}^{10} 0.8^i \cdot U(\epsilon^{(i)}; H, W)$, where U is a bilinear operator that upscales the image to dimensions $H \times W$, ϵ^i represents Gaussian noise with dimensions $h_i \times w_i$, and 0.8 being the scaling factor, and Simplex $\epsilon \sim \text{Simplex}(\nu = 2^{-6}, N = 6, \gamma = 0.8)$ where ν is the starting frequency of noise regions, N is the number of layers of noise with different frequency, and γ is the decay of noise throughout the layers of noise. A DDPM is trained for each noise type using the ID training set, following the same model architecture and hyperparameters as in [23], using 500 diffusion steps, and training for 200K iterations with batch size 20. Following [7], during reconstructions with Pyramid noise, we corrupt images with Gaussian noise to better allow the model to remove anomalous image features.

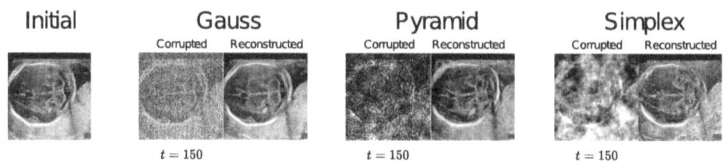

Fig. 2. Reconstruction of a normal fetal brain from corruption level $t = 150$.

Evaluation of DDPMs. The ability to reconstruct ID images with high fidelity is an essential part of the approach, hence, we evaluate DDPMs both for generation and reconstruction. Table 1 compares DDPMs trained with different noise types for image generation based on FID using the external ID test and for image reconstruction across different corruption levels in terms of SSIM using the ID validation set. We observe that the reconstructive ability of DDPMs trained with Simplex and Pyramid decreases faster than Gaussian and they generate samples with lower fidelity. An example reconstruction is shown in Fig. 2.

Table 1. Evaluation for generation and reconstruction of normal fetal brains.

Model	FID	SSIM for different noise step levels t						
		50	75	100	150	200	250	300
DDPM-Gaussian	**48.39**	**0.989**	**0.984**	**0.979**	**0.968**	**0.955**	**0.933**	**0.897**
DDPM-Pyramid	57.89	0.980	0.968	0.955	0.928	0.892	0.830	0.752
DDPM-Simplex	199.40	0.981	0.967	0.948	0.905	0.836	0.753	0.702

Supervised Baseline. A Resnet-18 [9] architecture is used as a supervised baseline in the form of a binary classifier (normal/abnormal). We group all anomalies into one class due to the per-class scarcity. The model is initiated with ImageNet pre-trained weights and fine-tuned for 60 epochs using random augmentations during training, on the validation set (250 ID/250 OOD cases). We evaluate its performance on the final test set (250 ID/242 OOD cases).

Results. We evaluate iNAAD with different noise types for all anomalies and subsets of the most frequent diagnoses, by grouping the infrequent ones into "Others". Area Under the Receiver-Operator-Characteristic curve (AUROC) is reported in Table 2 and examples of ROC curves in Fig. 3. Average Precision (AP) is reported in the Appendix. The performance of both iNAAD and the supervised vary across different anomaly groups. All iNAAD variants match or exceed the supervised baseline for anomalies that manifest in a localized way, e.g., cerebral cysts, ventriculomegaly, and corpus callosum agenesis. For microcephaly, hydrocephalus, and spina bifida, supervised performance is better.

Table 2. AUROC results on the test set (250 ID/242 OOD cases) for iNAAD, and the Resnet-18 supervised baseline trained for binary classification, per anomaly group. The best scores are in bold, second best are underlined.

Model	AUROC per anomaly group							
	Microcephaly (n=40)	Hydrocephalus (n=64)	ACC (n=38)	Cerebr. cyst (n=43)	Ventriculomegaly (n=69)	Spina bifida (n=39)	Others (n=93)	All (n=242)
Resnet-18	**0.63**	**0.69**	0.63	0.60	0.71	**0.78**	**0.65**	**0.67**
iNAAD-Gaussian	0.60	0.62	**0.76**	0.53	**0.74**	0.57	0.60	0.62
iNAAD-Simplex	0.56	0.65	0.69	**0.61**	0.69	0.62	0.56	0.58
iNAAD-Pyramid	0.60	0.64	0.68	0.57	0.69	0.62	0.56	0.57

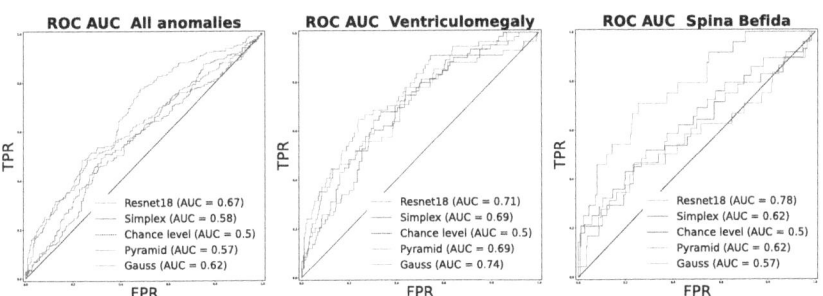

Fig. 3. ROC curves on the test set for the different models.

Table 3. Ablation study for iNAAD. AUROC and AP results are reported on all anomalies of the validation set (250 ID/250 OOD cases).

$\mathcal{P}$	$\mathcal{S}$	Similarity Metric	Inpainting	AUROC	AP
Gaussian	{150}	LPIPS	✗	0.54	0.53
	{150}	DeepSim	✗	0.54	0.52
	{150}	SSIM	✗	0.58	0.59
	{150}	SSIM	✓	0.65	0.65
	{75, 100, 150, 200, 250}	SSIM	✓	**0.68**	**0.68**
Simplex	{50}	LPIPS	✗	0.51	0.53
	{50}	DeepSim	✗	0.49	0.49
	{50}	SSIM	✗	0.56	0.54
	{50}	SSIM	✓	**0.59**	**0.58**
	{50, 75, 100}	SSIM	✓	0.58	**0.58**
Pyramid	{75}	LPIPS	✗	0.55	0.54
	{75}	DeepSim	✗	0.52	0.50
	{75}	SSIM	✗	0.57	0.55
	{75}	SSIM	✓	0.61	0.57
	{50, 75, 100}	SSIM	✓	**0.62**	**0.58**

Ablation Study. We conducted an ablation study to assess the components of iNAAD. Table 3 reports AUROC and AP for different similarity metrics and the impact of inpainting and aggregated reconstructions. Note that iNAAD-Gaussian with LPIPS metric, without inpainting, is similar to the method proposed in [8]. We observed that the optimal noise level s differs for each noise type $\mathcal{P}$, and pixel-based SSIM outperforms LPIPS and the semantic similarity metric DeepSim [4] with pre-trained SonoNet-64 [2] as feature extractor. Inpainting the fetal head removes reconstruction errors from anatomically unrelated regions while aggregating reconstruction results in better performance for all noise types.

Localization and Explanability. Reconstruction-based methods can be used to segment anomalous regions. Our framework can provide anomaly heatmaps from the reconstruction error offering explainability for localized anomalies such as dandy-walker syndrome, cysts, and hydrocephalus. However, these are less valuable for structural anomalies affecting the entire head, such as microcephaly. Examples of heatmaps for normal and abnormal cases are shown in Fig. 4.

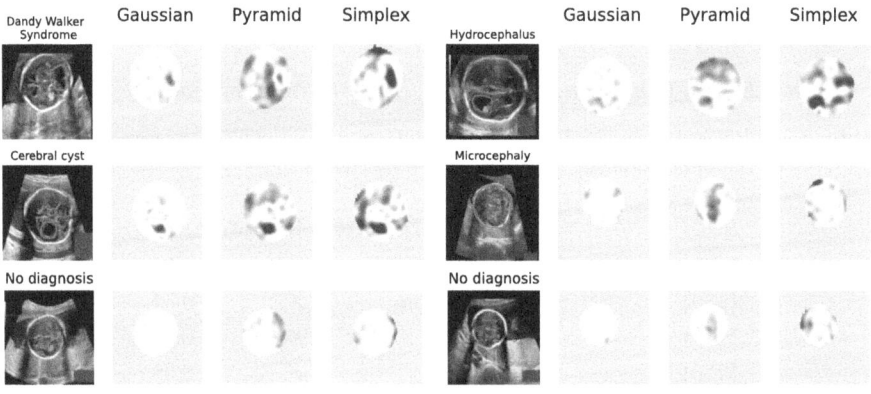

Fig. 4. Heatmaps and annotated anomalies by an MD with 3 years of experience in prenatal ultrasound imaging. More examples are available in the Appendix.

5 Discussion and Conclusion

Our findings indicate that unsupervised reconstruction-based methods can achieve comparable, in some cases even superior performance, compared to supervised approaches for anomaly detection in medical imaging tasks that are characterized by a scarcity of labeled data for supervised training, but a relative abundance of normal data. Our ablations demonstrate that incorporating inpainting and SSMI as a similarity metric enhances OOD detection of fetal brain anomalies across all noise types. The proposed method reconstructs normal brains with negligible reconstruction error while providing inherent explainability for localized anomalies as shown in Fig. 4. Our experiments on the effect of different noise types show that Gaussian is better on average for the fetal ultrasound setting for image generation, reconstruction, and anomaly detection, unlike MRI settings where Simplex and Pyramid perform best for anomaly detection [7,30]. Yet, Simplex noise is better at identifying highly localized anomalies, e.g., cerebral cysts, demonstrating the differences between noise types. Given the low signal-to-noise ratio, anisotropic noise pattern, and orientation-dependence of ultrasound imaging [1], adapting the noise process for different noise types in fetal ultrasound requires further exploration in future work.

Limitations. We rely on an automated data extraction process by sampling images from unique patients without manual validation, beyond anatomy identification, to confirm that anomalies are visible in the OOD images. Yet, ensuring non-overlapping patients and diversity in our data splits together with the absence of extensive prepossessing, e.g., including multiple high-quality planes sampled from the same patient videos [32], and removing images with shadows [31], likely increases the difficulty of our dataset, as reflected by the relatively low performance of our supervised baseline compared to previous studies [15,31,32], whose performance should be interpreted with caution as discussed in [32]. Notably, our data reflects real-world conditions, sourced from a national ultrasound screening database, rather than in-depth referral examinations by fetal medicine experts thoroughly examining the brain with the suspicion of an anomaly. Since previous works rely on extensive annotation, our data may better reflect clinical challenges, emphasizing the need for further clinical validation of all methods.

Conclusion. We present iNAAD as a proof-of-concept for unsupervised OOD detection using DDPMs to identify fetal brain anomalies. iNAAD can serve as a general framework for diffusion-based unsupervised medical anomaly detection with arbitrary noise types and post-hoc adjustments for explainability.

Acknowledgements. This work was supported by the Pioneer Centre for AI (DNRF grant nr P1), the DIREC project EXPLAIN-ME (9142-00001B), the Novo Nordisk Foundation through the Center for Basic Machine Learning Research in Life Science (NNF20OC0062606), and SONAI, an AI signature project from the Danish Agency for Digital Government.

References

1. Asgariandehkordi, H., Goudarzi, S., Basarab, A., Rivaz, H.: Deep ultrasound denoising using diffusion probabilistic models. In: 2023 IEEE International Ultrasonics Symposium (IUS). pp. 1–4. IEEE (2023)
2. Baumgartner, C.F., Kamnitsas, K., Matthew, J., Fletcher, T.P., Smith, S., Koch, L.M., Kainz, B., Rueckert, D.: Sononet: real-time detection and localisation of fetal standard scan planes in freehand ultrasound. IEEE transactions on medical imaging **36**(11), 2204–2215 (2017)
3. Chen, X., Konukoglu, E.: Unsupervised detection of lesions in brain mri using constrained adversarial auto-encoders. In: Medical Imaging with Deep Learning (2018)

4. Czolbe, S., Pegios, P., Krause, O., Feragen, A.: Semantic similarity metrics for image registration. Medical Image Analysis **87**, 102830 (2023)
5. Dhariwal, P., Nichol, A.: Diffusion models beat gans on image synthesis. Advances in neural information processing systems **34**, 8780–8794 (2021)
6. Fort, S.: Adversarial vulnerability of powerful near out-of-distribution detection. arXiv preprint arXiv:2201.07012 (2022)
7. Frotscher, A., Kapoor, J., Wolfers, T., Baumgartner, C.F.: Unsupervised anomaly detection using aggregated normative diffusion. arXiv preprint arXiv:2312.01904 (2023)
8. Graham, M.S., Pinaya, W.H., Tudosiu, P.D., Nachev, P., Ourselin, S., Cardoso, J.: Denoising diffusion models for out-of-distribution detection. In: Proceedings of the IEEE/CVF CVPR. pp. 2947–2956 (2023)
9. He, K., Zhang, X., Ren, S., Sun, J.: Deep residual learning for image recognition. In: Proceedings of the IEEE/CVF CVPR. pp. 770–778 (2016)
10. Ho, J., Jain, A., Abbeel, P.: Denoising diffusion probabilistic models. Advances in neural information processing systems **33**, 6840–6851 (2020)
11. Iskandar, M., Mannering, H., Sun, Z., Matthew, J., Kerdegari, H., Peralta, L., Xochicale, M.: Towards realistic ultrasound fetal brain imaging synthesis. In: Medical Imaging with Deep Learning, short paper track (2023)
12. Kascenas, A., Sanchez, P., Schrempf, P., Wang, C., Clackett, W., Mikhael, S.S., Voisey, J.P., Goatman, K., Weir, A., Pugeault, N., et al.: The role of noise in denoising models for anomaly detection in medical images. Medical Image Analysis **90**, 102963 (2023)
13. Komatsu, M., et al.: Detection of cardiac structural abnormalities in fetal ultrasound videos using deep learning. Applied Sciences **11**(1), 371 (2021)
14. Li, J., Cao, H., Wang, J., Liu, F., Dou, Q., Chen, G., Heng, P.A.: Fast non-markovian diffusion model for weakly supervised anomaly detection in brain mr images. In: MICCAI. pp. 579–589. Springer (2023)
15. Lin, M., He, X., Guo, H., He, M., Zhang, L., Xian, J., Lei, T., Xu, Q., Zheng, J., Feng, J., et al.: Use of real-time artificial intelligence in detection of abnormal image patterns in standard sonographic reference planes in screening for fetal intracranial malformations. Ultrasound in Obstetrics & Gynecology **59**(3), 304–316 (2022)
16. Lin, M., Ambsdorf, J., Sejer, E.P.F., Bashir, Z., Wong, C.K., Pegios, P., Raheli, A., Svendsen, M.B.S., Nielsen, M., Tolsgaard, M.G., et al.: Learning semantic image quality for fetal ultrasound from noisy ranking annotation. In: 21st international symposium on biomedical imaging (ISBI 2024) (2024)
17. Lin, M., Feragen, A., Bashir, Z., Tolsgaard, M.G., Christensen, A.N.: I saw, i conceived, i concluded: Progressive concepts as bottlenecks (2022)
18. Lin, M., Zepf, K., Christensen, A.N., Bashir, Z., Svendsen, M.B.S., Tolsgaard, M., Feragen, A.: Dtu-net: learning topological similarity for curvilinear structure segmentation. In: International Conference on Information Processing in Medical Imaging. pp. 654–666. Springer (2023)
19. Lugmayr, A., Danelljan, M., Romero, A., Yu, F., Timofte, R., Van Gool, L.: Repaint: Inpainting using denoising diffusion probabilistic models. In: Proceedings of the IEEE/CVF CVPR. pp. 11461–11471 (2022)
20. Mishra, D., Zhao, H., Saha, P., Papageorghiou, A.T., Noble, J.A.: Dual conditioned diffusion models for out-of-distribution detection: Application to fetal ultrasound videos. In: MICCAI. pp. 216–226. Springer (2023)
21. Nalisnick, E., Matsukawa, A., Teh, Y.W., Lakshminarayanan, B.: Detecting out-of-distribution inputs to deep generative models using typicality. arXiv preprint arXiv:1906.02994 (2019)

22. Naval Marimont, S., Baugh, M., Siomos, V., Tzelepis, C., Kainz, B., Tarroni, G.: Disyre: Diffusion-inspired synthetic restoration for unsupervised anomaly detection. In: International Symposium on Biomedical Imaging. IEEE (2024)
23. Pegios, P., Lin, M., Weng, N., Svendsen, M.B.S., Bashir, Z., Bigdeli, S., Christensen, A.N., Tolsgaard, M., Feragen, A.: Diffusion-based iterative counterfactual explanations for fetal ultrasound image quality assessment. arXiv preprint arXiv:2403.08700 (2024)
24. Pilu, G., et al.: Sonographic examination of the fetal central nervous system: guidelines for performing the 'basic examination' and the 'fetal neurosonogram'. Ultrasound in Obstetrics & Gynecology **29**(1), 109–116 (2007)
25. Płotka, S., Włodarczyk, T., Klasa, A., Lipa, M., Sitek, A., Trzciński, T.: Fetalnet: Multi-task deep learning framework for fetal ultrasound biometric measurements. In: Neural Information Processing: 28th International Conference, ICONIP 2021, Proceedings. pp. 257–265. Springer (2021)
26. Ren, J., Liu, P.J., Fertig, E., Snoek, J., Poplin, R., Depristo, M., Dillon, J., Lakshminarayanan, B.: Likelihood ratios for out-of-distribution detection. Advances in neural information processing systems **32** (2019)
27. Sinclair, M., Baumgartner, C.F., Matthew, J., Bai, W., Martinez, J.C., Li, Y., Smith, S., Knight, C.L., Kainz, B., Hajnal, J., et al.: Human-level performance on automatic head biometrics in fetal ultrasound using fully convolutional neural networks. In: 40th EMBC. pp. 714–717. IEEE (2018)
28. Wolleb, J., Bieder, F., Sandkühler, R., Cattin, P.C.: Diffusion models for medical anomaly detection. In: MICCAI. pp. 35–45. Springer (2022)
29. Wu, Y., Shen, K., Chen, Z., Wu, J.: Automatic measurement of fetal cavum septum pellucidum from ultrasound images using deep attention network. In: 2020 International Conference on image processing (ICIP). pp. 2511–2515. IEEE (2020)
30. Wyatt, J., Leach, A., Schmon, S.M., Willcocks, C.G.: Anoddpm: Anomaly detection with denoising diffusion probabilistic models using simplex noise. In: Proceedings of the IEEE/CVF CVPR. pp. 650–656 (2022)
31. Xie, B., Lei, T., Wang, N., Cai, H., Xian, J., He, M., Zhang, L., Xie, H.: Computer-aided diagnosis for fetal brain ultrasound images using deep convolutional neural networks. Int. Journal of Computer Assisted Radiology and Surgery **15**, 1303–1312 (2020)
32. Xie, H., Wang, N., He, M., Zhang, L., Cai, H., Xian, J., Lin, M., Zheng, J., Yang, Y.: Using deep-learning algorithms to classify fetal brain ultrasound images as normal or abnormal. Ultrasound in Obstetrics & Gynecology **56**(4), 579–587 (2020)
33. Yang, J., Zhou, K., Li, Y., Liu, Z.: Generalized out-of-distribution detection: A survey. arXiv preprint arXiv:2110.11334 (2021)

Diffusion Models for Unsupervised Anomaly Detection in Fetal Brain Ultrasound

Hanna Mykula[1], Lisa Gasser[3], Silvia Lobmaier[3], Julia A. Schnabel[1,2,4], Veronika Zimmer[1], and Cosmin I. Bercea[1,2(✉)]

[1] Technical University of Munich, Munich, Germany
cosmin.bercea@tum.de
[2] Helmholtz AI and Helmholtz Center Munich, Munich, Germany
[3] Klinikum rechts der Isar, Technical University of Munich, Munich, Germany
[4] King's College London, London, UK

Abstract. Ultrasonography is an essential tool in mid-pregnancy for assessing fetal development, appreciated for its non-invasive and real-time imaging capabilities. Yet, the interpretation of ultrasound images is often complicated by acoustic shadows, speckle, and other artifacts that obscure crucial diagnostic details. To address these challenges, our study presents a novel unsupervised anomaly detection framework specifically designed for fetal ultrasound imaging. This framework incorporates gestational age filtering, precise identification of fetal standard planes, and targeted segmentation of brain regions to enhance diagnostic accuracy. Furthermore, we introduce the use of denoising diffusion probabilistic models in this context, marking a significant innovation in detecting previously unrecognized anomalies. We rigorously evaluated the framework using various diffusion-based anomaly detection methods, noise types, and noise levels. Notably, AutoDDPM emerged as the most effective, achieving an area under the precision-recall curve of 79.8% in detecting anomalies. This advancement holds promise for improving the tools available for nuanced and effective prenatal diagnostics.

Keywords: Fetal Ultrasound Screening · Medical Imaging

1 Introduction

Ultrasonography (US) is an indispensable tool in prenatal care, widely used for monitoring fetal development due to its safety, real-time imaging capabilities, and cost-effectiveness [17]. Particularly, the mid-pregnancy US scan at around 22 weeks is crucial for assessing fetal growth and identifying potential anomalies, including those affecting the brain. However, interpreting US images remains

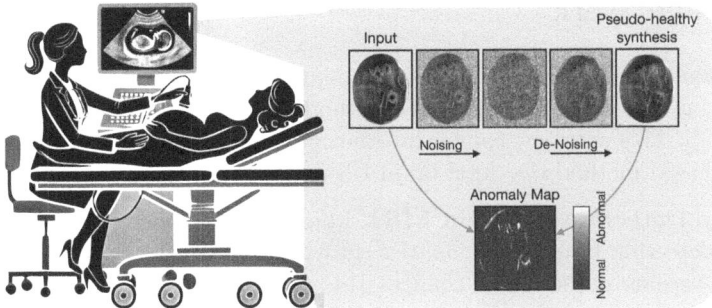

Fig. 1. Workflow for screening and monitoring fetal brain anomalies in ultrasound images during pregnancy. Diffusion models generate pseudo-healthy synthesis to effectively identify potential developmental anomalies.

challenging due to artifacts such as acoustic shadows, speckle, and motion blurring. These issues arise from the complex interactions between US waves and biological tissues, which can obscure critical diagnostic details and complicate both manual and automated analyses [15] (Fig. 1).

The application of deep learning (DL) in fetal US image analysis has shown significant promise, enhancing the ability of clinicians to detect anomalies [11]. However, supervised DL methods face considerable challenges due to the anatomical diversity and the imbalance between healthy and anomalous samples [16,25]. Given these limitations, unsupervised anomaly detection (UAD) emerges as a viable alternative. UAD methods train exclusively on healthy samples, establishing a baseline for normality without the need for labeled anomaly data. Even though this approach offers better generalization across various pathologies [21], it remains largely unexplored for fetal brain US.

In this study, we propose a novel UAD framework aimed at detecting brain anomalies in fetal US images. Our framework incorporates several innovative techniques to enhance the quality and consistency of the US scans. Specifically, we filter by gestational age, detect and localize standard planes using SonoNet [2], and remove background noise to focus on the brain region. Furthermore, we pioneer the application of denoising diffusion probabilistic models (DDPM) in this context. DDPMs have shown exceptional performance in capturing complex distributions and generating high-fidelity images, making them suitable for identifying previously unseen anomalies in fetal US scans [12].

We thoroughly evaluated our framework using various diffusion-based UAD methods, noise types, and noise levels to understand their performance and robustness. Among these, AutoDDPM [4] demonstrated superior performance, achieving an area under the precision-recall curve of 79.8% in anomaly detection.

2 Related Work

This section reviews existing research on anomaly detection (AD) in brain imaging, focusing on two main areas: AD methods for brain MRI and AD methods for fetal US. This overview establishes the context for our novel approach using diffusion-based methods for fetal brain US anomaly detection.

Anomaly Detection in Brain MRI. Magnetic resonance imaging (MRI) is vital for detecting brain abnormalities, providing detailed tissue contrasts and revealing various pathological changes [14]. Traditional AD methods in brain MRI include Autoencoders [5,9,27] and Generative Adversarial Networks [1,19], which learn the distribution of healthy anatomy by compressing and decompressing image data. Recently, diffusion models have demonstrated superior performance by offering better mode coverage and sample quality. Denoising diffusion probabilistic models (DDPMs) iteratively learn the data distribution through noising and denoising processes, showing significant success in brain MRI applications [3,4,22]. However, their application to fetal brain US remains unexplored.

Anomaly Detection in Fetal Images. There has been significant focus on other fetal organs, particularly the heart, for detecting anomalies in fetal imaging. In heart imaging, Chotzoglou et al. [10] proposed an unsupervised approach for detecting Hypoplastic Left Heart Syndrome from fetal US images. Research on AD for fetal brain imaging has also seen notable contributions. FOAC-NET, a supervised convolutional neural network (CNN) architecture, has been developed for detecting fetal organ anomalies in MRI [13]. In fetal brain US, H. N. Xie et al. [24] developed a CNN-based system to classify US images into normal and abnormal categories, achieving high accuracy. However, unsupervised anomaly detection remains largely unexplored in fetal brain US.

3 Methods

3.1 Background

Denoising Diffusion Probabilistic Models (DDPMs) use a forward diffusion process, $q(x_t|x_{t-1})$, to incrementally corrupt data from a target distribution, $q(x_0)$, to a normal distribution. A reverse process, $p(x_{t-1}|x_t)$, generates samples by transforming noise back to $q(x_0)$. The forward process is defined as:

$$q(x_t|x_{t-1}) = \mathcal{N}(x_t|x_{t-1}, \sqrt{1-\beta_t}, \beta_t I), \qquad (1)$$

with a variance schedule, $\beta_t \in (0,1)$, increasing linearly from $\beta_1 = 10^{-4}$ to $\beta_T = 0.02$ [12]. The reverse generative model, with parameters θ, begins with $x_T \sim \mathcal{N}(0, I)$ and proceeds from T to 1:

$$p_\theta(x_{t-1}|x_t) = \mathcal{N}(x_{t-1}|\mu_\theta(x_t, t), \tilde{\beta}_t I), \qquad (2)$$

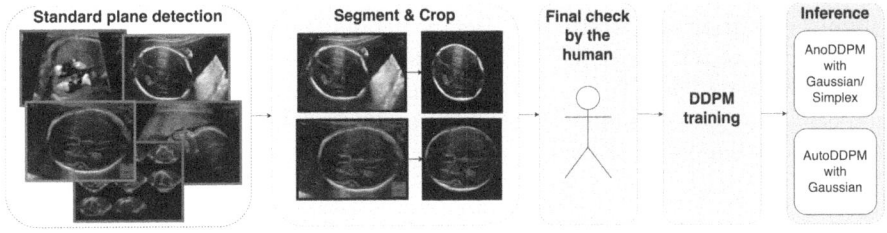

Fig. 2. Overview of the proposed framework for detecting brain anomalies in fetal ultrasound scans. The process includes: (1) detecting standard fetal planes (green boxes indicate correct detections, red boxes incorrect) using SonoNet [2]; (2) segmenting and cropping brain regions from these planes [7,20]; (3) performing a final quality check by a human expert; (4) using the curated dataset to train and evaluate diffusion-based anomaly detection methods; and (5) applying diffusion-based models for anomaly detection through iterative noising and denoising. (Color figure online)

where $\tilde{\beta}_t = \frac{1-\bar{\alpha}_{t-1}}{1-\bar{\alpha}_t}\beta_t$, $\alpha_t = 1 - \beta_t$ and $\bar{\alpha}_t = \prod_{i=0}^{t} \alpha_i$. A U-Net [18] is used to learn the noise $\epsilon_\theta(x_t, t)$ and approximate μ_θ as follows:

$$\mu_\theta(x_t, t) = \frac{1}{\sqrt{\bar{\alpha}_t}}\left(x_t - \frac{\beta_t}{\sqrt{1-\bar{\alpha}_t}}\epsilon_\theta(x_t, t)\right). \quad (3)$$

The loss function, $\mathcal{L}_t$, targeting the marginal likelihood $p_\theta(x_0)$, is:

$$\mathcal{L}_t = D_{KL}(q(x_{t-1}|x_t, x_0)||p_\theta(x_{t-1}|x_t)), \quad (4)$$

where D_{KL} is the Kullback-Leibler divergence. We use Ho et al.'s simplified objective [12]:

$$\mathcal{L}_s = \mathbb{E}_{x_0 \sim q(x_0), \epsilon \sim \mathcal{N}(0,I)}\left[\|\epsilon - \epsilon_\theta(x_t, t)\|^2\right]. \quad (5)$$

AnoDDPM [23] leverages DDPMs with either Gaussian or Simplex noise for anomaly detection segmentation. A more recent method proposes a conditional diffusion model to produce more accurate pseudo-healthy counterfactuals, known as AutoDDPM [4].

3.2 Fetal Brain UAD Framework

Selecting US data from the initial dataset requires meticulous attention to ensure the high quality of the training, validation, and testing data. This selection process must meet specific criteria, such as the correct gestational age, the transventricular plane view, and the visibility of key brain structures. To diminish the noise inherent in US images, segmentation into brain and background is necessary. Manually performing this selection process can be extremely time-consuming. Therefore, we propose a semi-automatic data preprocessing pipeline (see Fig. 2) that aids in the data curation process, thereby enhancing the quality of the data in the training dataset. Following the construction of the final training, validation, and testing datasets using our semi-automatic pipeline, we train DDPMs to remove artificially added noise and reconstruct pseudo-healthy images. The modular inference setup of our method allows us to test different inference strategies, including AnoDDPM and AutoDDPM, with various noise types such as Simplex and Gaussian.

Standard Plane Detection. We utilize SonoNet [2] to automatically select images with the correct transventricular plane view of the fetal brain. SonoNet is designed for the real-time detection of fetal standard scan planes in US images and classifies images into one of 13 standard plane categories, including the brain view at the posterior horn of the ventricle (Brain (tv.)). The core of the method is a CNN inspired by the VGG16 architecture. For our experiment, we employed SonoNet-32, equipped with 32 kernels, achieving an F1-Score of 0.798 in plane classification. SonoNet also provides a confidence score for its predictions, enabling a more rigorous selection of candidate images. We eliminate all images that are not labeled as "Brain (tv.)" or have a corresponding confidence score lower than 0.9.

Brain Segmentation. In the second step of our pipeline, we segment and crop all the images to eliminate background noise. We use a probabilistic deep learning approach with a U-Net segmentation network to mask the head from US images. Although in [7,20] ellipses are fitted to the segmented contours for biometric measurements, we only utilize the segmentation model. A manual review is performed to verify the quality of the data that has been automatically selected and preprocessed.

Diffusion-Based Anomaly Detection. The final step in our methodology involves the use of DDPMs for anomaly detection. The inference phase of our method is modular, allowing the use of different strategies for anomaly detection. We explore the use of both AnoDDPM and AutoDDPM methods.

By comparing the performance of AnoDDPM [23] and AutoDDPM [4] with different types and levels of noise, we aim to evaluate the effectiveness of different diffusion-based methods for fetal brain US anomaly detection.

4 Experiments and Results

4.1 Experimental Setup

Datasets. For our experiments, we utilized data from both public [8] and private clinical datasets. The clinical dataset comprised 234 control patients, from which only those within a gestational age range of 19 to 22+6 weeks were selected for inclusion. Consequently, our final dataset for training, validation, and testing included 76 patients from the clinical dataset and 19 from the public dataset, totaling 252 images. For the evaluation of the downstream task, we chose 8

Table 1. Anomaly detection performance. Best results are shown in **bold** and second-best are <u>underlined</u>.

Method	Healthy		Pathological	
	SSIM ↑	LPIPS ↓	AURPC ↑	AUROC ↑
AnoDDPM [23] with Simplex(t = 50)	0.81 ± 0.05	0.26 ± 0.05	<u>78.9</u>	**70.8**
AnoDDPM [12] with Gaussian(t = 250)	**0.88 ± 0.01**	**0.05 ± 0.01**	73.0	63.8
AnoDDPM [12] with Gaussian(t = 300)	0.87 ± 0.02	**0.05 ± 0.01**	73.5	57.4
AutoDDPM [4] with Gaussian(t = 300)	**0.88 ± 0.02**	**0.05 ± 0.02**	**79.8**	<u>66.6</u>

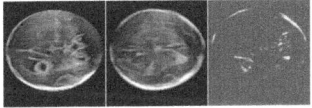

AutoDDPM
(t=300)
Gaussian

(a) Healthy example. (b) Pathological example.

Fig. 3. Anomaly detection performance for healthy and pathological fetal brain ultrasound images using AutoDDPM with Gaussian noise at noise level 300. From left to right, the row shows the original image, the generated reconstruction, and the anomaly map.

anomalous and 5 healthy control patients from the private clinical dataset, yielding 18 and 12 images, respectively. We adjusted the input pixel values to fall within the range of $(0, 1)$ for Gaussian noise and $(-1, 1)$ for Simplex noise. We normalized the images to the 98th percentile, resized them to a resolution of 128×128, and applied rotations and horizontal and vertical flips as data augmentation.

Evaluation Metrics. To evaluate the performance on healthy scans, we utilized several metrics, including mean absolute error (MAE) as a measure of reconstruction error, structural similarity index (SSIM), and learned perceptual image patch similarity (LPIPS) [26] for reconstruction accuracy. For anomaly detection performance, we assessed the algorithm's ability to correctly classify images as either healthy or anomalous using true positives, true negatives, false positives, and false negatives. We calculated the Area Under the Precision-Recall Curve (AUPRC) and the Area Under the Receiver Operating Characteristic (AUROC) curve to provide a comprehensive view of the classification performance. All experiments were conducted using an NVIDIA RTX A6000 GPU.

4.2 Anomaly Detection Performance

We assessed the performance of AnoDDPM employing both Gaussian and Simplex Noise, alongside AutoDDPM, as detailed in [4]. The evaluation focused on various noise levels ($t = 50, 100, 150, 200, 250, 300$), analyzing the model's robustness under different conditions.

The classification outcomes are succinctly summarized in Table 1, with the most effective noise variations and types for both AnoDDPM and AutoDDPM highlighted. Corresponding visual results for the best variation of AutoDDPM are depicted in Fig. 3. For a thorough examination of all noise levels and types, including metrics on reconstruction errors and accuracy, readers are directed to the supplementary materials, which provide an extensive overview of all conducted experiments.

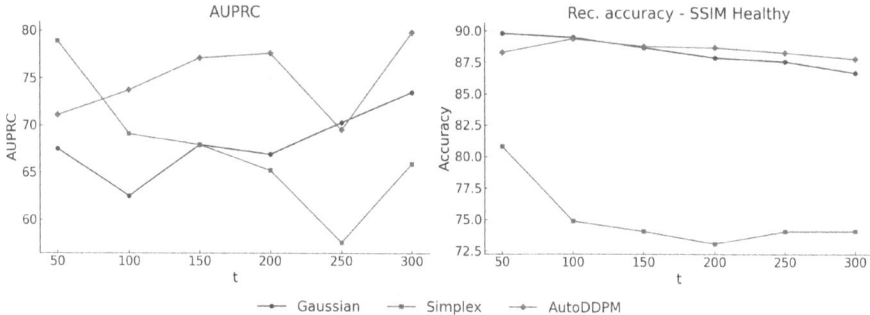

Fig. 4. AURPC and reconstruction accuracy (SSIM) for Gaussian, Simplex, and AutoDDPM models at various noise levels t. The graphs illustrate the performance in terms of reconstruction accuracy (SSIM) for healthy data and AURPC for anomaly detection capabilities.

Influence of Noise Type and Levels. We evaluated AnoDDPM using Gaussian and Simplex noise at various noise levels as depicted in Fig. 4 and detailed in Tables 1, 2 and 3 in the supplementary materials. While Gaussian noise at a level of $t = 50$ yields the best performance in terms of reconstruction for healthy images (MAE of 0.013, SSIM of 0.898), it demonstrates limitations in anomaly detection with modest scores (67.5 AUPRC and 43.5 AUROC). This reflects a typical challenge in medical imaging: achieving minimal alteration in input images often compromises the effectiveness of anomaly detection. In contrast, higher noise levels ($t \geq 250$) show improved anomaly detection results, reaching up to 73 AUPRC and 63.8 AUROC, despite the compromise in image quality metrics. This observation aligns with the 'noise paradox' discussed in. [4], illustrating the complex trade-off between achieving optimal reconstruction of healthy images and effective anomaly detection in pathological cases. This paradox can also be observed in Fig. 5, where higher noise levels enable the detection of the pathology but introduce false positive detections.

At a noise level of $t = 50$, AnoDDPM with Simplex noise achieves its most effective reconstruction capabilities for healthy images, recording MAE values of 0.034 and SSIM scores of 0.808. These significantly lag behind the results obtained with Gaussian noise, highlighting a substantial disparity in denoising effectiveness. As noise levels increase, both MAE and SSIM metrics for Simplex noise exhibit gradual deterioration, e.g., for $t = 300$, the MAE increases to

0.045, while SSIM scores decrease to 0.741. In terms of anomaly detection capabilities, Simplex noise at $t = 50$ delivers the most impressive results, achieving an AUPRC of 78.9 and an AUROC of 70.8. These figures are the highest among all configurations and noise types tested, underscoring the superior ability of Simplex noise to detect anomalies under specific conditions, despite its lower reconstruction performance.

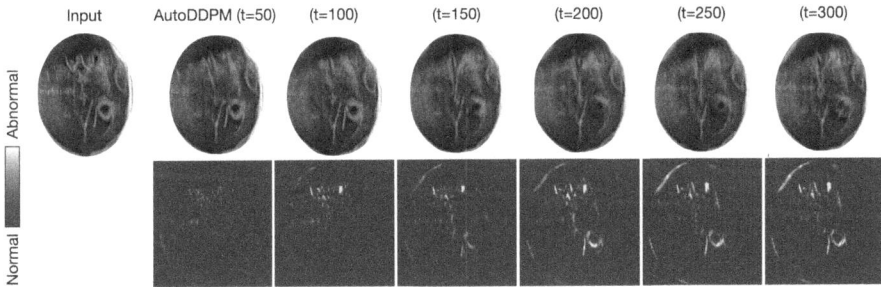

Fig. 5. Performance of AutoDDPM [4] on pathology under multiple noise levels t. The top row displays the input image followed by the reconstructed images at different noise levels ($t = 50, 100, 150, 200, 250, 300$). The bottom row shows the corresponding anomaly maps.

Figure 3 illustrates that AutoDDPM withGaussian noise achieves high-quality reconstructions and effectively highlight anomalies in fetal brain US images.

Influence of Anomaly Maps. We analyzed the impact of different anomaly maps—MAE, LPIPS [6], and their combination (MAE*LPIPS)—on anomaly detection performance. Detailed results are shown in Table 4 and Figures 1 and 2 in the supplementary materials. The combined anomaly maps yield the best performance overall, proving to be more precise in balancing the identification of pathological regions and reducing false positive detections.

5 Discussion

Our study into the automatic anomaly detection pipeline for fetal brain US using DDPMs demonstrates effective pseudo-healthy synthesis and precise anomaly localization. Notably, newer diffusion models such as AutoDDPM [4] show significant promise in enhancing these capabilities. However, the performance of Simplex noise raises specific concerns; its interaction with the inherent noise characteristic of US images suggests it may not be ideally suited for these applications. This behavior necessitates further analysis to fully understand and mitigate adverse effects caused by this type of artificial noise.

Although the results are promising and the dataset was large enough for the models to be able to capture the underlying normative distribution, the statistical validation of these findings requires more extensive datasets. This project is part of an ongoing initiative within the clinic, with continuous efforts to collect more US images to enrich our dataset. Additionally, assessing the clinical utility of this automated screening for pathologies is vital. Evaluating how well our pipeline supports operators and sonographers in detecting and diagnosing conditions will help determine the practical benefits of integrating this technology into everyday clinical practice.

Future research directions will focus on evaluating our pipeline on US video data to simulate real clinical environments more accurately. This includes capturing the dynamic aspects of fetal movements and variations in US probe positioning, which can significantly impact image quality and diagnostic accuracy. Moreover, expanding the diversity of the dataset with images from different US machines and settings will help improve the generalizability and robustness of the proposed methods.

6 Conclusion

In this work, we introduced a novel framework to enable fetal brain anomaly detection on US scans. We designed the framework to automatically reduce the noise and randomness inherent in the US images, allowing models to learn the normative distribution effectively. For the first time, we applied diffusion-based models to automatically processed fetal brain US scans and evaluated their performance under different noise types and levels. Our results indicate that diffusion models, particularly AutoDDPM, hold significant potential for improving the accuracy and reliability of fetal brain anomaly detection in clinics.

Acknowledgments. C.I.B. is funded via the EVUK program ("Next-generation AI for Integrated Diagnostics") of the Free State of Bavaria and partially supported by the Helmholtz Association under the joint research school 'Munich School for Data Science'.

References

1. Akcay, S., Atapour-Abarghouei, A., Breckon, T.P.: Ganomaly: Semi-supervised anomaly detection via adversarial training. In: Computer Vision–ACCV 2018: 14th Asian Conference on Computer Vision, Perth, Australia, December 2–6, 2018, Revised Selected Papers, Part III 14. pp. 622–637. Springer (2019)
2. Baumgartner, C.F., Kamnitsas, K., Matthew, J., Fletcher, T.P., Smith, S., Koch, L.M., Kainz, B., Rueckert, D.: Sononet: Real-time detection and localisation of fetal standard scan planes in freehand ultrasound. IEEE Transactions on Medical Imaging **36**(11), 2204–2215 (2017). https://doi.org/10.1109/TMI.2017.2712367
3. Behrendt, F., Bhattacharya, D., Krüger, J., Opfer, R., Schlaefer, A.: Patched diffusion models for unsupervised anomaly detection in brain mri. International Conference on Medical Imaging with Deep Learning (2023)

4. Bercea, C.I., Neumayr, M., Rueckert, D., Schnabel, J.A.: Mask, stitch, and resample: Enhancing robustness and generalizability in anomaly detection through automatic diffusion models. ICML 3rd Workshop on Interpretable Machine Learning in Healthcare (IMLH) (2023)
5. Bercea, C.I., Rueckert, D., Schnabel, J.A.: What do aes learn? challenging common assumptions in unsupervised anomaly detection. In: Medical Image Computing and Computer Assisted Intervention – MICCAI 2023. pp. 304–314. Springer Nature Switzerland, Cham (2023)
6. Bercea, C.I., Wiestler, B., Rueckert, D., Schnabel, J.A.: Generalizing unsupervised anomaly detection: towards unbiased pathology screening. In: Medical Imaging with Deep Learning (2023)
7. Budd, S., Sinclair, M., Khanal, B., Matthew, J., Lloyd, D., Gomez, A., Toussaint, N., Robinson, E.C., Kainz, B.: Confident head circumference measurement from ultrasound with real-time feedback for sonographers. In: Medical Image Computing and Computer Assisted Intervention – MICCAI 2019. pp. 683–691. Springer International Publishing, Cham (2019)
8. Burgos-Artizzu, X.P., Coronado-Gutierrez, D., Valenzuela-Alcaraz, B., Bonet-Carne, E., Eixarch, E., Crispi, F., Gratacós, E.: FETAL_PLANES_DB: Common maternal-fetal ultrasound images (Jun 2020). https://doi.org/10.5281/zenodo.3904280
9. Chen, X., You, S., Tezcan, K.C., Konukoglu, E.: Unsupervised lesion detection via image restoration with a normative prior. Medical Image Analysis **64** (2020)
10. Chotzoglou, E., Day, T., Tan, J., Matthew, J., Lloyd, D., Razavi, R., Simpson, J., Kainz, B., et al.: Learning normal appearance for fetal anomaly screening: Application to the unsupervised detection of hypoplastic left heart syndrome. Machine Learning for Biomedical Imaging **1**(September 2021 issue), 1–25 (2021)
11. Fiorentino, M.C., Villani, F.P., Di Cosmo, M., Frontoni, E., Moccia, S.: A review on deep-learning algorithms for fetal ultrasound-image analysis. Medical Image Analysis **83**, 102629 (Jan 2023). https://doi.org/10.1016/j.media.2022.102629
12. Ho, J., Jain, A., Abbeel, P.: Denoising diffusion probabilistic models. In: Proceedings of the 34th International Conference on Neural Information Processing Systems. NIPS '20, Curran Associates Inc., Red Hook, NY, USA (2020)
13. Lo, J., Lim, A., Wagner, M.W., Ertl-Wagner, B., Sussman, D.: Fetal organ anomaly classification network for identifying organ anomalies in fetal mri. Frontiers in Artificial Intelligence **5** (2022). https://doi.org/10.3389/frai.2022.832485
14. Luo, G., Xie, W., Gao, R., Zheng, T., Chen, L., Sun, H.: Unsupervised anomaly detection in brain mri: Learning abstract distribution from massive healthy brains. Computers in Biology and Medicine **154**, 106610 (2023). https://doi.org/10.1016/j.compbiomed.2023.106610, https://www.sciencedirect.com/science/article/pii/S0010482523000756S0010482523000756
15. Meng, L., Zhao, D., Yang, Z., Wang, B.: Automatic display of fetal brain planes and automatic measurements of fetal brain parameters by transabdominal three-dimensional ultrasound. Journal of Clinical Ultrasound **48** (07 2019). https://doi.org/10.1002/jcu.22762
16. Pang, G., Shen, C., Cao, L., Hengel, A.V.D.: Deep learning for anomaly detection: A review. ACM Computing Surveys **54**(2), 1–38 (2021). https://doi.org/10.1145/3439950
17. Reddy, U., Filly, R., Copel, J.: Prenatal imaging: Ultrasonography and magnetic resonance imaging. Obstetrics and gynecology **112**, 145–57 (08 2008). https://doi.org/10.1097/01.AOG.0000318871.95090.d9

18. Ronneberger, O., Fischer, P., Brox, T.: U-net: Convolutional networks for biomedical image segmentation. In: Medical Image Computing and Computer-Assisted Intervention – MICCAI 2015. pp. 234–241. Springer International Publishing, Cham (2015)
19. Schlegl, T., Seeböck, P., Waldstein, S.M., Langs, G., Schmidt-Erfurth, U.: f-AnoGAN: Fast unsupervised anomaly detection with generative adversarial networks. Medical Image Analysis **54**, 30–44 (2019)
20. Sinclair, M., Baumgartner, C.F., Matthew, J., Bai, W., Martinez, J.C., Li, Y., Smith, S., Knight, C.L., Kainz, B., Hajnal, J., King, A.P., Rueckert, D.: Human-level performance on automatic head biometrics in fetal ultrasound using fully convolutional neural networks. In: 2018 40th Annual International Conference of the IEEE Engineering in Medicine and Biology Society (EMBC). pp. 714–717 (2018). https://doi.org/10.1109/EMBC.2018.8512278
21. Tschuchnig, M.E., Gadermayr, M.: Anomaly Detection in Medical Imaging - A Mini Review, p. 33-38. Springer Fachmedien Wiesbaden (2022). https://doi.org/10.1007/978-3-658-36295-9_5
22. Wolleb, J., Bieder, F., Sandkühler, R., Cattin, P.C.: Diffusion models for medical anomaly detection. Medical Image Computing and Computer Assisted Intervention pp. 35–45 (2022)
23. Wyatt, J., Leach, A., Schmon, S.M., Willcocks, C.G.: Anoddpm: Anomaly detection with denoising diffusion probabilistic models using simplex noise. In: 2022 IEEE/CVF Conference on Computer Vision and Pattern Recognition Workshops (CVPRW). pp. 649–655 (2022). https://doi.org/10.1109/CVPRW56347.2022.00080
24. Xie, H.N., Wang, N., He, M., Zhang, L.H., Cai, H.M., Xian, J.B., Lin, M.F., Zheng, J., Yang, Y.Z.: Using deep-learning algorithms to classify fetal brain ultrasound images as normal or abnormal. Ultrasound in Obstetrics & Gynecology **56**(4), 579–587 (2020). https://doi.org/10.1002/uog.21967
25. Zhang, H., Guo, W., Zhang, S., Lu, H., Zhao, X.: Unsupervised deep anomaly detection for medical images using an improved adversarial autoencoder. Journal of Digital Imaging **35** (01 2022). https://doi.org/10.1007/s10278-021-00558-8
26. Zhang, R., Isola, P., Efros, A.A., Shechtman, E., Wang, O.: The unreasonable effectiveness of deep features as a perceptual metric. In: 2018 IEEE/CVF Conference on Computer Vision and Pattern Recognition (CVPR). pp. 586–595. IEEE Computer Society, Los Alamitos, CA, USA (jun 2018). https://doi.org/10.1109/CVPR.2018.00068
27. Zimmerer, D., Isensee, F., Petersen, J., Kohl, S., Maier-Hein, K.: Unsupervised anomaly localization using variational auto-encoders. In: Medical Image Computing and Computer Assisted Intervention – MICCAI 2019. pp. 289–297. Springer International Publishing, Cham (2019)

Correction to: Unsupervised Physics-Inspired Shear Wave Speed Estimation in Ultrasound Elastography

Ali Kafaei Zad Tehrani, E. G. Sunethra Dayavansha, Yuyang Gu, Ion Candel, Michael Wang, Rimon Tadross, Yiming Xiao, Hassan Rivaz, Kai Thomenius, and Anthony Samir

Correction to:
Chapter 1 in: A. Gomez et al. (Eds.): *Simplifying Medical Ultrasound*, LNCS 15186,
https://doi.org/10.1007/978-3-031-73647-6_1

The original version of Chapter 1 was inadvertently published without the below reference. The reference has now been added.

Chen, X.: Enhancing ultrasound shear-wave viscoelastography by advanced signal processing and deep learning. Ph.D. dissertation, Eindhoven University of Technology (2024)

The updated version of this chapter can be found at
https://doi.org/10.1007/978-3-031-73647-6_1

Author Index

A

Ahmetovic, Dragan 198
Albaiges, Gerard 88
Aleef, Tajwar Abrar 14
Alomar, Antonia 88
Ambsdorf, Jakob 209
Andreassen, Børge Solli 122
Arenas, Gabriel 132
Azampour, Mohammad Farid 35

B

Bagyura, Zsolt 167
Banerjee, Rohini 143
Barkhau, Carlotta 101
Beqiri, Arian 157
Bercea, Cosmin I. 220
Bettini, Claudio 198
Black, David 14
Black, Peter C. 14
Bransby, Kit M. 157
Byram, Brett 132

C

Candel, Ion 3
Chartsias, Agisilaos 157
Chen, Wanwen 47
Christensen, Anders Nymark 209
Civitarese, Gabriele 198
Collins, D. Louis 68
Colussi, Marco 198

D

Dannlowski, Udo 101
Desaigoudar, Vedanth 14
Dorent, Reuben 78
Dubrawski, Artur 143
Duelmer, Felix 35

E

Ernsting, Jan 101

F

Fábián, Alexandra 167
Fehrentz, Maximilian 78
Feragen, Aasa 209
Fisch, Lukas 101
Frisken, Sarah 78

G

Gasser, Lisa 220
Golby, Alexandra 78
Gomez, Alberto 157
Gu, Yuyang 3
Gualtierotti, Roberta 198
Gueziri, Houssem-Eddine 68

H

Hacihaliloglu, Ilker 24
Hahn, Tim 101
Haouchine, Nazim 78
Huang, Gao 58

I

Islam, Iman 112

J

Jia, Ning 58
Jiang, Haojun 58
Jiang, Xiaoyi 101
Jiao, Jianbo 187

K

Kafaei Zad Tehrani, Ali 3
Kapur, Tina 78
Karlas, Angelos 35
Kersten-Oertel, Marta 68
Kim, Woo-Jin Cho 157
King, Andrew P. 112
Konowski, Maximilian 101
Kovács, Attila 167

© The Editor(s) (if applicable) and The Author(s), under exclusive license to Springer Nature Switzerland AG 2025
A. Gomez et al. (Eds.): ASMUS 2024, LNCS 15186, pp. 231–233, 2025.
https://doi.org/10.1007/978-3-031-73647-6

L

Ladányi, Zsuzsanna   167
Lakatos, Bálint K.   167
Leenings, Ramona   101
Léger, Étienne   68
Li, Hao   132
Li, Meng   58
Lin, Manxi   209
Lobmaier, Silvia   220
Lügering, Andreas   101
Luo, Shaqi   58

M

Magyar, Bálint   167
Mannas, Miles   14
Mascetti, Sergio   198
Merkely, Béla   167
Moceri, Pamela   177
Morales, Cecilia G.   143
Mousavi, Amin   24
Mykula, Hanna   220

N

Najafi, Niki   68
Navab, Nassir   35
Nielsen, Mads   209
Noble, J. Alison   187

O

Oguz, Baris   132
Oguz, Ipek   132
Oliveira, Jorge   157
Olsen, Markus Ditlev Sjøgren   209

P

Payà, Antoni   88
Pegios, Paraskevas   209
Peyvandi, Flora   198
Piella, Gemma   88
Pouch, Alison   132
Prisman, Eitan   47
Puyol-Antón, Esther   112

R

Rasheed, Hassan   78
Reader, Andrew J.   112
Rivaz, Hassan   3

Rocher, Marie   177
Rubio, Ricardo   88
Ruijsink, Bram   112

S

Salcudean, Septimiu E.   14, 47
Salmanpour, Mohammad R.   24
Salort, Laura   88
Samir, Anthony   3
Samset, Eigil   122
Schmidt, Adam   47
Schnabel, Julia A.   78, 220
Schwartz, Nadav   132
Sermesant, Maxime   177
Simson, Walter   35
Solberg, Anne H. Schistad   122
Solyman, Aiman   198
Song, Shiji   58
Sukno, Federico   88
Sun, Yu   58
Sun, Zhenguo   58
Sunethra Dayavansha, E. G.   3
Svendsen, Morten Bo Søndergaard   209
Szeier, Thomas Á.   167
Szijártó, Ádám   167

T

Tadross, Rimon   3
Taksøe-Vester, Caroline   209
Thomas, Sarina   122
Thomenius, Kai   3
Thorley, Alex   157
Tokodi, Márton   167
Tolsgaard, Martin Grønnebæk   209
Tolvaj, Máté   167

V

Vassallo, Reid   14
Völgyes, David   122

W

Wang, Jiacheng   132
Wang, Michael   3
Weeks, William B.   24
Wells III, William M.   78

Author Index

Winter, Nils R. 101
Wodlinger, Brian 14
Wysocki, Magdalena 35

X
Xiao, Yiming 3
Xu, Yixi 24

Y
Yang, Yingyu 177
Yao, Xing 132

Z
Zeng, Qi 14
Zhang, Kangning 187
Zimmer, Veronika 220

The manufacturer's authorised representative in the EU is Springer Nature Customer Service Centre GmbH, Europaplatz 3, 69115 Heidelberg, Germany. If you have any concerns regarding our products, please contact ProductSafety@springernature.com

Printed and bound by CPI Group (UK) Ltd, Croydon, CR0 4YY

26/03/2026

02078973-0002